Conspiracy Theories in the United States and the Middle East

linguae & litterae 29

linguae & litterae

Publications of the School of Language & Literature
Freiburg Institute for Advanced Studies

29

De Gruyter

Conspiracy Theories in the United States and the Middle East

A Comparative Approach

Edited by

Michael Butter and Maurus Reinkowski

De Gruyter

ISBN 978-3-11-030760-3
e-ISBN 978-3-11-033827-0
ISSN 1869-7054

Library of Congress Cataloging-in-Publication Data

A CIP catalog record for this book has been applied for at the Library of Congress.

Bibliographic information published by the Deutsche Nationalbibliothek

The Deutsche Nationalbibliothek lists this publication in the Deutsche Nationalbibliografie; detailed bibliographic data are available on the internet at http://dnb.dnb.de

Typesetting: Dörlemann Satz GmbH & Co. KG, Lemförde
Printing and Binding: Hubert & Co. GmbH KG, Göttingen
© Printed on acid free paper

Printed in Germany

www.degruyter.com

Acknowledgments

Many people have "conspired" to make this volume possible. The Schools of History and Language & Literature of the Freiburg Institute for Advanced Studies (FRIAS) generously funded the 2011 conference where most of the articles collected here were first presented. We are especially indebted to the Schools' directors, Peter Auer, Werner Frick, Ulrich Herbert, and Jörn Leonhard, and their coordinators, Gesa von Essen and Uta Grund. Heike Meier, Simone Erdenberger and Jasmin Gauch took the logistics of hosting an international conference of our hands, and our research assistants Regine Egeler and Amelie Sing were of invaluable help during both the conference and the work on this volume. We are also indebted to the copy-editors of the Linguae & Litterae series, Frauke Janzen and Sara Landa. Finally, special thanks are due to Katharina Thalmann for her meticulous proof-reading and formatting.

Michael Butter and Maurus Reinkowski

Contents

V. Theorizing Conspiracy Theory

Michael Butter (Freiburg) and Maurus Reinkowski (Basel)

Introduction: Mapping Conspiracy Theories in the United States and the Middle East

Conspiracy theories hold that evil agents, the conspirators, secretly control or are plotting to gain control over an institution, a region, a nation, or the world. Over the past five decades such projections have received a considerable amount of scholarly attention. In fact, ever since Richard Hofstadter explored "The Paranoid Style in American Politics" (1964) in his by now classic essay, the field of conspiracy theory research has steadily grown.[1] But whereas Hofstadter and most others who studied the attractions, mechanisms, and effects of conspiracism from the 1960s to the mid-1990s tended to pathologize conspiracy theories, the past twenty years have seen a reevaluation of conspiracist visions, their origins, and their cultural, social, and political functions. As a number of recent studies have shown, conspiracy theories have both a long history and were and are far more widely spread than previously assumed.[2] While it is still unclear since when conspiracy theories have been part of Asian, Arab, and African cultures, in the western world at least they can be traced back to antiquity.[3] What is more, such theories were and are not only believed on the fringes, but were and still are an integral part of most, if not all, societies. Finally, scholars today may differ considerably in their overall evaluations of conspiracy theory, but most would surely agree with Mark Fenster's assessment that conspiracy theories "may sometimes be on to something".[4] What Fenster means is that some

1 Cf. Richard Hofstadter, "The Paranoid Style in American Politics", in: *The Paranoid Style in American Politics and Other Essays*, Cambridge 1995, pp. 3–40.

2 Cf., for example, Barry Coward/Julian Swann (eds.), *Conspiracies and Conspiracy Theory in Early Modern Europe: From the Waldensians to the French Revolution*, Aldershot 2004; Rogalla von Bieberstein, *Der Mythos von der Verschwörung: Philosophen, Freimaurer, Juden, Liberale und Sozialisten als Verschwörer gegen die Sozialordnung*, Wiesbaden 2008; Peter Robert Campbell/Thomas E. Kaiser/Marisa Linton (eds.), *Conspiracy in the French Revolution*, Manchester 2007; Robert Alan Goldberg, *Enemies Within: The Culture of Conspiracy in Modern America*, New Haven, CT 2001.

3 Cf. Joseph Roisman, *The Rhetoric of Conspiracy in Ancient Athens*, Berkeley, CA 2006; Victoria Emma Pagán, *Conspiracy Narratives in Roman History*, Austin, TX 2004.

4 Mark Fenster, *Conspiracy Theories: Secrecy and Power in American Culture*, rev. ed., Minneapolis, MN 2008, p. 90.

conspiracy theories are simply reflections of racism or anti-Semitism, whereas others are voiced, for purely manipulative reasons, by people who do not believe in the claims themselves. But conspiracy theories are also frequently articulations of and distorted responses to existing problems, needs, and anxieties. Thus, they must not be dismissed out of hand and ridiculed but have to be taken seriously.

In this vein, historians investigate the effects of conspiracist visions in past ages, while political scientists do the same for the present, with both of them paying special attention to conspiracy theories' role in stabilizing or destabilizing political systems. Sociologists examine the shifting status of the knowledge that conspiracy theories produce and represent and question how the Internet eases the distribution of such theories or how they contribute to the creation of counter-publics. Psychologists seek to understand if there are personality types or groups particularly prone to conspiracy theorizing, and analytical philosophers are currently struggling with the question if all conspiracy theories are intrinsically flawed, or if there are criteria by which one could distinguish between legitimate and unwarranted suspicions. Anthropologists and ethnologists investigate if conspiracy theories existed in indigenous cultures before they came into contact with the western world, how western visions of conspiracy have subsequently merged with other belief systems, and how conspiracist discourse allows people to make sense of their daily lives and to understand their position with regard to both the local and the global. Literary critics analyze the traces that conspiracist visions leave in fictional texts of all kinds, whereas scholars from cultural studies explore projections of conspiracy outside the realm of the literary, conspiracy theorizing as a cultural practice, and conspiracy theory's role in the formation of individual and collective identity.[5]

---

[5] It is impossible to list all relevant studies here but they are included in the bibliography of conspiracy theory research at the end of this book. For historical studies, cf., for example, Coward/Swann, *Conspiracies and Conspiracy Theory*; Campbell/Kaiser/Liton, *Conspiracy*; Geoffrey Cubitt, *The Jesuit Myth: Conspiracy Theory and Politics in Nineteenth-Century France*, Oxford 1993; Markus Hünemörder, *The Society of the Cincinnati: Conspiracy and Distrust in Early America*, New York 2006. For political science, cf. Michael Barkun, *A Culture of Conspiracy: Apocalyptic Visions in Contemporary America*, Berkeley, CA 2003; Matthew C. Gray, *Conspiracy Theories in the Arab World: Sources and Politics*, London 2010. For sociological contributions, cf., for example, Michael Schetsche/Ina Schmied-Knittel, "Verschwörungstheorien und die Angst vor über- und unterirdischen Mächten", in: *kuckuck: Notizen zur Alltagskultur*, 1/2004, pp. 24–29; Andreas Anton, *Unwirkliche Wirklichkeiten: Zur Wissenssoziologie von Verschwörungstheorien*, Berlin 2011. For current research in psychology, cf. Viren Swami/Rebecca Coles, "The Truth Is Out There: Belief in Conspiracy

This growing body of scholarly work has immensely increased our understanding of conspiracy theory. However, there is still a lot of work left to be done. Since most extant research focuses on one single region or culture – with the vast majority of studies examining various aspects of conspiracy theorizing in the United States or drawing on American examples when examining conspiracy theory in general – we do not yet know enough about how conspiracist visions differ from one region or culture to the other, how they travel from one culture or region to the other, or how this transfer affects their forms and functions. We also possess only a very rudimentary understanding of the reasons why conspiracy theories quite obviously figure more prominently in some regions and cultures than in others. And we also do not know for certain yet if conspiracy theories are an anthropological given, as some scholars assume, or if, at least in their modern form, they emerged with the Enlightenment and spread from Europe all over the world, as the editors of and most contributors to this volume think. The situation is further aggravated by the fact that there have not been many inter- or transdisciplinary efforts to study conspiracy theories so far. In fact, scholars often seem unaware of the insights already gained in neighboring disciplines. For example, historians and political scientists working on American conspiracy theories of the nineteenth and twentieth centuries have usually neither drawn on or historicized, nor explicitly rejected what cultural studies scholars have argued about contemporary American culture. They sometimes acknowledge their work in passing but hardly ever engage with their findings or the theoretical models they have proposed.

Theories", in: *The Psychologist*, 23/2010, pp. 560–563; Marina Abalakina-Paap et al.,"Beliefs in Conspiracies", in: *Political Psychology*, 20/1999, pp. 637–647; Ted Goertzel, "Belief in Conspiracy Theories", in: *Political Psychology*, 15/1994, pp. 731–742. Most work done in analytical or political philosophy has been collected in David Coady, *Conspiracy Theories: The Philosophical Debate*, Aldershot 2006. For contributions from anthropology and ethnology, cf. the essays collected in Harry G. West/Todd Saunders (eds.), *Transparency and Conspiracy: Ethnographies of Suspicion in the New World Order*, Durham, NC 2003. For literary studies, cf., among many others, Albert D. Pionke, *Plots of Opportunity: Representing Conspiracy in Victorian England*, Columbus, OH 2004; Adrian S. Wisnicki, *Conspiracy, Revolution, and Terrorism from Victorian Fiction to the Modern Novel*, New York 2008; Samuel Chase Coale, *Paradigms of Paranoia: The Culture of Conspiracy in Contemporary American Fiction*, Tuscaloosa, AL 2005. For cultural studies, cf. Fenster, *Conspiracy Theories*; Jodi Dean, *Aliens in America: Conspiracy Cultures from Outerspace to Cyberspace*, Ithaca, NY 1998; Peter Knight, *Conspiracy Culture: From Kennedy to* The X-Files, London 2000; Timothy Melley, *Empire of Conspiracy: The Culture of Paranoia in Postwar America*, Ithaca, NY 2000.

Focusing on the United States and the Middle East, two regions where conspiracy theories have been prominent for a long time, *Conspiracy Theories in the United States and the Middle East* constitutes a step toward closing some of the gaps thus left. Its perspective is both comparative and interdisciplinary, as it concentrates on two different regions of the world that are nevertheless connected in manifold ways, and as it brings together scholars from Middle Eastern Studies, Anthropology, History, Political Science, Cultural Studies, and American Studies. Taken together, the essays collected in this volume offer a nuanced image of the workings of conspiracy theory in the United States and the Middle East. Because of their focus on individual cases and local conditions, they dispel a number of myths about conspiracism, especially with regard to the Middle East, by complicating the pictures painted by previous research. Since a number of contributions address conspiracy theorizing prior to 1960, they add a historical perspective much needed in a field where most research still focuses on the present. Most importantly, they help us understand how conspiracy theories operate in different historical, cultural, political, and social contexts, alerting us to the commonalities and differences in conspiracist thinking both between the United States and the Middle East and within these nations or regions.

The volume is organized into five thematic sections. Section 1, "The United States and the Middle East", contains four essays that explore how the Middle East figures in conspiracist accounts prominent in the United States and vice versa, and how (alleged) actions by actors from one region have affected conspiracy theories circulating in the other. Aaron Winter focuses on the extreme right in the United States, Schirin Fathi on Iran, André G. Sleiman on Lebanon, and Brian Johnsrud on Dan Brown's *The Da Vinci Code* and its relationship to post-9/11 medievalism in the United States. The three essays in section 2, "The Politics of Conspiracy Theory", are case studies of how different kinds of political actors deploy conspiracy theories consciously or unconsciously in order to achieve their goals, that is, how they at times adapt certain theories for strategic purposes while rejecting others for the same reason. Christopher Herbert deals with vigilante committees in nineteenth-century California, Türkay Salim Nefes with political parties in contemporary Turkey, and Stephan Schmid with the Lebanese Hizbollah. Section 3, "The Promises of Conspiracy Theory", investigates different ways in which people utilize the knowledge offered by conspiracy theory to make sense of their lives. Sebastian M. Herrmann explores how the epistemic crisis to which conspiracy theory answers is dramatized in fiction, Annika Rabo examines the role of conspiracy talk in everyday discourse in Syria, and Christoph Herzog engages with visions of the "deep state" in Turkey. Section 4, "Travelling Theories", is dedicated to the transnational dimension of both conspiracy theorizing and conspiracy theory research. Andrew McKenzie-McHarg explores how the Illuminati conspiracy theory traveled from Europe to the United States at the end of the eighteenth century and how it was transformed during this process. In similar fashion, Barbara De Poli examines the transfer of Masonic and anti-Semitic conspiracy theories to the Arab world. Matthey Gray, by contrast, is not concerned with conspiracy theories, but discusses to what degree theories of conspiracy theory developed with regard to the United States can be used to shed light on conspiracist visions in the Middle East. His contribution thus forms a bridge to section 5, "Theorizing Conspiracy Theory", which contains four essays that consider the state of current research, including that collected in this volume, from a meta-position. Alexander Dunst argues that contemporary research has still not gone beyond pathologizing conspiracy theories; Birte Christ exposes the gendered biases of both conspiracy theory and conspiracy theory research; Mark Fenster uses recent discussions about how states might react to accusations of conspiracy to reject calls for one singular theory of conspiracy theory; and Peter Knight, finally, looks ahead and maps areas of future research. First of all, however, the introduction lays the foundation for what follows by providing an overview of the histories, forms, and origins of conspiracy theories in the United States and the Middle East, and the highly imbalanced relationship between these two regions.

1. The Forms and Functions of American Conspiracy Theories

From a certain perspective, the history of the United States is the history of a series of subsequent conspiracy theories that have decisively shaped the course of the country. In fact, more than a century before the nation was founded, the Puritan settlers in New England saw themselves as threatened by a devilish plot in the literal sense. Conceiving of themselves as God's chosen people, the Puritans believed that they were at the forefront of a cosmic struggle between God and Satan. Accordingly, they thought that all their enemies – for example, Native American tribes or Catholics from French Quebec – were secretly collaborating under the lead of the devil, and that all hardships that befell them – for example, epidemics or natural disasters – were moves in this battle.[6] This fear of conspiracy, as Robert Levine puts it,

[6] On Puritanism in general, cf. the contributions to John Coffey (ed.), *The Cambridge Companion to Puritanism*, Cambridge 2008. On Puritan conspiracy theories, cf. Goldberg, *Enemies Within*, pp. 1–4; Robert S. Levine, *Conspiracy and Romance: Studies*

"helped the Pilgrim and Puritan colonists to create and define their community".[7] As long as the enemy was located (largely) outside the community, the conspiracy theory that the Puritans believed in stabilized their community. However, when during the Salem witchcraft crisis of 1692 the enemy seemed to have infiltrated the community, the conspiracy theory fueled a mass panic and shook the community to its very foundations.

During the eighteenth century, metaphysical conspiracy theories featuring the devil were increasingly replaced by secular accounts that focused exclusively on human actors. But conspiracist fears remained important to American culture and continued to function as means of collective self-definition.[8] Indeed, one can make a strong case that the United States only came into being because of a conspiracy theory. Bernard Bailyn already argued during the 1960s that

> [t]he fear of a comprehensive conspiracy against liberty throughout the English-speaking world – a conspiracy believed to have been nourished in corruption, and of which, it was felt, oppression in America was only the most immediately visible part – lay at the heart of the Revolutionary movement.[9]

According to Bailyn's influential study, from the late 1750s onward, the colonists increasingly gained the impression that the king, his ministers, and the Church of England were conspiring against their and all other people's liberty – an idea that not only fueled but justified their rebellion and created a sense of collective identity. As Jodie Dean puts it, "Distrust of British authority helped produce a new 'we,' a 'we' constituted out of those sharing a fear of corruption and ministerial conspiracy, a 'we' hailed in the Declaration as those who might believe that the king was plotting against their liberty".[10]

---

in Brockden Brown, Cooper, Hawthorne, and Melville, Cambridge 1989, pp. 6–8; as well as chapter 2 in Michael Butter, *Plots, Designs, and Schemes: American Conspiracy Theories from the Puritans to the Present*, Berlin/Boston 2014.

7 Levine, *Conspiracy and Romance*, p. 6.

8 For more extended histories of American conspiracy theories than the one provided here, cf. David Brion Davis (ed.), *The Fear of Conspiracy: Images of Un-American Subversion from the Revolution to the Present*, Ithaca, NY 1971; Goldberg, *Enemies Within*. For the Early Republic, cf. also J. Wendell Knox, *Conspiracy in American Politics 1787–1815*, New York 1972; for the twentieth-century, cf. Kathryn S. Olmsted, *Real Enemies: Conspiracy Theories and American Democracy, World War I to 9/11*, Oxford 2009.

9 Bernard Bailyn, "Foreword", in: Bailyn (ed.), *Pamphlets of the American Revolution 1750–1776*, vol. 1, Cambridge, MA 1965, pp. vii–xii, p. x. Cf. also Bailyn, *The Ideological Origins of the American Revolution*, Cambridge, MA 1967.

10 Jodie Dean, "Declarations of Independence", in: Dean (ed.), *Cultural Studies & Political Theory*, NY 2000, pp. 285–304, p. 297.

As a consequence, it is hardly surprising that the Founding Fathers saw the newly established nation constantly threatened by plots involving internal or external enemies or a combination of both. This fear found its most pronounced expression in George Washington's *Farewell Address* of September 1796 in which Washington admonished Americans to stand united because their unity was "the point in your political fortress against which the batteries of internal and external enemies will be most constantly and actively (though often covertly and insidiously) directed [...]".[11] This warning did not go unheard but proved extraordinarily prophetic. Displaying the "uniform vigilance"[12] that Washington demanded, until into the second half of the twentieth century, conspiracy theorists worried about exactly that which Washington had worried about. In the 160 years after the issuing of the *Farewell Address*, American conspiracy theories revolved predominantly around alleged plots by domestic and/or foreign agents against the government. In these conspiracist visions, the government was almost always in great peril but had not yet fallen to the conspirators.

One prominent example of such fears occurred very shortly after the publication of the *Farewell Address*: the Illuminati scare of 1798–1799.[13] A number of Federalist politicians and New England ministers, most prominently Jedidiah Morse, charged that the secret order of the Illuminati, driven by the desire to abolish all religion and social order, had first caused the French Revolution and was now, in league with the Democratic Republicans, busy to subvert the American republic. Motivated at least in part by these claims, Congress passed the Alien and Sedition Acts, a set of bills that allowed the president to suppress critical opinions about the government in the press and to deport foreigners suspected of subversion. In his contribution to this volume, Andrew McKenzie-McHarg investigates how the Illuminati conspiracy theory traveled from Europe to the United States, why it fell on fertile ground there, and how Jedidiah Morse adapted the arguments of European conspiracy theorists in order to make them meaningful for the new context.

In many ways, the Illuminati scare provided the pattern which most conspiracist fears would follow over the nineteenth century, as the idea that a domestic faction was actively collaborating with a foreign power and thus com-

---

11 George Washington, "Farewell Address", in: Don Higginbotham (ed.), *George Washington: Uniting a Nation*, Lanham, MD 2002, pp. 137–155, p. 140.

12 George Washington, "Farewell Address", p. 147.

13 The classic study of this scare is Vernon Stauffer, *New England and the Bavarian Illuminati*, Diss. Columbia University, New York, 1918.

mitting what J. Wendell Knox has called the "cardinal sin in the United States" proved highly influential.[14] Throughout the 1800s and 1810s Democratic Republicans and Federalists continually accused each other of this crime. The Federalists usually claimed that the Democratic Republicans were conspiring with the French, and the Democratic Republicans claimed that the Federalists and the British were plotting the destruction of the American republic. The motivation of foreign powers to engage in such conspiracies was, however, only rarely seen as an anarchic desire for the destruction of social order as such (as in the case of the Illuminati). Far more frequently (as in the case of Britain and Napoleonic France), foreign powers were accused of planning the destruction of the United States in order to disqualify the unwelcome example in democracy that the country was setting to Europe where, in the eyes of the Americans, people were slaves to autocratic regimes.

Such strategic foreign conspiracies also featured prominently in various countersubversive scenarios that emerged from the 1820s onward. With the exception of the rather short-lived fear of a Masonic conspiracy and Jacksonian anxieties about the workings of a mysterious Money Power, all major conspiracy theories of the antebellum period revolved to varying degrees around exactly such foreign attempts. Between the 1830s and 1850s a considerable number of Americans became convinced that recently arrived Catholic immigrants as well as Catholics who had come to the United States before were not loyal to the republic and the Constitution but only to the pope. The pope and the monarchs of Europe, the conspiracy theorists believed, had devised a vicious plan to undermine the democratic system of the United States because they were concerned that the people in their own countries would soon demand the rights guaranteed to American citizens.[15]

In similar fashion and exactly at the same time, abolitionists and later Republican politicians as well were cast by proslavery activists as the (sometimes) knowing or (usually) unwitting participants in a British plot to drive the country into a civil war. According to these conspiracy theorists, the British fueled the abolitionist fervor because the internal conflict it would inevitably lead to would not only disqualify the democratic example America was set-

---

14 Knox, *Conspiracy in American Politics*, p. 316.

15 On the anti-Catholic conspiracy theory, cf. also Ray A. Billington, *The Protestant Crusade 1800–1860: A Study of the Origins of American Nativism*, Chicago, IL 1964; John Higham, *Strangers in the Land: Patterns of American Nativism, 1860–1925*, rev. ed., New Brunswick, NJ 2008; David Brion Davis, "Some Themes of Counter-Subversion: An Analysis of Anti-Masonic, Anti-Catholic, and Anti-Mormon Literature", in: *The Mississippi Valley Historical Review*, 47/1960, pp. 205–224; Susan M. Griffin, *Anti-Catholicism and Nineteenth-Century Fiction*, Cambridge 2004.

ting the world but also destroy the economic threat that the South allegedly posed for Great Britain.[16]

Opponents of slavery, however, also harbored a conspiracy theory. According to Republicans like Charles Sumner or Abraham Lincoln, an organization of slaveholders, the Slave Power, was plotting to nationalize slavery and possibly to extend it to the white working class. The Slave Power, these conspiracy theorists believed, had already brought the federal government under its control. Presidents, congressmen, or Supreme Court judges were either members of the Slave Power or its powerless puppets. In the accounts of these countersubversives, then, we no longer encounter a conspiracy directed against the state but one conducted by it. Apart from this deviation, however, the Slave Power conspiracy theory has a lot in common with those conspiracy theories of the time that regarded the state as not yet quite captured. Even though Lincoln and others contended that the Slave Power controlled all branches of government, they retained faith in the democratic process and held that change for the better could be brought about by elections. In fact, the Republican Party was founded exactly in this spirit. This confidence in elections distinguishes the opponents of the Slave Power from post-1960 countersubversives who usually claim that elections are only staged by those who control the government and thus offer no possibility to amend things. It aligns anti-Slave power activists with other conspiracy theorists of their time, for example with anti-Masons and anti-Catholics who also founded new parties to further their ends.

But these national, and sometimes even international, conspiracies were by no means the only ones that haunted the countersubversive imagination of antebellum America. Christopher Herbert demonstrates in his essay that the newly founded state of California experienced a series of conspiracy scares during the 1850s. Anglo-American merchants repeatedly convinced themselves that secret societies comprising Australian and Mexican immigrants, but also politicians, were trying to or had already gained control over cities and counties. These local conspiracy theories were disconnected from those that played out on the national stage, but they followed similar patterns and articulated the same anxieties and convictions. As Herbert puts it,

---

16 On conspiracy theories revolving around slavery, cf. David Brion Davis, *The Slave Power Conspiracy and the Paranoid Style*, Baton Rouge, LA 1970; Leonard L. Richards, *"Gentlemen of Property and Standing": Anti-Abolition Riots in Jacksonian America*, New York 1970; Richards, *The Slave Power: The Free North and Southern Domination, 1780–1860*, Baton Rouge, LA 2000; Michael Pfau, *The Political Style of Conspiracy: Chase, Sumner, and Lincoln*, East Lansing, MI 2005; Eric Foner, *Free Soil, Free Labor, Free Men: The Ideology of the Republican Party Before the Civil War*, New York 1995.

> While arising out of pragmatic interests of a certain group of middle-class Anglo-American merchants, these conspiracy theories gained widespread traction and credibility because they confirmed what Anglo-Americans already "knew": that the republic depended on free independent (white) men, and that social ills were symptomatic of challenges to the republic.

After the Civil War the fear of conspiracy diminished considerably on both the local and the national level for a couple of decades. David Brion Davis writes that "When compared with the stormy antebellum decades, the period from 1865 to 1890 exhibits a façade of stability, moderation, and pragmatic balance"[17] in which conspiracist visions did not thrive. Conspiracy theories, however, gained new prominence during the economic crisis at the end of the century. For the next couple of decades they did not only follow the established pattern and blamed internal and external enemies for conspiring against the government; in many cases they also revived old enemies. Turn-of-the-century conspiracy theories targeted Masons, Catholics, bankers, blacks, and various kinds of foreigners. But new villains were also added to the picture. Due to a wave of immigration from Eastern Europe, anti-Semitic conspiracy theories emerged for the first time on a larger scale in the United States. These theories have survived until today, and because of the genocidal history of the twentieth century they have received a lot of attention. Unlike in Europe, however, anti-Semitic conspiracy theories have, except for the late nineteenth century, never enjoyed much success in the United States. They have always appealed to the Ku Klux Klan and other groups on the extreme right, but overall their importance pales in comparison with conspiracist fears of Catholics or Communists.

Concerns about Communists also first emerged in the final quarter of the nineteenth century, but they only took on a conspiracist garb during the 1930s when Americans also began to worry about infiltration by Nazis. With the emergence of the Cold War, then, Communists became the primary target of American conspiracy theories.[18] Whereas during the Red Scare of 1918–1919 the Communists had been cast as foreigners who wanted to instigate open insurrection, anti-Communists now worried about American-born Communists who secretly plotted America's doom in allegiance with

---

17 Davis, *Fear*, p. 149.

18 On American anti-Communism, cf. Richard M. Fried, *Nightmare in Red: The McCarthy Era in Perspective*, New York 1990; Michael J. Heale, *American Anticommunism: Combating the Enemy Within 1830–1970*, Baltimore, MD 1990; Heale, *McCarthy's Americans: Red Scare Politics in State and Nation 1935–1965*, Basingstoke 1998; David Oshinsky, *A Conspiracy So Immense: The World of Joe McCarthy*, Oxford 2005.

and directed by the Soviet Union. Thus, during the 1950s, American conspiracy theories still followed the pattern that had emerged at the turn to the nineteenth century: anti-Communists fought a conspiracy that united a treacherous faction of "un-American" traitors on the inside with a foreign power in an attempt to capture the government.

During the 1960s, however, the thrust of American conspiracy theories changed significantly. If earlier conspiracy theories were almost exclusively concerned with plots against the state, and in particular the federal government, recent visions of conspiracy have predominantly revolved around plots by the state, and in particular the federal government.[19] No matter whether they concern the Kennedy assassination, the moon landing, the New World Order, the so-called Zionist Occupied Government (ZOG), 9/11, or the Obama presidency, post-1960 conspiracy theories usually hold that the federal government has already fallen to the conspirators and that they have effectively transformed the machinery of the state into an apparatus of oppression and exploitation. Although occasionally fueled, as in the case of Obama and ZOG conspiracy theories, by overt racism and anti-Semitism, these conspiracy theories invariably articulate a profound distrust of the forces of globalization, centralized power, and the state of American democracy in general. At the same time, they often express confidence that the wrongs can still be righted and that the values of republicanism can be restored through individual human agency.

Conspiracy theories that target the federal government and other state agencies have left a broad mark on film and fiction. There are innumerable movies and novels of all kinds that foster and negotiate the fascination with plots by government officials. In his essay on Larry Beinhart's two novels about White House conspiracies – one of which was adapted into the film *Wag the Dog* – Sebastian M. Herrmann investigates the cultural work that these novels, and, by implication, much non-fictional conspiracy theorizing, perform. Beinhart's conspiratorial plots, Herrmann argues, are "indicative of an 'epistemic panic', a widespread cultural anxiety about the limitations of knowledge and the elusiveness of the 'real' as a fundamental social category". In similar fashion, Birte Christ also draws on fictional representations of conspiracy, Oliver Stone's film *J.F.K.* (1991) and Sidney Pollack's *3 Days of the Condor* (1975), in order to highlight another important cultural function of conspiracist visions: the reaffirmation of a traditional, hegemonic notion of masculinity that, as the plots of these films show, disempowers women and works to restrict them to the private sphere. What is

---

19 On this shift, cf. Olmsted, *Real Enemies*, p. 4; and Knight, *Conspiracy Culture*, p. 58.

more, Christ also shows that most conspiracy theory scholarship does not critique but unwittingly contributes to this project by dismissing female visions of conspiracy as hysteria and ennobling male ones by considering them interventions, however misguided and distorted, in the political sphere.

That conspiracy theory scholarship these days regards American conspiracy theories as symptomatic expressions of deeper anxieties shows that not only the parameters of conspiracist visions but also their status has changed considerably since the 1960s. Whereas conspiracy theories that saw the state threatened but not yet captured represented a legitimate form of knowledge that was articulated in farewell addresses and on the Senate floor by some of the nation's most revered leaders, those more recent theories that accuse the government of conspiring against the people constitute what Michael Barkun calls "stigmatized knowledge".[20] Whereas in previous ages, accusations of conspiracy were an integral part of mainstream discourse, the term "conspiracy theory" now functions as a powerful instrument of dismissal. As Peter Knight puts it, "Calling something a conspiracy theory is not infrequently enough to end discussion".[21] Accordingly, while visions of conspiracies by the state are omnipresent in contemporary American culture, they have also increasingly moved to the margins of society. One group among which they thrive is the extreme right where the feeling that the federal government is secretly controlled by Zionists or the New World Order is particularly pronounced. Aaron Winter's essay, however, does not focus on these conspiracy theories directly but explores how the extreme right, before and after 9/11, tried to forge alliances with Islamists in Arab countries and why these attempts, which have caused much concern among liberal commentators, have been almost completely unsuccessful.

The attacks of 9/11 and their aftermath are also a powerful reminder that despite the paradigm shift of the 1960s there are still American conspiracy theories concerned with plots by – largely – external enemies directed against the state. While the attacks of September 11, 2001 were no doubt an actual conspiracy masterminded by Osama bin Laden and carried out by nineteen Arab men, the George W. Bush administration responded to these attacks with concocting a conspiracy theory that claimed that al-Qaeda and Iraq were secretly aligned and plotting America's doom. As this example shows, what is considered a conspiracy theory is not only determined by its internal characteristics but also by the position of those who voice it in public discourse. And while conspiracy theories that target the government are

20 Barkun, *Culture of Conspiracy*, p. 5.

21 Knight, *Conspiracy Culture*, p. 11.

usually labeled "conspiracy theories" and thus disqualified, conspiracy theories that target "enemies" of the state frequently escape this designation.

Two contributions to this volume engage with this official conspiracy theorizing, albeit in very different fashion. By way of a close analysis of Dan Brown's megaseller *The Da Vinci Code* (2002) and Ron Howard's movie adaptation (2006), Brian Johnsrud explores the medievalism that permeated both American culture in general and the Bush administration in particular in the first years after 9/11, arguing that Brown's novel confirms the idea that the crusades are essential to understanding the current conflict between the West and the Middle East, but that it complicates the view of the Middle East that has become an integral part of much institutional historiography and of the Bush administration's conspiracy theory. By contrast, Alexander Dunst takes this conspiracy theory as the point of departure for a general critique of conspiracy theory scholarship. Even the revisionist studies written since the mid-1990s, he argues, continue to pathologize one form of conspiracy theorizing and thus overlook the omnipresence of another form in mainstream discourse.

2. The Origins of American Conspiracy Theories

"Conspiracy theories are inseparably connected with conspiracies", German sociologist Michael Schetsche contends, thereby not only implying that conspiracy theories and real conspiracies are often difficult to tell apart but also that they condition each other.[22] Schetsche's argument is indeed one often made in conspiracy theory research. Trying to explain why conspiracy theories occur more frequently at certain historical moments than at others and figure more prominently in some cultures than in others, many scholars – and for good reasons, as our discussion of Middle Eastern conspiracy theories below will show – point to the existence of real conspiracies. However, as far as the United States is concerned, it is difficult to explain the lasting appeal of conspiracist visions in this way. Not only is the history of the United States, especially when compared to that of Europe or the Middle East, relatively devoid of real plots; what is more, the conspiracies that did occur were usually small in scale and only fueled already existing conspiracy theories, if they had any impact on conspiracy theorizing at all. The two most prominent plots of the nineteenth century, for example – the attempt of the

---

22 Michael Schetsche, "Die ergooglete Wirklichkeit: Verschwörungstheorien und das Internet", in: Kai Lehmann/Michael Schetsche (eds.), *Die Google-Gesellschaft: Vom digitalen Wandel des Wissens*, Bielefeld 2007, pp. 113–120, p. 114.

abolitionist John Brown to instigate a slave uprising by staging a raid on Harper's Ferry in 1859 and the assassination of Abraham Lincoln – were both carried out by only a handful of people and merely confirmed the conspiracy theories that the defenders of slavery and its opponents had harbored for many years.[23]

Accordingly, if one wants to explain "America's special relationship to conspiracy theory"[24] one has to look elsewhere. We do not wish to foster notions of American exceptionalism, but we would like to suggest that the popularity and power of conspiracy theories in American culture from Puritan times to the present can be explained by the longevity and co-presence of the heritage of Puritanism, the ideology of republicanism, and an epistemological paradigm that presupposes a direct link between cause and effect and thus holds that everything that occurs has been intended exactly that way. We do not contend that these three factors are the only sources of American conspiracism, but we consider them the most important ones. We are convinced that they explain why conspiracy theories, which were as popular in France, England, and most other European countries as they were in the United States during the eighteenth and nineteenth centuries, have retained their appeal in America but not in Europe.[25]

Over the past decades, scholars from different disciplines have demonstrated the importance of Puritanism for numerous aspects of American life.[26] Many Puritan ideas have been secularized over the centuries and thus continue to shape American culture and identity until today. For example, the notion of American exceptionalism has its roots in the Puritans' self-understanding as God's chosen people. Much the same is true for the American propensity for conspiracy theorizing. Displaying the Manichean thinking

---

23 The perception of real conspiracies was, however, a factor, albeit not the only one, in bringing about the shift from conspiracy theories that detect plots against the state to those that are concerned with plots by the state during the 1960s and 1970s. As Kathryn Olmsted puts it, "government officials provided fodder for conspiracism by using their powers to plot – and to conceal – real conspiracies" (*Real Enemies*, p. 234).

24 Olmsted, *Real Enemies*, p. 3.

25 Within the scope of this introduction it is impossible to explore these three factors and their complex interplay in detail. For a far more detailed version of the argument made here, cf. chapter 1 in Butter, *Plots, Designs, and Schemes.*

26 Cf. Sacvan Bercovitch, *The Puritan Origins of the American Self*, New Haven, CT 1975; Tracy Fessenden/Nicholas F. Radel/Magdalena J. Zaborowska (eds.), *The Puritan Origins of American Sex: Religion, Sexuality and National Identity in American Literature*, New York 2001; George McKenna, *The Puritan Origins of American Patriotism*, New Haven, CT 2007.

characteristic of conspiracy theorizing, the Puritans saw themselves at the forefront of the struggle between good and evil, and they were convinced that all their enemies were secretly aligned. Moreover, they believed that history unfolded according to a divine plan. Nothing happened by chance but because it had been predestined by an inscrutable God. Thus, Puritan thinking was organized along the parameters that Michael Barkun has identified as characteristic of all conspiracism: nothing happens by accident, nothing is as it seems, and everything is connected.[27]

The major difference between the Puritans' metaphysical conspiracy theory and later secularized versions is that the Puritans believed that ultimately God controlled the conspirators. Whereas accounts from the eighteenth century onward usually do without supernatural actors and regard the conspirators as those who are pulling the strings, the Puritans held that God allowed the devil and his minions to torment the Puritans whenever his chosen people was not living up to his high expectations. They conceived of their affliction as a corrective punishment that was meant to make them mend their ways and not to destroy them. Thus, for the Puritans, the detection of conspiracies was both a cause of concern and a confirmation of their sense of election and mission. Albeit in a modified form, the same still is true today. Contemporary conspiracy theorists worry about the plots they reveal, but the very fact that they have been capable of detecting these plots signals that they are different. They may not have been elected by God, but they are elevated from the unsuspecting masses because of their special knowledge and thus have the obligation to fight the conspiracy. Accordingly, historian Robert Alan Goldberg considers the originally religious and later nationalized sense of mission the most important source of American conspiracism.[28]

The second major influence on American conspiracy theories has been the ideology of republicanism, which was an important element of eighteenth- and nineteenth-century American political culture and whose impact, much like Puritanism's, is still discernible today.[29] The prototypical American fear of political parties, for example, which dominated American politics far into the nineteenth century and fueled various conspiracy theories, resulted from this political theory which the American colonists adopted from the

---

[27] Cf. Barkun, *Culture of Conspiracy*, pp. 3–4.

[28] Goldberg, *Enemies Within*, p. 1.

[29] On republicanism, cf. Gordon S. Wood, *The Creation of the American Republic, 1776–1787*, New York 1972; J. G. A. Pocock, *The Machiavellian Moment: Florentine Political Thought and the Atlantic Republican Tradition*, Princeton, NJ 1975.

English Whig party. Unlike liberalism, republicanism conceived of humans as social beings that formed communities not out of necessity, but because it was a part of their nature. Accordingly, the proponents of republicanism demanded that everybody should have the common good in mind at all times – a principle they saw violated by political parties. As Michael Pfau puts it, "parties were naturally suspect because they represented only a part of the people – a faction – that was likely to look to its own good in preference to the good of the whole".[30]

Parties, however, were only the most obvious and outward manifestation of a danger that adherents of republicanism worried about in more general terms: "corruption". In the ideology of republicanism, corruption figured as diametrically opposed to the one value the success of a republic hinged on: "virtue". Republican ideology postulated a perpetual struggle between virtue and corruption and held that only the former could prevent the rise and eventual triumph of the internal and external enemies that the latter would inevitably lead to. In this rather pessimistic view, adherents of republicanism were confirmed by the study of history. Even more so than their predecessors in Renaissance Italy, whose destinies they had carefully examined, Americans were aware that "traditionally republics were short-lived, subject to cyclical decline, and vulnerable to the plottings of internal and external enemies".[31] Because of their form of government, their openness when compared with autocratically ruled nations, and the absence of standing armies, republics were seen as all too quickly destroyed through the conspiracies of corrupted individuals and groups on the inside and outside.

The fear of plots and schmemes, then, was inscribed into the ideology of republicanism, and since republicanism was so important for eighteenth- and nineteenth-century American political culture, conspiracy theories were widespread, as various scholars have observed. Robert Levine, for example, writes that "Republican ideology and discourse [...] played a crucial role in perpetuating the fear of conspiracy in early national and antebellum culture"; and Daniel Walker Howe even speaks of a "conspiracy paradigm" when discussing republican ideas among the American Whigs, a political party of the 1830s and 1840s.[32]

Levine's and Howe's references to the antebellum period indicate that republicanism did not, as an earlier generation of scholars had assumed,

---

30 Pfau, *Political Style*, p. 41.

31 Levine, *Conspiracy and Romance*, p. 10.

32 Levine, *Conspiracy and Romance*, p. 40; Howe, *Political Culture*, p. 79.

rapidly lose in importance at the beginning of the nineteenth century.[33] Indeed, republicanism changed over the course of the nineteenth century but it remained highly influential until the Civil War after which the fear of party together with many other elements of republican thought slowly waned. Republicanism's basic tenet, however, the conflict between virtue and corruption, has survived and continues to fuel conspiracy theories until today. As J. G. A. Pocock, one of the most influential scholars of republicanism, has convincingly argued, it is still palpable in President Eisenhower's warnings against the workings of the "military-industrial complex", a concept that is integral to countless contemporary conspiracist visions.[34]

The final factor in accounting for American culture's predilection for conspiracy theories is an epistemological paradigm that emerged in the eighteenth century and that also remains influential in the United States until today. This paradigm has been most thoroughly described by Gordon Wood in his essay "Conspiracy and the Paranoid Style: Causality and Deceit in the Eighteenth Century". As Wood demonstrates, throughout this century, conspiracy theories produced officially accepted knowledge. The most enlightened thinkers of the age had abandoned the idea that history was unfolding according to a divine plan, but they were not ready yet to accept the impact of chance, contingency, or of systemic factors. Instead they propagated a mechanistic worldview in which "[a]ll human actions and events could now be seen scientifically as the products of men's intentions".[35] Assuming that "cause and effect were so intimately related that they necessarily shared the same moral qualities",[36] these thinkers dismissed the possibility that intentions and results could be more than occasionally at odds. If a group's actions constantly produced effects different from those the group allegedly wanted to produce, one was justified to assume that the group was hiding their real intentions. Hence, when faced with series of harmful events

---

33 Other scholars that make a strong case for the survival of republicanism far into the nineteenth century are Linda Kerber, *Women of the Republic: Intellect and Ideology in Revolutionary America*, 5th ed., Chapel Hill, NC 1997; Jeffrey Ostler,"The Rhetoric of Conspiracy and the Formation of Kansas Populism", in: *Agricultural History*, 69/1995, 1, pp. 1–27; Sean Wilentz, *Chants Democratic: New York City and the Rise of the American Working Class, 1788–1850*, New York 1984; Jean H. Baker, *Affairs of Party: The Political Culture of Northern Democrats in the Mid-Nineteenth Century*, Ithaca, NY 1983.

34 Pocock, "Civic Humanism and Its Role in Anglo-American Thought", in: *Politics, Language and Time: Essays on Political Thought and History*, London 1971, pp. 80–103, p. 97.

35 Wood, "Conspiracy", p. 416.

36 Wood, "Conspiracy", pp. 417–418.

whose originators denied all evil intentions, people were compelled to conclude that a conspiracy was underway. As Wood puts it: "The belief in plots was not a symptom of disturbed minds but a rational attempt to explain human phenomena in terms of human intentions and to maintain moral coherence in the affairs of men".[37]

This epistemological paradigm proved remarkably resilient in both Europe and America. Whereas Wood suggests that it disappeared early in the nineteenth century, Geoffrey Cubitt (for France) and Ralf Klausnitzer (for Germany in particular and Europe more generally) have demonstrated that it continued to generate knowledge considered legitimate until the early twentieth century.[38] According to Klausnitzer, it only lost its influence in Europe when the social sciences began to offer systemic explanations for effects hitherto ascribed to the hidden intentions of individuals. This, however, might be exactly the reason why the paradigm retained its hegemonic position far longer in the United States and why it continues to produce appealing, albeit by now disqualified, knowledge there until today. After all, resistance to structural explanations of all kinds is deeply ingrained in American culture because they would shake one of its central pillars: the belief in the power of individuals to shape not only their own lives but the course of history. During the 1950s, for instance, many social scientists claimed that brainwashing was possible because, as Timothy Melley has shown, this assumption allowed them to discuss systemic effects on individuals without giving up the belief in a self-contained, autonomous self (which was seen as being manipulated by an even stronger self, that of the brainwasher).[39] Unsurprisingly, therefore, politicians also still rejected systemic factors. As Senator Joseph McCarthy, one of America's most notorious conspiracy theorists of that period, put it, "History does not just happen. It is made by men – men with faces, and the only way the course of history can be changed is by getting rid of the specific individuals who we find are bad for America".[40]

---

[37] Wood, "Conspiracy", p. 429.

[38] Whereas Cubitt explicitly rejects Wood's argument ("Quite simply, this recession [that Wood postulates] shows very little signs of having happened during the nineteenth and early twentieth centuries" ["Conspiracy Myths", p. 18]), Ralf Klausnitzer does not refer to Wood at all (cf. *Poesie und Konspiration: Beziehungssinn und Zeichenökonomie von Verschwörungsszenarien in Publizistik, Literatur und Wissenschaft 1750–1850*, Berlin 2007). However, focusing on Germany, he discusses the emergence of the same epistemological paradigm (esp. pp. 66–98) and traces its repercussions into the twentieth century.

[39] Cf. Timothy Melley, "Brainwashed! Conspiracy Theory and Ideology in the Postwar United States", in: *New German Critique*, 35/2008, 1, pp. 145–164.

[40] McCarthy qtd. in Olmsted, *Real Enemies*, p. 107.

Since then, of course, even American culture has become more receptive to structural explanations, and naïve insistence on the power of individuals to shape the course of history is no longer acceptable in scientific as well as in parts of public discourse. But as the traditional *post hoc ergo propter hoc* logic of contemporary conspiracy theories shows, the eighteenth-century paradigm discussed here remains attractive. In fact, as Peter Knight has demonstrated, the idea that individuals can put their intentions into practice without any unwarranted side-effects both informs and is confirmed by the official (al-Qaeda did it) and unofficial (the government did it) conspiracy theories about 9/11. The two narratives of what happened that day and who is to be held responsible for it may be diametrically opposed as far as the allocation of guilt is concerned. Structurally, though, both rely "on a traditional model of highly efficient individual intentional action" and thus affirm "a vague ideological disposition toward understanding causality and responsibility in terms of pure intentional agency".[41]

Puritanism, republicanism, and the specific epistemology just discussed can be considered the most important origins of the American propensity for conspiracy theorizing, especially since these three factors did not exist in isolation next to each other. On the contrary, the epistemological paradigm, for example, provided the underpinning for republican fears of conspiracy, while the fact that the political theory facilitated conspiracist visions surely stabilized the epistemological paradigm. Moreover, from the eighteenth century onward, virtually all non-fictional indictments of conspiracy can be said to have assumed the form of the "republican jeremiad", a blend of the jeremiad, the narrative mode in which the Puritans expressed their fear of declension, and republican concerns about corruption.[42] Republican jeremiads bemoan the present state of society by contrasting it with the glorified time before the conspiracy began, but they also express the hope that the conspiracy can still be foiled if only the people wake up to the danger and begin to actively resist it. Jedidah Morse's exposure of the Illuminati plot, Abraham Lincoln's "House Divided" speech, Joseph McCarthy's Wheeling speech, and the online documentary *Loose Change* are all republican jeremiads, and they all assume that individuals can shape history by putting their plans into practice. Thus, it is the combination of Puritanism, republicanism, and a par-

---

41 Peter Knight, "Outrageous Conspiracy Theories: Popular and Official Responses to 9/11 in Germany and the United States", in: *New German Critique*, 35/2008, 1, pp. 165–193, pp. 176, 178.

42 Sacvan Bercovitch, *The American Jeremiad*, Madison, WI 1978, p. 128.

ticular epistemological paradigm that accounts for the continued presence of conspiracy theories in American culture.

3. The United States and the Middle East

The United States is both a clearly defined geographical unit and a nation state; the "Middle East", a term coined by Alfred Thayer Mahan, an American historian, in 1902, is neither. It comprises a great variety of states and, reaching from the Eastern Mediterranean to the western parts of South Asia, is characterized by the blurredness of its geographical boundaries. In a certain sense, therefore, the Middle East only exists from a western point of view.[43] Thus, for the scholar of conspiracy theory, speaking of "the Middle East" only makes sense when talking about American conspiracy theories that imagine the region precisely as homogeneous as the term implies, or when one is very generally concerned with processes of transfer from the "West", an equally fuzzy term, to the region. If one is interested, however, in the precise mechanisms and functions of conspiracy theories within the Middle East, one needs to look at individual states or specific local contexts. Accordingly, except for Barbara De Poli and Matthew Gray who seek to establish a general (historical respectively contemporary) framework, the other six contributions on the Middle East are dedicated to various states within the region.

What is more, a comparative approach to conspiracy theories in the United States and the Middle East must take into account the imbalance of power, in political, economic, academic-scientific, military, and many other terms, between these two entities. But not only is the United States far more powerful than the Middle East; it also exerts more power in and on that region than any other western country. While this may sound like a truism, it is worth remembering that the predominant role of the United States within the region was established only relatively recently. While U.S. special envoy Patrick Hurley noticed as early as May 1943, after visiting Egypt, that Great Britain would soon "no longer possess within herself the essentials of power needed to maintain her traditional role as the dominant influence in the

---

[43] On the genesis of the term "Middle East" which in today's usage roughly encompasses Syria, Palestine, Israel, Jordan, Iraq, the Arabian peninsula, Egypt, Turkey, Iran, and possibly also Afghanistan and Pakistan, cf. Roderic Davison and his fatalistic statement on the obvious unpracticability *cum* unavoidability of the term "Middle East": "Intentional vagueness sometimes has advantage as a tent-like cover for unformulated possibilities of future action or inaction" ("Where is the Middle East?", in: *Foreign Affairs*, 38/1959–1960, pp. 665–675, p. 675).

Middle East area",[44] it was only at the end of the 1970s – and after some intermittent steps such as Britain's renunciation of the Palestine mandate in 1947 and its disastrous involvement in the failed Suez intervention of 1956 – that the United States, under the impression of the Soviet invasion of Afghanistan, finally assumed "the lonely burden of protecting western interests in the Persian Gulf that Great Britain had shouldered" throughout the preceding decades.[45] The demise of the Soviet Union during the early 1990s then removed the United States' lone remaining competitor for influence in the region. In recent years, since the attacks of September 11, 2001, the Middle East has become more important than ever for the United States. It has become not only the central focus of American foreign policy,[46] but, as Melanie McAlister argues, it has come to perform an important function for America's self-understanding: faced with its own internal diversity and race issues, the United States "needed an 'outside' to mark its boundaries; that outside was the Middle East".[47]

The imbalance of power between the United States and the Middle East is mirrored by how they figure in each other's conspiracy theories. For American conspiracy theories, the Middle East is only of very limited importance. Of course, after 9/11 the Bush administration promoted the conspiracy theory that Osama bin Laden's al-Qaeda and Saddam Hussein's Iraq were secret allies, but, as Alexander Dunst reminds us in his contribution, this fantasy escaped the label "conspiracy theory". In narratives that are labeled accordingly, the Middle East features occasionally, but even then its inhabitants are bereft of agency. Many American post-9/11 conspiracy theories revolve

44 Qtd. in Douglas Little, *American Orientalism: The United States and the Middle East Since 1945*, Chapel Hill, NC 2008, p. 119.

45 Little, *American Orientalism*, p. 147.

46 Cf. also Brian Johnsrud's article in this volume. Emmanuel Todd argues, very much in the vein of intellectual French anti-Americanism, that it is the military decline of the U.S. that obliges it to make the Middle East an object of its aggression as it is a region known for its military incapabilities (*Weltmacht USA: Ein Nachruf*, München 2003, p. 172).

47 Melanie McAlister, *Epic Encounters: Culture, Media, and U.S. Interests in the Middle East, 1945–2000*, Berkeley, CA 2001, p. 259; she also comments on the importance of the Middle East for the racialized and gendered discourse of nationalist expansion in the United States (p. 275). What is more, even U.S. political scientists who sympathize with the basic tenets of U.S. policy in the Middle East will agree that in many ways not only political Islam, but also "September 11 was the price [the United States] paid for winning the Cold War and the strategies [it] chose" (Rachel Bronson, *Thicker Than Oil: America's Uneasy Partnership with Saudi Arabia*, Oxford 2006, p. 9).

around the Middle East, claiming, for example, that the attacks on the Pentagon and the World Trade Center were orchestrated in order to wage war in Iraq and Afghanistan, but in these accounts the Arab terrorists, if they are part of the scenario at all, are merely puppets whose strings are pulled by Americans. At first sight, Arabs are given a more active role in religious conspiracy theories as they circulate among millennial Christians in the United States.[48] Much like the Puritans three hundred years ago, these fundamentalist Christians believe in a cosmic struggle between the forces of good and evil. More precisely, they are convinced that the Anti-Christ will spearhead a plot against Israel and the United States in which many Middle Eastern countries will be involved. However, the Anti-Christ is rarely ever imagined as coming from a Middle Eastern country; reflecting remnants of the Cold War he is far more frequently imagined to be Russian, for example in Tim La Haye's immensely successful *Left Behind* series. Thus, Arabs tend to be reduced to mere pawns in this scenario as well.

By contrast, the United States has been crucial to conspiracy theories circulating in the Middle East during the last decades. In fact, one might argue that it is amply proven – for example, by many contributions to this volume – that one cannot write a history of U.S.-Middle Eastern relations without taking conspiracy theories into account. As we discuss in detail below, the real and alleged plots of the United States are one of the most important reasons why conspiracy theories are so prominent in the region. Yet, before we delve deeper into Middle Eastern conspiracy theories it must be stressed that, just as there must be histories of the United States in which conspiracy theories are merely a footnote, there *must* be histories of U.S.-Middle Eastern relations and the Middle East itself that pay no heed to conspiracy theories.[49] This is not the right place to address in detail the question of Orientalism but we should keep in mind Said's remark that Orientalism can be an academic discipline, a binary way of thinking that essentializes "the West" and "the East", and a medium of control and dominance.[50] Since conspiracy theories in the Middle East reflect the serious imbalance of power between the United States and the Middle East, speaking about their relationship in terms of conspi-

---

48 For an extended discussion of metaphysical New World Order conspiracy theories, cf. Barkun, *Culture of Conspiracy*, pp. 39–64.

49 A number of recent works prove that this is well possible. Cf., for example, Rashid Khalidi, *Resurrecting Empire: Western Footprints and America's Perilous Path in the Middle East*, London 2004; Ussama Samir Makdisi, *Faith Misplaced: The Broken Promise of U.S.-Arab Relations: 1820–2003*, New York 2010.

50 Edward W. Said, *Orientalism*, New York 1978, p. 2.

racy theory alone runs the danger of contributing to the cementation of this hierarchy. The same is true, however, for touching on Middle Eastern conspiracy theories in passing only or ignoring them altogether, which is why we turn to them now.

4. The Origins of Middle Eastern Conspiracy Theories

If one believes Daniel Pipes, whose study *The Hidden Hand: Middle East Fears of Conspiracy* was until recently the only monograph available in English on the subject, the matter is very simple indeed. For Pipes, Middle Eastern conspiracy theories are not the "result of political structures, which in turn are the result of historical impacts, the effects of external dynamics, state-society relations, and political culture", as Matthew Gray has recently argued,[51] but the result of regional idiosyncrasies, originating from "Zoroastrian, Manichean, and Mazdak sources" and a deep-seated psychological disorder, that is, paranoia.[52] Somewhat contradictorily, though, Pipes also argues that these conspiracy theories are at the same time strategically deployed: they function as a perilous weapon to attack the state of Israel. In order to prove this, Pipes repeatedly unfolds a panorama of ill-founded Middle Eastern anxieties about an alleged plan to conquer large parts of the Middle East in order to establish a "Greater Israel".[53]

As many critical commentators have observed, Pipes, a prominent spokesman of the neo-conservative camp in the U.S., known amongst other as founder of the inquisition-minded institution *Campus Watch*, does so for strategic reasons himself. Driven by the desire to disqualify any justified objections against Israel's policies, he focuses only on exaggerated and extremely vicious Arab positions vis-à-vis Israel, thereby both simplifying and distorting the complex Middle Eastern political landscape, and laying a smokescreen over the real reasons of the Israel-Arab conflict. In fact, while Pipes draws on an astounding variety of sources (including many newspapers in Arabic language) and thus presents conclusive evidence of the Middle Easterners' proneness to conspiracy theorizing, he comes dangerously close to the techniques of conspiracism himself in that he uses a continuous time frame, a universalizing geographical perspective, and assumes the ubiquity of conspiracism. At one point, for example, he deals with Egypt in the years

51 Gray, *Conspiracy Theories*, p. 8.

52 Pipes, *The Hidden Hand: Middle East Fears of Conspiracy*, Basingstoke 1996, p. 292.

53 Cf., for example, Pipes, *Hidden Hand*, pp. 49, 68–69.

1952, 1981 and 1990, with Iran in the years 1979 and 1989, and finally with Jerusalem in 1929 and 1969 on one page.[54]

Pipes is right in one respect, though: Israel and the Palestine question are of immediate relevance to the history and politics of the Middle East and in particular to U.S.-Middle Eastern relations, and therefore also to the forms and functions of conspiracy theories in the region. Pro-Israeli voices, anti-Zionists and the (larger or smaller) rest may not be able to agree on much, but they would all agree that "No matter how one turns the kaleidoscope of U.S.-Arab relations, one always returns, or is returned to, the picture of Palestine".[55] As a consequence, much Middle Eastern conspiracy theorizing is connected to the heated debates about Israel's legitimacy. But, first, the matter is far more complex than Pipes insinuates; and, second, there are other factors that need to be taken into account if one wants to understand the prominence of conspiracy theories in the Middle East.

Although the history of conspiracy theories in the Middle East prior to the second half of the twentieth century has yet to be written, it is clear that such theories circulated in the region before the foundation of the state of Israel in 1948. Yet, just as with anti-Semitism and Arab nationalism more generally, conspiracy theories became virulent and powerful only with the rise of the Zionist-Palestinian struggle.[56] Barbara De Poli demonstrates in her contribution to this volume that conspiracy theories were absorbed in

---

[54] Cf. Pipes, *Hidden Hand*, p. 14. Cf. Aaron Winter's piece in this volume for a similar assessment of this point. It also has to be noted that Pipes' pro-Zionism has not remained uncontested. It finds its counterpart in the academic world in scholars such as John Esposito who tend to idealize or at least belittle militant Islam. As Henry Munson pointedly puts it: "Reading Pipes, one could easily believe that Muslim hostility toward Israel is simply a matter of anti-Semitism. Reading Esposito, one would never know that anti-Semitism is indeed a serious problem in the Islamic world" ("Between Pipes and Esposito", in: *ISIM* [*International Institute for the Study of Islam in the Modern World*] *Newsletter*, 10/2002, p. 8.)

[55] Makdisi, *Faith Misplaced*, p. 5.

[56] For a general outline of the trajectory of anti-Semitism in the twentieth-century Middle East and a rich bibliography on the topic, cf. Gudrun Krämer, "Antisemitism in the Muslim World: A Critical Review", in: *Die Welt des Islams: International Journal of the Study of Modern Islam*, 46/2006, pp. 243–276. Cf. also Klaus Faber et al. (eds.), *Neu-alter Judenhass: Antisemitismus, arabisch-israelischer Konflikt und europäische Politik*, Berlin 2006; Meir Litvak/Esther Webman, *From Empathy to Denial: Arab Responses to the Holocaust*, New York 2009. Recent debates in the United States have stressed allegedly new "Islamofascists". Cf., for example, the polemical work by Norman Podhoretz, *World War IV: The Long Struggle Against Islamofascism*, New York 2007.

Arabic-speaking countries only slowly, but then with a sudden outburst of productivity from the 1940s onwards. De Poli identifies two main routes of the Arab world's appropriation of "western" conspiracy theories: on the one hand, anti-Masonic literature that traveled to Arab lands in the late nineteenth and early twentieth centuries, and, on the other hand, full-blown anti-Semitism injected by German Nazi propaganda from the 1920s onward. De Poli shows that both anti-Masonic and anti-Semitic writings were initially received only at the margins of society, but with the Jewish-Arab war and the proclamation of the state of Israel both became closely linked and have received much attention from the Arab media ever since. Especially the notorious *Protocols of the Elders of Zion* have since the 1950s become the centerpiece of conspiracy theorizing in the Arab world.

It would be wrong to say, though, that the Arab world thus still clings to a conspiracy theory that has, thankfully, long lost its mainstream appeal in Europe and North America. For once, as De Poli also shows, Arab conspiracy discourse constitutes a unique blend of anti-Semitism and anti-Masonism that does not only rely on European texts such as the *Protocols* but that has, in recent decades, been affirmed and embellished by countless Arab texts, many of them openly fictional, others allegedly factual. Moreover, Middle Eastern anti-Semitic conspiracy theories have different targets and different motivations than the ones that once thrived in Europe and North America and continue to exist there on the margins of society. Matthew Gray points out in his contribution that whereas anti-Semitic arguments in the United States these days focus on Jewish banking, finance, and informal power, Middle Eastern anti-Semitic conspiracy theories concentrate very specifically on Israel's actions and intentions.

However, even though the Israeli-Palestinian question as the central pivot of U.S.-Middle Eastern relations for now and for the foreseeable future is an important engine of conspiracist visions in the regions, there are others forces driving such visions that one needs to take into account as well. To begin with, there are the strategic interests of the United States, as well as of other western nations, in the region – for example, in a steady and cheap oil supply – that exist independently of the alliance with Israel and are at times even at odds with it. To protect these interests, the United States in particular launched a couple of clandestine operations in the region in the years following World War II, the most notorious of them being the CIA-led coup d'état of 1953 that removed Iran's prime minister Mohammad Mosaddeq from power. Unlike in the United States where, as we have argued, the impact of real plots on conspiracy theories has been negligible, the impact of such "real conspiracies" on the Middle Eastern predilection for conspiracy theorizing cannot be overestimated.[57] Next to the conflict with Israel, it is the single most important source of Middle Eastern conspiracism. The occurrence of actual plots in the past nourishes the belief in conspiracies, as it fosters the tendency to interpret convoluted and undesired political circumstances in conspiratorial terms and makes the public receptive to the "exposure" of new schemes by well-established villains. In this situation, political leaders are naturally tempted to articulate conspiracy theories, whether they believe in them themselves or not.

The case of Iran, a country where conspiracy theories are propagated on a large scale by the state, illustrates well both the significance of past plots and the strategic deployment of conspiracist discourse in the present. Mahmoud Ahmadinejad may refer to Zionism as a major evil in the world, but he can only do this so frequently because the history of Iran, and especially the public memory of not only the coup of 1953 but also the coups of 1908 and 1921, which were also exerted under strong foreign influence, provides a fertile ground for a public mobilization of this kind. Schirin Fathi, in her contribution to this volume, shows that conspiracy theories have been part of Iranian nationalism even before the time of the Shah. Refuting the idea that Iran is "addicted" to conspiracy theories because of the Shia's marginalization and persecution by the Sunni majority in early Islamic history,[58] she singles out the CIA's Operation Ajax of 1953, which has left deep scars in collective memory, as the major influence on Iranian conspiracism.

But Iran is not only the country in the region where conspiracy theories are handled as an important tool of political mobilization. The Lebanese Hizbollah is another striking example. Hizbollah, a radical military-political Shia movement that came into being in the early 1980s in southern Lebanon as a resistance movement against Israeli occupation, defined itself from the start as a close ally of Iran and adopted its grand theories of conspiracy. However, as Stephan Schmid demonstrates in his essay, in particular from

---

57 The United States also have to shoulder the historical burden of French and British imperialism, in particular the secret Sykes-Picot treaty of 1916 in which Great Britain and France defined their respective spheres of imperialist control. Bassam Tibi argues (not really convincing, though) that – when the document was diclosed by the Soviets in 1917 – the public outrage in the Middle East was the starting point for conspiracism in the region (*Die Verschwörung: Das Trauma arabischer Politik*, Hamburg 1993, p. 3).

58 This argument is implied by Sadik J. al-Azm who writes that "power was in fact usurped from Imamu Ali and his heirs through a series of dirty conspiracies" ("Orientalism and Conspiracy", in: Graf/Fathi/Paul (eds.), *Orientalism and Conspiracy*, p. 18).

the 1990s onwards, Hizbollah has put less emphasis on grand theories in the Iranian fashion and come to use "operational" conspiracy theories, or, as he puts it, theories that are "not the reflection of a bizarre, irrational, and intransigent anti-western and anti-Zionist outlook, but a very rational medium of propaganda and political maneuvering adopted by the Party of God in the course of its changing role in the domestic and regional political arena". Whereas all of Hizbollah's conspiracy theories excoriate Israel, they are primarily addressed at the internal public and meant to strengthen Hizbollah's political position within Lebanon and its political landscape.

Lebanon is also the subject of André G. Sleiman's essay, which delves deeply into the intricacies of the country's civil war (1975–1990) and investigates how international power politics, which regarded Lebanon as a theater for proxy wars in the Middle East and beyond, were perceived from different Lebanese perspectives and interpreted in conspiracist fashion. Henry Kissinger, U.S. Secretary of State in the years 1973–1977, was identified by major Lebanese politicians, of both Christian and Muslim denomination, as a vile manipulator. A widespread, but unsubstantiated persuasion existed in Lebanon according to which Kissinger had not only triggered the civil war but intended to destroy the Lebanese model of Muslim-Christian conviviality by dividing Lebanon into two confessional states. While the Christian narrative centers on the fatal consequences of a Christian exodus from Lebanon, the Muslim one stresses the potential advantages for Israel's policy. Such a scheme, thus ran the conviction of many in Lebanon, was to stabilize Israel's position in the Middle East as its sectarian identity would then have seemed less peculiar.

Besides demonstrating how the Israeli question and the experience of real plots interact in fueling conspiracy theories in the region, these three examples show that the conspiracist visions circulating throughout the Middle East are far from simplistic or uniform, as Pipes would have it. They are highly complex projections that are at times strategically deployed and at others naively believed, but that are invariably adapted to the specificities of the national, and at times even local, contexts from which they emerge and for which they perform various kinds of cultural work. It is therefore of the utmost importance to proceed with due caution when generalizing about the forms and functions of Middle Eastern conspiracy theories.

5. The Forms and Functions of Middle Eastern Conspiracy Theories

Generalizing about conspiracy theories in the Middle East, one could also assume, is so difficult because the region's conspiracist visions have been far less well researched than those of the United States. We may not know enough about American conspiracism yet, but we know far more about it than about the Middle Eastern variant. Moreover, whereas scholars from different disciplines have over the past decades developed theories and models to account for and describe American conspiracy theories, no such models exist for the Middle Eastern context. As Matthew Gray argues in his article, scholars can draw on concepts developed for the United States (and other western countries) and originally applied to cases of conspiracism there, and he encourages them to do so because it will prevent them from falling into the trap of essentializing Middle Eastern conspiracy theories. Gray thus sees "potential for […] the transferability and transposability of explanations for conspiracy theories across any cultures, not least of all the U.S. and the Middle East". Nevertheless, he also sees "strict limitations" for such transfers, as they run the danger of disregarding local specificities. What is needed, one might therefore conclude, is more research that draws on detailed case studies to theorize Middle Eastern conspiracism in general.

However, from our vantage point, the opposite is the case. The more we know about specific Middle Eastern conspiracy theories, their structures, targets, and audiences, the more difficult it becomes to identify characteristics shared by all of them. Apart from the observations that conspiracy theories are not native to the Middle East, but that this way of making sense of the world has traveled there from Europe and has then been adapted to regional circumstances, and that Middle Eastern conspiracy theories reflect and to a certain extent cement the imbalance of power between the United States (and "the West" in general) and the region, no generalizations are possible. The essays on the Middle East collected in the volume at hand challenge, rather than confirm existing generalizations. Thus, instead of defining general characteristics that do not stand closer scrutiny, we wish to stress four features that, from our current position, are integral to many, but not to all Middle Eastern conspiracy theories, and we discuss how the case studies presented here complicate them.

First, Middle Eastern conspiracy theories, as Ervand Abrahamian observed almost twenty years ago, treat interior "politics as a puppet show in which foreign powers control the marionettes – the local politicians – by invisible strings".[59] Although Abrahamian referred only to Iran, his observation is certainly true for many, maybe even for most conspiracy theories circulating in the region. No matter whom or what the conspiracy theory focuses on,

[59] Ervand Abrahamian, "The Paranoid Style in Iranian Politics", in: Abrahamian (ed.), *Khomeinism: Essays on the Islamic Republic*, Berkeley, CA 1993, pp. 111–131, p. 111.

the American government, or at least parts of it, or "the West" more generally is almost always lurking somewhere in the background and usually cast as the mastermind behind the plot. However, not all conspiracy theories follow this pattern, as Annika Rabo and Christoph Herzog show in their contributions to the volume. Rabo demonstrates that people in Syria share conspiracy narratives that articulate dissatisfaction with the malfunctioning of the state and that blame corruption among Syrian politicians, rather than the schemes of foreign powers. Christoph Herzog shows that despite Turkey's strong democratic record and viable press, conspiracy theories abound in that country. They revolve not only around "outward forces", but also engage with the "deep state" – a concept that relates to power groups, particularly in the adminstration and the military, accused of steering state and society according to their allegedly privileged understanding of what Turkey is meant to be. Drawing on the work of the Turkish writer and intellectual Erol Mütercimler, Herzog admits that, of course, Turkish conspiracy theories also occasionally accuse foreign forces of meddling with Turkey's fate. But, for one, Herzog argues that Mütercimler's conspiracist master narrative of "the West against Turkey" follows classical anti-imperialist lines of argumentation and thus could be regarded as "essentially a nationalist vulgarization that is ultimately derived from the Marxist theoretical debate on imperialism and reinforced by the popularization of the Huntington thesis of the clash of civilizations". Moreover, even in Mütercimler's account, not all Turkish nationals are merely pawns; some of them are actors pursuing goals of their own.

Second, Matthew Gray has recently argued, and indeed does so in this volume, too, that a distinguishing feature of conspiracism in the Middle East is that conspiracy theories serve as a powerful tool of political mobilization for the state or powerful state-like organizations. Faced with a continuously diminishing legitimacy, Gray suggests, "[states] have adopted their own conspiracism also as a tool of state symbolism, legitimacy-building and control".[60] Indeed, Middle Eastern state machines frequently deploy conspiracy theories for political ends, and the invectives of Gaddafi, Assad, or Ahmadinejad, who habitually blame(d) foreign agents for causing internal unrest, are often reported on by the media in Europe and North America. However, Gray's valid observation has to be modified in two respects. As Alexander Dunst reminds us in his essay, the Bush government, continuing a longstanding American political tradition, also formulated a conspiracy theory when it suggested that Iraq and al-Qaeda were secretly plotting against the

60 Gray, *Conspiracy Theories*, p. 12; also cf. chapter 5 in this volume, pp. 272–289.

United States. He suggests that the only difference between the Bush administration's conspiracist vision and the visions of Middle Eastern leaders was that the former was not labeled "conspiracy theory" whereas the latter were. Accordingly, he concludes that, as in the Middle East, conspiracy rhetoric "has been part of mainstream politics from its beginnings, and continues to be so today". Moreover, conspiracy theories articulated by the state to maintain control are not always as successful as western news reporting tends to imply. As Schirin Fathi shows, state conspiracy propaganda in Iran may have strongly increased under the Ahmadinejad regime, but there are indicators that it has at the same time lost much of its appeal among the Iranian public, in other words, that it falls on deaf ears.

Third, and closely related to the previous point, one might think that unlike in the western world, conspiracy theorizing is not a fringe phenomenon in the Middle East, but that it permeates society on all levels and independent of affiliation with political camps. Again, there is much to be said in favor of this observation, since Middle Eastern conspiracy theories are often uncritically believed not only by the disempowered but also by political and cultural elites. Yet, as we pointed out above, at least as far as the United States is concerned, the delegitimization of the knowledge produced by conspiracy theorizing is a fairly recent development. Until the 1950s, American conspiracy theories, too, permeated all levels of society and all political camps, and as the example of the Bush administration shows, this has not completely changed until today, the only difference being that some visions do and others do not escape the derogatory label "conspiracy theory". Moreover, the observation that in the Middle East conspiracy theories are ubiquitous often implies the assessment that Middle Easterners cast themselves invariably as the passive and helpless victims of foreign plots. This, however, is not necessarily the case. As Annika Rabo's contribution makes clear, Middle Eastern conspiracy theories do not only occasionally revolve around domestic villains. Rabo's analysis of "conspiracy talk" in Syria, that is, everyday talk of ordinary Syrians about conspiracies by powerful others, shows that such talk is often quite prosaic and frequently deals with tangible threats. In fact, many people, especially educated males, tend to invent new elements and bring the conspiracy narratives into a direct and meaningful relationship with their personal lives as a form of entertainment, thus giving in to what Mark Fenster, for the American context, has described as the "conspiracy rush", as playful engagement with an alleged plot as if it was real.[61] What is

---

[61] Fenster, *Conspiracy Theories*, p. 156.

more, when people say that "It has all been planned" they stress not only their powerlessness vis-à-vis "the system" or "the authorities" but combine it with confessions of intense self-flagellation. "Blaming 'us' is the flip side of blaming 'them'", Rabo concludes, and so her study confirms that conspiracy theories indeed permeate society, but in a fundamentally different way than it is generally assumed.

Fourth, and finally, it has been argued that whereas western conspiracy theories from the eighteenth century onward have been an epiphenomenon of secularization, that indeed conspiracy theories emerged in their modern form only because of the secularizing force of the Enlightenment, Middle Eastern conspiracy theories are different in that they are metaphysical conspiracy theories because of their connection to political Islam. While it is true that political Islam, thriving since the 1970s, has taken up conspiracy theorizing and made it even more pervasive in the public realm, the matter is, once again, more complex. To begin with, as the example of fundamentalist Christians in the United States mentioned above indicates, religious conspiracy theories continue to exist in the western world as well. In addition, political Islam, roughly defined as an ideology which strives to base politics on the premises and prescriptions of the Islamic religion, emerged in the nineteenth century. Thus, there is no natural link between political Islam and conspiracy theorizing, as the latter became part of the former's agenda only recently. Moreover, political Islam must be understood as an attempt of the Muslim world to come to terms with the challenges of modernity. "Islam", whatever it may mean to the individual person, is thus conceived by Muslims as an essential part of the Muslim heritage and identity. Accordingly, "political Islam", far from corroborating a case of Islamic exceptionalism, is intrinsic to the Muslim experience of a secularizing world. Much of Islamic ideology today is nothing else but an "islamicizing" discourse that provides a religious garb for secular themes. Finally, there is no compulsory link between political Islam and conspiray theories. Türkay Nefes' essay on the *Dönme* shows that the mainstream Islamic Justice and Development Party (AKP), in power in Turkey since 2002, explicitly distances itself from certain conspiracy theories. Nefes describes how the very small crypto-religious group of the *Dönme* (allegedly pretending to be Muslims, but practicing a particular version of Judaism inside the group) have, because of their religious and cultural liminality, been regarded as potentially disloyal to the Turkish "nation-state" since the 1920s and have become a central element in Turkish conspiracy theories. Interviews that Nefes led with important representatives of major political parties corroborate that conspiracy theories revolving around the *Dönme* are propagated by radical parties of nationalist

(National Action Party, MHP) or Islamist (Felicity Party, SP) leanings, whereas the AKP has moved away from such interpretations.[62]

Middle Eastern conspiracy theories, then, are publicly acceptable forms of interpreting political, economic, and social contexts within the region and in its relation to the world beyond. They are containers or vehicles for specific arguments and specific anxieties, and they help to arouse the feeling of a commonly shared destiny. Contrary to common assumptions, they do not automatically render Middle Easterners the passive victims of foreign plots but also imbue them with agency. And as everywhere else, Middle Eastern conspiracy theories must be taken seriously and have to be studied closely because they often "address real structural inequities, albeit ideologically, and they may well constitute a response, albeit in a simplistic and decidedly unpragmatic form, to an unjust political order, a barren or dysfunctional civil society, and/or an exploitative economic system".[63] This is not to say that conspiracy theories in the Middle East, as well as elsewhere, are not at times vicious and dangerous. The problematic role that conspiracy theories, particularly in their many anti-Semitic variations, play in Middle Eastern societies is not to be belittled. The same, however, is true for the United States where the media and large parts of the public accepted and helped promote the Bush administration's "official" conspiracy theory about Iraq in 2002 and 2003. But that conspiracy theories at times have fatal consequences is one more reason why they have to be taken seriously by academics.

---

62 This is, of course not to deny that the conspiracy theories promoted by radicalized Islam are often of the especially vicious and anti-Semitic kind. The major producer and exporter of "classical" crude anti-Semitic conspiracy theories is Saudi Arabia and its role in this regard would have deserved closer scrutiny.

63 Fenster, *Conspiracy Theories*, p. 90.

I. The United States and the Middle East

Aaron Winter (Abertay)

My Enemies Must Be Friends: The American Extreme-Right, Conspiracy Theory, Islam, and the Middle East

That's really a true American: George Lincoln Rockwell
I know for a fact he hates Commies cus he picketed the movie Exodus
Bob Dylan, "Talkin' John Birch Paranoid Blues"

Whether they articulate fears about freed slaves, Jews, freemasons, communists, civil rights, the federal government, the "New World Order", or "Zionist Occupied Government" (ZOG), conspiracy theories have always been central to the American extreme-right. The extreme-right is a diverse group of right-wing movements, most notably white supremacists, white nationalists, white separatists, and neo-Nazis such as the Ku Klux Klan, American Nazi Party, National Alliance, Aryan Nations, and others who hold racist and/or anti-Semitic views, ideologies, and conspiracist interpretations and theories of history and power.[1] Such extreme-right movements and organizations have emerged and proliferated at different points throughout American history whenever they perceive social, political, or economic developments as detrimental to the white race and/or America, from Reconstruction in the 1860s and 1870s through civil rights in the 1960s and the farm crisis in the 1980s to the election of Barack Obama in 2008.

Conspiracy theories have provided a vehicle for the expression and representation of the extreme-right's fears about threats to white supremacy and America and served as justification for their political mobilization, activism, and violence. While the conspirators in such theories have included internal and external enemies or threats, there has been a consistent stable of usual suspects that relate to America's racial, political, ideological, and regional fault-lines. Even though there have been both internal enemies and allies in such theories, external forces are rarely portrayed as anything but a threat. Following 9/11, al-Qaeda, 'Islamist' Extremists, the Middle East, and the wider Muslim and Arab world began to feature more prominently in ex-

---

1 Cf. Martin Durham, *The Christian Right, the Far Right and the Boundaries of American Conservatism*, Manchester 2000, p. xii.

treme-right conspiracy theories and literature. While the mainstream right feared the threat posed by this region and people, the extreme-right saw them as potential allies in their war against the American government and Zionism. In response, watchdogs, academics, and other commentators have made a great deal about the link between extreme-right and Islamist conspiracy theories and potential alliances between the two movements, not just post-9/11 but retrospectively throughout the post-war era.

In this chapter, I examine American extreme-right conspiracy theories concerning the Middle East and the Muslim and Arab world, attempted alliances with Islamists, and the relationship between such theories and alliances, as well as the work by commentators who attempt to establish links between the extreme-right and Islamists based on their shared penchant for conspiracy theories and efforts towards alliance building. I argue that in spite of claims about overlap and alliances, attempts to forge alliances between the extreme-right and Islamists have been unidirectional, originating with the extreme-right, and largely unsuccessful. Moreover, they have tended to occur during (and thus reflect) periods of movement realignment or crisis, when the extreme-right is seeking political direction and relevance. These are periods which correspond to developments and realignments in American foreign policy and international relations that concern the Middle East and Islam. In Part One, I examine attempts by commentators to establish links between conspiracy theories, extremism, and political alliances, *and* between the extreme-right and Islamists. This is followed in Part Two with an examination of attempts by the extreme-right to form alliances with movements in the Arab and Muslim world, as well as conspiracy theories about them, in five specific periods of realignment or crisis in the post-war period: post-World War II, post-Civil Rights, post-Cold War, post-9/11, and following the election of Barack Obama.

1. Conspiracies, Theories, and Alliances

Since the events of 9/11, a great amount of attention has been paid not only to Islamist terrorism and extremism in the Middle East, Arab and Muslim world, but to conspiracy theories about 9/11, American foreign policy, and Jews, Zionism, and Israel. High-profile examples include theories that claim 9/11 was an American and/or Israeli plot, the anti-Semitic conspiracy theory *Protocols of the Elders of Zion* promoted on jihadist websites, Radio Islam, and, in a dramatization, on Hizballah TV soon after 9/11, as well as the Holocaust denial by Iranian President Mahmoud Ahmadinejad in a 2005 speech and during his 2006 Holocaust conference in Iran. In a speech made at the UN in New York in September 2010, Ahmadinejad also claimed that the U.S. government was behind 9/11 in order to prop up Israel.

Since 9/11, this phenomenon has been examined and commented on in numerous books and articles on Islamist extremism, conspiracy theory, and the relationship between them – a topic first written about by Daniel Pipes in *The Hidden Hand: Middle East Fears of Conspiracy* (1996) –, most notably Matthew Gray's *Conspiracy Theories in the Arab World: Sources and Politics* (2010). The link has also been discussed in the increasing number of books and articles on conspiracy theory that came out post-9/11, such as David Aaronovitch's *Voodoo Histories: How Conspiracy Theory Has Shaped Modern History* (2009). Aaronovitch argues that "all sorts of conspiracy theories were springing up around the attack on the World Trade Center and the subsequent invasion of Afghanistan, theories that seemed to me potentially dangerous in the world view they expounded".[2] Aaronovitch views conspiracy theory as an attack on enlightenment reason and democratic discourse and practice, targeting in particular the West, Israel and Zionism, the Anglo-American coalition, and the war on terror. Aaronovitch posits, in agreement with Daniel Pipes, that the Middle East is "awash" with conspiracy theories,[3] but that post-9/11 "we in the West are currently going through a period of fashionable conspiracism" as well.[4] Thus, in addition to his examination of conspiracy theory in the Middle East and amongst Islamists, he also looks at the 9/11 'Truthers', the anti-war left, and the extreme-right in the West.

Aaronovitch sees an overlap between Islamism and the extreme-right in anti-Semitic conspiracy theories such as the *Protocols of Zion*,[5] as does Mark Levin in the HBO documentary *Protocols of Zion* (2004). In the film, which begins in New York City at the site where the World Trade Center stood, Levin traces 9/11 conspiracy theories concerning Jews back to the original *Protocols*, a forged document about a meeting between Jewish leaders in which they formulate a plot for world domination, first published in Russia by agents of the Czar in 1905. Levin then traces the *Protocols* to its publication in the U.S. in 1919 in the form of Henry Ford's "The International Jew" in the *Dearborn Independent*, to its instrumentalization by Nazi Germany and eventually its revival, dissemination and use by contemporary Muslim leaders,

---

2 David Aaronovitch, *Voodoo Histories: How Conspiracy Theory Has Shaped Modern History*, London 2009, p. 3.
3 Aaronovitch, *Voodoo Histories*, p. 8.
4 Aaronovitch, *Voodoo Histories*, p. 3.
5 Cf. Aaronovitch, *Voodoo Histories*, p. 1.

Jihadist websites, and American neo-Nazis such as Shaun Walker of the National Alliance and Frank Weltner of Jew Watch.[6]

Aaronovitch and Levin are not alone in linking conspiracy theory and extremism and finding overlap between Islamists and the extreme-right. Others include Martin Lee in "The Swastika and the Crescent" (2002), George Michael in *The Enemy of My Enemy: The Alarming Convergence of Militant Islam and the Extreme Right* (2007), and Daniel Pipes in "The Far Right and Jihadis in Alliance", "More Ties between Islamists and Neo-Nazis", and "CAIR Promotes and Hosts William W. Baker, Neo-Nazi".[7] Yet, these three find more than overlap between the two movements: they are concerned about alliances between them. This concern emerged almost immediately following 9/11, when extreme-right activists issued statements which not only celebrated the attacks, but also extended a hand of friendship to al-Qaeda and other Islamists. One example cited by these and other commentators came from Billy Roper of the National Alliance:

> The enemy of our enemy is, for now at least, our friend. We may not want them marrying our daughters, just as they would not want us marrying theirs. We may not want them in our societies, just as they would not want us in theirs [...] But anyone who is willing to drive a plane into a building to kill jews is alright by me. I wish our members had half as much testicular fortitude.[8]

The notion that shared enemies provide a basis for an alliance between the extreme-right and Islamists is central to the analysis of Lee, Michael, and

---

6 Cf. Mark Levin, *The Protocols of Zion*, HBO, USA, 2004. It should be noted that there is a lack of consensus on the origins of the *Protocols* with some scholars putting them in France in the eighteenth century and others in Russia in the nineteenth or early twentieth century.

7 Martin A. Lee, "The Swastika and the Crescent", in: *Intelligence Report*, 105/2002, http://www.splcenter.org/get-informed/intelligence-report/browse-all-issues/2002/spring/the-swastika-and-the-crescent/ (accessed Dec. 10, 2010); George Michael, *The Enemy of My Enemy: The Alarming Convergence of Militant Islam and the Extreme Right*, Lawrence 2006; Daniel Pipes, "The Far Right and Jihadis in Alliance", Mar. 9, 2005, updated Apr. 15, 2011, http://www.danielpipes.org/blog/2005/03/the-far-right-jihadis-in-alliance (accessed Dec. 16, 2011); "More Ties between Islamists and Neo-Nazis", Jan. 8, 2004, http://www.danielpipes.org/blog/2004/01/more-ties-between-islamists-andneo-nazis (accessed Aug. 16, 2010); "CAIR Promotes and Hosts William W. Baker, Neo-Nazi", Mar. 9, 2004, http://www.danielpipes.org/blog/2004/03/cair-promotes-and-hostswilliam-w-baker-neo-nazi (accessed Aug. 16, 2010).

8 Roger qtd. in Southern Poverty Law Center (SPLC), "Extremist Groups React to the 9/11 Attacks", in: *Intelligence Report*, 104/2001, http://www.splcenter.org/get-informed/intelligence-report/browse-all-issues/2001/winter/reaping-the--whirlwind#.UXUBB0ockt0 (accessed Dec. 16, 2011).

Pipes. Despite focusing primarily on the European extreme-right, Lee discusses the American scene as well and argues that "the peculiar bond between white nationalist groups and certain Muslim extremists derives in part from a shared set of enemies – Jews, the United States, race-mixing and ethnic diversity".[9] This point not just ignores the racial, ethnic, and national diversity of Islam, but also implies that in principle both the extreme-right and Islamists would oppose any co-existence, if not also co-operation, with each other based on their respective racial and ethnic differences. In addition to this, Lee argues that "both sets of groups also have a penchant for far-flung conspiracy theories that caricature Jewish power". He claims that "the psychological dynamics that propel the actions of Islamic terrorists have much in common with the mental outlook of neo-Nazis" since, he writes, "both glorify violence as a regenerative force and both are willing to slaughter innocents in the name of creating a new social order".[10] Although initially merely stating that the two movements are a peculiar match due to their shared insularity and xenophobia, he eventually argues that because of these common characteristics and historical links between Nazis and Muslims "the potential for an alliance between American neo-Nazis and Islamic terrorists – an alliance that could develop into strong operational ties – cannot be ruled out".[11]

Like Lee, Michael holds that, in spite of clear differences on issues of race and religion, the two movements have a clear overlap if not convergence on several important issues, such as their utopian desire for homogeneous societies and support for Palestinian independence, their critique of American foreign policy and military intervention in the Middle East, the American media, modernity, secularism, and globalization, and their anti-Semitic conspiracy theories about Jewish and/or Zionist control over the U.S. and the New World Order.[12] Michael argues that such overlap "could presage greater cooperation between the two movements in the future. Such an alliance, if properly organized and coordinated, could pose a significant challenge to the status quo not only in the United States but in Europe as well",[13] and that "by aligning itself with militant Islam, the extreme-right could conceivably ride on the coattails of a dynamic movement".[14] What was clear from Roper's statement and his expression of both admiration for 9/11 and regret that his

---

9 Lee, "The Swastika and the Crescent".
10 Lee, "The Swastika and the Crescent".
11 Lee, "The Swastika and the Crescent".
12 Cf. Michael, *The Enemy of My Enemy*, pp. 2–3, 9.
13 Michael, *The Enemy of My Enemy*, p. 3.
14 Michael, *The Enemy of My Enemy*, p. 172.

movement lacked the "testicular fortitude" to do so, was that he wanted to ride on al-Qaeda's coattails and become friends if not allies.

While Lee and Michael look for potential alliances between the extreme-right and Islamists, Pipes investigates what he terms "the neo-Nazi affection for radical Islam", and tries to prove existing alliances and conspiracies between them.[15] In his various articles, Pipes cites as evidence their shared anti-Semitism and conspiracy theories, statements issued by right-wing extremists following 9/11, reports from Europe, anecdotes, Michael's book,[16] as well as the example of Canadian right-wing extremist William Baker visiting alleged Islamists in America.[17] One could argue that by imagining plots and accumulating evidence from diverse and somewhat unconnected sources in order to prove the existence of these plots, Pipes is operating as a conspiracy theorist himself.

In such work about alliances, the authors look not only at statements of intent – such as Roper's – and common characteristics, but for concrete evidence. Looking at history, they attempt to construct a narrative of overlap, relations, and alliances between Nazis and Arabs and Muslims. For Lee, the origins of the overlap and potential for alliances lie in the fact that the growth of the Muslim Brotherhood in Egypt, which had a "fascistic ideology", and fascism in Europe not only coincided historically, but that the Brotherhood's founder Hassan al-Banna allegedly collaborated with the Third Reich and the Grand Mufti of Jerusalem supported Hitler. According to Lee, Hitler overcame his dislike of Arabs because both had the same enemies – British, communists, and Jews –, and thus formed an alliance articulated by "the old Arab adage […] 'the enemy of my enemy is my Friend'".[18] That connection even entered the popular vernacular following 9/11 when the term "Islamo-fascist" came into use, creating a direct link between America's greatest enemies of the twentieth and twenty-first century, Nazism and Islamism. Following this example from World War II, both Lee and Michael travel through America, Europe, and the Muslim world, from the Cold War to 9/11, citing examples of statements of intent to establish links between American right-wing extremists, Arab and Muslims leaders, and Islamists.

Yet, Michael argues that attempts to build alliances in the Middle East have produced few tangible results. "Although the extreme-right and militant Islam on occasion share rhetoric", Michael writes, "what admiration does

---

15 Pipes, "The Far Right".
16 Cf. Pipes, "The Far Right"; Pipes, "More Ties".
17 Cf. Pipes, "CAIR Promotes".
18 Lee, "The Swastika and the Crescent".

exist tends to move in one direction: selected extreme-right activists voice support for militant Islam, but the latter rarely voices support for the former".[19] He also points out that some Islamists have reached out in an effort to build a "broad-based anti-Zionist coalition",[20] but concrete examples have mainly been in the area of Holocaust denial (e.g. Ahmed Rami of Radio Islam speaking at the *Historical Review* conference in 1992 and David Duke attending Ahmadinejad's Holocaust conference in 2006) and conspiracy theory.

As noted, Aaronovitch, Pipes, Michael, and Lee all argue that conspiracy theory (specific theories, overlapping theories, or the mere penchant for them) is a significant link between Islamists and the extreme-right and evidence of potential or actual alliances. Conspiracy theories are significant as they are widely viewed by commentators and watchdogs as embodying and thus serving as evidence of a movement's anti-democratic and anti-Semitic persuasion, if not also their irrationality, paranoia, and extremism which hold the potential for violence. According to Mark Fenster in *Conspiracy Theories: Secrecy and Power in American Culture* (1999), "the term 'conspiracy theory' serves as a strategy for delegitimization in political discourse. [... it] has come to represent a political Other to a 'proper' democratic politics".[21] The fact that movements who have committed acts of terrorism also have a penchant for conspiracy theories and the targets of the former tend to be the scapegoats in the latter completes the circle of evidence. According to Chip Berlet, the employment of conspiracy theory and inclination towards conspiracism by social and political movements and activists has historically been used by the state, law enforcement agencies, watchdog groups, and commentators to represent them as irrational, paranoid, and a threat to the liberal consensus if not also the government, nation, and/or democracy itself, and thereby not only to demonize and de-legitimize them and their political causes, but also to justify repressive state measures.[22]

It is thus unsurprising that during periods when oppositional social and political movements that engage in conspiracy theory are on the rise or in the news, there is a proliferation in books, articles, and commentaries about conspiracy theory which demonize it and its adherents. Peter Knight, a critic

---

19 Michael, *The Enemy of My Enemy*, p. 138.

20 Michael, *The Enemy of My Enemy*, p. 130.

21 Mark Fenster, *Conspiracy Theories: Secrecy and Power in American Culture*, Minneapolis 1999, p. xiii.

22 Cf. Chip Berlet, "Three Models for Analyzing Conspiracist Mass Movements of the Right", in: E. Ward (ed.), *Conspiracies: Real Grievances, Paranoia, and Mass Movements*, Seattle 1996, pp. 47–50.

of such demonization like Berlet, argues that "the prominence of conspiracy theories in American politics and culture has generated much anxious discussion in recent years, not least in the aftermath of the Oklahoma bombing and its panicked revelations about the rise of the paranoia-promoting militias".[23] In this case, Knight is referring specifically to the work of Daniel Pipes in *Conspiracy: How the Paranoid Style Flourishes and Where It Comes From* (1997). This pattern, he holds, occurred again in the aftermath of 9/11 with more writing from Pipes and Aaronovitch, but has its roots in Richard Hofstadter's "The Paranoid Style in American Politics". Berlet cites Hofstadter's essay as the foundational text for this delegitimation of conspiracy theory, particularly its psycho-pathologization, which exerted a great influence on Pipes as his title indicates. Hofstadter's piece was first published in *Harper's Magazine* in 1964 in the context of civil rights, the Cold War, and at the same time as the FBI's COINTELPRO was investigating and trying to suppress both the Klan and the left. In it, Hofstadter argued that conspiracy theory is a combination of "distorted judgment" and "demonological fervor".[24]

Pipes' *Conspiracy* picks up on Hofstadter's "paranoid style" and defines conspiracy theory as a "fear of a non-existent conspiracy",[25] thus confirming the irrationality, instability, and illegitimacy of the theory and theorist within the very definition. Although Pipes was responding to the rise of the American extreme-right in the 1990s and used Hofstadter's thesis, written in response to McCarthyism in the 1950s and examining what he saw as a particularly American phenomenon with a far longer history, he states that he happened upon the topic of conspiracy theories when he was writing about their prominence in the Middle East in his study *The Hidden Hand*.[26] Writing about conspiracy theory and alliances between Islamists and the extreme-right following 9/11 thus brought Pipes full circle and allowed him to bring the two movements together. In *Conspiracy*, Pipes cites Hitler and Stalin as examples of the danger posed by conspiracism.[27] Linking conspiracism to two symbols of evil in the twentieth century, it becomes by example, if not also by definition, anti-democratic, anti-Semitic, genocidal, and both right and left. According to Pipes, the contemporary targets of

---

23 Peter Knight, *Conspiracy Culture: From Kennedy to the "X-Files"*, London 2000, p. 5.

24 Hofstadter qtd. in Knight, *Conspiracy Culture*, pp. 5–6.

25 Daniel Pipes, *Conspiracy: How the Paranoid Style Flourishes and Where It Comes From*, New York 1997, p. 21.

26 Cf. Pipes, *Conspiracy*, p. xii.

27 Cf. Pipes, *Conspiracy*, p. xi.

conspiracists include the democratic governments of Britain, America, and Israel,[28] with the latter representing the relation between conspiracy theory, anti-democracy, and anti-Semitism.

The key theme of conspiracy theory which links it to both the extreme-right and Islamism is anti-Semitism. This link is based on the prevalence of anti-Semitism in conspiracy theories and the penchant for conspiracy theories amongst anti-Semitic movements (e.g. the extreme-right and Islamism). Differentiating between two types of conspiracy theory – those about secret societies from the crusades and those about Jewish conspiracies such as the *Protocols* – Pipes argues that modern conspiracy theory is fueled by anti-Semitism. This argument has been pushed even further by Leonard Zeskind who holds that the *Protocols* are not only the source and foundation for modern conspiracy theory, but also anti-Semitism.[29] Conspiracy theory is not only anti-Semitic in terms of content and history, he argues, it is itself "structurally anti-Semitic".[30] Thus, the mere presence of conspiracy theory is used as evidence of anti-Semitism, and each is seen as constitutive of the other.

Berlet develops on the relationship between racism, anti-Semitism, extremism, violence, and conspiracy theory in his essay "Three Models for Analyzing Conspiracist Mass Movements of the Right" (1996) and his report for Political Research Associates (PRA) *Toxic to Democracy: Conspiracy Theories, Demonization, & Scapegoating* (2010). Both texts were written in response to the proliferation of conspiracy theories and right-wing extremism leading up to and following the Oklahoma City bombing in the case of the former and following both 9/11 and the election of Obama in the case of the latter.[31] For Berlet, conspiracism is "[a] distinct narrative form of scapegoating, [...] [that] uses demonization to justify constructing the scapegoats as wholly evil while reconstructing the scapegoater as a hero. [It] [s]ees secret plots by tiny cabals of evildoers as the major motor powering important historical events".[32] Moreover, he views conspiracy theories as "tools of fear", rooted in and drawing on anti-Semitism and racism, which "build structures of vi-

---

28 Cf. Pipes, *Conspiracy*, p. xi.

29 Cf. Leonard Zeskind, "Some Ideas on Conspiracy Theories for a New Historical Period", in Ward, *Conspiracies*, pp. 11–35, pp. 16–17.

30 Zeskind, "Some Ideas", p. 17.

31 Cf. Berlet, "Three Models"; Berlet, "Toxic to Democracy: Conspiracy Theories, Demonization, & Scapegoating", June 2010, http://www.publiceye.org/conspire/toxic2democracy/index.html (accessed Oct. 12, 2010).

32 PRA, "Big Glossary", http://www.publiceye.org/glossary/glossary_big.htm (accessed July 21, 2002).

olence" that are directed towards these scapegoated groups.[33] Unlike Hofstadter and Pipes, however, Berlet does not demonize or psycho-pathologize conspiracy theories and theorists, but argues that they constitute reified symptoms – not causes – of underlying social tensions, and that the basis of the grievances needs to be revealed and resolved.[34]

While Berlet, as a left-wing progressive, tries to recover material reality from the conspiracy theory, Mark Fenster tries to recover conspiracy theory for left-wing progressive politics. Fenster argues that conspiracy theory articulates a populist antagonism between "the people" and "power" by critiquing the dominant political order and its representation of reality. It represents both an expression of contemporary subjectivity as well as a condition of political insignificance and the manifestation of political life "in-significance" and asserts the utopian desire for political transparency, which could make it a critical vehicle for the left or progressives.[35] The problem is that because of their criticism of the war on terror and Israel, the left and their conspiracy theories also become targets for Aaronovitch, Pipes, and neo-conservatives such as David Horowitz, along with Islamists and the extreme-right.[36]

If attempted alliances between the latter two are indeed unidirectional, unsuccessful, and the function of such overtures is coattail-riding, as Michael has argued, and if one agrees with Fenster that conspiracy theories are about political "in-significance", then the extreme-right's attempted alliances are of the same order as their conspiracy theories. This is not because such attempts prove an alliance, but because they are both about political insignificance and the fantasy of being IN-significance (as a movement). As I have already suggested, they occur at specific moments in American post-war history when the extreme-right is experiencing a period of realignment or crisis in which they are seeking to establish their relevance and which corresponds almost directly to developments in American foreign policy that relate to the Middle East and Islam. The realignment or crisis in question may also be brought on by the mere fact that the extreme-right and the domestic issues

33 PRA, "PRA Releases New Study, Toxic to Democracy", June 4, 2009 www.publiceye.org/conspire/toxic2democracy/media.html (accessed Oct. 12, 2010); Berlet, "Toxic to Democracy", p. 5.

34 Cf. PRA, "Big Glossary".

35 Fenster, *Conspiracy Theories*, pp. vii–xiv, 55–59.

36 Cf. Pipes, "The Left Love CAIR, MPAC, et al.", Aug. 19, 2003, www.danielpipes.org/blog/2003/8/the-left-9829-cair-mpac-et-al, Aug. 19, 2003 (accessed Oct. 12, 2010); David Horowitz, *Unholy Alliance: Radical Islam and the American Left*, Washington 2004.

which concern or interest them are marginalized in favor of more pressing or high profile foreign policy issues and interests in the Middle East or involving Muslims or Arabs, such as 9/11. Because the extreme-right is traditionally anti-Semitic, American foreign policy in the Middle East, Arab or Muslim world, and conflicts that involve Israel or its "enemies" are highlighted and made relevant. The extreme-right attempts to establish alliances with Arabs, Muslims, and Islamists at such moments in order to insert themselves into the political landscape and a position of significance. Yet, in the absence of such alliances or recognition in reality, they construct conspiracy theories in which they present themselves as agents, targets, or merely theorists who have access to the truth. This function has a parallel in the work of many of those who use the extreme-right's penchant for conspiracy theory to suture the gaps in their narrative of alliances when the reality is that these attempted alliances have been unsuccessful. In a sense, both want real alliances, but all there may be are conspiracy theories. In order to illustrate this thesis, in the next section, I will examine five periods in the post-war history of extreme-right conspiracy theories about and attempted alliances with Islamists and the wider Arab and Muslim world.

2. Conspiracy Theories, Alliances, and Axes in History

2.1. Post-War

For American fascist organizations, such as the National Renaissance Party (NRP), the German-American Bund, and William Dudley Pelley's Silver Shirts, who had been on the rise during the depression, but were seriously diminished by the anti-fascist Brown Scare following Pearl Harbor and America's entrance into the war, the defeat of the Nazis and establishment of Israel represented serious blows. Yet, these events mapped easily on to existing conspiracy theories about Jewish plots for global power, such as the *Protocols* and Ford's "The International Jew", which was circulated by the Klan and American fascists prior to and throughout the war.[37] While the establishment of Israel could be integrated into existing theories, it also represented a paradigm shift in anti-Semitic theories and representations, as the traditional diasporic stateless Jew was replaced by one with formal political power and military might in a new post-war global order.

---

[37] Cf. Martin Durham, *White Rage: The Extreme-Right and American Politics*, London 2007, p. 12.

With world powers realigning in the post-war, and later Cold War, period, not only did America want a foothold and allies in the Middle East (e.g. Israel), but so did the extreme-right. In the late 1940s and early 1950s, Gerald L. K. Smith of the Union Party, America First Committee/Party, and Christian Nationalist Crusade/Party met with a representative of the Egyptian embassy, and Robert Williams, a former military intelligence officer and pioneer of Holocaust denial, met with a Syrian Minister to discuss the translation of his writings on the "Jewish Problem" into Arabic.[38] Also in the 1950s, the NRP which, like other American fascist organizations, had declared its support for National Socialism against what was seen as Jewish communism, now expressed support for Stalin as a bulwark against the international Jewish "menace" and extended that support to the Middle East, including the Baathists in Iraq and Nasser's progressive nationalism in Egypt. The NRP even sold Nasser's publications in America and invited Egyptian UN press attaché Abdul Mawgoud Hassan to speak at their meeting.[39] The NRP also looked closer to home, establishing links with the Greenshirts, a New York based Islamist group led by white convert John Hassan and inspired by the Muslim-Bosnian SS who were endorsed by the Grand Mufti of Jerusalem.[40] The NRP saw Muslim and Arab movements as the frontline of resistance against colonialism and other newer forms of global imperialism such as Zionism.[41] In fact, the NRP were calling for a nationalist revolution in the third world and linked it to the anti-colonialism of the American Revolution, thus making America and American movements (including themselves) relevant. According to the NRP, these revolutionaries in the third world want: "to throw off the oppressive yoke of foreign colonialism just as our heroic American ancestors rebelled against the unjust taxation and repressive laws of the British Empire in 1776".[42]

In spite of courting movements in the Middle East and Arab and Muslim world, the extreme-right received very little response or reciprocation. Instead, those with whom the extreme-right did form links or alliances were domestic American Muslim groups such as the Greenshirts, and in the case of George Lincoln Rockwell's American Nazi Party (ANP), the organization most widely cited for forming alliances with Muslims, it was the Black American Nation of Islam (NOI). Although Rockwell also allegedly made

---

[38] Durham, *White Rage*, pp. 14, 16.

[39] Nicholas Goodrick-Clarke, *Black Sun: Aryan Cults, Esoteric Nazism and the Politics of Identity*, New York 2002, pp. 78–79.

[40] Cf. Goodrick-Clarke, *Black Sun*, pp. 78–79; Durham, *White Rage*, p. 19

[41] Cf. Goodrick-Clarke, *Black Sun*, pp. 78–79.

[42] Durham, *White Rage*, p. 19.

overtures to United Arab Republic President Gamal Abdel Nasser in 1959,[43] it was his speech at a NOI rally in 1961 and attendance at their 1962 convention that are most often used as evidence of his alliance with Muslims.[44] The example also testified to the ANP's focus on domestic American politics – in fact they had rejected the NRP for its anti-Americanism –,[45] and domestic developments that concerned race and which not only overshadowed international issues but also made the extreme-right relevant again. In this case, these domestic developments were battles over desegregation and civil rights in the 1950s and 1960s

2.2. Post-Civil Rights

With the passing of the Civil Rights Act in 1964, the extreme-right entered a decisive period. The Civil Rights Act appeared to represent the end of white supremacy that the ANP, Klan, and others had mobilized to defend. At the same time, the Klan was under investigation by the FBI's COINTELPRO and the HUAC, which published its indictment of the Klan in 1967,[46] the year that Rockwell was assassinated. Such developments saw the movement marginalized, without a cause, and in search of a new direction. Events in the Middle East, such as the 1967 Arab-Israeli War, expansion of Israel with U.S. support, and the Middle East becoming a major Cold War front, provided material. For an already anti-Semitic extreme-right, they confirmed the belief in a Zionist plot for domination of America and the world and allowed for the incorporation of Israel and the Middle East into existing anti-Semitic conspiracy theories and the creation of new ones. It was at this time that the extreme-right picked up the conspiracy theory "The Soviet-Israelite Class Strangles the Arabs" (1969) by Polish anti-Semite Louis Bielsky, in which he outlines the plans that "Jewish imperialism and the communist revolution have for the conquest of the Arab states and the Islamic world".[47]

The direction of the extreme-right was also greatly influenced by developments within the movement itself. One significant example occurred in

---

43 Cf. Michael, *The Enemy of My Enemy*, p. 124.

44 Cf. Durham, *White Rage*, p. 21.

45 Cf. Durham, *White Rage*, p. 21.

46 Cf. U.S. Government, *The Present-Day Ku Klux Klan Movement*, Hearings Before the Committee On Un-American Activities, House of Representatives, Ninetieth Congress, Dec. 11, 1967.

47 Louis Bielsky, "The Soviet-Israelite Class Strangles the Arabs", in: Donald T. Critchlow et al. (eds.), *Political Conspiracies in America: A Reader*, Bloomington 2008, pp. 130–133.

1973, the same year as the next Arab-Israeli War and oil crisis which hit closer to home, when William Pierce, a former ANP member and editor of their *National Socialist World*, took over the National Youth Alliance (NYA).[48] The NYA was formed the year after Rockwell's assassination in 1968 to counter the student movement on the left, but had also been subject to battles over the future of National Socialism, between an American-style national socialism of Rockwell and Willis Carto and a German style-national socialism of Francis Yockey.[49] Under Pierce, the former was adopted and American foreign policy became one of the NYA's key interests. Israel in particular became a more significant issue following the 1967 and 1973 wars respectively and the oil crisis. In 1973, the NYA testified before the Senate Committee on Foreign Relations, arguing that Henry Kissinger should not be appointed Secretary of State as he would support Israel over America.[50]

The following year, the NYA was renamed the National Alliance which would become infamous for Pierce's advocacy of an anti-government insurgency and his novel *The Turner Diaries*, which at least partially inspired the Oklahoma City bombing in 1995. Pierce's enmity with the government and his calls for armed insurgency were part of a wider trend amongst the extreme-right in the 1970s and early 1980s, as it was trying to adapt to the post-civil rights era. While Klansman David Duke pursued a mainstreaming electoral strategy, another Klansman, Louis Beam, would issue his call-to-arms "where ballots fail, bullets will prevail".[51] What followed in the wake of Beam's appeal was the paramilitarization of the Klan and emergence of a new breed of insurgent anti-government, anti-Semitic white supremacist and separatist groups such as Posse Comitatus, Aryan Nations, The Order, The Covenant, the Sword and the Arm of the Lord, and White Aryan Resistance.

It was at this time that conspiracy theories concerning the ZOG controlling the United States became prominent and pervasive. ZOG, which exemplified the post-war shift from the traditional representation of the diasporic Jew to that of a contemporary political force seeking global political domination, was popularized by the Christian Identity movement,[52] which had a long-standing interest in Israel and Zionism. Its anti-Semitic religion had been popular amongst national socialists of the pre- and post-war period with adherents such as Gerald L. K. Smith and the Silver Shirts and

---

48 Cf. Durham, *White Rage*, p. 27.

49 Cf. Durham, *White Rage*, p. 27.

50 Cf. Durham, *White Rage*, p. 27.

51 Qtd. in James Ridgeway, *Blood in the Face: The Ku Klux Klan, Aryan Nations, Nazi Skinheads, and the Rise of a New White Culture*, New York 1990, p. 87.

52 Cf. Durham, *White Rage*, p. 69.

came to dominate the post-civil rights era through adherents such as Beam, William Potter Gale, and former Silver Shirt Richard Butler, who was a member of Posse Comitatus, founder of Aryan Nations and mentor to The Order. The Christian Identity movement has its theological roots in nineteenth century British Israelism which migrated to the U.S. in the 1930s, taking the name Christian Identity and becoming popular amongst the extreme-right.[53] According to Identity theology, Aryans are Yahweh's chosen people, the offspring of the original tribes of Israel, and hence the true Israelites, who have been spread across the world, wandering in search of the Promised Land.[54] In the American version, the U.S. is depicted as the "NEW JerUSA-lem".[55] Jews, on the other hand, are neither the true Israelites nor God's chosen people, but the spawn of the serpent (or Satan) who have no legitimate claim on Palestine or America.[56] They have not only occupied Israel/Palestine, but seek to extend their power globally and over the U.S. in particular, leaving the Aryans without a nation. This not only makes the U.S. more central, it also reverses the logic of anti-Semitism, portraying Aryans as the diasporic stateless other and Jews as political oppressors, imperialists, and fascists. This is exemplified in Identity Pastor William LeGrande's theory that "Jewish 'Fascism' Governs the U.S.A.",[57] and Aryan Nations' R. F. Masker's "International Marxist/Zionist Program for World Domination", in which the *Protocols* inspired "International Rabbinical Talmudism" meets "International Political Zionism" to form a "Zionist Controlled One-World Government".[58]

In addition to promoting ZOG conspiracy theories, Identity activists also attempted to establish alliances with Islamists. According to Richard Scutari of The Order, in 1984 the group met with members of the Egyptian Islamic Group who were responsible for the 1981 assassination of Anwar Sadat.[59] It was also alleged that Order leader Robert Mathews approved a plan to seek funding for their white revolution from oil-rich Arab countries, but Michael states that little is known about their progress or if the plan was a fabrication

---

53 Cf. Durham, *White Rage*, p. 67.

54 Cf. Betty Dobratz/Stephanie L. Shanks-Meile, *The White Separatist Movement in the United States*, Baltimore 2000, p. 76.

55 Durham, *White Rage*, p. 67.

56 Cf. Dobratz/Shanks-Meile, *The White Separatist Movement*, p. 76.

57 William S. LeGrande, "Jewish 'Fascism' Governs the U.S.A.", in: *Calling Our Nation*, 41, pp. 9–10.

58 R. J. Masker, "International Marxist/Zionist Program for World Domination", in: *Calling Our Nation*, 54, p. 15.

59 Cf. Michael, *The Enemy of My Enemy*, p. 31.

or pipe dream.[60] Another example of an attempted alliance between Identity activists and movements in the Middle East and Arab and Muslim world occurred in 1989 when Louis Beam announced the formation of the New Right, an alliance between the American extreme-right and "liberation movements" against Zionism in Syria, Libya, Iran, and Palestine.[61] Although remaining unrealized, Beam's attempt to ally himself and his cause with movements in the Middle East occurred at a significant time when the region became more central in American foreign policy and political debates with the end of the Cold War, the Gulf War, and "Clash of Civilizations".

2.3. Post-Cold War

The Gulf War of 1990–1991 would prove a significant factor in increasing extreme-right enmity toward the government and mainstream right, as well as providing further material for conspiracy theories. President George H. W. Bush's decision to go to war against Iraq, an enemy of Israel, in defense of Kuwait, split the right between the neo-conservatives supporting it and paleo-conservatives, such as Pat Buchanan, as well as extreme-right activists, such as David Duke, opposing it as a Zionist war.[62] The notion that America was fighting a Zionist war was something that extreme-right conspiracy theorists believed was proven by the Jewish presence in the neo-conservative movement, which they believed was gaining too much of an influence over American foreign policy. This was an issue that originally came up in the 1970s when the Liberty Lobby expressed concerns over an alleged Jewish infiltration of conservatism,[63] and would come up again following the Oklahoma City bombing and during the war on terror. In response to the Gulf War, Garry Schroeder of Posse Comitatus went to the Iraqi embassy in Washington DC to protest, while Oklahoma Klansman Dennis Mahon organized a demonstration in support of Saddam Hussein in Tulsa.[64] According to George Michael, "like previous attempts to build alliances in the Middle East, the extreme right's support for Saddam Hussein appears to have produced few tangible results".[65]

---

60 Cf. Michael, *The Enemy of My Enemy*, p. 31.
61 Nicholas Chriss, "Beam Says His 'New Right' Has Middle East Links", in: *Houston Chronicle*, Apr. 2, 1989, p. 16A.
62 Cf. Durham, *White Rage*, p. 121; Michael, *The Enemy of My Enemy*, pp. 288–289.
63 Cf. Durham, *White Rage*, p. 123.
64 Cf. Michael, *The Enemy of My Enemy*, p. 138; Lee, "The Swastika and the Crescent".
65 Michael, *The Enemy of My Enemy*, p. 138.

At the same time as the Gulf War, Bush's gave his "New World Order" speech on September 11, 1990.[66] In the absence of the communist evil empire following the end of the Cold War, Bush's speech was seen as an announcement of its replacement by a New World Order led by ZOG. In fact, a Patriot monthly at the time claimed that the *Protocols* were "the blueprint used for the New World Order".[67] Evidence for the New World Order included not only the war, but the FBI/ATF sieges at Ruby Ridge, the Idaho home of Randy Weaver, in 1992 and the Branch Davidian compound in Waco, Texas in 1993. This led to a significant backlash by the extreme-right which included the emergence of the militia movement and the Oklahoma City bombing by Gulf War veteran Timothy McVeigh. He claimed that his attack was a "retaliatory strike" for the actions of the federal government at Ruby Ridge and Waco,[68] and that his experience as a soldier in the Gulf War, Iraqi deaths, and U.S. foreign policy in the Middle East informed his beliefs and activism.[69]

Following his conviction, McVeigh spoke out against U.S. foreign policy, including the 1998 missile strikes on Afghanistan and Sudan following al-Qaeda bombings in Kenya and Tanzania. On April 21, 2001, he also expressed approval of Ramzi Yousef's 1993 attack on the World Trade Center.[70] In a conspiracy theory about an alliance between the extreme-right and Islamists, this attack and McVeigh's Oklahoma City bombing have been linked together. This conspiracy theory originated in McVeigh's lawyer Stephen Jones's investigation and book *Others Unknown: Timothy McVeigh and the Oklahoma City Bombing Conspiracy* (1998) and the documentary *Conspiracy? The Oklahoma City Bombing* (2007). The documentary also attempts to incorporate 9/11, which occurred a mere three months after McVeigh was executed by lethal injection at Terre Haute Indiana Federal Prison on June 11, 2001, by asking if there is a "single thread that ties [all three of] them altogether?"[71] This conspiracy theory tries to prove that Oklahoma City, the only one of the three not involving al-Qaeda, was committed by them, negating the aberration and establishing continuity. Evidence for such a link includes eyewitness accounts of two Middle Eastern looking men, one of whom was alleged

---

66 Sara Diamond, *Roads to Dominion: Right-Wing Movements and Political Power in the United States*, New York 1995, p. 286.

67 Durham, *White Rage*, p. 137.

68 SPLC, "Bombs, Bullets, Bodies: The Decade in Review", in: *Intelligence Report*, 97/2000, pp. 8–39, p. 21.

69 Cf. Michael, *The Enemy of My Enemy*, p. 135.

70 Cf. Michael, *The Enemy of My Enemy*, p. 135.

71 History Channel, *Conspiracy? Oklahoma City Bombing*, A&E, 2007.

to be the suspect John Doe 2, who were in the vicinity, but sped off in a car before the blast. The theory also argues that McVeigh and his accomplice Terry Nichols had little experience with bombs and thus could not have executed the plot without help. The fact that the same method of attack was used in the first World Trade Center attack and the Oklahoma City bombing – Ryder trucks with ammonia nitrate bombs – is taken as proof of al-Qaeda's involvement. The theory also claims that Nichols traveled to the Philippines to meet with Yousef and Abu Sayyaf and receive bomb making training.[72]

In another theory, Jayna Davis, a former reporter for KFOR-TV in Oklahoma City, claimed that the Iraqi government was involved in the bombing. She argued that former Iraqi Republican Guard Hussain Hashem al-Hussaini met with McVeigh and was in fact the mysterious John Doe 2.[73] The extreme-right *American Free Press* suggested, in return, that Davis had been duped into believing Arabs were behind the bombing, when it was the Israelis. The paper argued that the Iraq connection theory was propagated by Jewish neo-conservatives such as Paul Wolfowitz in an attempt to justify an invasion back in the 1990s.[74] While McVeigh accepted full responsibility and never implicated al-Qaeda, he and the extreme-right were soon overshadowed by the events of 9/11.

2.4. Post-9/11

Following the Oklahoma City bombing, the extreme-right had the eyes of the nation on them: senate subcommittee hearings on domestic terrorism and extremism were held from 1995 to 1996,[75] books written, and anti-terror legislation was passed.[76] Yet, increased pressure, aging leadership, lawsuits, and a lack of purpose pushed them into the political wilderness, which 9/11 and the focus on Islamist extremism would compound. Some extreme-right activists criticized the attacks on 9/11, such as a contributor to the Stormfront website who stated that although he opposed "Jewish schemes" like Islamists, "no one who flies airplanes full of ARYANS into buildings full of

---

72 Cf. History Channel, *Conspiracy*; Stephan Jones/Peter Israel, *Others Unknown: Timothy McVeigh and the Oklahoma City Bombing Conspiracy*, New York 1998.

73 Cf. Michael, *The Enemy of My Enemy*, pp. 132–133.

74 Cf. Michael, *The Enemy of My Enemy*, pp. 134–135.

75 Cf. *Combating Domestic Terrorism*; *The Militia Movement in the United States*; and *Nature and Threat of Violent Anti-Government Groups In America* (1995).

76 Cf. 1995 Antiterrorism Bill/1996 Antiterrorism Act.

ARYANS is a friend of the ARYANS".[77] The majority, however, were more in line with the National Alliance's Billy Roper who has been quoted above. There were many more such statements which, like Roper's, explicitly acknowledged that the extreme-right had been overshadowed, feared obsolescence, and were eager to ride al-Qaeda's coattails and enter the battlefield. For example, Rocky Suhayda of the American Nazi Party said:

> [W]hat's wrong with just ACCEPTING the FACT that a HANDFUL of VERY BRAVE PEOPLE were WILLING TO DIE FOR 'WHATEVER' THEY BELIEVED IN [...] and DID IT? [...] All I can say is that it's a DISGRACE that in a population of at least 150 MILLION 'White/Aryan Americans' [...] we provide so FEW that are willing to do the same. [...] [A] bunch of 'towel head/sand niggers' put our great 'White Movement' to SHAME.[78]

In similar fashion, Paul R. Mullet of Aryan Nations declared:

> [T]he current events in Jew York city have caused me to activate my unit. We are preparing a strike here in Minnesota and other surrounding areas. Please be advised that the time for ALL ARYANS TO ATTACK IS NOW NOT LATER. Our opportunity may never be the same.[79]

Following from such statements, there were numerous attempts by the extreme-right at alliance building. The most notable and vocal example was Aryan Nations. The organization had been prominent and influential in the 1980s and 1990s, but between the Oklahoma City bombing and 9/11 it had lost its compound to a Southern Poverty Law Center (SPLC) lawsuit and experienced leadership struggles. With founder Richard Butler in ill health at the time of 9/11, a breakaway faction led by former webmaster August Kreis attempted to grab the momentum by trying to establish an alliance with al-Qaeda. Soon after 9/11, Kreis's website posted the piece "Why Islam Is Our Ally".[80] While President Bush and others were attempting to differentiate between true moderate Islam and extremist Islam, Kreis argued that it is "the Islam of Al-Qaida, of the Taliban, of Hamas" that is the true and authentic Islam as it rejects compromise with Zionism and the decadence of the West, and that Aryans should respect it just as Hitler had the Grand Mufti of Jerusalem.[81] Aryan Nations also recommended that Aryans take up arms in support of Muslims, arguing that while a "Turner Diaries scenario" is possible, it

---

[77] Qtd. in Durham, *White Rage*, p. 112.
[78] Qtd. in SPLC, "Extremist Groups React".
[79] Qtd. in SPLC, "Extremist Groups React".
[80] SPLC, "Extremist Groups React".
[81] Qtd. in SPLC, "Extremist Groups React".

was up to Yahweh, because Muslims not Aryans were now the "conduits for his wrath".[82]

In the lead-up to the Iraq invasion, Aryan Nations confirmed their willingness to support al-Qaeda with a call for volunteers: "Will the sons and daughters of YHVH God be joining with the zealous soldiers of Mohammed, rising up in righteous indignation?"[83] In 2005, Kreis announced that "the cells are out there and they are already in place. They may not be cells of Islamic people, but they are here and they are ready to fight".[84] That same year, Aryan Nations went beyond the offering of mere suicide bombers by creating the position of "Minister of Islamic Liaison".[85] While nothing came out of any of these offers, they remain central to the alliance thesis.

William Pierce, on the other hand, not only condemned the attacks, but criticized the extreme-right itself for bandwagon-jumping:

> We must not foolishly imagine that we can achieve some quick and easy victory by building alliances with people whose goals or interests are essentially different than our own – Middle Easterners or other non-whites for example.[86]
>
> I have no real fondness for anyone in the Middle East. I do not believe that Middle Easterners, Arabs, and Jews – especially Jews – should be permitted to live in America or Europe. I have no sympathy for Islam or any other Semitic religion from the Middle East.[87]

Pierce's fellow Alliance member and successor as host of *American Dissident Voices* Kevin Strom did express sympathy, if not identification:

> It is not the white separatists who are the violent threat to the non white races. […] It is the Jewish power structure, not white separatists, which routinely pumps Palestinian children full of bullets, tortures them, and keeps them behind barbed wire in what ought to be called concentration camps. It isn't white people who commit drive-by shootings and drug murders in our streets, but the Jewish establishment which has supported the browning of America […] It's the Jewish establishment that insists that no white nation on earth can keep itself white. That's genocide, Palestinians and whites are in the same boat.[88]

While in most of the statements the extreme-right celebrated, supported, and even expressed envy that Islamists committed the 9/11 attacks, most of their conspiracy theories suggested the plot originated elsewhere, with the

---

82 Qtd. in SPLC, "Extremist Groups React".
83 Qtd. in SPLC, "Extremist Groups React".
84 Qtd. in SPLC, "Extremist Groups React".
85 SPLC, "Extremist Groups React"; *White Rage*, p. 79.
86 Qtd. in Michael, *The Enemy of My Enemy*, p. 165.
87 Qtd. in Michael, *The Enemy of My Enemy*, p. 166.
88 Qtd. in Michael, *The Enemy of My Enemy*, p. 289.

American government and/or Israel. The belief that the American government was behind the attacks is something that the extreme-right shared with more mainstream 9/11 conspiracy theories such as *Loose Change* and theorists such as Alex Jones and David Ray Griffin. The extreme-right *Free American* conceded that bin Laden played a role, but argued that he was used by FEMA to establish a "military police state" and implement counterterrorism measures designed to control opponents of the New World Order.[89] Mike Piper of *American Free Press* claimed that "Mossad ultimately orchestrated the 9–11 terrorist attacks in order to spark U.S. outrage against the Arab world".[90] He argued that:

> on September 11, Israel was faced with world opprobrium for its treatment of the Palestinian uprising, and public opinion was turning against Israel. A small-scale 'suicide' operation (that is, [Israeli operatives] crashing planes into the World Trade Center and pinning the blame on Arabs) would have been a small cost to Israel.[91]

After abandoning his mainstreaming strategy in the 1990s, David Duke now emerged as one of the most vocal of the extreme-right 9/11 conspiracy theorists. According to Duke, al-Qaeda was behind the attack, but Mossad had prior knowledge of it and did not warn the U.S. so that it would retaliate against enemies of Israel in the Middle East.[92] Duke cites several pieces of 'evidence', including disputes about how many Jews died or were missing, claims that Jews owned the World Trade Center, an alleged witness statement that Mossad agents were seen filming the attacks and had been living near Muhammed Atta.[93] Duke also charged that U.S. Attorney Michael Chertoff released an Israeli spy ring from prison immediately following 9/11 in order to conceal Israeli complicity.[94] While Aaronovitch, Pipes, and others attempt to link extreme-right conspiracy theories to those from the left and Islamists, Duke also devotes attention to debunking left-wing conspiracy theories which hold that 9/11 was staged by the U.S. government to justify a war for oil, claiming that these theories were created by Jews to divert attention from their plot.[95]

---

89 Michael Barkun, *A Culture of Conspiracy: Apocalyptic Visions in Contemporary America*, Berkeley 2003, p. 161.

90 Qtd. in Michael, *The Enemy of My Enemy*, p. 229.

91 Qtd. in Michael, *The Enemy of My Enemy*, pp. 229–230.

92 Cf. Michael, *The Enemy of My Enemy*, p. 230; Kathryn S. Olmsted, *Real Enemies: Conspiracy Theories and American Democracy, World War I to 9/11*, Oxford 2009, p. 221.

93 Cf. Michael, *The Enemy of My Enemy*, p. 230.

94 Cf. Michael, *The Enemy of My Enemy*, pp. 190–191.

95 Cf. Michael, *The Enemy of My Enemy*, p. 163.

Duke was also one of the few extreme-right activists to not only court Islamists, but be invited to the Middle East, usually to present his conspiracy theories in person. In 2002, Duke gave two lectures in Bahrain, "The Global Struggle against Zionism" and "Israeli Involvement in September 11".[96] He also published his conspiracy theory in the Saudi-based *Arab News* under the title "The Worlds Most Dangerous Terrorist", appeared on al-Jazeera's *Without Borders*,[97] and attended Ahmadinejad's 2006 Holocaust conference. The Duke case is widely taken as the best example of the alliance forged between extremists through conspiracy theory, yet none of those examples constituted a formal alliance beyond the sharing of conspiracy theories.

2.5. Obama and Conspiracy Theory

It may seem surprising that in a country that had been attacked by terrorists and fighting a war on terror, the extreme-right, with its own history of terrorism and attempts to join the conflict, did not make more of an impact on the American security services, media, and popular consciousness. This was in spite of the extreme-right courting Islamists and Pipes and others claiming that the two movements could form or had formed an alliance. There are many possible factors contributing to this lack of impact. Most notably, the extreme-right was already in decline following the Oklahoma City bombing and 9/11 compounded this, creating a prolonged crisis. The reason for this was that in an America under attack, not only were Islamist terrorism and foreign antagonisms more pressing concerns, but as America was also unified by the attack, domestic antagonisms were largely ignored. This was particularly the case when the domestic antagonists in question were, as in the case of the extreme-right, white Christian right-wing American terrorists who did not fit easily into a conservative schema in which America was under attack by and at war with foreign, non-white Muslim terrorists.

In this context, the election of Barack Obama as the first African-American President seemed to offer the racist extreme-right an opportunity for relevance. Almost immediately following the election, statements were issued by extreme-right activists such as Thom Robb of the Knights of the Ku Klux Klan who claimed: "It could mean a reawakening of our spirit and blood.

---

96 Michael, *The Enemy of My Enemy*, p. 161.
97 Michael, *The Enemy of My Enemy*, p. 161.

Every time the television shows an image of Obama it will be a reminder that our people have lost power in this country".[98]

According to the SPLC, 2007–2008 saw a 4% rise in hate groups, with over 900 active, and attributed this reversal of the decline experienced since 2000 partly to Obama's election.[99] The revival of such groups continued through 2008–2009 with the number increasing to 932.[100] Yet, the greatest increase was with the anti-government patriot movement, which experienced a rise of 244% from 149 to 512 groups.[101] Such developments caused the U.S. Department of Homeland Security, which was formed following 9/11 to combat Islamist terrorism, to issue the 2009 report *Rightwing Extremism: Current Economic and Political Climate Fueling Resurgence in Radicalization and Recruitment*.[102] There were also growing concerns about the proliferation of anti-government conspiracy theories from The Anti-Defamation League (ADL) in their report *Rage Grows in America: Anti-Government Conspiracies* (2009), and PRA in *Toxic to Democracy*. The ADL argue that:

> Since the election of Barack Obama as president, a current of anti-government hostility has swept across the United States [...]. What characterizes this anti-government hostility is a shared belief that Obama and his administration actually pose a threat to the future of the United States. Some accuse Obama of plotting to bring socialism to the United States, while others claim he will bring about Nazism or fascism. [...] Some of these assertions are motivated by prejudice, but more common is an intense strain of anti-government distrust and anger, colored by a streak of paranoia and belief in conspiracies.[103]

Although both reports look at extreme-right *and* mainstream right-wing theories (and theorists), it is the latter that have dominated the post-election period. The loudest voices are not Nazis claiming that Obama is a tool of the Zionists, but the more populist mainstream conservative movements, such as the Tea Party, Freedomworks, and Birther movement, which emerged in

---

98 Qtd. in SPLC, "In Their Own Words: Hating Barack Obama", 2009, www.splcenter.org/intel/intelreport/article.jsp?sid=442&printable=1 (accessed Oct. 12, 2009).

99 Cf. David Holthouse, "The Year in Hate", 2009, http://www.splcenter.org/intel/intelreport/article.jsp?aid=1027 (accessed Nov. 19, 2009).

100 Cf. Mark Potok, "Rage on the Right", 2010, http://www.splcenter.org/get-informed/intelligence-report/browse-all-issues/2010/spring/rage-on-the-right (accessed July 14, 2010).

101 Cf. Potok, "Rage on the Right".

102 Cf. Department of Homeland Security, *Rightwing Extremism: Current Economic and Political Climate Fueling Resurgence in Radicalization and Recruitment*, Apr. 7, 2009.

103 ADL, "Rage Grows in America: Anti-Government Conspiracies", Nov. 16, 2009, http://www.adl.org/special_reports/rage-grows-in-america/default.asp (accessed Nov. 23, 2009).

the post-election realignment of the right and mobilized support by exploiting conservative fears of Obama, usually planted through conspiracy theories. These theories hold that Obama is a Nazi, socialist, Muslim, or Kenyan, and not American (as the Birthers claim), and thus a threat to America. Interestingly, the claim that Obama is a Nazi *and* Muslim *as well as* a socialist plays on the discursive schema that was developed to allege a connection between Nazis and Islamists as well as the left post-9/11.

The notion that Obama is a closeted Muslim or sleeper Islamist is widespread in the right-wing press and tied to conspiracy theories about the wider "Islamicization" of America, the most notable proponents of which are Pam Geller and Robert Spencer of Stop Islamicization of America. Specific plots within this alleged conspiracy include the building of the "Ground Zero Mosque", the establishment of Sharia Law in America, and the infiltration of the government and security services by interns from the Council on American-Islamic Relations (CAIR), which is also said to fund or function as a front for terrorists. The latter theory is propagated by Daniel Pipes, who had also previously claimed that CAIR is in league with both Hamas and neo-Nazis.[104] While Pipes is making a link between the extreme-right and Islamists through this theory, he fails to account for what the neo-Nazis may think about the fact that their supposed allies at CAIR are involved with an African-American President, even if he is allegedly Muslim.

Beyond conspiracy theory, such claims about Muslims have had an impact on public and political debates, notably in opposition to the mosque and Sharia law, the latter of which has been the subject of pre-emptive bans in two states (and attempted bans in sixteen others).[105] There were also calls from GOP House members to investigate the CAIR intern allegations,[106] and in 2010 Republican Congressman Peter King, Chairman of the House Homeland Security Committee, held McCarthy-like hearings on "The Radicalization of American Muslims and response of the community". It seems that the extreme-right has been overshadowed yet again, this time, however, not by Islamist conspiracy theorists, but by Islamophobic conservative ones.

---

104 Cf. Pipes, "CAIR"; "More Ties"; "CAIR: 'Moderate' Friends of Terror", in: *New York Post*, Apr. 22, 2002, http://www.danielpipes.org/394/cair-moderate-friends-of-terror (accessed Aug. 16, 2010).

105 Cf. Tim Murphy, "Has Your State Banned Sharia?", in: *Mother Jones*, Feb. 11, 2011, http://www.motherjones.com/mojo/2011/02/has-your-state-banned-sharia (accessed Sept. 5, 2011).

106 Cf. Glenn Greenwald, "GOP House members call for investigation of Muslim political activity", in: *Salon*, Oct. 15, 2009, http://politics.salon.com/2009/10/15/investigation/ (accessed Sept. 5, 2011).

Schirin Fathi (Hamburg)

From Mosaddeq to HAARP: Some Aspects of the Conspiratorial Component of U.S.-Iranian Relations

When Barack Obama delivered his highly acclaimed speech at Cairo University in June 2009, he seemed well aware that the balance sheet of U.S. relations with the Middle East was not a positive one. In particular the dealings with Iran are marred by a history of direct and covert meddling, crowned by the coup d'état against Prime Minister Mohammad Mosaddeq in 1953. Obama directly referred to this incident when he affirmed:

> For many years, Iran has defined itself in part by its opposition to my country, and there is indeed a tumultuous history between us. In the middle of the Cold War, the United States played a role in the overthrow of a democratically-elected Iranian government. Since the Islamic Revolution, Iran has played a role in acts of hostage-taking and violence against U.S. troops and civilians. This history is well known. [...] it will be hard to overcome decades of mistrust, but we will proceed with courage, rectitude and resolve.[1]

The content and intention of this speech has since been rendered moot; what persists, especially in the relations between Iran and the U.S., is an atmosphere of mistrust and conspiracy.

1. A History of Mutual Distrust

A precursory perusal of internet pages under the heading of "Iran – U.S. – conspiracy" reveals a plethora of pages dealing with all sorts of issues that are the ingredients of this atmosphere of distrust. They range from "real" issues, such as the hostage crisis, the U.S. involvement in the war between Iran and Iraq from 1980 to 1988,[2] the Iran-Contra affair, and evidence that points to arms deals and illegal sales of technology to Iran.[3] But there are

---

1 U.S. Department of State, "President Obama's Speech in Cairo: A New Beginning", Cairo University, June 4, 2009, http://www.state.gov/p/nea/rls/rm/2009/124342.htm (accessed Sept. 24, 2010).

2 Cf., for example, Brian Becker, *U.S. Conspiracy to Initiate the War Against Iraq*, 1992, http://deoxy.org/wc/wc-consp.htm (accessed Sept. 24, 2010).

3 Cf. "US Charges Six in Iran Satellite Conspiracy", in: *BBC News*, June 8, 2010, http://www.bbc.co.uk/news/10270537 (accessed Sept. 24, 2010).

also websites that can quickly and easily be detected as pure fabrication, as the stuff sensational conspiracy theories are made of. They allege, for instance, that it is really the Illuminati who are behind the possibility of war between Iran and the U.S.,[4] or they refer to Iranian accusations voiced on state television that the occurrence of the swine flu is actually nothing but a U.S. Zionist plot to advance the medication "Tamiflu" which is produced by a Zionist company owned by Zionist shareholders and Donald Rumsfeld, of course, who is a major share-holder.[5] Another conspiracy theory of the sensational, fabricated type can be found on *Jihad Watch*, and it reads as follows:

> A fundamentalist Iranian News Service Jahan News, has discovered a new plot by American troops in Pakistan to subvert Islam. Jahan News claims that U.S. troops, to promote Christianity, distribute a free mixture of sweet milk chocolates and dark bitter chocolates to Pakistani kids, but wrap the bitter chocolates in labels imprinted with the name of the Islamic prophet, Mohammad, to leave a 'bad taste' with children about Islam![6]

I believe these few examples suffice to illustrate the range of topics and to show some of the elements of fantasy employed in these "theories".

It is important to note and probably needless to mention here that the accuracy of these websites unless they are quoted by known and respected news agencies or academic institutions (and sometimes even then!) is generally subject to doubt. The other important introductory remark that may be superfluous but has to be made is that conspiracy thinking is not a one-way street and not limited to Iranians thinking of conspiracy whenever the U.S. is involved, rather, the thinking goes both ways. However, in this paper, I will limit myself to the Iranian view of the U.S. Two questions come immediately to mind: how do these "theories" work? And why do people believe in them?

---

4 Cf. Henry Makow, "Illuminati War Conspiracy: Shakedown of US & Iran", in: *Conspiracy Planet*, 2009, http://www.conspiracyplanet.com/channel.cfm?channelid=126&contentid=4302 (accessed Sept. 27, 2010).

5 Cf. Memri TV, *Iranian TV: Swine Flu – A Zionist/American Conspiracy*, 2009, http://www.youtube.com/watch?v=5qrp63L1R4Y (accessed Sept. 27, 2010).

6 "Iranian media: American troops subverting Islam with bitter 'Muhammad' chocolates", in: *Jihad Watch*, Aug. 20, 2010, http://www.jihadwatch.org/2010/08/iranian-media-american-troopssubverting-islam-with-bitter-muhammad-chocolates.html (accessed Sept. 27, 2010).

2. The Make-Up of Conspiracy Theories

I would like to deal with the first question very briefly and devote the rest of the paper to attempting to offer some explanations toward the second question. How do these narratives work? A qualificatory note to start with: strictly speaking, conspiracy theories are not theories, among other reasons because they cannot be verified. I will nevertheless, for the sake of simplification, continue to speak of them as "conspiracy theories", bearing in mind the limitations. Generally speaking, conspiracy theories follow their own logic and structure. They always come into play when complex questions ask for easy answers. They rely on seemingly irrefutable assumptions, their chain of arguments leads to an infinite loop, and they move in closed, self-referential systems that do not need a direct reference object – it may be helpful to link up with an existing historical or current conspiracy,[7] but at some point the theory disengages itself from the conspiracy and enters the realm of abstraction. Then, the slightest allusion to known events or recourse to historical wrongs suffices to cement the viability of the theory – a condition that lies at the basis of the Iranian propensity to readily suspect evil machinations in dealing with the US.

Conspiracy theories usually align and try to make sense of eclectic evidence from very different frames of reference. They construct causally determined linkages among observed phenomena without any critical questioning.[8] So-called "errant data" are, according to Brian Keeley,[9] a main ingredient of conspiracy theories that aim to construct a holistic system embracing those facts that support a theory as well as those that may contradict it. As a matter of fact, those data that stand in contradiction to the theory add the ultimate stamp of credence. Moreover, standards that are usually binding for any argumentative alignment, such as chronological order and conceptualisation, are meaningless in the construction of such a theory.[10]

---

7 For a further elaboration on the distinction between and the interplay of real conspiracies and conspiracy theories, cf. Kerstin Johannsen/Nikolai Röhl, "Definitionen und Vorbetrachtungen", in: Schirin Fathi (ed.), *Komplotte, Ketzer und Konspirationen: Zur Logik des Verschwörungsdenkens – Beispiele aus dem Nahen Osten*, Bielefeld 2010, pp. 17–32.

8 Cf. Rudolf Jaworski, "Verschwörungstheorien aus psychologischer und aus historischer Sicht", in: Ute Caumanns/Mathias Niendorf (eds.), *Verschwörungstheorien: Anthropologische Konstanten – historische Varianten*, Osnabrück 2001, pp. 11–30, p. 17.

9 Brian L. Keeley, "Of Conspiracy Theories", in: *Journal of Philosophy*, 96/1999, 3, pp. 109–126, p. 117.

10 Cf. Jaworski, "Verschwörungstheorien", pp. 17–18.

Conspiracy theories aim to avoid responsibility for failure, to explain great calamities, or simply to make life more meaningful and comprehensible. Ruth Groh calls this a special variant of a "teleologische Weltdeutung",[11] and Brian Keeley endorses this view, stating that conspiracy theorists are "some of the last believers in an ordered universe. By supposing that current events are under the control of nefarious agents, conspiracy theories entail that such events are *capable of being controlled*".[12] In this way, there is a linkage between religion and conspiracy theories, and some authors have put forward the idea that conspiracy thinking is the secular and pseudo-scientific answer to the loss of religious thinking. However, I will leave it to other scholars to further ponder this idea.

By way of illustration of how conspiracy theories work, let us take the above-mentioned example of an article dealing with the Illuminati and their involvement in U.S.-Iranian relations. The author of said article is quoted as Henry Makow, PhD. His academic credentials, whether real or imagined, are of course listed to lend added credibility, despite the fact that the news item or article, whatever one wants to call this, is found on a website called *Conspiracy Planet: The Alternative News and History Network*. The item starts by saying: "If Russian warnings are correct, at this time next week the US could be at war with Iran". The opening sentence serves two purposes: first, it stirs up fears, and, second, it quotes supposedly reliable inside information. Makow goes on to state:

> Let us understand that this war is really an assault by the Illuminati on both countries.
>
> The top rung of Freemasonry, the Illuminati Order is an international satanic cult that aims to subdue humanity by pitting nations against each other. It represents an ancient occult conspiracy of international finance and many 'leading families' of Europe and America.[13]

Here, everything is mixed together with no regard for historical evidence or logical correlation; catchwords are taken out of their context for maximum effect. Thus, the Illuminati, the Freemasons, Satanic cults, an occult conspiracy, and Zionist allusions by mentioning international finance and 'leading families' in Europe and America are presented as a cocktail that assures the highest recognition value. The article makes sure that the statement strikes a

---

11 Ruth Groh, "Verschwörungstheorien und Weltdeutungsmuster: Eine anthropologische Perspektive", in: Caumanns/Niendorf (eds.), *Verschwörungstheorien*, pp. 37–45, p. 38.

12 Keeley, "Of Conspiracy Theories", p. 123; emphasis in the original.

13 Makow, "Illuminati War Conspiracy".

chord with everybody. The mix of antagonists corresponds to the way actors in conspiracy thinking are often presented, namely in vague terms: the infamous "them". At the same time, however, they are omnipotent and ever-present. To top all this, the article is graced by "pictures of Bush and Ahmadinejad giving the satanic 'goat's head' sign [to] suggest Iranians are as ignorant as Americans of their President's true loyalty".[14] This suggestion is augmented by the slight resemblance in looks between Bush and Ahmadinejad. Now, granted that this article is an extremely obvious and suggestive example, it nonetheless serves the point of illustration well, even if it does not explicitly address the issue of Iranian conspiracist views of the U.S., to which we will now turn.

3. The Propensity to Believe in Conspiracy Theories

The other question that I have mentioned before addresses the propensity to believe in conspiracy theories. I am no adherent of culturalism; I do not believe that certain cultures are more prone to conspiratorial thinking than others. On the contrary, I would agree with authors who define conspiracy theories in terms of an anthropological constant, meaning that conspiracy thinking can be found in all cultures, but that its prevalence depends on historical circumstances. Dieter Groh talks about a "welcome orientation and structure" that facilitates the mechanism of interplay between reality and conspiracy theory.[15] Using the analogy of a key fitting into the key-hole, he explains that for this mechanism to work, conspiracy theories have to correlate with the prevalent interpretative pattern of a group, party, nation, culture, or religion.

This cautionary introductory note notwithstanding, many scholars attest the Middle East a higher propensity for conspiracy thinking than other regions. Daniel Pipes and Bassam Tibi are among the best known, even if they are not considered quote-worthy by all.[16] Other academics like Asef Bayat believe that it is the authoritarianism of Middle Eastern governments that

---

[14] Makow, "Illuminati War Conspiracy".

[15] Dieter Groh, "Verschwörungstheorien revisited", in: Caumanns/Niendorf (eds.), *Verschwörungstheorien*, pp. 187–196, p. 189.

[16] Cf. Bassam Tibi, *Die Verschwörung: Das Trauma arabischer Politik*, Hamburg 1994. One of the best known authors is Daniel Pipes who mentions several reasons for this assumption in his well-known monograph: *The Hidden Hand: Middle East Fears of Conspiracy* (Basingstoke 1996). Among these are the decline in power among Muslims, the special nature of regional politics, the influence of European thinking, and the large incidence of actual conspiracies in the Middle East.

sets the ground for conspiratorial thinking,[17] but stress that the experience of real and successful conspiracies and the inability to fight them off is more important. In this context, it is interesting to add that most theories in circulation in the Middle East do not originate in the region but were imported from the "West" by the agency of missionaries, students, adventurers – the known mix of agents that are made responsible for so much of the transfer of ideas. The fact that these theories resonate more strongly in the Middle East has to do with the built-up resentment and the feeling of helplessness in view of a real or perceived stronger Other, be that the "West" or obscure and sinister powers. The cumulative effect of the coup d'état against Mosaddeq, the Eli Cohen spy affair, and the wars in Iraq and Lebanon – just to quote a few – has provided proof for the people in the Middle East that the "West" or certain groups in the West have successfully conspired against the "Orient". This might explain why, for example, Muslims in South East Asia, even though they have experienced direct colonial intervention and drawn-out wars, are less prone to believe in conspiracy thinking.[18] Even the intellectual Sadiq Jalal al-Azm attests the experience of historical conspiracies or "dirty dealing" some value in laying the ground for the propensity to believe in conspiracy theories:

> This set me thinking about the role of Shiʿism, for example, in intensifying this Iranian super addiction to conspiracy explanations, considering that power was in fact usurped from Imamu ʿAli and his heirs through a series of dirty conspiracies.[19]

When al-Azm speaks about the "Iranian super addiction to conspiracy explanations" he echoes a consensus that Iranians are more willing than others to suspect evil machinations behind events that lie beyond their capability to understand. Ahmad Ashraf, author of the well-known article about "Conspiracy Theories" in the *Encyclopædia Iranica*, testifies to this view and states that:

> Particularly since the beginning of the 20th century Persians from all walks of life and all ideological orientations have relied on conspiracy theories as a basic mode of understanding politics and history. The fact that the great powers have in fact intervened covertly in Persian affairs has led ordinary people, political leaders, even the rulers themselves to interpret their history in terms of elaborate and devious conspiracies.[20]

---

17 Cf. Asef Bayat, "Conspiracies & Theories", in: *ISIM Review*, 18/2006, p. 5.

18 Cf. Bayat, "Conspiracies & Theories", p. 5.

19 Sadiq al-Azm, "Orientalism and Conspiracy", Hamburg University, June 23, 2005.

20 Ahmad Ashraf, "Conspiracy Theories", in: *Encyclopædia Iranica*, Dec. 15, 2009, http://www.iranicaonline.org/articles/conspiracy-theories (accessed Sept. 24, 2010).

He elaborates that the acceptance of these theories has reinforced the feeling of helplessness vis-à-vis great power interference, a highly dysfunctional mechanism that leads to a sense of resignation and apathy which in turn facilitates the longevity of repressive regimes. Thus, he concludes: "The acceptance of such theories has in itself influenced the course of modern Persian history".[21]

4. The Trauma of a Real Conspiracy

Even though Iran has never experienced formal colonisation, it has nonetheless had its share of great power meddling and rivalry. In particular, Russian and British designs on Iranian sovereignty – cumulating in the Anglo-Russian Convention of 1907 by which Persian territory was divided into spheres of influence and subsequent occupation by Great Britain and Russia during WWI and WWII – have left their mark on the Iranian mentality. The myths surrounding British dominance of all Iranian affairs are abundant and need not be reiterated here.[22] One point, however, is important to note: these theories were believed in by all sectors of society and even by the rulers. Suspicions of the British pervaded every aspect of Iranian politics, and the Shahs themselves were not immune to this virus.

But it proved to be another incident that has conditioned Iranian politics to this day. The CIA-engineered coup d'état that overthrew the democratically elected prime minister Mohammad Mosaddeq in 1953 not only remains deeply-ingrained in the Iranian psyche, but it has also been taken as proof of American omnipotence, the U.S. thus taking the place of the British and Russians before them. The 1953 coup is deemed so important for U.S.-Iranian relations that it warrants a closer look.

But first, a brief discussion of the terms "conspiracy" and "conspiracy theory" is needed for our purpose. Often, these two terms are used interchangeably, despite the fact that they connote very different phenomena. A conspiracy is a real occurrence involving two or more (but not too many in order to safeguard the secrecy) actors that reach a secret understanding involving secret action or a concerted plan either to either achieve power, or

---

21 Ashraf, "Conspiracy Theories".

22 It suffices to point to the role the British have played in the years preceding the Constitutional Revolution, the acquisition of special concessions (i.e. tobacco), and the early years of the oil industry. In addition, one of the alleged myths concerns the establishment (creation) of the Baha'i faith.

to maintain or expand it.[23] Pipes, in his polemic style, manifests the apparent omnipotence of the conspirators when he insists: "The conspirator never rests, never falters, never makes mistakes and never shows fear".[24] Conspiracies are real, and knowledge of this real existence is a precondition to understand conspiracy theories. Conspiracy theories, on the other hand, are fabricated, invented, or assumed, but they thrive in an atmosphere that has been shaped by real conspiracies, even if the theory is in no way related to or the result of the real conspiracy. With their particular logic and structure the theories take on a life of their own. Therefore, in the last analysis, conspiracy theories are self-referential systems, yet, they cannot be thought independently of real conspiracies and of pre-existing fears, enemies, bogeymen, and out-groups. One of the central characteristics of conspiratorial thinking is the attempt to explain complex developments and to break down difficult chains of events to monocausal and easily understandable steps. There seems to be an obsession to want to explain everything and to imbue meaning to the most unrelated events.

Let us now resume the discussion of the defining moment in Iranian history, namely the real conspiracy surrounding the 1953 events in Iran that set the stage for the multitude of conspiracy theories that have marred American-Iranian relations for more than half a century. The short period of government under Mosaddeq can be subsumed under one word: self-determination.[25] As such, it symbolised the apex of a movement against autocracy and foreign domination which had been the rule in much of Iran's modern history. It also crystallizes the turmoil that Iran found itself in by the middle of the twentieth century. This period was as much disruptive as it presented Iran a rare chance to become a self-sufficient, independent player on the

---

[23] Cf. Eduard Gugenberger/Franko Petri/Roman Schweidlenka, *Weltverschwörungstheorien: Die neue Gefahr von rechts*, Wien 1998, p. 22.

[24] Pipes, *The Hidden Hand*, p. 180.

[25] There are various sources about the coup against Mosaddeq and the political situation, the most important of which are: Ervand Abrahamian, *Iran Between Two Revolutions*, Princeton 1988; Sharoukh Akhavi, *Religion and Politics in Contemporary Iran: Clergy-State Relations in the Pahlavi Period*, Albany, NY 1980; Houchang E. Chehabi, *Iranian Politics and Religious Modernism: The Liberation Movement of Iran under the Shah and Khomeini*, London 1990; Hamid Dabashi, *Theology of Discontent: The Ideological Foundations of the Islamic Revolution in Iran*, New Brunswick 2006; Nikki R. Keddie, *Roots of Revolution: An Interpretative History of Modern Iran*, New Haven 1981; Ali Rahnema, *An Islamic Utopian*, London 2000; Asghar Schirazi, *Modernität und gestörte Wahrnehmung: Eine Fallstudie über die Tudeh-Partei des Iran und ihr Verhältnis zur Demokratie*, Hamburg 2003; Marvin Zonis, *Majestic Failure: The Fall of the Shah*, Chicago 1991.

world scene. In May 1951, Dr. Mohammad Mosaddeq and his National Front, a grouping of constitutionalist and nationalist politicians and technocrats, won a majority in the Iranian parliament, the *Majlis.* Mosaddeq was made prime minister based on popular support for his platform that was dominated by a nationalist agenda. As early as 1944, he had, then as a member of the *Majlis*, worked toward a parliamentary bill to prevent the granting of any more oil concessions to foreign powers, and hence, the nationalization of the oil industry became the driving force of his political programme. The other pillar on which his popularity rested was the movement to widen the participatory system by electoral reform, among others granting women the right to vote and to restore the constitutional character of the monarchy, which in effect meant to curb the powers of the Shah.

There had been sporadic opposition to the national Iranian sell-out since the beginning of the twentieth century. These opposition attempts were conditioned by a gradual shift in the composition of the politically aware population that had been in effect since the mid-nineteenth century when a very thin segment of the Iranian population began to seek education abroad and was introduced to western bodies of thought. Realization dawned on these intellectuals, together with more traditional segments such as the religious establishment, the bazaar merchants, and dissatisfied bourgeois elements, that Iran was in dire need of reforms in all spheres in order to guarantee its survival as an independent nation state and to stop the national sell-out by the ruling elites. Thus, as in much of the Middle East, a period of instability was ushered in as a direct result of the clash of modernity with a traditional system that was deeply aware of its culture and former significance.

The fault lines along which loyalties were aligned in this conflict were not always clear-cut. As one of the main actors one can identify the monarchy, trying to hold on to its traditional power base and role while at the same time embarking on a massive, orchestrated modernization program. The opposition was made up of varying alliances between the clergy (although there were elements of the clergy that had always been loyal to the monarchy), the nationalists, and later the leftist movements. Mosaddeq's National Front initially united the disparate elements of the opposing forces. This was as much its strength as it was ultimately its downfall, when the National Front disintegrated into warring factions. More than anything, it was the figurehead that kept this loose alliance together. Mohammad Mosaddeq came from a family of influential and wealthy state servants and great land-owners. His bourgeois background and almost noble demeanour made up part of his charisma together with the ability to make flaming speeches and certain acting skills that he utilised at will. But above all, Mosaddeq had his fingers on the pulse of his time by forcefully calling for the expulsion of foreign interests from Iran and the restoration of full powers of the *Majlis*. In that sense, he incorporated the attributes of a true nationalist and constitutionalist.

The story is known: the intense power struggles between the Shah and Mosaddeq eventually led to a brief interlude of self-imposed exile on part of the Shah and subsequent ousting of Mosaddeq in August 1953 by a direct CIA coup d'état – known as "Operation Ajax", self-professed by the CIA to have been the most inexpensive coup performed in any third world country. The American involvement has to be seen in the context of the incipient Cold War and the threat of the spread of Communism, fed mostly by British instigation. Upon the Shah's return, Mosaddeq was tried for high treason by a military tribunal, imprisoned, and spent the last years of his life until his death in 1967 under house arrest in his village outside Tehran. The monarchical regime re-established itself with an autocratic grip and firm backing by the United States. The arrogance of power demonstrated by the U.S. was reinforced by Mosaddeq's acting potential, showcasing the feeling of helplessness of a whole nation.

If these facts in themselves were not enough to raise the spectre of conspiracy, they were aided by a CIA document that has been spread since by American sources. The document is called "Overthrow of Premier Mossadeq [sic] of Iran" and can be found to date under the heading "Secrets of History" on the website of the *New York Times*.[26] This "Clandestine Service Historical Paper No. 208" was written by Donald N. Wilber who was responsible for the planning of "Operation AJAX". Mr. Wilber, shown on the website in an almost parodistic way in traditional Arab garb, seemed like the perfect person for this operation. Due to his occupation as a historian of Middle Eastern architecture he did not even need a camouflage; working for the CIA became a lucrative side job. The study was written:

> because it seemed desirable to have a record of a major operation prepared while documents were readily at hand and while the memories of the personnel involved in the activity were still fresh. In addition, it was felt advisable to stress certain conclusions reached after the operation had been completed and to embody some of these in the form of recommendations applicable to future, parallel operations.[27]

---

26 James Risen, "Secrets of History: The C.I.A. in Iran", in: *New York Times on the Web*, 2000, http://www.nytimes.com/library/world/mideast/041600iran-cia-index.html (accessed Sept. 29, 2010).

27 "Introduction: The C.I.A. in Iran", in: *New York Times on the Web*, 2000, http://www.nytimes.com/library/world/mideast/iran-cia-intro.pdf (accessed Sept. 30, 2010).

It is this attitude, more than anything else, that undermines any "good intentions" that the United States might have had toward Iran. An attitude that is echoed by Kermit Roosevelt, Jr., responsible for the execution of "AJAX":

> Not wishing to be accused of trying to use the Americans to pull British chestnuts out of the fire, I decided to emphasize the Communist threat to Iran rather than the need to recover control of the oil industry. I argued that even if a settlement of the oil dispute could be negotiated with Musaddiq [sic], which was doubtful, he was still incapable of resisting a coup of the Tudeh Party, if it were backed by a Soviet support. Therefore he must be removed.[28]

Even worse in hurting any Iranian feeling of self-worth were American newspaper commentators who prophesied that the new Iranian government of General Zahedi after the overthrow "won't be with us long, unless it can prove that being nice to the West is more profitable for Iran than being as consistently nasty as Old Mossy was".[29] All the more as the Shah was deemed to require "special preparation. By nature a creature of indecision, beset by formless doubts and fears, he must be induced to play his role".[30]

5. Mosaddeq as a Point of Reference

The brief interlude of a nationalist government remains a point of reference for all Iranians, albeit of different significance. For most of the nationalist and secular-minded population in Iran and in exile, Mosaddeq has not forfeited his popularity to date. This was especially visible during the Islamic revolution of 1978–1979 when he became a rallying point for the voicing of anti-American and anti-Shah protest. Even in the aborted Green Revolution of 2009, the nationalist element was strengthened vis-à-vis the religious establishment. The experience of clear-cut foreign interference and domination has caused part of the Iranian trauma until today.[31] In retrospect, the short period of rule under Mosaddeq is viewed by many, admittedly in an idealistic way, as Iran's only true chance at democracy, and the coup is regarded as a setback to the country's political development.

Even in some circles of the current Iranian government, Mosaddeq seems too important to be ignored and thus there is recourse to the events of

---

28 James A. Bill, *The Eagle and the Lion*, New Haven 1988, p. 86.
29 Qtd. in Bill, *The Eagle*, p. 96.
30 Risen, "C.I.A. in Iran".
31 For an interesting and enlightening comment by an exiled Iranian professor, cf. Sasan Fayazmanesh, "In Memory of August 19, 1953: What Kermit Roosevelt Didn't Say", in: *Counterpunch*, Aug. 18, 2003, http://www.counterpunch.org/2003/08/18/what-kermit-roosevelt-didn-t-say/ (accessed Sept. 28, 2010).

1953.[32] However, this effort rather commemorates the important event of the oil nationalization programme concurrent with anti-monarchical sentiments, while at the same time shifting the focus of the protest movement away from the nationalists and toward the religious establishment of the time. As mentioned before, the nationalization movement was an alliance of many opposition forces. In official communiqués and news items today, the role and importance of the religious establishment under Ayatollah Kashani is weighted far more than the role of the nationalists. In fact, a current news item commemorating the events portrayed the role of Ayatollah Kashani as so prominent that it relegated Mosaddeq to a lower rank.[33] This is also achieved by placing most emphasis on commemorating the events of July 1952 rather than the coup d'état of August 19, 1953. In July 1952 Mosaddeq resigned because of the economic and political turmoil and ostensibly because of the Shah's refusal to relinquish the power to appoint the Minister of War and the Chief of Staff, a constitutional prerogative of the prime minister. Mosaddeq was reinstated as prime minister due to pressure from the street instigated by the communist party, the Tudeh, as well as the religious establishment. In today's regime discourse, it is of course the role of Ayatollah Kashani that is the most decisive.

Another news item published by the same news agency close to the government lays emphasis on the diverse character of Mosaddeq's national alliance, pinpointing especially the role of the Tudeh and alluding to the ideological proximity between Mosaddeq and the Tudeh. But the main gist of the article goes toward blaming Mosaddeq for a certain naivité in believing the good intentions of the U.S.-Americans and seeking their help against the British, thus having assisted in establishing American hegemony over Iran in particular and the Middle East in general. According to the article, Mosaddeq exchanged one for the other, and this is deemed a lesson of history to be learned.[34]

---

32 I am indebted to Ramin Shaghaghi for providing me with the relevant websites that discuss the role of Mosaddeq in Iran today. He was also very helpful in drawing my attention to some of the current conspiracy theories circulating in Iranian regime discourse.

33 Accordingly, it was Kashani who stood firmly in front of the Shah and his apparatus while Mosaddeq had retreated to his family home outside of Tehran. Kashani pronounced an ultimatum and thus forced the monarchy to relinquish. After Mosaddeq was reinstalled, his relationship with Kashani deteriorated (*Salrūz-e Qīyam-e 30 Tīr* [*The Anniversary of the Uprising of 30 Tir*], 2010, http://www.khabaryaab.com/News/162308.htm [accessed Oct. 2, 2011]; translation is my own).

34 Cf. Fars News Agency, *Mosaddiq as Šarr-e Inglīs be Āmrīka Panāh Mibarad* [*Mosaddeq turned from the Evils of the English to the Americans*], 2011, http://www.khabaryaab.com/News/384033.htm (accessed Oct. 3, 2011); translation is my own.

In even stronger words, Ayatollah Jannati, the conservative chairman of the Guardian Council and considered a hard-line fundamentalist Shiʿi cleric, commemorates the events of the coup d'état, directly blaming Mosaddeq for having attempted to separate state and church and indirectly making him responsible for the continuation of the corrupt Pahlavi regime. He says specifically:

> Ayatollah Kashani, after enduring many difficulties, started a movement against the regime and effected Mosaddeq to be reinstated as prime minister. But Mosaddeq did not appreciate Ayatollah Kashani, became imbued by his power, turned into a megalomaniac and thought that henceforth he did not need religion and the religious establishment. Thus he put forward the idea of a separation of politics and religion which led to his isolation from the population and resulted in the continuation of the corrupt and cruel regime of the Pahlavis for years to come.[35]

This quote is illustrative for many reasons: again, of course, it stresses the role of Kashani as the main factor for reinstating Mosaddeq, ignoring the existence of a diverse array of opposition forces. More than that, in this reading, Ayatollah Kashani becomes the instigator of a movement that eventually led to the downfall of the Pahlavis, the precursor of the movement that led to the establishment of the Islamic Republic. In this narrative, the coup of 1953 is not a nationalist coup anymore but the seed that later developed into the Islamic Revolution of 1978–1979. The attempt to discredit Mosaddeq is exacerbated by the claim that it was actually Kashani's idea to nationalize the oil industry and that Mosaddeq had to be persuaded to include it in his agenda.[36]

Obviously, revisionist historical narratives are part and parcel of any government strategy,[37] and the Iranian regime is no exception. The only excep-

---

35 Found on the website of the Guardian Council: *Text of Friday Prayer*, 2010, http://www.shora-gc.ir/Portal/Home/ShowPage.aspx?Object=NEWS&CategoryID=1649831b-f60a-44a8-ac21-51d63e34cdb9&LayoutID=70c93d9a-5354-4235-85ec-da6cb1b9dc1b&ID=3395770045ba-4fe1-a269-6b88302d0fc8 (accessed Oct. 2, 2011); translation is my own.

36 Found on the website of the FARS News Agency (http://www.farsnews.com/newstext.php?nn=870208074 [accessed Oct. 4, 2011]).

37 More of these may be found on the following websites: Alireza Mohammadi, *Kāšānī wa Nehżat-e Melli Šodan-e San'at-e Naft* [*Kashani and the Movement for the Nationalization of the Oil Industry*], 2005, http://www.hawzah.net/fa/MagArt.html?MagazineID=0&MagazineNumberID=5034&MagazineArticleID=445; *Tekīye-ye Mosaddiq be Fadaīyan-e Eslām* [*Mosaddiq's Leanings toward the Fedayin of Islam*], 2010, http://www.rasekhoon.net/Article/Show-49146.aspx; Student News Agency, *Mosaddiq wa Melli Šodan-e San'at-e Naft* [*Mosaddiq and the Nationalization of the Oil Industry*], 2010, http://snn.ir/news.aspx?newscode=13891228084; Fars News Agency, *Hošdār-e Tārīkhī* [*A Historical Warning*], 2010, http://www.farsnews.com/newstext.php?nn=8805261295, (all accessed Oct. 4, 2011).

tion is that the purpose behind the discourse becomes all too obvious at times, such as when this issue is discussed on the website of the Supreme Leader of Iran, Ayatollah Khamene'i. He points to Mosaddeq as the main agent responsible for the frictions within the opposition front and goes on to issue a thinly veiled warning for current Iranian opposition figures: "in any movement divisions ease the way for the conspiratorial plans of the enemy, and the one sowing the discord, either consciously or unconsciously, becomes an ally to the conspirators".[38]

6. The Present-Day Debate: Strong State and Strong Society?

The regime of Shah Mohammad Reza Pahlavi, due to its close association with the West, became the main object of conspiracy theories among the Iranian population which were rampant during the reign of the Pahlavis. But what about the current regime in Iran, a regime that is not on western payroll (even though ardent conspiracy theorists would see the extreme anti-western slant of the Islamic Republic of Iran as the proof for its being a covert ally)? What role do conspiracy theories play today, and are they as prevalent? I would say even more so, but their domain has changed. Under the current regime, and particularly in view of the international opposition to its nuclear programme, conspiracy theories have become a government tool. The Islamic Republic has not shied away from using even the most despicable instruments in an attempt to denounce its adversaries and to solidify the support of its populace, as the Holocaust deniers' conference in Tehran in December 2006 has shown. The more pressured the regime in Tehran feels, the more likely it is to reload the conspiracy matrix, capitalize on the fertile conspiratorial breeding ground, and point to the "U.S.-Zionist camp", in an attempt to thus garner loyalty and solidarity.

This kind of manoeuvring is typical for autocratic regimes. They use conspiracy theories to distract from their own structural weaknesses, to legitimise their unjust rule, or to achieve other goals. Conspiracy theories are quite often instrumentalised by repressive regimes; one welcome option is to make outside actors or inside agents responsible for the problems besetting the society and thus to deny all responsibility. There is a possibility, of course, that members of the ruling elite themselves believe in the conspiracy theories. Nonetheless, to contend that there exists a conspiracy directed against the well-being of the nation – or, as in the case of the following example,

---

[38] Ali Ma'sumi, *Kudeta-ye 28 Mordad* [*The Coup of Mordad 28th*], 2010, http://farsi.khamenei.ir/others-article?id=9137 (accessed Oct. 3, 2011).

against the whole world – furnishes a good reason for that regime to vehemently counteract the conspiracy, be it by mass imprisonment or whatever measure the regime may deem necessary. Should all these actions fail to produce the desired results, then it is just one more proof of the saturnine machinations of the conspirators that pervade every sphere.[39]

We have two mechanisms at play here: one is the lack of "state-society dialogue",[40] that may account for the occurrence of conspiracism on part of the populace directed toward the governing circle that "is distant and opaque",[41] and, on the other hand, we have a government that makes ample use of conspiracy theory as a tool of keeping the population at bay, an instrument of rule. While the first mechanism was more prevalent during the regime of the Shah, the regime of the Islamic Republic of Iran has undergone several phases since its inception. Most notable has been the shift from emphasizing dialogue and rapprochement under President Khatami to the presidency of Ahmadinejad that has drastically reversed this course of opening avenues toward the western world. Not only has the current regime again gone into open opposition to the "West", most pronouncedly the U.S., but it has also managed to isolate itself in the domain of foreign affairs as well as at home among its own population, even more so after the allegations of fraud involving Ahmadinejad's re-election in June 2009 began to circulate. Conspiracy theories, and especially those launched by the regime, thrive in such an atmosphere.

One of the latest of such state-launched conspiracy theories involves HAARP (High-Frequency Active Auroral Research Program) which is made responsible by official Iranian circles for the earthquake in Haiti in January 2010 and the cold front in Europe in the winter of that same year.[42] Now, HAARP is not an Iranian invention. Like all conspiracy theories, it refers to actually existing circumstances or has a kernel of truth. HAARP is run by the Office of Naval Research, affiliated with the Pentagon, and it is a high-powered transmitter, an ionospheric research facility, based in Alaska. Its actual function and scope eludes my knowledge and is not subject to debate

---

39 Cf. Karl Popper, *The Open Society and Its Enemies: 2, The High Tide of Prophecy: Hegel, Marx, and the Aftermath*, New York 2005, p. 105.

40 For more information on this cf. Matthew Gray, "Political Culture, Political Dynamics, and Conspiracism in the Arab Middle East", in: Arndt Graf/Schirin Fathi/Ludwig Paul (eds.), *Orientalism and Conspiracy*, London 2011, pp. 105–125, p. 120.

41 Gray, "Political Culture", p. 120.

42 Cf. *The High Frequency Active Auroral Research Program*, 2011, http://www.haarp.alaska.edu/ (accessed Oct. 3, 2011).

here. There have been widespread rumours and conspiracy theories about its range and function in cyberspace for some time,[43] but all of these acquire a different quality if the country's state-run media point to it as yet another proof of "U.S.-Zionist" omnipotence. The article appeared in *Kayhan*,[44] the most authoritative Iranian state-run newspaper with a wide circulation, on January 21, 2010 and was titled "Serious Doubts Among Academic Circles in the World of Science: the Earthquake of Haiti is Not Natural but the Making of HAARP" (own translation). The semi-scientific tone of the headline is quickly superseded by blatantly conspiracist language and content in the article itself. Among other allegations it contends that it is the "American-Zionist Empire" which uses HAARP as a weapon, a weapon that not only sent an incredible cold wave to Europe in the winter of 2009–2010 in order to silence the critics of climate change but also triggered the earthquake of Haiti. The reason behind this devastating earthquake was, according to *Kayhan*, to provide a camouflage for the presence of the American navy in the Caribbean with the ultimate goal of occupying Haiti (since large oil reservoirs are believed to exist off-shore), Cuba, and Venezuela (the latter for its oil resources, too, of course). The article goes on to cloak its blatantly conspiracist views with pseudo-scientific explanations and quotes by such well-known "scientists" like Zbigniew Kazimierz Brzeziński, security advisor under Jimmy Carter and a "special friend" of Iranian conspirators.

It might seem a long way from Mosaddeq to HAARP. However, my contention is that without Mosaddeq, HAARP would probably be more easily relegated to the world of pure fabrication in Iran. Instead, the government dares to instrumentalise it, relying on the fertile ground of conspiracism in Iran, in order to divert from its own technological problems (that is, the issue of its nuclear program). The question is: are these theories still believed in by the population? The answer to this question has to remain purely speculative, as with so many issues involving the topic of conspiracy theories.

---

[43] Cf., for example, *Was ist Haarp?*, http://www.wahrheitssuche.org/haarp.html; Nick Begich/Jeane Manning, *The Military's Pandora's Box*, http://www.haarp.net/; *Klimaerwärmung und das Haarp-Projekt*, http://www.klimaforschung.net/haarp/; or Andreas Bunkahle, "AARP-Projekte auch mitten in Berlin? Codename 'Teddybär' – Geheime militärische Anlage in Berlin-Tempelhof gefährdet die Gesundheit der Berliner", http://www.bunkahle.com/Aktuelles/Astromedizin/HAARP_Tempelhof.html (all accessed Sept. 25, 2010).

[44] Kayhan News, *Tardīd-e Jeddi-ye Mahāfel-e Elmī-e Jahān* [*The Serious Doubts of World Academic Circles*], 2010, http://www.kayhannews.ir/881101/16.htm#other1604 (accessed Sept. 29, 2010).

There is no doubt that we are dealing with a strong state in Iran. Strong in this regard does not necessarily mean the popularity of the state, but rather that the state possesses the means a repressive apparatus needs to stay in power. At the same time, as the events after the latest election campaign have shown, we are also dealing with a strong society – or a strong society in the making. This seems to be the main dilemma of the Iranian reality today: the clash of a strong state with a strong society, and all concomitant phenomena. Analysts of Iran have observed a reversal of public and private spheres for some time, most prominently regarding the role of religion. Ever since the regime has engaged religion for its own purposes, so that religion dominates the public space, the role of religion in the private sphere has been diminishing. So much so that some argue that Iran is the most secular society in the Middle East, and since the 1990's there has been talk of "din-gorizi",[45] a flight away from religion. One may speculate, and I would like to posit this idea for further research, that a similar phenomenon is occurring regarding the role of conspiracism in Iran. By over-using conspiracy theories as a government tool of manipulation, and, as the examples have shown, doing it so blatantly, the propensity to believe in these theories among the populace might also dwindle away in the generations to come – and Iranians might shed their "super-addiction" to conspiracy thinking after all.

---

[45] I benefited from a conversation with Prof. Ludwig Paul on this issue.

André G. Sleiman (Paris)

"Zionising" the Middle East: Rumours of the "Kissinger Plan" in Lebanon, 1973–1982

1. Introduction

The partition of Lebanon into ethno-confessional cantons has been a persistent theme in the country's political history since its accession to independence in 1943. The "threat" of cantonisation has been felt like a sword of Damocles since the establishment of the dual *qā'imaqāmiyya* system in 1843 and the establishment of the *mutasarrifiyya* system in 1861 – both in the Ottoman province of Mount Lebanon. Even the proclamation of the State of Greater Lebanon by French authorities in 1920 was the result of a delicate confessional arithmetic.

The proclamation of the state of Israel in May 1948 and the protracted Arab-Israeli conflict has constantly fuelled – and will fuel – a plethora of conspiracy theories in the Arab countries. In a situation of stark polarisation resulting from the Cold War, from the 1950s through the 1980s, between the U.S. and its allies on the one hand and the Soviet Union and its allies on the other one, American foreign policy chose a different path during the 1960s by opting for *détente.*

In January 1969, President Richard Nixon appointed Henry Kissinger as the head of the National Security Council, the institution supervising all military and diplomatic actions of the U.S. In September 1973, after Nixon's re-election, Kissinger became Secretary of State. He was awarded the Nobel Peace Prize the following month for having helped to negotiate a ceasefire between the U.S. and Vietnam. In the wake of the Watergate scandal, Nixon resigned in August 1974 and Gerald Ford succeeded him while Kissinger remained in office and resumed the policy of *détente* towards the Soviet Union. He was quickly forced to deal with the Arab-Israeli conflict, striving to reach disengagement agreements between the warring parties (mainly Israel, Egypt under Anwar Sadāt, and Syria under Hāfez al-Asad). His efforts eventually bore fruit with the 1978 Camp David Accords and the ensuing Egypt-Israel Peace Treaty in 1979, which are both considered to have won Egypt over to the western camp. U.S. diplomacy in the Middle East cannot be studied regardless of the Cold War context and Soviet-American give-and-take during that period.

In the 1970s and 1980s, a widespread persuasion existed in Lebanon that Kissinger himself, an "evil in disguise", had started the civil war. "Since 1974", people would say, "something has been cooked for Lebanon". The objective, they said, was to suppress the Lebanese model of Muslim-Christian conviviality by dividing the country into two confessional states. Lebanon's liberal democracy and religious pluralism both bothered the monolithic Arab regimes, in particular Syria and Israel.

These fears of partition have been projected on U.S. Secretary of State Henry Kissinger primarily because of his personal traits – his Jewish affiliation, his outstanding tactical skills as a negotiator and mediator, his finesse and intelligence – and also because his diplomacy was greatly detrimental to Lebanon. In 1975–1976, the Christian and the Muslim parties felt abandoned, betrayed, and vulnerable; in the complex war fabric, woven by alliances and enmities between local and foreign actors, all of the parties felt targeted. The conspiracy theory that emerged may thus have been the outcome of an understandable paranoia.

Such a conspiracy theory flourished because it was – and still is – able to express everybody's fears. It is also a way of proving one's patriotism and attachment to the integrity of the homeland (for the Christians) or the Arab soil (for the Muslims). Third, this theory serves as a useful political and ideological instrument against a foreign policy that is perceived as hostile to the Lebanese cause, or the Arab cause, depending on the actors. Fourth, many local and foreign observers view the balkanisation of the Middle East, and of Lebanon in particular, as a process of normalising the existence of the state of Israel as a confessional state, thereby contributing to its security.

As in any other conspiracy theory, the Kissinger conspiracy theory involves an external schemer with dreadful attributes (obscure, clever, devilish, all-mighty, and tentacular), local agents or traitors, and a righteous victim. The combination of collective emotional tensions, global and local contexts (in the Cold War and the Arab-Israeli War), internal and external factors (Lebanese sectarianism, Palestinian armed activity) contributed to produce this successful conspiracy theory.

This paper examines the rumours and conspiracy theories about partition that emerged in Lebanon in the wake of the 1973 Arab-Israeli War. In the first part, I will address the common Lebanese perceptions of Henry Kissinger and the assumptions about the "Kissinger Plan" to partition Lebanon into two states, starting in 1975. In the second part, I will go through the rumours about the implementation of this plan by the U.S. Department of State Special Envoy to Lebanon L. Dean Brown in the spring of 1976.

Finally, I will compare these rumours to the common Arab views of Israel's policy towards Lebanon and the Middle East, based on Israeli documents.

2. Henry Kissinger's Diplomacy in the Middle East and Its Perception

Appointed Secretary of State on the eve of the Arab-Israeli War of October 1973, Henry Kissinger quickly became in charge of Near-Eastern affairs. He pursued a "small steps" diplomacy consisting in finding a common ground between Israel and the belligerent Arab states through bilateral negotiations. His first success was a military disengagement agreement, called the "Sinai Separation of Forces Agreement" (later known as Sinai I), in January 1974. Under its terms, Israel withdrew its forces from the areas west of the Suez Canal held since the October 1973 ceasefire and also pulled back several miles on the Sinai front east of the canal, while it was left in control of certain parts of Sinai. Egypt regained control of all Egyptian territory west of the canal and also of the whole of the eastern bank. Further intense "shuttle diplomacy" by Kissinger resulted in the signature of the Agreement on Disengagement by Syria and Israel concerning the Golan front in May 1974, which led Israel to withdraw from all the territory it had captured in the October 1973 war as well as from some areas it had occupied since the 1967 war.

A second Egyptian-Israeli disengagement agreement, the Sinai Interim Agreement (Sinai II) was formally signed in Geneva in September 1975, again after protracted diplomatic efforts by Kissinger. Under this agreement, Israel withdrew its forces from the remaining occupied zone. Among other things, both sides agreed to refrain from the use or threat of force or military blockade and to observe the ceasefire scrupulously. This agreement thus virtually consists in an agreement to demilitarisation and renouncement of violence between Israel and Egypt.

Arab leaders deemed this "step-by-step diplomacy" to be too favourable to Israel and detrimental to their own national interests, as it only reached agreements on a few limited points (territorial concessions, neighbourly relations, and 'good fences' policy). At the same time, it suspended the Palestinian question and constantly eluded a global settlement. Thus, the PLO was indeed excluded from the peace talks.[1]

---

[1] "Kissinger had a blind spot toward the Palestinian issue. He knew that at some point it would have to be confronted [, …] but he geared much of his diplomacy to trying to circumvent this crucial issue, to putting off the moment of truth, to weakening the appeal of the Palestinian movement" (William B. Quandt, *Decade of Decisions: American Policy Toward the Arab-Israeli Conflict, 1967–1976*, Berkeley, CA 1977, p. 286).

3. Kissinger's Only Visit to Lebanon

Compared to Vietnam, East Timor, and other countries, Lebanon takes up a very small part in Kissinger's diplomacy and thus appears of secondary interest. In his memoirs *Years of Upheaval* (1982), Kissinger recounts his first and last visit to Lebanon on Sunday, December 16, 1973.[2] The U.S. Secretary of State met with President Frangieh and the Lebanese Minister of Foreign Affairs at Riyāq Air Base in the Beqāʿ Valley, which is located 61 km from Beirut and only 6 km from Syria, for security reasons: demonstrations that were held in Beirut protesting the visit and the presence of Palestinian camps near the Beirut airport obliged the Lebanese government to change the place of the meeting. Karim Pakradouni, a Katā'eb leader, believes that Kissinger decided to stir up a conflict in Lebanon from that moment onwards.[3] He had reportedly said to a member of his staff: "What kind of a state is that, where the President cannot receive me at the airport of its capital?"[4] Kissinger never saw Beirut, but his brief visit was enough for him to understand Lebanon's regional situation, as he later revealed in his memoirs.

4. April 1975: Lebanon at War

Since 1943, major demographic changes in favour of the Muslims – the Shīʿis in particular – had occurred. Therefore, starting in 1970, the Lebanese political order became the target of boycotts and increased dissent by the left-wing parties, which were Muslim in majority but counted an important number of Christians among their leadership, as well as the Sunni conservative establishment which protested against Christian domination of the state and against the control of all key positions in the republic by the Maronites. The left-wing opposition advocated for political reforms in the name of "secular Arab nationalism" and "better participation". Some, such as the Lebanese Communist Party and the Progressive Socialist Party (PSP), called for complete secularisation. Others, such as the Amal Movement and the conservative Sunni establishment, rejected secularism, believing that it was contradictory to Islam, and called for the "abolition of political sectarianism" only (that is, the abolition of the principle of representation of religious sects in state institutions, in force since 1926, consecrated in 1943).

---

2 Cf. Henry Kissinger, *Years of Upheaval*, Boston 1982, pp. 787–789.

3 Cf. Karim Pakradouni, *Le Piège: De la malédiction libanaise à la guerre du Golfe*, Paris 1991, pp. 84–85.

4 Cf. Pakradouni, *Le Piège*, p. 85; unless otherwise indicated, all translations are my own.

By 1975–1976 this polarisation had created two warring camps: (1) the Lebanese Front, led by former President Camille Chamoun, which backed the existing political order and was attached to Lebanon's sovereignty. Predominantly Christian, it was composed, *inter alia*, of Chamoun's National Liberal Party (NLP), the Katā'eb party, and current President Suleiman Frangieh's supporters. (2) The Lebanese National Movement, presided by Kamāl Junblāt, which contested the political order and supported the Palestine Liberation Organisation. Predominantly Muslim, it brought together, *inter alia*, the PSP, the Amal Movement, the Communist Party, the Sunni conservatives, and Arafāt's PLO. During that period, President Frangieh faced an acute crisis of legitimacy as the Lebanese opposition demanded his resignation.

American policy in Lebanon at the time was mainly characterised by indifference and a lack of consideration. The U.S. avoided intervening politically in Lebanon in order not to compromise their peace-making efforts in the Middle East after the 1973 war. They favoured an internal compromise between the Lebanese sects without siding with a specific program.[5] The political reform that the U.S. would support had to correspond to the new demographic and political realities while respecting the ethics of Muslim-Christian partnership peculiar to Lebanon.

The Muslim leaders' calls for a "better participation" seemed legitimate to the Americans. U.S. Ambassador to Lebanon George Godley manifested his disagreement with Maronite President Frangieh and maintained distant relations with him, while ostensibly being in dialogue with Sunni Prime Minister Rashīd Karāmeh.[6] Furthermore, on November 6, 1975, Kissinger sent a letter of support to the Lebanese government conspicuously addressed to Karāmeh.[7]

The Lebanese perceptions of Henry Kissinger are by and large similar and refer compulsively to his Jewishness and cynical pragmatism. Kamāl Junblāt, a fervent believer that the war in Lebanon had been schemed after 1967 by the "imperialists" who wanted to partition the country and subsequently all the Arab states,[8] wrote:

---

[5] Cf. Edward P. Haley/Lewis W. Snider, *Lebanon in Crisis: Participants and Issues*, Syracuse, NY 1979, p. 234; Fadia Nassif Tar Kovacs, *Les rumeurs dans la guerre du Liban: Les mots de la violence*, Paris 1998, p. 188.

[6] Cf. Haley/Snider, *Lebanon in Crisis*, p. 235; Nassif, *Rumeurs*, p. 190.

[7] James M. Markham, "U.S. and Lebanon: Echoes of 1958; Americans Still Try to Live Down Old Phalangist Link", in: *New York Times*, Nov. 28, 1975, p. 2; *An-Nahār*, Nov. 7, 1975, pp. 1, 8.

[8] Cf. the first chapter of Kamāl Junblāt's *Pour le Liban* (Paris 1978): "Le complot", pp. 15–59.

> Kissinger, ce Sémite germain, rompu aux fers de la dialectique orientale, de la philosophie de Hegel et des stratèges politiques et militaires, avait très habilement saisi l'occasion pour faire renaître le mythe [d'inclusion des Palestiniens dans le Royaume hachémite jordanien dans un État sur la rive ouest du Jourdain,] et pousser au jeu de la réalité objective. Il encouragea l'intervention [syrienne] au Liban.[9]

The Lebanese author Georges Corm, a critic of the Maronite establishment and of leftist inclination depicts the American diplomat in a similar fashion, emphasising his ethnic and religious origins: "Dr. Kissinger, this obscure professor of political science, of Germanic origin and Jewish confession who has, within a few years, attained the summit of international politics".[10] Although he was an "assimilated Jew" *par excellence*, Kissinger remained associated to a religion he did not practice but with which he often identified. In any event, his Judaism is the key to understanding the reactions of the Arab world to him; it fired the imagination of the abounding Judeophobes in the Arab world. Arab spokesmen are anxious to explain that they distinguish between Jews and Zionists, but most Arabs use these terms interchangeably, or at least believe, deep down inside, that they are synonymous. (Besides, most Jews openly proclaim their support for the Zionist cause and the state of Israel.)

Lebanese conspiracy theories about Kissinger did not emerge until late in 1975, but rapidly proliferated afterwards. The Lebanese press disseminated a comment of his, made in September 1975, when Kissinger had stated that he considered the change of national borders, the disappearance of certain states and the emergence of others, a natural thing.[11] This being said, his statement is hardly a sufficient proof for the existence of a conspiracy. Kissinger, originally a history and political science professor at Harvard, was conscious of the incalculable destiny of nations, the fluctuation of power, the turnarounds of politics, and the ephemeral character of empirical givens. He was thus establishing a historical fact, but the Lebanese thought they were being targeted. Similar *post facto* interpretations of statements that Kissinger had made earlier burgeoned. On January 7, 1975, Kissinger had declared in Stockholm that "the gravity of the situation in Lebanon carries the germs of a world conflagration", whereby he was again making an analysis. The Lebanese press, quoting this passage a year later and for several years afterwards,[12]

---

9 Junblāt, *Pour le Liban*, p. 33.

10 Georges Corm, *Le Proche-Orient éclaté: 1956–2007*, Paris 2007, p. 357.

11 Qtd. in Nassif, *Rumeurs*, p. 201.

12 Cf. Nassif, *Rumeurs*, pp. 201–202; Benassar (Béchara Ménassa), *Anatomie d'une guerre et d'une occupation: Événements du Liban de 1975 à 1978*, Paris 1978, pp. 59, 147.

led its readers to believe that this premonitory observation was in fact a premeditated one. It is worth noting that both statements had gone unnoticed in Lebanon until the rumours of the "Kissinger Plan" began to circulate.

5. Raymond Eddé's Accusations

Starting in 1975, Raymond Eddé, Maronite deputy of Jbeil, repeatedly accused the U.S. and Israel of contriving a plot to partition Lebanon. Eddé made the first public statement in that direction in an interview conducted by Éric Rouleau on December 16, 1975,[13] which was published in the French daily *Le Monde*. Eddé declared:

> I still argue that there is an American plan aiming at the partition of Lebanon, which will lead, in a more or less short term, to the disintegration of Syria. The objective is to create several states of sectarian character alongside Israel, buffer states which would contribute to the security of the Jewish state. In short, the plan is to balkanise the region.[14]

Apparently, Eddé was in the possession of the partition map, which he never disclosed publicly. Sources report that he had obtained it from an American journalist, who had told him about the "Kissinger Plan" for Lebanon. The map showed Lebanon divided into two states demarcated by the Damascus Road connecting Beirut to Damascus, with a Christian state in the North and a Muslim one in the South, where the 400,000 Palestinian refugees on Lebanese soil would establish their state – a scenario close to what happened in Cyprus in 1974. Furthermore, Eddé claimed that the "Christian extremists" (Katā'eb and NLP) were actively working for the partition of Lebanon alongside the Americans and Israelis.[15] He accused Katā'eb founder Pierre Gemayel, for instance, to be supportive of partition for declaring that "Palestinian presence in Lebanon was becoming unbearable".[16]

Eddé was born on March 15, 1913 in Alexandria, Egypt. He was the son of Émile Eddé, former President of the Lebanese Republic under the French

---

13 Rouleau (b. 1926) is a French journalist and diplomat, then known for his left-wing views and sympathies for the PLO.

14 The translation of the interview was published in: Éric Rouleau, "Civil War in Lebanon", in: *SWASIA*, 41/1975, 2, pp. 5–6.

15 Following these accusations, Eddé's party issued a short study highlighting the perils of partition (cf. Hizb al-Kutla al-Wataniyya/Maslahat Tullāb Keserwān-al-Ftūh, *At-Taqsīm: Al-Azma al-Lubnāniyya 'alā Daw' at-tajāreb al-ʿālamiyya* [*Partition: The Lebanese Crisis In the Light of International Experiences*], 1976).

16 *Le Monde*, Dec. 15, 1975.

Eddé's partition map, showing the Christian and Muslim states, as well as Syria's and Israel's share, with the mention, in French: "I am of course against the partition of Lebanon"[17]

Mandate (1936–1941), and Laudi Sursock, a Greek-Orthodox aristocrat. After Émile's death in 1949, Raymond took the lead of the National Bloc (NB), founded by his father two years earlier. He was elected deputy of Jbeil in 1953 and was re-elected several times. Both proponents of Lebanese nationalism and strongly attached to Lebanon's full sovereignty, father and

17 Author's private collection (photocopy of original document). A picture of the map was republished in Nabīl Khalīfeh, *Lubnān fī Istrātījiyyat Kissinger: Muqāraba siyāsiyya wa geo-strātījiyya* [*Lebanon in Kissinger's Strategy: Political and Geostrategic Approach*], Byblos 1991, p. 314.

son agreed on many political issues. Émile remained a pro-French Christian politician, steeped in French culture and concerned with the fate of the Lebanese Christians, especially the Maronites. He was against Lebanese independence from France in 1943. After his father's death, Raymond sought to win more credibility among his Muslim fellow citizens and tried to make himself a national leader accepted and supported by Christians and Muslims alike.

The NB's 'corporate image' was moderation; it maintained a critical stance towards the other mainstream Christian parties and sought to distinguish itself from them. But, although it had some Muslim supporters, the NB could not get rid of its predominantly Christian character. Eternal candidate for the Presidency of the Republic and eternal runner-up, Raymond Eddé was nicknamed the "Lebanese Poulidor" in reference to the French bicycle racer Raymond Poulidor, who never wore the yellow jersey despite his persistency. In the spring of 1976, a few months after his interview with Rouleau, Eddé was a candidate to replace Frangieh (elected in 1970), competing with the Syrian-backed Eliās Sarkīs. In the same interview, the 'Amīd ("dean" in Arabic) of the NB, as he was called, confessed that he was unable to provide concrete proofs to support his allegations. He contended, however, that: "The best proof of the existence of this plan is that Washington did not issue any denial, despite everything that has been said and written about the subject, which seems highly suspicious to me".[18]

As the Syrian intervention in Lebanon started on May 31/June 1, 1976, Raymond Eddé saw the fulfilling of his prophecies. He sent an open letter to Henry Kissinger on June 12, reiterating his accusations which built on Kissinger's own statement that: "in order to have peace, [one should] give Lebanon to Syria".[19] According to him, Kissinger's plan for the Middle East was to delay indefinitely any Israeli-Palestinian settlement, establish a status of non-belligerency between Israel and Syria, while keeping Lebanon as the only and perpetual battlefield in the region.

Quite unexpectedly, Kissinger's reply came very quickly. It was published in the next issue of the Arabic-speaking biweekly *Al-Hawādeth*,[20] on the cover of which the Secretary of State was pictured under the heading: "Architect of the war in Lebanon!" The alleged letter was written in New Mexico on June 14, translated into Arabic, and published "literally conform to the original". In the letter, Kissinger frankly admits to having triggered the Lebanese crisis and striving to destroy the Christian-Muslim coexistence, inspired

18 *Le Monde*, Dec. 16, 1975.

19 *An-Nahār*, June 12, 1976, p. 3; *L'Orient-Le Jour*, June 12, 1976, pp. 1, 2.

20 *Al-Hawādeth*, June 18, 1976, p. 11.

by a 1954 correspondence between David Ben-Gurion and Moshe Sharett, where the former pleads passionately for the partition of Lebanon.

Assuredly, the reply is a *faux*, as the following should demonstrate:

(1) There was no mention of the letter anywhere in the press at the time, even in the most prestigious dailies such as *An-Nahār* and *As-Safīr.*
(2) It is highly improbable that Kissinger received Eddé's letter translated into English and replied within two days.
(3) There is no trace of such a letter in the archives of the U.S. diplomatic records.[21]
(4) Kissinger's fake confession in the letter is diametrically opposed to what he wrote about Lebanon in his memoirs.
(5) A diplomat who makes such a public statement can be indicted by the International Court of Justice.
(6) No American statesman in office can openly and naively proclaim his loyalty to the state of Israel and call America his "third country" (after Israel and Germany) as did the Kissinger in the letter.
(7) *Al-Hawādeth* was a Saudi-funded magazine close to the pro-Palestinian and leftist milieus, where the 1954 correspondence between the two Israeli leaders widely circulated.
(8) Eddé himself never saw nor received the "original" letter.[22]

As the Ford Administration was soon coming to an end, president-elect Jimmy Carter symbolised a ray of hope for Eddé, who could still not convincingly corroborate his claims. In another statement given to *Le Monde* in 1977, he expressed his hopes that the new Carter Administration would revise Henry Kissinger's policy by putting an end to the "plot against Lebanon".[23] However, upon noticing President Carter's lack of response during the first months after taking office, Eddé, who was known to be an obstinate

---

21 As recently evidenced by the publication, in April 2013, of 1.7 million formerly confidential "Kissinger Cables" dated from 1973 to 1976. Cf. "Wikileaks Publishes 1.7 million 'Kissinger Cables'", in: *Al Akhbar English*, Apr. 8, 2013, http://english.al-akhbar.com/node/15465 [accessed Oct. 28, 2013].

22 As was confirmed by his nephew Carlos Eddé (who inherited his uncle's archives) and the author of the fake letter himself (cf. footnote 20). I have elaborated on this argument providing more details and documents on my blog (cf. André Sleiman, *Kissinger's Reply to Eddé: A Beautiful Hoax*, Nov. 14, 2010, http://sleimans.wordpress.com/2010/11/14/henry-kissingers-fake-reply-to-raymond-edde/ [accessed Mar. 13, 2012]).

23 Jean Gueyras, in: *Le Monde*, Jan. 14, 1977.

man, tried to undergird his claims with indirect clues. "The way the civil war is unfolding", he said, "with its many twists and turns, and the interplay of the two powers directly involved, Syria and Israel, there seem to be many irrefutable elements which, for me, point to the existence of a plot aiming at assassinating Lebanon".[24]

The ʿAmīd then quickly turned his criticism towards the Syrian President Hāfez al-Asad, whom he accused of carrying out the American conspiracy in Lebanon. He thought that in order to have peace with Syria, Kissinger would have told Asad to compensate his loss in the Golan by annexing parts of Lebanon, as a first step towards the establishment of Greater Syria:

> Everything went on *as if* Mr. Kissinger said to President Asad: "Keep the ʿAkkār with Tripoli [North of Lebanon] and the Beqāʿ [West], and leave the Golan to Israel." I was asked if I had any proofs. My reply is that these proofs will perhaps be suddenly brought to light, exactly like the Watergate scandal or the CIA's remittances to King Hussein of Jordan.[25]

According to him, "it was in Asad's utmost interest to spark off a conflict between Lebanese and Palestinians, after having provided weapons for the latter and then flying to the rescue of the endangered Christians, while occupying all of Lebanon until the Litani River, which marks the 'red line' not to be crossed drawn by Israel".[26] He brought two major arguments into consideration: first, that Syria had never recognized Lebanon's independence and national sovereignty; second, that it needed Washington's green light in order to intervene.

6. Speculations about Dean Brown's Mission

From the start, Syria had a clear desire to play an active role in the Lebanese crisis, while the U.S. demonstrated caution, a lack of interest, and even a lack of understanding of the local issues.[27] The first Syrian attempt to end the Lebanese crisis came in February 1976 through the Constitutional Document (*al-Wathīqa ad-Dustūriyya*). Immediately labelled a "Syrian reform program", the Document was rejected by the majority of the warring parties. Having had the confirmation that a purely political solution in Lebanon was impossible, the Syrian President realised the necessity of a military solution to achieve the

---

24 "Pour comprendre la tragédie libanaise", in: *Le Trimestre du Monde*, 3/1989, pp. 107–117.

25 *Le Monde*, Mar. 10, 1977; emphasis added.

26 *Le Monde*, June 29, 1977.

27 Cf. Ronald D. McLaurin, "Lebanon and the United States", in: Edward E. Azar (ed.), *Lebanon and the World in the 1980s*, College Park, MD 1983, pp. 87–112.

country's ambitions. Parallel to that, Syria tried to present itself as a "wise" arbitrator before the U.S. and France – a stratagem that would soon bear fruit.

On March 30, 1976, the U.S. Department of State announced that L. Dean Brown had been appointed by Kissinger as his representative and sent as a special envoy to Lebanon.[28] Brown recounts: "This decision was taken during a half-hour conversation with Henry Kissinger who told me he had no idea of what was going on, nor what the diverse forces on the ground represented, and if this had any sort of importance".[29] According to Brown himself, he was given no instructions, except that he was to give a quick outline of the situation and to submit his suggestions, if he had any. The special envoy arrived in Lebanon the next day. He met with Kamāl Junblāt and other Muslim leaders on April 2, and with the two main presidential candidates, Raymond Eddé and Eliās Sarkīs, the following day. On April 5, Brown met with President Frangieh, before seeing Junblāt again on April 8 and 12, and Prime Minister Rashīd Karāmeh on April 9.

Brown's mission to Lebanon consisted in collecting information rather than suggesting solutions. Unlike Ambassador Robert Murphy in 1958,[30] he came as a mere diplomat who had no military assistance to offer.[31] The Maronite establishment realised that the Americans were neither able nor willing to support their war effort; even worse, they seemed to share most of the Muslims' views. Rumours started circulating that Kissinger's emissary had been ordered to carry out the famous "Kissinger Plan". Brown had purportedly told Frangieh that "there would be ships waiting for the Christians to take them to the U.S. or Canada, and that the U.S. were willing to pay thousands of dollars for each immigrant".[32] The Christians gone, Lebanon would be turned into a Muslim-Palestinian state serving the interests of Israel.

Multiple versions of the conspiracy theory circulated among the Lebanese population. One of them stated that Brown had proposed that 30,000 dollars and a Green Card should be issued per immigrant and a street in the U.S. be named "Green Lebanon".[33] To be sure, the "man of the situation" was

---

28 Lewis Dean Brown (1920–2001) was the president of the Middle East Institute and U.S. Ambassador to Jordan from 1970 to 1973. He played a noticeable role in the events of Black September, which drove the Palestinians out of Jordan to Lebanon.

29 L. Dean Brown, "La politique des États-Unis au Liban", in: Bassma Kodmani-Darwish (ed.), *Liban: espoirs et réalités*, Paris 1987, pp. 183–189, p. 183.

30 Not to be mistaken for Richard Murphy, U.S. Ambassador to Syria at the time (1974–1978).

31 Cf. Brown, "Politique", p. 184.

32 Cf. Nassif, *Rumeurs*, p. 218.

33 Cf. Nassif, *Rumeurs*, p. 218.

Suleiman Frangieh. The rumours portrayed him as a Christian hero, standing against foreign powers and defying Lebanon's enemies, at odds with the whole world. By refusing to resign and by rejecting Brown's offer he had preserved the Christians' honour and thwarted the trap that had been set for them – a trap leading them into exile to Canada and resulting in the constitution of Lebanon as a surrogate country for the Palestinians.

Frangieh kept on proclaiming openly and frequently, until his death in 1992, that Brown had *literally* proposed to "ship the Christians away". During the Conference of National Dialogue held in Lausanne in March 1984, he brought up his version of his meeting with Brown again and called to sever diplomatic ties with the U.S.[34] In reality, all the available sources firmly deny that Brown ever made such a statement. In his memoirs, Abbot Būlos Naʿmān, a major witness in the Dean Brown affair, refutes Frangieh's conspiracy theory. He argues that Brown's approach to the Lebanese crisis was circumspect, to say the least; his mission seemed only to have helped "calming down the situation" in a way that served the interests of his country.[35] The most ambitious part in the "American plan" back then seemed to favour the holding of early presidential elections and a reform plan reflecting the new Lebanese realities, which explains the congruence of interests between the American diplomats and the Lebanese opposition.

No confirmation of Frangieh's theory can be found in the diary of Camille Chamoun either, who held several meetings with Brown.[36] According to him, Brown first enquired about the Christians' situation and assured the Christian leadership that his government was aware of the military imbalance in favour of the Palestinians. He promised to help them to exert pressure on the Palestinians, while he clearly alluded to the decisive role of the Syrian troops as an essential part of a peacekeeping force. To Chamoun's disappointment, Brown left no room for exegesis: there would be no American intervention, and Syria had a certain role to play. Many other witnesses noted Brown's obsessive asking about "how long the Christians could stand against the Palestinians". Fawaz Traboulsi, a Lebanese leftist intellectual in-

---

34 Cf. Talāl Salmān (ed.), *Genève-Lausanne: Al-Mahāder as-sirriyya al-kāmila* [*The Complete Minutes*], Beirut 1984, p. 312. Frangieh mentioned the conspiracy theory throughout the two conferences (cf. Salmān, *Genève-Lausanne*, pp. 129, 270, 288, 391). Also cf. *As-Safīr*, July 3, 1985.

35 Abbot Būlos Naʿmān, "Dean Brown fī al-Kaslīk" ["Dean Brown in Kaslīk"], in: *Al-Insān, al-Watan, al-Hurriyya: Mudhakkirāt al-Abātī Būlos Naʿmān* [Man, Nation, Liberty: The Memoires of Abbot Būlos Naʿmān], Beirut 2009, pp. 111–114.

36 Cf. Camille Chamoun, *Crise au Liban (14 janvier–10 novembre 1976)*, Beirut 1977, pp. 89–90, 93, 99–100, 103–104, 110–111.

volved in the military hostilities, aptly writes that Brown's mission consisted in "selling" the Syrian solution to the Lebanese,[37] an option that the Christians were ready to embrace as they were bending under the Palestinians' yoke.

This misinterpretation of Brown's words by Frangieh is certainly not due to an error of translation – Dean Brown was fluent in French. Frangieh may have used his allegations as a political manoeuvre to highlight his rectitude, as the discord between him and Prime Minister Karāmeh had reached its peak. In an attempt to strengthen his position and increase his popularity among the Christians against Karāmeh (who benefited directly and indirectly from Palestinian, Arab, and American support), Frangieh pictured himself as the saviour of the Christians. A similar misunderstanding occurred with Kamāl Junblāt: "Visiting Junblāt in his castle of Mukhtāra,[38] [Brown] expressed gloom about the coexistence between Druzes and Maronites which Junblāt took to mean American sanction for partition".[39]

7. Between Official and Unofficial Diplomacy: The Red Line Agreement and Its Lethal Consequences for Lebanon

On April 11, 1976, the Israeli cabinet discussed the entry of Syrian units into Lebanon. The next day, Syrian units were sighted digging in 10 km into Lebanon, and there were conflicting reports of Syrian movement elsewhere. On April 13, Asad declared that Syria had "total freedom of movement" in Lebanon. On the other hand, U.S. Secretary of State Henry Kissinger said that Syrian military moves in Lebanon were "getting very close to the borderline" of Israeli tolerance (April 14), while Israeli Premier Yitzhak Rabin warned Syria against overstepping "a definite red line" which would "prompt an Israeli action".[40]

On April 23, U.S. Special Envoy to Lebanon Dean Brown met with Kissinger in London. Kissinger later said the U.S. position was that "there would be no intervention by any outside powers". In his own memoirs, Kissinger is quite

---

37 Fawwaz Traboulsi, "Un certain Mr. Brown", in: *Identités et solidarités croisées dans les conflits du Liban contemporain*, Diss. Université Paris VIII-Sorbonne, 1993, pp. 484–490, p. 486.

38 Junblāt mentioned some of his conversations with Brown (cf. *Pour le Liban*, pp. 23, 36, 39).

39 Patrick Seale, *Asad of Syria: The Struggle for the Middle East*, Berkeley, CA 1989, p. 280.

40 "Arafat Assumes Peacemaker Role", in: *Sarasota Herald-Tribune*, Apr. 15, 1976, p. 2A.

ambivalent concerning the situation in Lebanon. He claims that he insisted on Lebanon's sovereignty while he accepted the Syrian role of arbitration:

> To achieve all [his] aims, Asad was prepared to bolster the Maronite community and its institutions against the Muslim majority. In this manner, he found himself in an unlikely, uneasy, and spasmodic cooperation with the Israelis. [...] We had a traditional policy of supporting the Christian community; opposed Syrian hegemony in Lebanon; *saw a role for Syria in balancing the radical Muslim groups* so long as this did not cause Israel to preempt and start a Middle East war. [...] *We opposed foreign intervention while seeking to balance the various forces so that none would gain a decisive advantage.*[41]

He also quotes statements he made during two press conferences on January 14 and 20, 1976, where he expressed his total support for the independence and sovereignty of Lebanon and his opposition to any foreign intervention, "which would involve the greatest threat to peace and stability in the Middle East".[42]

Despite all these official statements, U.S. support for Lebanese independence and sovereignty remained a rhetorical one. Concerning the fate of Lebanon, "sordid arrangements", as Raymond Eddé would say, did exist between the U.S., Syria, and Israel,[43] but the war was not the outcome of a Zionist or imperialist plot. In reality, these arrangements were built on the events generated by the war, not the other way around. There was no "plan" conceived by Kissinger and carried out by the successive American administrations. The U.S. gave Syria and Israel the "responsibility" of managing the Lebanese quagmire, since Lebanon was – and still is – crucial for their security. A perennial victim due to its unfortunate location, Lebanon is the ideal buffer state. Eliās Sarkīs was elected President on May 8. Backers of Eddé boycotted the presidential election protesting interference by Syria in favour of Sarkīs. Three days later, Brown concluded his mission to Lebanon, as the American goals had been met.

Despite his denials,[44] however, everything indicates that Kissinger was indeed, directly or indirectly, responsible for the Syrian and Israeli invasions

---

41 Kissinger, *Years of Renewal*, p. 1025; emphasis added.

42 Kissinger, *Years of Renewal*, p. 1025.

43 Cf. USADOS, *For Secretary from Brown* (Secret), Beirut 3545, Apr. 21, 1976.

44 "After a long meeting with [UN Secretary-General Kurt] Waldheim, Kissinger: 'We were given no notice with regard to the Syrian intervention'" (*An-Nahār*, June 6, 1976, front page). Kissinger denied being involved in the Syrian intervention and reiterated his country's unfaltering stance on the territorial integrity and sovereignty of Lebanon and his opposition to any foreign intervention. On the other hand, he again voiced his approval of the Constitutional Document sponsored by Syria.

of Lebanon in 1976 and 1978.[45] Patrick Seale provides an insightful analysis on the matter:

> The turnabout was heralded by a dramatic change of tune from Washington. Right up to the end of March the State Department publicly warned Damascus against intervention, but suddenly thereafter the White House, Kissinger himself, L. Dean Brown and the Damascus embassy started issuing expressions of approval for Syria's 'constructive' role. Kissinger's concern was to break the tidal wave of radicals and Palestinians, and the forces backed by the Soviets in general. The benefits for the U.S. and Israel could be great indeed: the Palestinians would be humbled, the left reined in, Moscow thwarted, and Asad himself tarnished by a deed heinous in Arab eyes. Syria had to be told that the U.S. would not disapprove of an intervention in Lebanon and that Israel would not contest it by force; Israel in turn had to be persuaded to accept the entry of a Syrian army into Lebanon; and in Lebanon itself the fighting between Christians and Palestinians would have to be kept going because if it stopped Syria would have no further cause to intervene.[46]

According to Seale, Kissinger successfully persuaded Asad to enter Lebanon: "Instead of saying to him, 'If you go in, so will Israel', the shrewder message was, 'If you *don't* go in, Israel certainly will'".[47] By that, not only would Syria be weakened by an additional military operation, it would also suffer from a lack of legitimacy in the eyes of the other Arab states (indeed, they immediately blamed Syria for its actions) and would forget about the Golan. This view is denied by Kissinger in his memoirs but generally accepted by Arab and pro-Arab commentators.

Kamāl Junblāt seems to have understood the Lebanese predicament, as evidenced by his testimonial book. Again becoming absorbed with the Jewishness of the "devilish schemer" and his zeal to serve Israel's interests above all consideration, the Druze leader first comments that "Kissinger, the Germano-Semite, had realised a clever magic trick" by allowing Syria to invade Lebanon. He then lingers over Kissinger's "famous" call to Rabin,[48] who was

---

45 This has been evidenced by the recent declassification of a new set of documents and minutes of meetings on the Lebanese crisis involving Kissinger. Cf. "Kissinger Saw the Benefits of Syrian Intervention in Lebanon", in: *The Daily Star*, Sep. 23, 2013, p. 3.

46 Seale, *Asad of Syria*, pp. 278–280. He quotes two important authors: Ze'ev Schiff ("Dealing with Syria", in: *Foreign Policy*, 55/1984, pp. 92–112) and Itamar Rabinovich ("The Lebanese Missile Crisis of 1981", in: Colin Legum/Haim Shaked/Daniel Dishon [eds.], *Middle East Contemporary Survey V: 1980–1981*, London 1982, pp. 167–181).

47 Seale, *Asad of Syria*, p. 279; italics in the original.

48 The two men had become friends since Rabin was Israel's Ambassador to the U.S. from 1968 to 1972.

worried by the Syrian intervention, during which Kissinger is reported to have said to Rabin: "Haven't you understood yet? Let it be!"[49]

The conspiracy theory of the "Kissinger Plan" is shared by both Muslim and Christian sides. However, the Christian narrative differs essentially from the Muslim one. The Christian versions centre on the Christian exodus and leave no doubt about the involvement of Syria and the Palestinians, alongside Israel, who aimed at settling the Palestinian question (incidentally, the dream of a Greater Syria) at the expense of the Christians and the sovereignty of Lebanon.[50] The Muslim versions stress the plan's advantageousness for Israel: the creation of a Christian state allied to Israel, and the debilitation of the PLO with the help of Syria. In both cases, the U.S. and Israel would be relieved of the "Palestinian burden". Nevertheless, the fact that different accounts of the same conspiracy exist is perhaps the best proof of its fallacy.

Another indicator of its fallacy is the absence of any trace, mention, or even allusion in the declarations and communiqués of both western and Soviet diplomats, pointing towards the existence of a Kissingerian partition plan readied for Lebanon in the 1970s. Moreover, Brown made it clear twice, after the end of his mission, that partition would not only be economically and politically disastrous for Lebanon, but that it would also render any attempt to reach a regional peace settlement more difficult.[51] As for Kissinger, the evidence shows that he considered Lebanon to be a minor actor in the Middle East – a frail, small, complicated state. Thus, he thought that direct diplomacy had to be exerted with the relevant (that is, strong) states, Syria and Israel, whereas an indirect diplomacy was to be left for the irrelevant (that is, weak) ones. In that respect, Kissinger's attitude towards Lebanon was one of *laissez faire*. He did not deliberately opt for partition, as that would have created too many enemies for the U.S. (an attentive reading of his memoirs clearly indicates that he was highly aware of such consequences). For Rabin and Kissinger, Syrian involvement in Lebanon, without the absorption of the latter, was a satisfactory option, as long as the Red Line Agreement was respected. Speculatively, however, had a *de facto* partition occurred, by

---

49 Junblāt, *Pour le Liban*, pp. 36, 33, 37.

50 The most widespread Christian version, which I have compiled from different written and oral sources, goes as follows: It is clear that the PLO accepted Kissinger's plan and started executing it. All parties involved were somehow satisfied: Syria would take the Beqāʿ and Tripoli as a bribe; Israel also accepted the plan since it would be relieved from the Palestinians and the latter would be isolated from Israel by future Shīʿite and Druze cantons. Most Arab states turned a blind eye and everybody thought they would live happily ever after.

51 Cf. Appendices I and II.

itself and independently of foreign influence, they probably would not have minded it and dismissed the issue as a mere domestic one.

Egypt was isolated after 1978 and the only regional party that seemed to be profiting from the Lebanon crisis, in the eyes of many Arabs, was Israel. In Lebanon, hence, the ground was fertile for such a conspiracy theory about Kissinger. However, the situation was indeed cataclysmic, but it was not the result of an American plan implemented by Israel and the Arabs – even though both Israel and Syria benefited from Lebanon's sufferings – but that of the combination of certain regional configurations, political ambitions, and a pragmatic U.S. diplomacy.

8. "An Old Zionist Dream"

Perhaps the most interesting feature of the "Kissinger Plan" conspiracy theory was its innate ability to develop a twin theory involving the neighbouring Zionist state. The "merit" of dovetailing between the two conspiracy theories is largely due to the Syrian President Hāfez al-Asad who said in his famous speech delivered at Damascus University on July 20, 1976:

> The partitioning of Lebanon is an old Zionist aim, as you know. Perhaps many of you have read the letters which were exchanged between the Zionist leaders, or some of them, in the 1950s on this subject, stressing the importance of partitioning Lebanon. [...] Israel wants the partitioning of Lebanon for a political, ideological reason. It is only natural that Israel wishes the establishment of sectarian statelets in this area so that Israel can remain the stronger state. [...] Israel seeks to partition Lebanon in order to defeat the slogan of the democratic secular state – the slogan which we raise. [...] When Lebanon is partitioned, the Israelis will say [...]: If they could not coexist together, if the Muslim Arab could not coexist with the Christian Arab, how then can they coexist with the Jews and the non-Arab Jews? [...] Israel wants partition to acquit itself of the charge of racism. [...] When Lebanon is partitioned between Christians and Muslims, Israel will say: Where is racism? Israel is based on religion, and in Lebanon there would be states or statelets based on religion.[52]

These views were not only those of the Syrian Baathist regime. They were held by many Lebanese as well. Indeed, the removal of Henry Kissinger from office by the Carter Administration in January 1977 (he was replaced by Cyrus Vance) did not ease their fears. The events in 1977 seemed to them as

---

[52] Cf. Itamar Rabinovich, *The War for Lebanon, 1970–1983*, Ithaca, NY 1984, pp. 183–218. An original version of this speech can be retrieved from the Foreign Broadcast Information Service (FBIS) that monitored the speech from Radio Damascus.

if the plans went like clockwork, long after their architect was gone. Kamāl Junblāt was assassinated in March 1977, while the deployment of Syrian troops and secret services on Lebanese territory and their ensuing active participation in the conflict increased. Although a ceasefire was established in 1977, ending what was called the Two-Year War, the Lebanese remained in a state of uncertainty until the Israeli intervention in March 1978, code-named "Operation Litani" (in reference to the Red Line Agreement), confirmed their apprehensions.

The second Israeli invasion of Lebanon in June 1982, code-named "Operation Peace for Galilee", gave a new impetus to the conspiracy theory of partition. Several Israeli documents envisaging the balkanisation of Lebanon and the whole Middle East were put in circulation, principally in the U.S. and in France and later on in the Lebanese press. One of the most famous ones was the article by Oded Yinon, an Israeli journalist and policymaker, written in Hebrew and entitled "A Strategy for Israel in the 1980s". It was published in *Kīvūnīm*, a Zionist journal, in February 1982.[53] The article, no less than a policy paper, had gone unnoticed in the Arab world until Israel Shahak provided an English translation and a foreword for it,[54] shortly after the Israeli invasion. In his foreword, Shahak quotes Ze'ev Schiff,[55] the military correspondent of *Ha'aretz*, saying that the "best" that could happen for Israeli interests in Iraq was "the dissolution of Iraq into a Shiite state, a Sunni state and the separation of the Kurdish part".[56] In the same vein, Yinon advocates the stimulation of disruptive ethno-religious nationalist sentiments, ultimately aiming at the creation of sub-national entities (Alawite, Druze, Kurdish, Maronite, Coptic, etc.) on the ruins of the Arab nation states.

---

53 Cf. Oded Yinon, "Estrategiah le-Yisrael bi-Shnot ha-Shmonim", in: *Kivunim*, 14/1982, pp. 49–59. Yinon was a senior Israeli Foreign Affairs Ministry official and a journalist for the *Jerusalem Post*. His only scholarly article was published the same year: "The Significance of Egypt's Population Problem", in: *Middle Eastern Studies*, 18/1982, 4, pp. 378–86.

54 Shahak (1933–2001), an Israeli professor and civil rights activist, enjoys a wide popularity in the Arab world, and his political essays are usually translated into Arabic.

55 Schiff (1932–2007) is also knowledgeable about the Lebanese question, as he co-wrote *Israel's Lebanon War* (Ina Friedman [ed. and trans.], New York, 1984) with fellow-journalist Ehud Ya'ari, one of the earliest accounts of the Israeli experience in Lebanon in 1982–1983.

56 "Beyn Shtey Raʿot: Ha-Interess ha-Yisraeli ba-Milchamat Iraq-Iran" ["Between Two Evils: Israel's Interest in the Iran-Iraq War".], in: *Ha'aretz*, June 2, 1982, p. 9.

Needless to say, these "revelations" triggered feelings of agitation and anxiety among the Arab press readers. However, they remained limited to some circles in Lebanon and did not spread to the entire population. In this highly apocalyptic scenario (which envisioned that the Palestinian fighters were driven out of Lebanon by the Israel Defence Force, that West Beirut was heavily bombarded, Bashir Gemayel was the newly elected President), the September 1982 issue of *Le Monde Diplomatique*, which showed hints of left-wing stances and pro-Arab sympathy throughout the 1970s and 1980s, added to the already tense situation. It published a column entitled "Un vieux rêve israélien" ("An Old Israeli Dream") which quoted excerpts from Moshe Sharett's diary pleading for the "redefinition of Lebanon's borders" – in other words, partition.[57]

These excerpts, dating back to February and May 1954, precisely the ones that Hāfez al-Asad had alluded to years earlier, recounted opinions expressed by David Ben-Gurion concerning the establishment of an Israel-friendly Christian – or alternatively Maronite – state in Lebanon. Ben-Gurion had argued that the state of Greater Lebanon, proclaimed in September 1920 by the French authorities at the request of influential Maronite elites, had been France's greatest error. In short, to him, the Lebanese state was fundamentally weak and the Lebanese nation a mere illusion. If Lebanon could not be partitioned, it had to be controlled by bribing or winning over a local officer, who would then proclaim himself Saviour of the Maronites. Although Major Saad Haddad (1938–1984), chief of the South-Lebanon Army and the "state of Free Lebanon", fit the description (even though he was not a Maronite), the anonymous author of the column in *Le Monde Diplomatique* clearly alluded to President-elect Bashir Gemayel.

Rumours and apprehensions about the "Kissinger Plan" in Lebanon never really dwindled. After Israel had entered the Lebanese scene and become a full-fledged actor in local politics, the attention shifted from one actor to another. For most Lebanese, the Zionist plan to balkanise the

---

57 *Le Monde Diplomatique*, Sept. 1982, p. 13. The excerpts were taken from anti-Zionist sources published by Jews, one of them an Israeli citizen; they were translated into French from the English translation of the original Hebrew text (cf. Livia Rokach, "Let Us Create a Maronite State in Lebanon", in: *Israel's Sacred Terrorism: A Study Based on Moshe Sharett's Personal Diary and Other Documents*, foreword by Noam Chomsky, Belmont, MA 1980, ch. 5 (available online at: http://chss.montclair.edu/english/furr/essays/rokach.html [accessed Mar. 12, 2012]). The direct source is Moshe Sharett's personal diary (cf. Yaakov Sharett [ed.], *Yoman Ishi*, Tel Aviv 1978). Sharett (1894–1965) was Prime Minister of Israel from 1953 until 1955.

Middle East was just an updated avatar of the Kissinger Plan, or vice versa, depending on the conspiracy theory. The origin of the plan mattered little as long as the conviction of its existence did not waver. It was as if Israel had taken over Kissinger's plan in 1978 and set about to realise it; the events of 1978 to 1982 thus appeared to be the sequel of the events of 1973 to 1977. After all, Israel and the U.S. are viewed as twins almost systematically; imperialism and Zionism used interchangeably. Besides, is not Kissinger himself a Jewish American, therefore considered as a pro-Zionist on two counts?

The circulation of these Israeli documents has contributed to reinforce the belief that an American-Israeli plan has been set up to partition Lebanon; a plan perhaps going beyond the scope of Henry Kissinger's influence. The documents do not, however, prove much more than the following fact: a tendency exists in Israeli policy-making to promote separatist movements based on ethno-religious *ʿasabiyya*s.[58] It does not indicate, however, that all the Israeli policies until now have been geared to that end. By way of example, Moshe Sharett was deeply sceptical of Ben-Gurion's projections. On the other hand, the state of Israel is by all means based on an ethno-religious nationalism. (Did not Herzl hold that the Jewish question was neither social nor religious, but a national one?) Therefore, the ethno-religious rationale is bound to persist in Israeli political thought. As for the Lebanese privy to these documents and believing in the accuracy of their claims, they consider having had their proofs. Raymond Eddé extensively relied on the excerpts published in *Le Monde Diplomatique* to underpin his allegations. He is not alone.

9. Conclusion

The "Kissinger plan" is a trivial, common, and established national myth in Lebanon, and its instrumental character seems clear. Three main figures contributed to its proliferation: Raymond Eddé, Suleiman Frangieh, and Kamāl Junblāt. The conspiracy theory since then has been relayed and perpetuated in the national press, in political discourse, and everyday conversations, which has etched it in the minds of the Lebanese.

There is a substantial semi-scholarship and pseudo-scholarship on the matter, but scholarly articles remain rare. Lebanese authors are divided over the authenticity of the "Kissinger Plan". Geo-strategist Nabīl Khalīfeh is a

---

[58] The term is used by Ibn Khaldūn and refers to social solidarity, internal cohesion, or *esprit de corps*.

firm believer in the theory, as well as Jules Bustānī, the former head of the Secret Services from 1972 to 1976 (close to Frangieh), the journalist Tony Mufarrej, and President Eliās Sarkīs. Farīd al-Khāzen, a Maronite deputy and professor of Political Science at the American University of Beirut, is not; just like the diplomat and editorialist Nagīb Dahdāh (a.k.a. Libanius) and the author Fadia Nassif.[59]

In a milestone speech, delivered on November 11, 2010, Hizbullah Secretary-General *sayyed* Hassan Nasrallah excessively quoted Kissinger's fake letter to Raymond Eddé, in an intention to "unveil" the Zionist-Imperialist plot against the coexistence of Muslims and Christians in Lebanon to strengthen the Zionist state. Nasrallah was not only trying to give legitimacy to his armed struggle against Israel; he was also trying to present himself, in front of his detractors, as a patriotic leader concerned with the fate of all the components of the Lebanese nation. The next day, the author of the document himself, a Lebanese journalist named Salim Nassar, appeared on television, 34 years after the affair had started. He openly denied the letter's authenticity,[60] but gave credit to Nasrallah's vision of the regional and international struggle. This event shows that the Kissinger conspiracy theory is still a coherent theory producing meaning, and therefore will always be part of the national mythology, no matter what "non-believers" say and despite the lack of evidence.

Both the "cyprianisation" of Lebanon (*qabrasa* in Arabic, meaning the division into two states, Christian and Muslim) and its partition into several entities are impossible to put into practice, for neither statelet would be able to survive. If a "Kissinger Plan" indeed existed, it did not deign to deal with Lebanon, but perhaps aimed at a more global political settlement in the region or an oil policy to manage (or control) the oil fields in the Gulf and the Arabian peninsula.

---

59 Cf. Khalīfeh, *Lubnān fī Istrātījiyyat Kissinger*; Jules Fu'ād Bustānī, *Aqdār wa Tawaqquʿāt, 1972–1976* [*Destinies and Previsions*], Beirut 1980; Tony Mufarrej, *Harb arradda* [*The War of Conversion*], Beirut 1979; Karim Pakradouni, *As-Salām al-Mafqūd: 'Ahd Eliās Sarkīs, 1976*–1982 [*The Lost Peace: Elias Sarkis's Mandate*], Beirut, 2009; Farīd al-Khāzen, "Al-ʿilāqāt al-lubnāniyya al-amīrikiyya fī siyāsat at-tawāzun al-iqlīmī, 1975–1989" ["The Lebanese-American Relations Within the Politics of Regional Balance"], in: *Ad-difāʿ al-watanī al-lubnānī*, 1/1989, pp. 10–29; Libanius (Nagīb Dahdāh), "Les erreurs du département d'État: L'action syrienne au Liban", in: *Le Réveil*, Mar. 2, 1979, pp. 463–466.

60 Nassar provided the full story behind his forgery during an interview which aired on *ANB TV* in November 2010 (cf. http://www.youtube.com/watch?v=6SqoDUEQqbA [accessed Jan. 23, 2012]).

Appendix I: Excerpts from the transcript of a TV interview with Dean Brown on Press Conference U.S.A. (an unrehearsed panel discussion program in Washington D.C.), aired on August 10, 1976[61]

[…]

D.B.: I see [no outlines of a settlement in Lebanon] whatsoever at this present moment. I see none in the few months to come. If very lucky, over a period of time, you might get a settlement which would be a return to somewhat like the *status quo ante*, that is within the constitutional framework of the country, because the only institution that's left in that country is the Constitution.

Henry Trewhitt (*Baltimore Sun*): As an outsider, now, it seems preposterous to me that the Moslems and the Christians in Lebanon could get together in a mixed, viable relationship for the short term. Am I wrong about that? And, is there some potential in what has become known in journalistic jargon as the Swiss canton proposal for creating a roof government in Lebanon in which I suppose the ceasefire lines, whatever they might be, would be held?

D.B.: I think that's probably the solution that will come out. In other words, it really won't be the *status quo ante*. The only reason I mentioned is simply that somewhere within the Constitution a solution can be found. But there will have to be large changes, both in the political setup of the country, but perhaps more important, in the division of the pie. The social and economic structure needs a great deal of change if there's going to be peace there. […] I think most countries share a general interest, and that is to see Lebanon not radicalized, not turned into a country divided in parts with one part, that on the Israeli border, run by a … run as a radicalized Moslem state, i.e. another Iraq or another Libya. I think this is an interest that we share with the Syrians, with the Israelis, probably the Soviet Union, certainly the Saudis and most of what we call the moderate nations of the Middle East. […]

Gerald Ter Horst (*Detroit News*): […] You had spoken earlier of the desirability, but perhaps the futility of a reunited Lebanon. Does this mean we ultimately must settle for something like partition? I'm aware, as we all are, that the terms Moslem and Christian are not religious terms in the context of the Lebanese struggle. And yet, here we find the United States, for example, seemingly helping Israel and Syria reach some sort of an accord between

---

[61] The excerpts were taken from the Lebanese English-speaking weekly political magazine *Monday Morning*, Aug. 1976, 219, pp. 10–15.

those two nations. The U.S. also has interests in bringing about some kind of a way of dealing the Palestinian question. How can we move [...] toward something that is [...] better than partition?

D.B.: Well, I think we have to be very careful about the partition thing. That is to say, the United States policy has always been for the unity and the territorial integrity of Lebanon. And I would hope it would maintain that policy. A split-up Lebanon, actually divided into separate countries would create another series of small, non-viable, economically non-viable, states in the area. Lebanon worked as an economic unity. But break it down, and we'll see created just the seeds of future strife. Now, I think in the infinite capacity of the Lebanese of the past for working out political compromises, they can work out something with a cantonal or a confederal system, but one which somehow maintains the territorial unity and does not allow the creation of what we mentioned before in response to a Maronite state in one part, a radicalized state in another part. [...]

Appendix II:
Excerpts from Dean Brown's analysis of the Lebanese situation shortly after the 1982 Israeli invasion[62]

"President Reagan has just told a cheering British Parliament that 'armed aggression must not be allowed to succeed'. He was talking about the Falkland Islands, not Lebanon.[63] [...] American presidents for decades have committed themselves to the territorial integrity, the unity and the political stability of Lebanon. That commitment appears faint today. What does the future hold? [...] The partition of Lebanon may well be the eventual outcome. Israeli control may stretch to Beirut plus a Maronite-controlled state to the north of that. A Moslem state, doubtless housing Palestinian refugees from the south, would be centered on Tripoli in the far north, while the Syrians remained in control of the Bekaa valley in the east. But this dismemberment will not bring peace to the Middle East or solve the Palestinian problem. Nor will it accord in any way with our history support of Lebanon. The Christian community, including the heavily armed Phalange, must tremble at the prospect, despite its hatred of the Palestinians and its cautious relationship with Israel. [...]"

---

62 L. Dean Brown, "The Cost of Israel's Attack", in: *The Washington Post*, June 10, 1982, p. A17.

63 The end of the Falklands War between the United Kingdom and Argentina (April 2 – June 14, 1982) was concomitant to the Israeli invasion of Lebanon.

Brian Johnsrud (Stanford)

The Da Vinci Code, Crusade Conspiracies, and the Clash of Historiographies

> History is to the nation rather as memory is to the individual. As an individual deprived of memory becomes disoriented and lost, not knowing where he has been or where he is going, so a nation denied a conception of its past will be disabled in dealing with its present or future.[1]

After 9/11, the history of the medieval Crusades became a historical and mnemonic benchmark in which disoriented Americans framed the traumatic event and the subsequent "war on terror". The "clash of civilizations" debate had been ignited almost a decade earlier by Bernard Lewis and Samuel P. Huntington, who both saw the Crusades as the quintessential example of the cultural divide between the "East" and "West".[2] As Lewis became a historical adviser to the George W. Bush administration after 9/11, it is perhaps unsurprising that medieval rhetoric was so quickly adopted by the President, Vice President Dick Cheney, Secretary of Defense Donald Rumsfeld, and his deputy, Paul D. Wolfowitz, among others in that administration.[3] A flurry of new academic and popular historiography of the Crusades also emerged, and in the months after 9/11 even President Bush read James Reston's *Warriors of God* (2001) about Richard the Lion Heart and Saladin.[4]

A reinvigorated interest in Crusades historiography, television documentaries, films, and other popular texts ensured that rhetoric surrounding the medieval holy wars continued to surface in American public and academic spheres. Of course, current political, cultural, and religious relations between the U.S. and the Middle East indelibly influenced each text's interpretation of

---

1 Arthur Meier Schlesinger, *The Disuniting of America: Reflections on a Multicultural Society*, New York 1998, pp. 51–52.

2 Bernard Lewis, "The Roots of Muslim Rage", in: *Atlantic Monthly*, 3/1990, 266, pp. 47–60; Samuel P. Huntington, *The Clash of Civilizations and the Remaking of World Order*, New York 2011, pp. 209–211.

3 Cf. Bruce Holsinger, *Neomedievalism, Neoconservatism, and the War on Terror*, Chicago 2007.

4 "Bush, Turning Over a New Leaf?", in: *BBC News*, Aug. 22, 2002, http://news.bbc.co.uk/2/hi/americas/2210185.stm (accessed Nov. 20, 2010).

the Crusades as well as their popular reception.[5] Perhaps, as Frederic Jameson claims, in the wake of the postmodern era's "end of history", "the recent past is always the most distant in the mind's eye of the historical observer".[6] To be certain, it is seemingly counterintuitive that the Crusades gained such popular historical significance when other, more recent and lived history (the *First* Gulf War, for example) was often overlooked in favor of medievalisms when discussing relations between the U.S. and the Middle East after 2001.

Part of the question, then, is how Crusades analogies and conspiracy theories became available, understandable, and viewed as relevant and useful in the U.S. after 2001. There have been a number of events that have aided in stirring the conspiratorial coals suggesting that the U.S.-led wars in Iraq and Afghanistan were religious wars continuing the medieval Crusading legacy. Some of the events exhibited characteristics that predisposed them to subsequent Crusades analogies; other events took place, in part, due to Crusades analogies already prevalent. While this list is not exhaustive, a few notable reported incidents include: President George W. Bush called the war on terror a "Crusade" in 2001;[7] Donald Rumsfeld's classified World Wide Intelligence updates to President Bush in 2003 with biblical verses and images on the title pages were leaked to *GQ* magazine in 2009;[8] Lt. Gen. William G. Boykin spoke to church congregations in 2003 in his military uniform, explaining that the U.S. was engaged in a holy war against Satan in Iraq and Afghanistan;[9] an undercover Al-Jazeera reporter filmed American troops proselytizing and distributing Christian bibles translated into local languages in Af-

---

5 Of course, historians (perhaps medieval historians in particular) are reluctant to admit that any events after the sixteenth century influence their "accurate" portrayals of the events. However, looking at their predecessors, some admit that *their* Crusade historiography was affected by global violence like World War II (cf., in particular, Thomas Madden, *The Crusades: The Essential Readings*, Oxford 2002, p. 6).

6 Fredric Jameson, "The End of Temporality", in: *Critical Inquiry*, 4/2003, 29, pp. 695–719.

7 George Bush, "Today We Mourned, Tomorrow We Work", http://www.whitehouse.gov/news/releases/2001/09/20010916-2.html (accessed Nov. 20, 2011).

8 Cf. Robert Draper, "And He Shall Be Judged", in: *GQ*, June 2009, http://www.gq.com/news-politics/newsmakers/200905/donald-rumsfeld-administration-peers-detractors (accessed Nov. 20, 2011).

9 Cf. Rebecca Leung, "The Holy Warrior: General Called a Religious Fanatic Finally Speaks Out", in: *CBS News*, Feb. 11, 2009, http://www.cbsnews.com/stories/2004/09/15/60II/main643650.shtml (accessed Nov. 20, 2011).

ghanistan in 2009;[10] former employees of U.S. military contractor Blackwater (now Xe Services) claimed in 2009 that the company founder, Erik Prince, "views himself as a Christian Crusader tasked with eliminating Muslims and the Islamic faith from the globe";[11] and in early 2010 it was discovered that biblical verses were engraved onto hundreds of thousands of U.S. rifle scopes used in Iraq and Afghanistan.[12]

Regardless of the accuracy of these events or the religious motivations attributed to them, after 2001, elected officials, members of the military, scholars, journalists, novelists, filmmakers, and the general American public began to revisit the history of the Crusades and to consider how useful "holy war", "medieval", or "Crusade" were as markers to situate the U.S. military presence in the Middle East.

Mark Fenster has outlined the interpretive practice and narrative structure of conspiracy theory in America, "a model of historical storytelling that allows a narrative assemblage of details from the past to be comprehensible and to appear real and true".[13] Dan Brown's *The Da Vinci Code* (2003) is a model of historical storytelling unique from other forms of "medievalism", a genre that anachronistically re-imagines the Middle Ages. Instead, the novel and subsequent film adaptation draw the Middle Ages to the present and bind the period through a historical continuity in the form of secretive orders such as the Knights Templar, the Priory of Sion, the Freemasons, and Opus Dei. *The Da Vinci Code* legitimizes and furthers a concept of historical continuity by arguing that the medieval conflict between the "East" and "West" is essential for comprehending the contemporary, post-9/11 American "plot".

Of course, if we believed that readers of popular novels and film audiences lack intellectual curiosity or the ability to assess competing forms of knowledge, then we would agree with the majority of critics that *The Da Vinci Code* phenomenon is nothing more than spoon-fed, conspiratorial rubbish

---

10 Cf. "The Crusade for a Christian Military", in: *Al Jazeera*, http://aljazeera.com/news/articles/42/The-Crusade-for-a-Christian-military.html (accessed Nov. 20, 2011).

11 "Blackwater Accused of Murder in 'Crusade to Eliminate Muslims'", in: *Times*, http://www.timesonline.co.uk/tol/news/world/us_and_americas/article6740735.ece (accessed Nov. 20, 2011).

12 Cf. Joseph Rhee/Tahman Bradley/Brian Ross, "U.S. Military Weapons Inscribed with Secret 'Jesus' Bible Codes", in: *ABC News*, Jan. 18, 2010, http://abcnews.go.com/Blotter/us-military-weapons-inscribed-secret-jesus-bible-codes/story?id=9575794 (accessed June 9, 2010).

13 Mark Fenster, *Conspiracy Theories: Secrecy and Power in American Culture*, Minneapolis 2008, p. 123.

destined to confuse and corrupt the paranoid, dim-witted masses. However, the "answers" the characters in *The Da Vinci Code* find are far from simple and rarely conclusive; neither are Americans without advanced academic degrees helplessly inane, as many critics of *The Da Vinci Code* would have us believe. Rather than providing irrefutable answers or clean-cut historical analogies, the *Da Vinci Code* novel and film – each in different ways – trust and encourage readers with the capacity to assess, agree with, refute, or otherwise frame historical narratives of the conflict between East and West and its relevance to their everyday lives.

1. *The Da Vinci Code*

Of all post-9/11 medievalisms, Dan Brown's wildly successful *The Da Vinci Code* was most influential in transforming the medieval Crusades and Knights Templar into daily conversational pieces for the millions of Americans captivated by the novel. By the time the film version was released in May 2006, the book had still not left the *New York Times* bestseller list since its release. The film (2006) premiered on 3,735 screens, grossing $77 million on its opening weekend and over $217 million during its three months in theaters.[14]

By late 2005, just two years after its release, 28.5 percent of Americans claimed to have read the novel,[15] and as of 2009, the novel had sold more than 80 million copies worldwide.[16]

The story continues where Brown's previous crime-thriller novel, *Angels and Demons* (2000), left off, with protagonist Robert Langdon, a mild-mannered Harvard "symbologist", about to publish a book on goddess-worship and the Sacred Feminine. After giving a lecture in Paris, he is confronted by local authorities to help them interpret odd symbols a curator inscribed onto his body after he was shot in the Louvre museum. The victim's granddaughter and police cryptographer, Sophie, arrives on the scene and surreptitiously delivers a note to Langdon warning him that he is the prime suspect and will need her help to escape arrest. Before fleeing the museum, however, the pair follows clues left by Sophie's grandfather, discovering a digital key

---

14 Cf. IMDb, *Box Office/Business for "The Da Vinci Code"*, 2011, http://www.imdb.com/title/tt0382625/business (accessed Nov. 20, 2011).

15 Cf. Jerry Z. Park/Scott Draper, "Religious-Media Consumption: The *Da Vinci Code* Effect", in: Rodney Stark (ed.), *What Americans Really Believe: New Findings from the Baylor Surveys of Religion*, Waco, TX 2008, pp. 167–175.

16 Cf. *The Official Website of Bestselling Author Dan Brown*, 2011, http://www.danbrown.com/#/davinciCode/resources (accessed Nov. 20, 2011).

and a sequence of numbers that lead to a bank deposit box. At the bank they find a sealed cryptex and enough symbolism to lead Langdon to believe that Sophie's grandfather was a member of the Priory of Sion, a secret medieval fraternity dating from the Crusades that protects the Holy Grail and a valuable secret about Jesus, which the Vatican is desperate to keep from the world.

The pair enlists the help of Langdon's colleague in France, Leigh Teabing, a British Royal Historian and expert on the Grail and the Priory of Sion. Teabing unveils the secret story of the Holy Grail for Sophie: Jesus was married to Mary Magdalene and their child and subsequent descendants are the *sangreal* (not "holy grail", but "holy blood"). Not only has the church hidden the secret by destroying gospels that portray Jesus as more human than divine since the fourth century, it has also driven Jesus and Mary's descendants into hiding. By the Middle Ages, the Priory of Sion founded the Knights Templar. During the Crusades, the Templars unearthed the grail documents that trace the ancestry in Jerusalem's temple mount; the Priory has protected the sacred bloodline ever since. Sophie's grandfather was the secret Grand Master of the Priory of Sion, and the clues he left should lead them to the tomb of Mary Magdalene, the grail documents, and perhaps the identities of the last scions of Jesus and Mary. With this revelation, the actions and schemes of the conspiratorial groups woven throughout the novel – including the Knights Templar, Priory of Sion, Freemasons, Illuminati, and Opus Dei – are incidental in comparison to the truth that they seek to destroy, keep hidden, or reveal. The slow unveiling of "truth" is the driving force of the novel. Therefore, while critiques of the narrative attack how the conspiratorial groups are portrayed, the "truth" that necessitates their presence in the novel is what ultimately captivates the *Da Vinci Code*'s audience and encourages them to continue their exploration after finishing the book or film.

It is a wonder that so many have decried the novel's fictional elements, as novels are – by definition – fictional. The controversy and hubbub surrounding the book is largely due to its preface: "FACT: The Priory of Sion – a European secret society founded in 1099 – is a real organization [...] All descriptions of artwork, architecture, documents, and secret rituals in this novel are accurate".[17] This, of course, is true – after a fashion. To be sure, the descriptions of da Vinci's *Mona Lisa* and *The Last Supper* are accurate; the interpretation of them, however, is debatable, as all interpretations are. What is more, neither Dan Brown nor his narrator make any historical claims; Brown's *characters* do, namely Langdon and Teabing. The mention of "FACT" in the preface (should we read this as a note from the narrator,

[17] Dan Brown, *The Da Vinci Code*, Special Illustrated Edition, New York 2004, p. 1.

Brown, or the publisher?) invites the reader from the beginning to sort out what is "historically" accurate, accepted, refuted, conjectural, or conspiracy. Far from claiming that the majority of the novel will be factually or historically accurate or even "based on a true story", the three paltry "facts" listed on the preface page indicate that any brief, verifiable history is far outweighed by crime-thriller characters, events, and plot devices.

Serious academic responses to *The Da Vinci Code* as an imaginative novel have been almost non-existent, with the exception of a few articles leveraging literary and feminist critiques on the characters' interpretations of the Sacred Feminine.[18] As historiography, it has been ruthlessly criticized, despite the obvious fact that no classification – from the Library of Congress to its shelving in a bookstore – would place it anywhere near non-fiction. The critiques – from religious scholars, the clergy, historians, and book critics – all mount their complaints against a novel they find to be unforgivably fictitious. Critics' primary concerns have been the novel's dubious combination of "confirmed" and conjectural history, that it is supposedly "built on a historical foundation that the reader was to accept as factual, not fictitious".[19]

The linking verb used in this critique ("the reader *was* to accept") by religious historian Bart Ehrman is too simplistic, however, and needs to be altered to reflect the agency that readers possess. "Could", "may", "refuses to", or "wholeheartedly decides to" are more reflective of the myriad of potential reader experiences. As this essay will show, critiques concerning readers' interpretive faculties, as well as a growing American concern with global terrorism and religious violence between the U.S. and the Middle East, did shape a number of key scenes in the imagining of the 2006 film version. However, if we put aside the elitist contention that average readers are not capable of dealing with historically accepted fact alongside fiction, the novel shows itself as something much more than a pathological conspiracy theory intended to be whole-heartedly accepted by anti-historical Americans. Rather, the novel and film are purposefully self-reflexive about the nature of

---

18 Cf. Bettina Bildhauer, *Filming the Middle Ages*, London 2011; Kristy Maddux, *The Faithful Citizen: Popular Christian Media and Gendered Civic Identities*, Waco, TX 2010; Bradley Bowers (ed.), *"The Da Vinci Code" in the Academy*, Newcastle 2007; Gwendolyn A. Morgan, *The Invention of False Authorities as a Literary Device in Popular Fiction: From Tolkien to "The Da Vinci Code"*, Lewistown, NY 2006. Even here, the majority of these authors confuse the protagonist, Langdon, with Brown and criticize the author for historical mistakes of his character, to say nothing of the narrator.

19 Bart D. Ehrman, *Truth and Fiction in "The Da Vinci Code": A Historian Reveals What We Really Know about Jesus, Mary Magdalene, and Constantine*, New York 2006, pp. xii–xiii.

historical "accuracy", documentary evidence, authority, and interpretation. This form of self-reflexivity does more than allow for an alternative or counter-history, as many conspiracy theories purport. The self-reflexive mode in *The Da Vinci Code* novel and film exposes and critiques traditionally limited semiotic authority, and provides new models for social conditions that limit what is endorsed as proper history, by whom and for whom, and how academia and the public should respond to proper or "invalid" historical narratives.

2. Historical Authority in the Novel

A historical continuity between the ancient, medieval, and modern is exposed in *The Da Vinci Code* by challenging established histories and historians, played out in the impromptu lectures and discussions that initiate Sophie and the reader into alternative, conspiratorial historiography. Of course, the protagonist of *The Da Vinci Code* is a Harvard professor, and the novel initially bestows Langdon with the same skepticism and distaste for anachronistic conspiracy or historical analogy that modern Crusade historians typically display.[20] Having "lectured often enough on the Knights Templar", Langdon laments that, for academics, "the Templar's history was a precarious world where fact, lore, and misinformation had become so intertwined that extracting a pristine truth was almost impossible", and even a mention of the Knights Templar to non-academics leads to a frustrating "barrage of convoluted inquiries into assorted conspiracy theories".[21] The narrator recounts a previous conversation between Langdon and his publishing editor in order to underscore and undermine the political and economic forces that endow histories with authority: if Langdon were to publish such "conspiratorial" ideas, his editor explains to him, "It will kill your reputation. You're a Harvard historian, for God's sake, not a pop schlockmeister looking for a quick buck".[22] *The Da Vinci Code* does not overtly reference American history after 9/11 in the way that Brown's later *The Lost Symbol* does, although

---

20 The most inflammatory academic critiques against comparisons between the Crusades and the contemporary period have been leveled by Christopher Tyerman, who claims, "the Crusades and their history were *hijacked* by western supremacists" who had "no rational or benign purpose" (*Fighting for Christendom*, New York 2004, pp. 199, 23; emphasis added). Crusade historians Jonathan Riley-Smith, Stephen Madden, and Thomas Asbridge have shared similar sentiments in their books, novels, and op-ed pieces after 9/11.

21 Brown, *The Da Vinci Code*, p. 167.

22 Brown, *The Da Vinci Code*, p. 163.

we should question how great the "barrage" of conspiracy theories regarding the Templars and Crusades would have been in the U.S. before 2001 and the publication of *New York Times* best-selling books like "pop schlockmeister" Robert Spencer's *Politically Incorrect Guide to Islam and the Crusades* (2005).[23]

The Da Vinci Code navigates the authority of established history in a number of ways, and ultimately the novel endows academics and non-academics alike with the semiotic faculty to assess the "pristine truth" that Langdon initially seeks in terms of its historical character and epistemological possibility. Langdon begins by providing his partner-in-crime, Sophie, with "the standard academic sketch of the *accepted* Knights Templar history",[24] as he fears that without "the *proper* historical background, Sophie would be left with a vacant air of bewilderment".[25] Sophie, a non-academic with no formal training in history, initially holds similar allegiances to official, authoritative interpretations of the past. She argues with Teabing that a documented genealogy of Christ's bloodline without genetic evidence is "not proof. Historians could not possibly confirm its identity".[26] Teabing, the lauded "British Royal Historian", undercuts the strength of "proof" and "authenticity" on which his academic field claims to purport. The legitimacy of conspiratorial history often cannot be confirmed any more than the bible, he remarks, as "history is always written by the winners [...] a one-sided account".[27] After Teabing deconstructs history's authoritative foundation, nothing separates Sophie from the other members of the Ivory Tower (including Langdon and Teabing) except her exposure to the hidden secrets and clues from the past that are necessary for interpreting the bewildering present.

In fact, Sophie has very little to learn, as the secret, conspiratorial history of Christ's bloodline is known to "almost everyone one earth", Langdon explains: "You're just used to hearing it called by the name 'Holy Grail'".[28] Observing the creative translation of the Latin *sangreal* does not simply pro-

---

23 It should be noted that while changing social conditions in the U.S. after 2001 allowed for analogies or metaphors like the Crusades to become more intelligible, they certainly had a currency in American culture alongside other medievalisms in the nineteenth and twentieth century as well. Similarly, propagandistic Crusade rhetoric is by no means limited to the "West" and has been commonplace and formidable in the Middle East at least since Gamal Abdel Nasser's comparison between himself and Saladin in the 1950s, a likeness later capitalized on by many heads of state in the Middle East.

24 Brown, *The Da Vinci Code*, p. 168; emphasis added.

25 Brown, *The Da Vinci Code*, p. 172; emphasis added.

26 Brown, *The Da Vinci Code*, p. 256.

27 Brown, *The Da Vinci Code*, p. 266.

28 Brown, *The Da Vinci Code*, p. 161.

vide Sophie with new information; it endows her with the semiotic interpretive faculty to discover other mistranslations or codes from the past that, once decoded, explain the present. And while an impromptu translation of Latin requires a formal background in the language, Sophie – like the reader – is equally if not more equipped than Langdon or Teabing to interpret the conspiratorial clues left by the medieval Knights Templar and their fraternal descendants. Despite his claims that historians are not endowed with a special authority, Teabing still off-handedly dismisses the possibility that Sophie could decipher a text "if a British Royal Historian and a Harvard symbologist could not even identify the language".[29] However, the "codex" requires no academic training or credentials for Sophie to solve it, just her semiotic instinct to reverse the mirror-image text Da Vinci also used and reveal its secret truths.

These parts of *The Da Vinci Code* speak to the postmodern condition that Linda Hutcheon outlines in her analysis of "historiographic metafiction". While reworking the past like typical historical fiction, the popular novels that constitute historiographic metafiction are also intensely self-reflexive.[30] Hutcheon applies her work to more "high brow" and less popular novels than *The Da Vinci Code*, though the formal elements and their impact in the texts she chooses to analyze and Brown's novel function similary. To be sure, the blend of "FACT" and fiction in *The Da Vinci Code* contributes to the self-reflexivity inherent to the novel's success. Formal, academic history has failed to illuminate ancient *gnosis* and its medieval legacy, yet Sophie and the reader discover the truth through a series of Langdon's ironic reenactments of generic, semi-formal history lessons. What is more, Dan Brown is aware that *his* lackluster academic pedigree and the international success of his novels could easily qualify him as one of the "pop schlockmeisters looking for a quick buck" that the narrator describes in the novel.

The Da Vinci Code expands Hutcheon's notion of self-reflexivity between the author and text by drawing readers themselves into the self-reflexivity within and beyond the novel. *The Da Vinci Code* asks the reader to continue the interpretive work of uncovering the truth by deciphering ubiquitous signs and reconstructing an alternative, hidden history. Illustrated editions of the novel include photographs, reprintings of paintings, and other visual "clues" that the novel's characters interpret so that the reader can equally and further engage with the symbols, perhaps to find something new. Ever since

---

29 Brown, *The Da Vinci Code*, p. 299.

30 Linda Hutcheon, *A Poetics of Postmodernism: History, Theory, Fiction*, New York 1988, p. 5.

its first printing, the novel's book jacket has included hidden longitude and latitude coordinates for the CIA, bolded letters that make references to Freemasonry, and codes that replace select page numbers and author headers inside the text. The novel's structure and interpretive elements provide the reader opportunities to read, then *read.* The reader (like the characters) is challenged to see the world, then *see* the world and its truth. In this way, the novel asks not that its readers become conspiracy theorists, but *critical* theorists: inquisitive, interpretive, questioning, skeptical, and concerned with the constant pursuit of oblique or furtive knowledge.

After all, any real conclusion suggesting that the interpretive work of the novel is finished at the close of the final page would disqualify *The Da Vinci Code* as truly conspiratorial. As Fenster describes, a narrative conclusion "would call a halt to interpretation – conspiracy theory's key practice and source of pleasure".[31] The abundance of extra-textual manifestations of *The Da Vinci Code* encourages readers to perform their interpretive agency beyond the original text. As Fenster notes, the corpus of "texts" based on the novel seems to suggest that "conspiracy is not a 'theory' – in fact, it is everywhere – once you learn to see and read the code".[32] By undercutting historical institutions, historians, and any inherent authority or superior interpretive skills they may have over non-academics, Sophie's success in decoding the past is rewarded by realizing that sacred knowledge and truth have – literally – been inside her all along: she embodies the *sangreal*/Holy Grail as the last scion of Christ and Mary Magdalene.

3. Illuminating the Past in the Film

The 2006 film version of *The Da Vinci Code* is incredibly true to the novel, although it notably emphasizes the act of debating and critically assessing historical claims and alternative history to a greater degree. The film also mimics a popular frustration with violence in the name of religion, echoing both the Crusades as they were utilized in the original novel as well as the rising awareness of global terrorism by the time of the film's release.

In the novel, Langdon and Teabing unfold layer after layer of the historical saga for Sophie, who Teabing describes as a grail "virgin" because of her ignorance, and because Langdon's unfinished education of Sophie when he brings her to Teabing has "robbed her of the climax!"[33] Langdon responds,

---

31 Fenster, *Conspiracy Theories*, p. 14.
32 Fenster, *Conspiracy Theories*, p. 7.
33 Brown, *The Da Vinci Code*, p. 236.

"I know, I thought perhaps you and I could …", and trails off. Priory members conducted sacred orgies to worship and reach the divine, and the triad invokes an awkwardly similar (if only metaphorically sexual) group initiation rite into the divine *gnosis* for Sophie. In the novel, Teabing tells his version of biblical historiography to Sophie, who interjects with occasional astonishment, questions for clarification, or rebuttals on behalf of the standard, accepted version she is familiar with. Langdon's role during this initiation session is back-up assistance for Teabing, offering an occasional "soft nod of concurrence" with the alternative historical narrative.[34]

If the novel presents Langdon and Teabing as complementary lovers co-seducing Sophie, the film places the two as diametrically opposed and rival knights vying for the lady's intellectual affections. Teabing begins his tale seated at a table with Sophie, while Langdon, immediately on the defensive, stands to the side ready to interject. Landon first interrupts that Constantine's council of Nicaea didn't "create Jesus' divinity", as Teabing claims, but sanctioned an idea already widely held. "Semantics", Teabing scoffs, and Langdon shouts back, "No, it's not semantics. You're interpreting facts to support your own conclusions!" This interlude on the importance of determining causation, one of the key components to conspiracy theories with grand historical depth, comes before any of the larger, more heavy-hitting elements of Teabing's tale and establishes a rubric for stringent standards for historical investigation.

Teabing counters Langdon's concern with causation by invoking the authoritative and controversial marker opening Dan Brown's novel: "FACT: for many Christians, Jesus was mortal one day and divine the next!" While the novel offers no qualification after its pronouncement of "FACT", Langdon immediately challenges Teabing's claim in the film, "For *some* Christians, his divinity was enhanced". Here, the qualifiers "many" in Teabing's statement and "some" in Langdon's can both be correct, and quantifying the true intentions of believers 1,600 years in the past is at the same time semantics, as Teabing claims, as well as interpreting facts to support your own conclusions, as Langdon contends.

Similarly, when Sophie responds in surprise at the suggestion that Jesus may have been married to Mary Magdalene, Teabing notes "There is much evidence to support it". Langdon quickly interjects, "*Theories.* There are *theories*". In the novel, Langdon is the one persuading Sophie that "the historical evidence supporting it is substantial".[35] In the film, his derogatory desig-

---

34 Brown, *The Da Vinci Code*, p. 233.

35 Brown, *The Da Vinci Code*, p. 254.

nation of "theory" is clearly in the same stratum as "conspiracy", unlike more accepted and reputable "theories", such as relativity or evolution. At the end of their discussion, it is not clear whether or not Sophie believes in Teabing's story, Langdon's redacted and qualified version of it, or either, giving the audience permission to continue the film's journey without pledging to belief or disbelief. Rather, the evidence is put forth by two opposing sides – Langdon and Teabing – for much of the film. Due to the short two-hour, uninterrupted experience of the film, the decision to clearly state two opposing views for the audience is effective and necessary structurally: viewers do not have the reader's luxury of intermittent circumspection between chapters, laying down the novel to go online and fact check or challenge uncomfortable revelations before continuing with the story, and Langdon's objections in the film that are absent from the novel provide the integral experience of investigative speculation. By the end of the film, Sophie and the audience have confronted and assessed enough opposing historical evidence that is forged or authentic, visible or concealed, conjectural or probable, that they learn to trust nothing as "FACT" without first adjudicating its merit with their own inherent and learned interpretive abilities.

The film is more self-reflexive than the novel due to choices made by the writer, director, and producer to acknowledge that the murders committed by religiously-inspired characters, medieval and modern, would strike a resonance with American audiences after 2001. During the historical debate between the three at Teabing's estate, the discussion of the Council of Nicaea, the Templars, Crusades, and religious violence becomes disturbingly "academic" for Sophie, who now realizes her grandfather's death resulted from someone's obsession with this secret history. Sophie interrupts an argument between Langdon and Teabing by shouting, "Excuse me! 'Who is God? Who is man?' How many have been murdered over this question?!" Teabing responds gravely, "As long as there has been a one true God, there has been killing in his name". Nothing like this conversation takes place in the novel, and while Sophie's frustration has been voiced for centuries, it carries a grim reverberation after 9/11 and other religiously influenced violence in the twenty-first century. Teabing's response also targets the audience's awareness of Islamic terrorism by appropriating the phrase "one true god", a reverberation of the Muslim *shahada*, or profession of faith, "there is one true God, and Mohammad is his messenger".

Aside from the Crusader history employed, there are no geographical connections to the Middle East in the novel, no mention of Islam, not even any Arab characters. However, the root of the revelation and subsequent concealment of the novel's grail documents occurred during the most notable holy wars, what Lewis and Huntington mark as the beginning of the clash of civilizations, the Crusades. The film creators intentionally utilizes the recent history of 9/11 and the popular understanding of *jihad* and religious violence to emphasize why, like Sophie, the audience should engage with arcane medieval history as something fundamentally relevant to their present.

Just as the original cover-art for *The Da Vinci Code* novel highlights letters to reveal clues, in the film Langdon visually "sees the light" with letters and images jumping out at him and rearranging themselves as he decodes messages and solves riddles. The film's director, Ron Howard, producer Brian Grazer, and writer Akiva Goldsman had recently used the same cinematic technique when they worked together on *A Beautiful Mind* (2001), the story of Nobel laureate and mathematician John Nash's struggle with schizophrenia. The cinematic borrowing between films has been interpreted awkwardly by one medieval scholar as "the championing of paranoia in both the [*Da Vinci Code*] novel and the film".[36] This odd appraisal clearly (and unfortunately) adopts Richard Hofdstadter's and Daniel Pipes's critiques of conspiracy theorists as clinically paranoid.[37] It also ignores other important ways that the film highlights vision and the perception of truth and knowledge by those *not* endowed with the semi-mystical sight of a Harvard symbologist.

For example, after Teabing leads them astray and Langdon cannot decipher the clue "in london lies a knight a pope interred [sic]", he and Sophie board a double-decker bus and he laments the half-hour journey from there to Chelsea Library. The camera then frames Sophie's eyes as she scans the bus, notices a teenager with a smartphone, and walks over to his seat, telling Langdon "I'm getting you a library card". The young man is equally skilled in seeing what Langdon cannot. With a surprisingly technical vernacular, he explains to Langdon that the web search on his smartphone keeps coming up with ostensibly off-target hits because of "a basic linguistic coincidence" from the keywords Langdon input. Of course, the "false results" turn out to reveal the puzzle's meaning: "a pope" is, in fact, a veiled allusion to Alexander Pope. To emphasize the young man's "alternative" technical intelligence that Langdon relies upon, the bus passenger's "proper" cultural education is found lacking when he regrets irrelevant search hits for "some

---

36 Nickolas Haydock, *Movie Medievalism: The Imaginary Middle Ages*, Jefferson, NC 2008, p. 195.

37 Cf. Richard Hofstadter, "The Paranoid Style in American Politics", in: *The Paranoid Style in American Politics and Other Essays*, London 1966, pp. 3–40; Daniel Pipes, *Conspiracy: How the Paranoid Style Flourishes and Where It Comes from*, New York 1997. While Hofstadter initially tries to distinguish between clinical and cultural paranoia, his rhetoric treats them both as a form of pathological neuroses, though the latter does not necessarily call for institutionalization or psychological treatment.

bloke named Alexander Pope". Throughout the film, Langdon and Sophie are joined by the visual perception and often surprising intelligence of other "observers". In this scene, the passenger in the bus seat also mimics the interpretive sight of the millions of filmgoers in cinema seats.

The film provides opportunities for the audience to focus their interpretive sight by recognizing symbols and encoded historical references that only those initiated into the conspiratorial history, that is, those who have read the novel before watching the film, would notice as meaningful and relevant. Executive producer Dan Brown, director Ron Howard, production designer Allan Cameron, and assistant Anna Culp intentionally planted subtextual visual references in the film as another way for audiences to engage with cryptology and historical symbolism. For instance, Sandro Botticelli's *The Birth of Venus* is on the cover of Langdon's book, *The Sacred Feminine,* and a marquee near the U.S. embassy displays an advertisement for the opera version of Victor Hugo's *Les Misérables.* Botticelli and Hugo were both, supposedly, members of the Priory of Sion. Like the Holy Grail, "hidden" knowledge in the film is displayed in plain sight, though only those initiated and possessing a sharp eye can discern it.

4. Conspiratorial Codebreakers

In terms of Hayden White's conception of "linguistic protocols", novels like *The Da Vinci Code* ignore the limits academic historians place on what is "thinkable" after 9/11. Instead, they create new linguistic protocols to characterize the past's relationship with the present "*in [their] own terms*".[38] If cultures experience trauma in an analogous manner to individuals, constructing and ordering narratives of the past is an essential part of "working-through" traumatic events of the present.[39] Rather than outsourcing that historical engagement to professional academics, popular narratives endow Americans with the semiotic agency to discover meaning in everyday ephemera. Historical inaccuracies and conspiratorial illusions become increasingly less urgent

---

38 Hayden White, *Metahistory: The Historical Imagination in Nineteenth-Century Europe*, Baltimore 1975, p. 30; italics in the original.

39 From the beginning of psychoanalysis to its critical adoption by narratology and cultural studies, trauma, memory, and sequencing or ordering have an established relationship. Cf. Sigmund Freud, *Civilization and Its Discontents*, New York 1961, p. 46; Peter Brooks, *Reading for the Plot: Design and Intention in Narrative*, New York 1984, pp. 100–102; Brian Johnsrud, "Putting the Pieces Together Again: Digital Photography and the Compulsion to Order Violence at Abu Ghraib", in: *Visual Studies*, 2/2011, 26, pp. 154–168.

if we value this interpretive response to national trauma as an ongoing process of healing rather than an authoritative pronouncement or an end in itself.

Of course, *The Da Vinci Code* is not primarily concerned with the past, just as interest in past events and history after a national tragedy is more than simple nostalgia. Various interpretations of the past and historical metaphors are often adopted in order to envision a future where those tragedies are avoided.[40] This is more than just traumatic repetition compulsion; in psychoanalytic terms (which are hard to escape when dealing with trauma theory), it is not the "death drive" but Freud's complementary "life drive", the creative impulse and "Eros of the poets and philosophers which holds all living things together".[41] The way that violent and conspiratorial history is interpreted in *The Da Vinci Code* highlights the agency of codebreakers and their ability to illuminate knowledge and improve their life. This is far from the "agency panic" that Timothy Melley ascribes to conspiracy theorists, which is an initial anxious and desperate reaction to believing one's actions are controlled by external, powerful agents or organizations.[42] Instead of a desperate, paranoid flight away from imaginary oppression, the protagonists in Brown's novels demonstrate intellectual daring toward a truth – an intuitive leap that disregards academic warnings of the dangers of untrained musings.

This is not to say that all conspiracy theorists or the consumption of conspiracy are inevitably benign, or that history cannot be misused in a hateful and violent manner. A good deal of cultural memory of the Crusades today is aligned with Lewis and Huntington's thesis to legitimize an inescapable future of conflict between the East and West. In its extreme, it encourages renewed, religiously inspired violence to condone racist and xenophobic practices. On July 22, 2011, Anders Behring Breivik electronically distributed his manifesto, *2083 – A European Declaration of Independence*, hours before bombing government buildings in Oslo, Norway and shooting dead 69 people on the nearby island Utøya. In it, he cites the medieval Crusades and

---

40 In classic psychoanalysis, Freud saw this in the many ways people, even children, imagine and rehearse traumatic experiences in order to prepare for or even prevent the future event. It is described most famously in his interpretation of the father's dream of a burning child and his grandson's *fort/da* game (cf. Sigmund Freud, *Beyond the Pleasure Principle*, New York 1961, pp. 12–17; James Strachey [ed. and trans.], *The Standard Edition of the Complete Psychological Works of Sigmund Freud*, London 1953–1974, vol. 5, pp. 547–548).

41 Freud, *Beyond the Pleasure Principle*, pp. 60–61.

42 Timothy Melley, *Empire of Conspiracy: The Culture of Paranoia in Postwar America*, Ithaca 2000, pp. 7–16.

contends that his actions reflect a continuation of the effort to defend Europe against malevolent Islamic and Arab influences, a thesis which draws heavily from Robert Spencer's *The Politically Incorrect Guide to Islam and the Crusades*, as well as a number of other popular American sources.[43] Months later, Britain's Home Secretary made membership to the Islamist group "Muslims against the Crusades" illegal after declaring that it was a successor to the already banned Islam4UK and other proscribed terrorist organizations.[44] If *The Da Vinci Code* in any way aligned with this deplorable use of history, there would be some justification for academic critiques that the novel is "as dangerous as the claims of the Freeman, various Citizen's Militia groups, Anarchists, or White Supremacists, to the legal government of the United States […] the result can easily be a dystopia".[45]

However, there are no calls for a renewal of historical violence in *The Da Vinci Code*, especially by the protagonists. In fact, even the novel's critics find admirable qualities in its overall pacifist, inquisitive, and knowledge-seeking thesis. One scholarly observer of an Assembly of God congregation, for instance, noted that the pastor was comfortable dismissing the novel and its character's historical postulations while simultaneously praising Robert Langdon and quoting his character verbatim as a source of wisdom: "the most important thing is what you believe".[46] There remains only the derogatory suggestion that "confused" readers and filmgoers would somehow completely misread and corrupt *The Da Vinci Code*'s overt message of religious liberalism to one of virulent intolerance. In response to this sort of claim, Dan Brown has cautioned: "I believe readers and movie-goers are a lot smarter than some people would have you believe".[47] In actuality, it was because of the intellectual curiosity of the millions of readers who planted down in bookstore readings, church discussion groups, and online forums to continue questioning that the book drew such notoriety, and these readers

---

43 Cf. Scott Shane, "Killings in Norway Spotlight Anti-Muslim Thought in U.S.", in: *New York Times*, July 24, 2011, https://www.nytimes.com/2011/07/25/us/25debate.html?pagewanted=1&_r=2&hp (accessed Nov. 20, 2011).

44 Alan Travis, "Muslims Against Crusades to Be Banned from Midnight", in: *Guardian*, Nov. 11, 2011, http://www.guardian.co.uk/uk/2011/nov/10/muslims-against-crusades-banned (accessed Nov. 20, 2011).

45 Morgan, *Invention of False Authorities*, p. 83.

46 Ellen E. Moore, "The Gospel of Tom (Hanks): American Churches and *The Da Vinci Code*", in: Christopher Deacy/Elisabeth Arweck (eds.), *Exploring Religion and the Sacred in a Media Age*, Burlington, VT 2009, pp. 123–140.

47 Laura Knoy, "Dan Brown Speaks: Writers on a New England Stage", in: *New Hampshire Public Radio*, Apr. 24, 2006, http://info.nhpr.org/node/10582 (accessed Nov. 10, 2011).

were then ironically dismissed as naïvely uninquisitive by many of *The Da Vinci Code*'s critics.

In his work on conspiracy culture, Peter Knight asks us to bear in mind, "In many instances consumers of conspiracy don't really believe what they buy, but neither do they really disbelieve it either. Often people believe rumors with a provisional commitment, believing them *as if* they were true".[48] Balancing belief with disbelief alongside "FACT" and "fact" is common practice for most Americans in the twenty-first century, an ability encouraged by postmodern, ironic, and self-reflexive cultural products.[49] Dan Brown was the son of an Episcopalian church organist and a mathematician, and he often speaks about the ability to simultaneously fully believe and be ultimately skeptical of claims about truth.[50]

Knight also distinguishes conspiracy culture from conspiracy theorists, and those who watch a conspiratorial film or read a similar book (consumers) are not "theorists" (producers) in his mind, a distinction shared by many scholars of conspiracy theory. Rather, conspiracy theorists are distinguished by the active work of searching for and developing conspiratorial information, not just the "passive" consumption of Oliver Stone's *JFK* (1991), for instance. When Knight notes that by 1992 three-quarters of Americans believed there was a conspiracy or official cover-up of the conditions surrounding President John F. Kennedy's assassination,[51] it is not intended to claim that three-quarters of Americans are conspiracy theorists, just "passive" consumers. Belief and action, in this image of conspiracy consumers versus conspiracy theorists, are separate and distinct categories. While this may sometimes be the case, belief and action are often accompanied, especially when we consider different forms of action and consumer agency.

The Da Vinci Code does not present conspiracy theory to be inertly consumed, but as information and questions to be acted upon through interpretation, discussion, research, and eventual belief, disbelief, or a mixture of the two. In the novel and film, as in the real world, knowledge itself is not power; the ability to act upon knowledge is power. When asked if he begrudged the critiques and negative attention garnered by *The Da Vinci Code*, Brown re-

48 Peter Knight, *Conspiracy Culture: From Kennedy to the "X Files"*, London 2000, p. 48; italics in the original.

49 Frederic Jameson, *Postmodernism or, The Cultural Logic of Late Capitalism*, Durham 1991; Linda Hutcheon, *A Poetics of Postmodernism. History, Theory, Fiction*, New York 1988; Umberto Eco, *Travel in Hyperreality*, London 1986, p. 1–73.

50 Cf. Knoy, "Dan Brown Speaks".

51 Cf. Knight, *Conspiracy Culture*, p. 78.

sponded, "The dialogue that's being created is powerful and positive. The more vigorously we all consider and debate these topics, the better our understanding of our own spirituality [...] religion only has one real enemy: apathy [...] debate forces us to *actively* explore our beliefs".[52]

5. Conclusion

After September 11, 2001, dozens of alternative histories and popular "conspiratorial" accounts sprung forth concerning the Crusades, Templars, religious violence, and a millennial "clash of civilizations". As an early part of and catalyst for this phenomenon, *The Da Vinci Code* is unique in its ability to endow readers, particularly non-academics, with an interpretive and semiotic agency to subvert institutional medieval historiography. Historical inaccuracies and conspiratorial ephemera, however seemingly anecdotal, deserve to be studied and placed within a larger cultural framework. The imaginative impulse surrounding popular histories, novels, and films, does more than draw from and reflect an existing cultural milieu of trauma and representation in a sort of feedback loop. They create new cognitive and historical frameworks and, more importantly, encourage non-academics to engage in the creative work of introducing the past to the present and ushering them into an imagined – and hopefully better – future.

52 Knoy, "Dan Brown Speaks"; emphasis added. The transliteration of his speech is my own.

II. The Politics of Conspiracy Theory

Christopher Herbert (Pasco, WA)

The Society of Death and Anglo-American Fears of Conspiracy in Gold Rush California, 1849–1858

In 1851, a Frenchman, Albert Benard de Russailh, wrote in his diary that in California, the "brigands" belong to "powerful secret organizations, such as the *Do or Die*, or *The Society of Death*, [that] bind them together, and they have a leader in Sacramento whom they obey unquestioningly".[1] Benard de Russailh's fears of a criminal conspiracy were shared by many of the new arrivals in California. Newspapers, private accounts, and correspondence all contain allusions to a conspiracy or conspiracies of criminals in San Francisco, and, to a lesser extent, Sacramento, and the mines. None of these conspiracies can be proved to have existed, and indeed, most sound like the imaginings of a bad fiction writer, yet the idea of criminal conspiracies would go on to have a profound impact on the political development of the state, particularly in its dominant city, San Francisco. For it was in San Francisco that fears of conspiracy contributed to the formation of the Vigilance Committees of 1851 and 1856.

The links between vigilantism in California and conspiracy is a relatively unexplored topic. Until the 1960s, most historians tended to rather uncritically accept the vigilante's claims that they were acting to suppress actual crime waves. In these early analyses, vigilance committees were a necessary, if regrettable, step to restore order in the "wild west" that was California.[2] More recently, historians have focused on the political, gender, and racial aspects of the vigilance committees, seeing in them an attempt by the middle-class white merchants, who made up the majority of the upper ranks of the Vigilance Committees, to maintain dominance when under economic threat.[3] Virtually no attention has been paid to the language and logic of

---

1 Albert Benard de Russailh, *Last Adventure: San Francisco in 1851; Translated from the Original Journal of Albert Benard de Russailh by Clarkson Crane*, San Francisco 1931, p. 33.

2 Cf., for example, Hubert Howe Bancroft, *History of California, 1848–1859*, San Francisco 1886, pp. 405–406, 742–768.

3 Cf. Robert M. Senkewicz, *Vigilantes in Gold Rush San Francisco,* Stanford, CA 1985, pp. 35–45, 75–77; Susan Lee Johnson, *Roaring Camp: The Social World of the California Gold Rush*, New York 2000, pp. 196–215.

these committees, however. But at a closer look they reveal the social conditions that engendered conspiracy theories among middle-class Anglo-American merchants and demonstrate the links between conspiracy theories, vigilance committees, and ideals of republican citizenship in the California gold rush.

Faced with a recently-conquered territory, a large minority of diverse "races" (including Chileans, Mexicans, Natives, Australians, French, and Chinese), and a lack of traditional social structures (church, family, state) that had shaped their lives in the Atlantic world, Anglo-Americans needed to find a way to understand the situation in which they found themselves. One of the strategies they settled on for producing such knowledge was to "know" society by "knowing" about a variety of conspiracies that threatened the social order they were attempting to create. These conspiracy theories targeted not only non- or off-whites like the Mexicans or Australians, but were also marshaled against elected officials.[4] While arising out of pragmatic interests of a certain group of middle-class Anglo-American merchants, these conspiracy theories gained widespread traction and credibility because they confirmed what Anglo-Americans already "knew": that the republic depended on free independent (white) men, and that social ills were symptomatic of challenges to the republic.

In this, the Anglo-American merchants of California were hardly on new ground. Americans had, by the mid-nineteenth century, a rich history of identifying conspiratorial threats to the republic.[5] In addition to the fears of British domination that had propelled the original thirteen colonies to revolution in 1776, in more recent times, Americans had become concerned about Masonic conspiracies, "Popish" plots, and the rise of the Slave Power or, if a southerner, the rise of the Abolitionists.[6] As I will discuss later, the conspiracy theories of California were distinct from, but also related to, these other conspiracy theories. While the tendency to identify conspiracies

---

[4] The term "off-white" (sometimes used as "not-quite-white") refers to a range of peoples occupying what Maria DeGuzmán calls the "critically unacknowledged third position" between a black-and-white binary understanding of race (cf. Maria DeGuzmaìn, *Spain's Long Shadow: The Black Legend, Off-Whiteness, and Anglo-American Empire*, Minneapolis 2005, p. xxvii).

[5] Indeed, Bailyn makes a convincing argument that conspiracy theory was central to the revolutionary project (cf. Bernard Bailyn, *The Ideological Origins of the American Revolution*, Cambridge, MA 1967.

[6] Cf., for example, Eric Foner, *Free Soil, Free Labor, Free Men: The Ideology of the Republican Party Before the Civil War*, New York 1970; Ray Allen Billington, *The Protestant Crusade: A Study of the Origins of American Nativism*, Chicago 1964; Mark C. Carnes, *Secret Ritual and Manhood in Victorian America*, New Haven 1989, pp. 24–25.

as a threat to the republic was not new, however, the specific conspiracies identified in California were extremely localized. As the Benard de Russailh quote suggests, even the most concerned commentators believed the conspiracy (or conspiracies) reached only to Sacramento, possibly throughout the state. These conspiracies were not national, and certainly not international. They were, to use the terminology of Daniel Pipes, "petty conspiracy theories", not "world conspiracy theories", with goals that fell well short of global domination.[7] However, just because the conspiracy was local did not make it any less powerful as a motivating force in social, political, and cultural discourse and action. Indeed, the experiences in San Francisco imply that petty conspiracy theories can influence the course of human events as much as world conspiracy theories.

The first waves of humanity left the Eastern United States early in 1849 following news of what President Polk called gold discoveries of "an extraordinary character as would scarcely command belief were they not corroborated by the authentic reports of officers in the public service".[8] The discovery of gold would eventually attract tens of thousands of migrants, mostly male, from around the world to California. From a very early point in the gold rush, the middle-class white merchants who were to make up the bulk of the Vigilance Committees singled out foreigners as likely to be criminals. Indeed, the 1851 Vigilance Committee specifically targeted "Sydney Ducks", that is, predominately Irish-born immigrants from Australia.[9] Other vigilance movements targeted Mexican, Chilean, and French nationals both in the gold fields and in the major cities.[10] Joaquin Murrieta is an excellent example of this. Murrieta, who may not even have existed, was believed to be responsible, either directly or indirectly, for virtually all banditry by Mexicans in California until a military expedition caught up with a man they believed

---

7 Daniel Pipes, *Conspiracy: How the Paranoid Style Flourishes and Where it Comes From,* New York 1997, pp. 21–22.

8 James Polk, "Message to Congress, 5 December, 1848", in: *Journal of the Senate of the United States of America, 1789–1873*, American Memory from the Library of Congress, http://memory.loc.gov/cgi-bin/query/r?ammem/hlaw:@field%28DOCID+@lit%28sj0404%29%29 (accessed July 12, 2010).

9 "The Excitement Yesterday", in: *The Daily Alta California*, Feb. 23, 1851, p. 2; "Incidents of Yesterday – Trial of Jas. Stuart", in: *The Daily Alta California*, Feb. 24, 1851, p. 2; "What Should our Citizens do?", in: *The Daily Alta California*, Feb. 23, 1851, p. 2; "Secret Organization", in: *The Daily Alta California*, June 11, 1851, p. 2.

10 Cf. Ernest de Massey and Marguerite Eyer Wilber, *A Frenchman in the Gold Rush; The Journal of Ernest de Massey, Argonaut of 1849*, San Francisco 1927, p. 36; J. M. E., "A Letter from the Mines", in: *The Daily Alta California*, Aug. 31, 1849, p. 1; Johnson, *Roaring Camp*, pp. 196–207.

was Murrieta and beheaded him.[11] Even in this example, for all his supposed fierceness, Murrieta was never reputed to have any broader connections outside of California. For the conspiracy-minded merchants, there was no world-encompassing conspiracy, there were only a series of loosely related social threats. In targeting foreigners, particularly non- and off-white and Roman Catholic foreigners, the middle-class Anglo-American merchants were acting in keeping with the received wisdom they had transported from the Atlantic world. In other words, ideas of racial, religious, and national distinctions – nicely summed up in the term "nativism" – still impacted how Anglo-Americans perceived the world in California, even if those understandings were manifested in a different, albeit as conspiratorial, manner as in the East.

Mark Fenster has correctly pointed out that "conspiracy theory *is* populist in its evocation of an unwitting and unwilling populace in thrall to the secretive machinations of power" and conspiracy theory in California was no exception.[12] The crux of the issue is, of course, who falls into the category of "the people" and, even more importantly, who gets to determine the boundaries of that category. Nor was the right to define who was and was not a member of "the people" uncontested in San Francisco. While many groups attempted to shape the political discourse to their ends, for our purposes, two groups were the most important: the white middle-class merchants and the Democratic Party. In San Francisco, both the conspiracy theories themselves and the reaction to those theories in the form of the Vigilance Committees were a way for middle-class, male merchants to deny political legitimacy to the Democratic party, which relied heavily on immigrant support.[13]

Over and over, accounts of criminal conspiracies emphasized the threat they posed to the respectable merchants of the city. Of particular concern were criminal conspiracies to "fire" the city.[14] These "secret bands of unmanly ruffians" were reputed to set fires "and under cover of the alarm and

---

11 Cf. Johnson, *Roaring Camp*, pp. 29–43.

12 Mark Fenster, *Conspiracy Theories: Secrecy and Power in American Culture*, Minneapolis 2008, p. 84.

13 African-Americans make up one of the most notable groups also seeking to influence the definition of "the people" to include themselves. For Democratic dependence on immigrant support, cf. Senkewicz, *Vigilantes*, pp. 123, 134–173.

14 Charles White, *St. Joseph Gazette*, July 28, 1848, Folder 1, Box 2168, California State Archives (CSA); "The Execution of Jenkins", in: *The Daily Alta California*, June 12, 1851, p. 2; "Mssrs. Editors", in: *The Daily Alta California*, June 10, 1851, p. 2; "Incendiarism in San Francisco", in: *The Daily Alta California*, Jan. 24, 1850, p. 2; "What Should our Citizens do?", p. 2; Senkewicz, *Vigilantes*, pp. 75–78.

confusion produced by which events, robberies could be carried on with impunity".[15] These conspiracies were concerning to commentators because they not only threatened the lives of respectable white men, they imperiled their economic well-being as well. The middle-class white men who formed a powerful community within California generally, but in trade-dominated San Francisco particularly, considered themselves the target of the conspiracy. To their minds, the merchant class was the backbone of respectable society in a particularly turbulent colonial setting and arsonist attacks threatened to rob respectable men of the financial independence that made them the leading citizens of California. That they would be the target of a conspiracy was not particularly surprising to them, after all, they represented the "good citizens" of San Francisco, and it was entirely in keeping with the logic of conspiracy and nineteenth-century ideals of morality and character that "bad men" preyed on "good citizens".[16] Indeed, that the conspiracy apparently targeted middle-class white men helped to prove their claim that they represented "the people" and that, therefore, political power should be in their hands.

Financial independence held a deep meaning for Anglo-American men in California, and throughout the United States, in the mid-nineteenth century. It was at the very core of what were believed to be the virtues necessary for a citizen to partake in a republican form of government. The republic, it was believed, functioned only because independent men exercised their political choice, free of the control of their employers, an aristocracy, or other despotic forces.[17] Americans likewise believed that a citizen was rational, cool,

---

15 Frank Soulei, *The Annals of San Francisco; Containing a Summary of the History of the First Discovery, Settlement, Progress, and Present Condition of California and a Complete History of All the Important Events Connected with its Great City to Which are Added Biographical Memoirs of Some Prominent Citizens*, New York 1855, p. 257; Alonzo W. Rathburn, *Diary 1849–1851*, May 9, 1851.

16 "[No Title]", in: *The Daily Alta California*, May 16, 1856, p. 2; "[No Title]", in: *The Daily Alta California*, May 20, 1856, p. 2; "The Law of the People is Supreme", in: *The Daily Alta California*, June 6, 1856, p. 2; "The Address of the Vigilance Committee", in: *The Daily Alta California*, June 9, 1856, p. 2; A Looker On, "Thoughts From a Looker-on, to Those in the Distance – No. 2", in: *The Daily Alta California*, July 22, 1856, p. 2.

17 Cf. Foner, *Free Soil*, pp. xi–xxvi; David Roediger, *The Wages of Whiteness: Race and the Making of the American Working Class*, New York 1991, pp. 50–51, 66–74; Philip J. Ethington, *The Public City: The Political Construction of Urban Life in San Francisco, 1850–1900*, Cambridge 1994, pp. 55–58; Sean Wilentz, *Chants Democratic: New York City & The Rise of the American Working Class, 1788–1850*, New York 1986, pp. 61–63, 92–94.

and fair; in other words, a citizen embodied the attributes of manliness. Women and children, both dependent on others and prone to irrationality, emotion, and selfishness, were incapable of fulfilling the role of citizens.[18] Race, class, and nationality also served to differentiate those who could be full citizens and those who lacked the necessary virtues. Elisha Capron bluntly highlighted the confluence of race, nationality, and gender in the hierarchy of California's colonial society when he argued that "all classes of Europeans are superior to them [the Chinese, South and Central American, and Mexican] in those qualities which are essential to the security of a republican form of government".[19] It was little surprise then, that middle-class white male merchants in California saw themselves as the embodiment of "the people" and the target of various criminal conspiracies.[20]

San Francisco was a particularly threatening place for respectable white men. In the mid-nineteenth century, most white Americans were from a rural background and evinced a profound discomfort with rapidly growing urban areas like New York and Boston.[21] This discomfort was only heightened in San Francisco. The "instant city" of San Francisco was an unprecedented experience, and more than one commentator remarked on the fast-paced life there.[22] Especially unsettling was the prominence of the

18 Cf., for example, Dana Nelson, *National Manhood: Capitalist Citizenship and the Imagined Fraternity of White Men*, Durham 1998; Anthony Rotundo, *American Manhood: Transformations in Masculinity from the Revolution to the Modern Era*, New York 1993; Nancy Isenberg, *Sex and Citizenship in Antebellum America*, Chapel Hill 1998. On the meaning of women in particular, cf. George Lakoff, *Women, Fire, and Dangerous Things: What Categories Reveal About the Mind*, Chicago 1987.

19 Elisha Smith Capron, *History Of California, From its Discovery to the Present Time: Comprising also a Full Description of its Climate, Surface, Soil, Rivers, Towns … Agriculture, Commerce, Mines, Mining, &C., With a Journal of the Voyage from New York, via Nicaragua, to San Francisco, and Back, via Panama …*, Boston 1854, p. 171.

20 Occasionally conspiracy theories arose, like that of "The Forty", that cast middle-class white men as the conspirators seeking to deprive, in this case, hard-working Hispanics of their wealth through whatever means necessary. The existence of this theory, and others like it, underscores that the populist basis of conspiracy is subjective, not objective. While these other conspiracy theories are important, they left little trace in the historical record and, ultimately, did not have the same impact as the theories of white middle-class merchants (cf. Ramón Gil Navarro/Maria del Carmen Ferreyra/David Sven Reher, *The Gold Rush Diary of Ramón Gil Navarro*, Lincoln 2000, pp. 29, 47–48.

21 For a discussion of this phenomenon on the East Coast of the United States, cf. John Kasson, *Rudeness & Civility: Manners in Nineteenth-Century Urban America*, New York 1990.

22 The term "instant city" is derived from Gunther Barth's classic study (cf. *Instant Cities: Urbanization and the Rise of San Francisco and Denver*, New York 1975).

gambling halls. By all accounts, these buildings were the most opulent buildings in San Francisco. Adorned with erotic pictures, luxurious decorations, and ablaze with light, these buildings literally and figuratively towered over much of San Francisco.[23] Respectable whites claimed that gamblers lured men inside where they manipulated them by over-exciting their senses, serving them alcohol, and playing on their sense of manliness by challenging them to prove themselves at the gambling table until they had lost all their money. Gambling halls, and to a lesser extent, drinking saloons, represented places where white men could lose the self-control that defined them as respectable and the wealth that would make them independent.[24] A loss of self-control could also make men vulnerable, and stories of men being mugged or murdered while drunk underscored the perception that criminal elements, possibly with the cooperation of gamblers or saloon-owners, were constantly watching, waiting for respectable white men to relax their vigilance and make themselves vulnerable.[25]

San Francisco, like all of California, was also far more racially diverse than what most Anglo-Americans were accustomed to. In addition to the large numbers of Europeans (in particular French and Germans), there were also sizable populations of Chileans, Peruvians, Mexicans, Kanakas (Hawaiians), and Chinese, among others. This diversity, combined with assumptions as to the proclivity of non-whites to criminal activity, made these groups particularly threatening to many white male commentators. California, it seemed to at least one commentator, "favored the freedom of criminals from arrest, [and] helped to extend their acquaintance among kindred rogues".[26]

---

23 Cf. E. Phelps to J.C. Ray, Nov. 23, 1850, Gold Rush Letters, mss C-B 547:136, Bancroft Library, Berkeley, CA.; James J. Ayers, *Gold and Sunshine, Reminiscences of Early California*, Boston 1922, pp. 37, 93; Capron, *History of California*, pp. 148–150; D. B. Bates, *Incidents on Land and Water*, New York 1974, pp. 202–203; John David Borthwick and Horace Kephart, *The Gold Hunters: A First-Hand Picture of Life in California Mining Camps in the Early Fifties*, Cleveland 1917, p. 64; George Payson, *Golden Dreams and Leaden Realities*, New York 1853, pp. 75–77.

24 Indeed, Charles Thompson describes himself as going "half-mad" while gambling. Thompson to Uncle, Sept. 10, 1850, Gold Rush Letters; John Findlay, *People of Chance: Gambling in American Society From Jamestown to Las Vegas*, New York 1986, p. 94; John M. Letts, *A Pictorial View of California: Including a Description of the Panama and Nicaragua Routes, with Information and Advice Interesting to all, Particularly Those Who Intend to Visit the Golden Region / By A Returned Californian*, New York 1853, pp. 48–50.

25 Cf. Frank Marryat, *Mountains and Molehills; or, Recollections of a Burnt Journal*, Philadelphia 1962, p. 17; "Bad Characters", in: *The Daily Alta California*, May 19, 1852, p. 2; "Immigration of Convicts", in: *The Daily Alta California*, Nov. 20, 1850, p. 2.

26 Souleì, *The Annals of San Francisco*, p. 564.

The diversity of San Francisco's population seemed to challenge the assumption that white middle-class men should be at the apex of colonial society. Though middle-class white men had no doubt that they *should* be in charge, they were concerned about their ability to maintain order. In other words, the social and racial diversity of San Francisco, combined with the tumultuous nature of gold rush society and the general weakness of the colonial state, meant that conspiracies of criminality seemed all the more plausible and threatening.

Although subsequent research has shown that San Francisco actually experienced the same amount of crime as other major American cities of its size, in the early years of the gold rush middle-class commentators began to complain with greater and greater frequency of a rising crime wave in the city.[27] Increasingly, middle-class white men criticized what they saw as the inability of the colonial government to protect their interests and deal with the crime wave. To these commentators, the weakness of the colonial state allowed the criminal conspiracy to grow to unprecedented proportions. As Frank Soulé summarized in his early and influential history of San Francisco:

> Thus there was gradually formed a secret combination among the chief thieves, burglars and murderers of the country, minute ramifications of which extended down to the pettiest pilferers. To occasionally cut off a single member of this class would do little good, so long as the grand gang was at large and in full operation.[28]

To destroy this conspiracy would require "nothing less than the complete extirpation of the whole body of miscreants, with their numerous supporters and sympathizers, aids and abettors". In other words, for "society" to be free from the "fearful incubus that [...] oppressed it," it would be necessary for "the people" to vest the authority of the colonial state directly in themselves through the formation of vigilance committees.[29]

The path to vigilance committees was not as straight-forward as later accounts would have it, of course. Initially, the white middle-class merchants who were to form the core of both the 1851 and 1856 Vigilance Committees were actually quite reluctant to take over the reins of the state, as evidenced by their reaction to the "Hounds" crisis of 1849. The "Hounds" were ostensibly a mutual benevolent society formed to give aid and protection to its members, most of whom were American veterans of the recent Mexican-

---

27 Cf. Senkewicz, *Vigilantes*, pp. 75–79.
28 Souleì, *The Annals of San Francisco*, p. 564.
29 Souleì, *The Annals of San Francisco*, p. 564.

American war.[30] By June 1849, however, the Hounds had begun to attack foreigners, particularly Chileans, claiming they were defending American citizens from "acts of violence committed by Chilenos and foreigners".[31] At first, both the authorities and merchants paid scant attention to the Hounds, seeing them as mostly harmless lower-class rowdies. However, on July 15, 1849 these perceptions radically changed in the aftermath of a brutal attack on the Chilean district of San Francisco that left four Chileans dead and thirteen wounded.[32]

The Hounds were caught off-guard by the response of the government and middle-class white merchants. The next day, a mass public meeting led to over two hundred "special deputies" being appointed to arrest the Hounds under the authority of the mayor, leading to the destruction of the gang.[33] The Hounds had not realized how much their behavior and dress marked them as "brawlers, gamblers, and drunkards", in other words, as not-quite-whites.[34] As off-whites, they could not act on behalf of the people (implicitly raced as white), and their attacks on the Chileans were therefore construed as a threat to the stability of the colonial society of respectable white men. The experience with the Hounds was important for how it informed the subsequent reactions of middle-class white merchants to perceived criminal conspiracies. Within months, the role of the mayor and other elected officials in organizing the response to the Hounds was forgotten, and instead the incident came to demonstrate that "the people" could act decisively to crush a group of organized criminals.

---

30 Cf. Joshua Paddison, *A World Transformed: Firsthand Accounts of California Before the Gold Rush*, Berkeley 1998, p. 311; "The Chilenos and other Foreigners in the City of San Francisco attacked by an Armed Party of Americans – Great Excitement – Meeting of the Citizens – Formation of a citizen armed Police – Arrest of the rioters – Their Trial and Sentence", in: *The Daily Alta California*, Aug. 2, 1849; Bancroft, *History of California*, pp. 211–212.

31 "The Chilenos and other Foreigners"; "More News from California – Illegal Assembly – Governor's Proclamation – Politics and the Gold Digging – Prospects for Emigrants – Goods for a Song, &c., &c", in: *New York Herald*, Sept. 17, 1849.

32 Cf. "More News from California"; "The Chilenos and other Foreigners".

33 "The Chilenos and other Foreigners".

34 William Ryan Redmond, *Personal Adventures in Upper and Lower California, in 1848–9*, New York 1973, pp. 257–258. Paul Spickard usefully notes that whiteness and Americanness are not absolute conditions, but instead are judged on the degree to which an individual or group conforms to the behavior of Americans of English descent. He labels this "Anglo-normativity" (*Almost All Aliens: Immigration, Race, and Colonialism in American History and Identity*, New York 2007, pp. 5–6). In California, criminal or anti-social behavior could make individuals or groups, even of Anglo-American descent, not-quite-white.

By early 1851 there was a growing perception that elected authorities had again lost control and this time attention focused on slung-shot wielding Australians. The Great Fire of May 4 proved to be catalyst for the formation of the first Vigilance Committee in San Francisco. Very quickly it became widely understood that the fire was the work of organized criminal "incendiaries" who were assumed to be Australians.[35] A group of middle-class Anglo-American merchants, fearful of interference by the state or criminals, organized itself secretly into the first Vigilance Committee, even going so far as to assign members numbers that were used in place of their names.[36] Unable to catch any arsonists, the Committee instead caught, tried, and executed a minor thief, John Jenkins, hanging him from a beam in the main Plaza.[37]

The trial and execution of Jenkins was a pivotal moment in establishing the legitimacy of the Committee of Vigilance and lynch law in San Francisco. This was despite the numerous unusual aspects of their action. The secret trial, lack of counsel, sentence of death, and manner in which Jenkins was executed all proved to be points where the Committee's legitimacy was both asserted and challenged.[38] The Committee acted quickly to explain the need for secrecy (it was to avoid "confusion, disorder, and irresolution")[39] and to publish the charter of the organization and a list of its members so as to "remove all the objections against secret organization and star-chamber proceedings".[40] The Committee asserted that the arrival of "large numbers of the most daring, depraved and reckless men" "from every part of the habitable globe, but more particularly from the British penal colonies", had left the city at "the mercy of organized gangs of the worst felons".[41] The courts and police had failed, "through want of energy or collusion", to protect the "good citizens" of San Francisco.[42] In response, the "good citizens", "men

---

35 Letts, *A Pictorial View of California*, p. 54; Senkewicz, *Vigilantes*, p. 81.

36 Cf. "The Vigilance Committee", in: *The Daily Alta California*, June 13, 1851, p. 2; "City Intelligence – The Coroner's Inquest Continued", in: *The Daily Alta California*, June 13, 1851, p. 2.

37 Cf. "Arrest of a Robber! Trial and Sentence by the Citizen Police. Execution on the Plaza!", in: *The Daily Alta California,* June 11, 1851, p. 2; "City Intelligence – Coroner's Inquest", in: *The Daily Alta California*, June 12, 1851, p. 2.

38 Cf. "The Execution of Jenkins", in: *The Daily Alta California*, June 12, 1851, p. 2; "City Intelligence – Coroner's Inquest"; "The Vigilance Committee".

39 "Law and Order", in: *The Daily Alta California*, June 14, 1851, p. 2.

40 "The Vigilance Committee".

41 "Law and Order"; "Organization of the Vigilance Committee", in: *The Daily Alta California*, June 12, 1851, p. 2; "The Execution of Jenkins".

42 "Law and Order".

of standing, character and influence",[43] "industrious, orderly and patriotic men",[44] that is, men who embodied republican virtues, were "compelled" to organize into a body to restore order to society.[45] In so doing, the Committee began a campaign to shape public perception of themselves as an organization in keeping with the forms of republican law in the country. The Committee was not, they claimed, a shadowy conspiracy of criminals, but an association of determined citizens compelled by necessity to temporarily assume the trappings of a conspiracy in order to counteract the considerable forces arrayed against them.[46] The Committee argued that the difference between their organization and the conspiracy against which they mobilized was that the need for secrecy had been a temporary expedient whose necessity had now passed, allowing the Committee and its members to emerge clearly as the embodiment of republican virtue.

It would be five years until the next Vigilance Committee would assemble, and in 1856, as in 1851, local merchant elites used the pretext of a supposed crime wave to justify their actions. Again, too, the Vigilance Committee drew heavily on the language and popular understandings of republicanism to legitimize its actions. This time however, the duration and extent of the Vigilantes' actions would far exceed the 1851 precedent. It began in late November, 1855, when the *Alta* newspaper and other supporters of lynch law began agitating about what they perceived as the sure-to-be biased trial of Charles Cora, a gambler reputed to have "friends, rich, powerful, influential, talented, fertile in expedients, active and determined to rob justice of its own".[47] Anger about Cora's trial and subsequent hung-jury failed to mobilize the population, however, and it was the death of James King of William, an anti-Democratic newspaper editor, at the hands of a rival newspaperman, James Casey, on May 14, 1856 that proved the flashpoint. King had been an active supporter of the 1851 Vigilance Committee, and his newspaper, the *San Francisco Daily Evening Bulletin* had been a leading voice in the anti-gambling hysteria of 1855 and 1856, focusing in particular upon the case of Charles

---

43 "Secret Organization".

44 "Law and Order".

45 "The Execution of Jenkins"; "Law and Order".

46 The Committee's disavowal of their own conspiratorial nature echoes Richard Hofstadter's claim that the countersubversives "emulate" the very conspiracies they seek to destroy ("The Paranoid Style in American Politics", in: *Harper's Magazine*, 11/1964, pp. 77–86, p. 83).

47 "The First Legal Execution", in: *The Daily Alta California*, Nov. 21, 1855, p. 2; "Progress of Civilization", in: *The Daily Alta California*, Jan. 28, 1856, p. 2.

Cora.[48] It took little incentive for many in the population to seize upon this coincidence as proof of a conspiracy between gamblers, arsonists, and corrupt politicians and officials.[49]

The second Vigilance Committee grew quickly out of the skeleton of the first.[50] By May 18, the Vigilance Committee claimed almost three-thousand men under arms, many of whom defected from militia units stationed in the city.[51] With the death of James King on May 20, the Vigilance Committee moved quickly to try both James Casey and Charles Cora. Both men were tried privately, found guilty, and hung by the Committee on May 22 from the windows of the Committee's headquarters.[52] From then until it disbanded on August 18, the Vigilance Committee executed two more men, caused the suicide of another, and banished, deported, or drove into hiding at least twenty-seven more.[53] However, although the committee had originally formed as a response to a supposed conspiracy linking gamblers, criminals, and corrupt politicians, it was the latter who became the primary targets of the committee. In particular, the 1856 Vigilance Committee systematically purged the Democratic Party in California.[54]

It turned out to be fairly easy to convince much of San Francisco that this shift was logical and justified. By 1856, many Anglo-Americans in San Francisco believed that the local authorities were at best hamstrung by the technicalities of the law or, at worst, were complicit in shielding criminals from justice. Corrupt officials, though hardly rare in the nineteenth century (indeed, more notable in their absence), were anathema to republican philosophy. As previously noted, at the core of American republicanism was the ideal of the independent man, free from encumbrances, exercising his political voice. Ballot-box stuffing and other forms of electoral fraud were therefore more

---

48 Cf. Findlay, *People of Chance*, p. 96; Frank F. Fargo, "A True and Minute History of the Assassination of James King of Wm. at San Francisco, Cal…", CSA, p. 2.

49 Cf. Frank F. Fargo, "A True and Minute History", CSA, pp. 2–3,.

50 Cf. "Incidents of Wednesday's Occurrence", in: *The Daily Alta California*, May 16, 1856, p. 2; Senkewicz, *Vigilantes*, pp. 134, 170.

51 Cf. "Events of Yesterday – Rescue of the Prisoners, Casey and Cora, Without Resistance", in: *The Daily Alta California*, May 19, 1856, p. 2; "Incidents of Wednesday's Occurrence".

52 Cf. "Events of Yesterday – Death of Mr. King – A Wonderful Sensation in the Community – The Whole City Draped in Mourning", in: *The Daily Alta California*, May 21, 1856, p. 2; "Events of Yesterday – Funeral of Mr. James King of Wm. – Execution of Casey and Cora by the Vigilance Committee!! – The Day", in: *The Daily Alta California*, May 23, 1856, p. 2.

53 Cf. "Events of Yesterday", in: *The Daily Alta California*, June 21, 1856, p. 2.

54 Cf. Senkewicz, *Vigilantes*, pp. 186–187.

than a danger to the legitimacy of the civil government; these actions threatened the racialized and gendered privileges upon which white men constructed their superiority. Without free elections, white men were no better than the women and non-whites to whom they denied a place in government. Even more striking, the loss of the vote through fraud reduced white men rhetorically to the slaves of corrupt politicians and their criminal allies.[55]

The Vigilance Committee presented an alternative for Anglo-American men who feared that they were losing the ability to be white men through the exercise of their franchise. In place of "slavery" at the hands of corrupt politicians and criminals, the Vigilance Committee offered "good citizens" the means by which "the people" could vest sovereignty directly in themselves, purify the political system, and impose a new order on San Francisco. This order would be one that was predicated on the rule of "good citizens", which, practically speaking, meant the political allies of the Vigilance Committee, but which rhetorically linked the racial and gender requirements of citizenship, the attributes of republicanism, and the moral code of Victorianism.

As with other conspiracy theories, members of the opposition tended to be dismissed as members of the conspiracy. According to the vigilantes, the opposition Law and Order party was made up of as "reckless men" who had "mercenary and corrupt motives", and sought to shape society for their own "private interests", rather than for the public good.[56] Interestingly, not all opposition was part of the conspiracy, as class lines and standards of respectable behavior made it necessary that the Committee acknowledge that some men of standing "*honestly* differed" in their opinions. However, these men, while not a part of the conspiracy, were unable to bring themselves to recognize the extraordinary measures necessary to deal with the threat to Californian society.[57] In other words, class and reputation acted to shield certain individuals from the becoming targets of the Vigilance Committee, instead earning them the only slightly better standing of being unwitting dupes. The reaction of the Federal government – who saw the Vigilance Committee as

---

55 For examples of the importance of the rhetoric of slavery for Anglo-Americans, cf. Roediger, *The Wages of Whiteness*, pp. 36, 55–60, 66; Edmund S. Morgan, "Slavery and Freedom: The American Paradox", in: *The Journal of American History*, 59/1972, pp. 5–29.

56 "To the People of California", in: *The Daily Alta California*, June 9, 1856 p. 2.

57 Cf. "The Executive Committee of the General Committee of Vigilance", in: *The Daily Alta California*, August 27, 1856, p. 2; "Adopted Citizens and the Vigilance Committee", in: *The Daily Alta California,* June 29, 1856, p. 2.

potentially revolutionary – and popular opinion in the Eastern states were also dismissed as being the result of misleading reports and an insufficient grasp of the situation.[58] At the same time, however, vigilantes remained concerned that the conspiracy theories that engulfed San Francisco were deemed blatantly preposterous by most outside observers and continually sought to sway public opinion in the East and in the Federal government to their side.[59]

Conspiracy theories are cultural productions and, as such, are subject to the same forces that affect the transmission and reproduction of other forms of cultural production. And while conspiracy theories have attracted little attention from scholars of the American West, the question of cultural transference in the American West has received numerous treatments. Recently, a consensus has begun to emerge among scholars that stresses that while Anglo-Americans looked eastward for models of society, the impact of local conditions and the distance from eastern sources of cultural production, meant that cultural productions in California, while clearly derived from eastern examples, differed in sometimes startling ways.[60] To put it another way, like other cultural productions, conspiracy theories were not carried across the continent intact. Instead, they were reshaped to fit local circumstances and conditions.

The subjects of the conspiracy theories themselves reflect the impact of the local: gamblers, immigrant criminals, and corrupt politicians. Even more significantly, these conspiracy theories did not significantly overlap with the major conspiracy theories of the time: namely popish plots, the slave power, and Masonry. Despite the preponderance of Roman Catholic immigrants and residents, religion was not a major issue in the California conspiracy theories, a situation that reflected the lack of concern with theological issues and a greater concern with simply getting the population to attend church,

---

58 Cf. "The Effect in the East", in: *The Daily Alta California*, June 20, 1856, p. 2; F. W. H., "News from California – The Revolution in San Francisco", in: *The New York Times*, June 30, 1856, p. 1; "Revolution in San Francisco", in: *The New York Times*, June 14, 1856, p. 4.

59 Cf. "The Effect in the East"; F. W. H., "News from California"; "Revolution in San Francisco"; Joseph Benton, "Sermon [Vigilance and Reform]", May 18, 1856, in: Joseph Augustine Benton Collection, Box 28, CSA; Christopher Waldrep, *The Many Faces of Judge Lynch: Extralegal Violence and Punishment in America*, New York 2002, pp. 51–58.

60 Cf., for example, Brian Roberts, *American Alchemy: The California Gold Rush and Middle-Class Culture*, Chapel Hill 2000; Elliot West, *Growing up with the Country: Childhood on the Far-Western Frontier*, Albuquerque 1989; John Mack Faragher, *Men and Women on the Overland Trail*, New Haven 1979; Barth, *Instant Cities*; Findlay, *People of Chance*.

any church. The institution of slavery was also a curious non-issue. California was a free state on paper, and yet African slavery was openly practiced in the southern mines and Indian slavery widely practiced throughout the state.[61] Masonic lodges were also fairly common in California, particularly as the 1850s wore on, and they too, caused little controversy.

Instead, conspiracy theories in California reflected what middle-class white merchants "knew" about their state. They knew that California's "anomalous condition", the weak state, a large and diverse international immigration, a resident native and Hispanic population, and supposedly young and transient Anglo-American population, fast-paced society, and less regulation of vice all set California apart from the rest of the republic.[62] The Californian conspiracy theories were a manifestation of intense concern about the stability of the colonial project in that state. They suggested a worst-case scenario: that criminally-inclined immigrants, degraded whites, and corrupt officials were allying together, effectively reversing the proper order of colonial society. In other words, the conspiracy theories were a nightmare tailor-made for white, middle-class, male merchants, all too aware of the very real precarious position in which they found themselves. Of course, to many outside observers it was the formation of the Vigilance Committees, with their apparent subversion of the state, that posed the greatest risk to the republic. While the vigilantes claimed to be acting in the best interests of the republic, viewed from the Eastern seaboard they seemed dangerously revolutionary and arbitrary.

Despite many notable differences, at their cores the conspiracy theories in California shared many structural similarities with other contemporary American conspiracy theories. During the period discussed, the East Coast of the United States saw the rise, crest, and collapse of one major conspiracy theory manifested in the nativist Know-Nothing Party, and the rise to dominance of two related conspiracy theories relating to the relationship between slave and free societies.[63] These were the Slave Power and Abolitionist con-

---

61 Cf. Albert Hurtado, *Indian Survival on the California Frontier*, New Haven 1988; Johnson, *Roaring Camp*, pp. 68–71; Rudolph M. Lapp, *Blacks in Gold Rush California*, New Haven 1977, pp. 65–78.

62 "Executive Committee of the General Committee of Vigilance"; Eliza Farnham, *California, In-doors and Out: or, How we Farm, Mine, and Live Generally in the Golden State*, New York 1856, p. 28; Howard C. Gardiner, *In Pursuit of the Golden Dream: Reminiscences of San Francisco and the Northern and Southern Mines, 1849–1857*, Stoughton, MA 1970, p. 81.

63 For a detailed discussion of the Know-Nothing Party's fears of immigrants, and particularly of Roman Catholic immigrants believed to be under the thrall of the Vatican, cf. Tyler Anbinder, *Nativism and Slavery: The Northern Know Nothings and the Politics of the 1850's*, New York 1992, pp. 103–126.

spiracy theories.[64] Given the political impact of these two bodies of theories, it is relatively easy to track their popularity and pervasiveness. The various conspiracy theories that focused on foreigners, especially Roman Catholics, found a welcoming home in the Know-Nothing party. The ideology of the Know-Nothing party was based in part on a belief that insidious foreign powers easily controlled child-like or conniving immigrants and therefore threatened the political, economic, and social basis of the republic. The success of the Know-Nothing party between 1854 and 1856, particularly in the northern states, is convincing evidence that during this period a conspiratorial view of immigration had considerable traction among Protestant Americans.[65]

Yet, even in 1856, the influence of the Know-Nothing party and of conspiracy views which focused on dangerous immigrants and foreign influence had begun to wane. As slavery became the primary political issue in both the North and the South, the inability and unwillingness of the Know-Nothing party to take a firm stance on the issue of slavery cost it all but its most loyal adherents. In the North, the Republican Party absorbed former Know-Nothing voters.[66] In turn, the Republican Party offered a different conspiracy theory to explain the nation's ills: the machinations of the Slave Power. To an increasingly large segment of the free states, the Slave Power sought to extend slavery, perpetuating the rule of an elite class of slaveholding oligarchs, at the cost of the freedom of northern whites who, forced to compete with slavery, would be reduced to little better than slaves themselves.[67] The rise of the Slave Power conspiracy theory was paralleled by a similar development in the slave states where an increasing segment of the white

---

64 As Robert Goldbert has argued, the North and the South increasingly came to know each other through these conspiracy theories in the 1850s and 1860s (cf. "Conspiracy Theories in America: A Historical Overview", in: Peter Knight [ed.], *Conspiracy Theories in American History: An Encyclopedia*, Santa Barbara 2003, pp. 4–5; David Brion Davis, *The Slave Power Conspiracy and the Paranoid Style*, Baton Rouge 1970; Leonard L. Richards, *The Slave Power: The Free North and Southern Domination, 1780–1860*, Baton Rouge 2000).

65 The standard study of the Know-Nothing party is Anbinder, *Nativism and Slavery*. Cf. also David Bennett, *The Party of Fear: From Nativist Movements to the New Right in American History*, Chapel Hill 1988, pp. 84–86; Billington, *The Protestant Crusade*, pp. 118–120, 193.

66 Cf. Foner, *Free Soil*, pp. 238–259; Anbinder, *Nativism and Slavery*, pp. 263–265.

67 The seminal work on the Slave Power conspiracy is Davis, *The Slave Power Conspiracy*. Another excellent resource is Foner, *Free Soil*. Foner's work gives the most elaborate understanding of the Free Soil ideology of which the Slave Power conspiracy was a part.

population began to see an Abolitionist "Black Republican" conspiracy to destroy slavery at all costs, forcing political and social equality with blacks upon the South.[68] The developments of the 1850s, and certainly after 1856, prove David Brion Davis's assertion that "conspiratorial imagery had become a formalized staple in the political rhetoric of both North and South" to be indisputable.[69]

The conspiracy theories of California, though differing in specific content, shared basic structural similarities with the conspiracy theories so prevalent on the East Coast, and particularly with the conspiracy theories in the northern states. Specifically, each of these theories was based in a worldview informed by republican ideology that held that the republic was a fragile creation, and only men who possessed a rational intellect, moral character, and the independence to exercise their free will in the political sphere should partake in civil society. This construction of citizenry was explicitly raced and gendered, so that most white Americans saw white men as the sole embodiment of the republican virtues necessary to preserve American liberty.[70] In other words, the republican government had to be secured by and for respectable white men. This understanding of society had several repercussions for conspiracy theories in California and the United States. First, the conspiracy theorists identified as good citizens and therefore tended to ascribe to themselves the traits supposedly embodied by white men. Second, in keeping with the logic of republican citizens having to be ever on-guard against the influence of "bad" men, they tended to ascribe the traits of non-citizens to those they believed behind the conspiracy. This is particularly evident in each conspiracy theory's concern with domination by a ruthless, cruel, and autocratic Other.[71] Third, each group of conspiracy theorists tended to see the crucial battleground as being over control of the state. Even the criminal conspiracies of California that did not explicitly seek to capture the state posed a challenge to its functioning and raised the possibility of an alternative social order, one in which various groups of bad men ruled over good citizens. Ultimately, a close examination of the conspiracy

---

68 Cf. Davis, *The Slave Power Conspiracy*, pp. 32–61.; Goldberg, "Conspiracy Theories in America", pp. 4–5.

69 Davis, *The Slave Power Conspiracy*, p. 7.

70 The writing linking concepts of American citizenship to whiteness has blossomed in recent years. A good introduction is Spickard, *Almost All Aliens.*

71 For examples of republican thought in the rhetoric of the Slave Power and Abolitionist conspiracy theories, cf. Davis, *The Slave Power Conspiracy*, pp. 14–21, 34–43, 47, 49–50. For similar examples of republican thought in the rhetoric of the Know-Nothing party, cf. Anbinder, *Nativism and Slavery*, pp. 104–108.

theories and anti-conspiracy movements of California, and particularly of San Francisco, reveals that while the basic structural logic of conspiracy theorizing remained relatively stable, the process of cultural transmission across the continent combined with a variety of local factors was crucial in determining the articulation, dissemination, and response to conspiracy theories in California.

Türkay Salim Nefes (Oxford)

The Function of Secrecy in Anti-Semitic Conspiracy Theories: The Case of Dönmes in Turkey

1. Introduction

Conspiracy theories are narratives that propose a hidden, deliberate, omnipotent agency of groups or individuals in society. They claim to explain social events and transformations as results of secret acts of cliques and individuals. In this regard, conspiracy theories are political narratives *par excellence* that provide accounts of how power relations operate in society. Unsurprisingly, they have been politically significant throughout history. For instance, the backbone of anti-Semitic ideologies relies on a conspiratorial view of the Jewish community. However, the academic literature has not given much attention to the socio-political impacts of conspiracy theories. There are not many comprehensive and empirical studies on the role and communication of conspiracy accounts. This paper aims to fill this gap by exploring the role of secrecy in the anti-Semitic conspiracy theories on Jewish converts, called Dönmes, in Turkey.

Secrecy is an indispensable aspect of the conspiratorial rhetoric. Historically significant conspiracy theories have most often been about secret societies such as the Illuminati. However, the function of secrecy in conspiracy theories has not been examined yet. This paper, then, investigates the role of the secret character of the Dönme community in the production and communication of conspiracy theories about the group. It draws on a historical analysis of the Dönme society and the conspiracy theories about them. Moreover, it evaluates interviews that have been conducted with representatives of different political parties from the Turkish parliament to assess their perception of the conspiracy theories and the Dönmes. The paper first discusses the relevant literature on conspiracy theories and secrecy before introducing the historical record of the Dönme community and the conspiracy theories about them. The next part evaluates the interviews with the political parties. Last, the paper outlines the findings and conclusions of the discussion.

2. Understanding Conspiracy Theories and the Social Significance of Secrecy

There are two main perspectives in the academic literature on conspiracy theories: the classical and the cultural approaches. The classical standpoint emphasises the political uses of conspiracy theories by extremist groups that propagate ideologies of prejudice and paranoia.[1] It views conspiracy theories as phoney accounts and political pathology. For example, Daniel Pipes describes conspiracy theories as ideological pathologies that could shape people's thinking: "conspiracy theories have a way of growing on a person, to the point that they become a way of seeing life itself".[2] The cultural approach takes a critical view on the classical understanding of conspiracy theories as political pathologies.[3] It attempts to understand conspiracy theories as social and political symptoms. Peter Knight thus claims that conspiracy theories are a symptom of people's quest to understand the socio-political reality, that is, "a do-it-yourself sociology in an age that finds any discussion of social causation deeply suspicious".[4]

On the one hand, while emphasising the political aspects of conspiracy thinking, the classical view denies the socio-political reasons and significance of conspiracy theories by labelling them as political pathologies. The approach

---

[1] Some of the works in the classical view are: David Aaronovitch, *Voodoo Histories: The Role of the Conspiracy Theory in Shaping Modern History*, London 2009; Hadassa Ben-Itto, *The Lie That Wouldn't Die: The Protocols of Elders of Zion*, London 2005; Stephen Bronner, *A Rumor About the Jews: Anti-Semitism, Conspiracy, and the Protocols of Zion*, New York 2003; Norman Cohn, *Warrant for Genocide: The Myth of the Jewish World Conspiracy and the Protocols of Elders of Zion*, Harmondsworth 1970; Richard Hofstadter, *The Paranoid Style in American Politics and Other Essays*, New York 1965; Karl Popper, *The Open Society and Its Enemies*, Princeton, NJ 1966; Robert Robins/ Jerrold Post, *Political Paranoia: The Psycho-Politics of Hatred*, New Haven 1997; Elaine Showalter, *Hystories: Hysterical Epidemics and Modern Culture*, London 1997.

[2] Daniel Pipes, *Conspiracy: How the Paranoid Style Flourishes and Where It Comes From*, New York 1997, p. 22.

[3] Some of the contributions from the cultural perspective are: Clare Birchall, *Knowledge Goes Pop: From Conspiracy Theory to Gossip*, Oxford 2006; Jack Bratich, *Conspiracy Panics: Political Rationality and Popular Culture*, Albany 2008; Mark Fenster, *Conspiracy Theories: Secrecy and Power in American Culture*, Minneapolis 1999; Matthew Gray, *Conspiracy Theories in the Arab World: Sources and Politics*, London 2010; Simon Locke, "Conspiracy Culture, Blame Culture, and Rationalisation", in: *The Sociological Review*, 57/2009, 4, pp. 567–585; Timothy Melley, *Empire of Conspiracy: The Culture of Paranoia in Postwar America*, London 2000; Timothy Melley, "Brainwashed! Conspiracy Theory and Ideology in the Postwar United States", in: *New German Critique*, 35/2008, 1, pp. 145–164.

[4] Peter Knight, *Conspiracy Culture: From Kennedy to* The X-Files, London 2000, p. 155.

does not provide a comprehensive analysis of why certain conspiracy theories prevail in specific contexts. For example, in the case of the conspiracy theories on the Dönmes, the approach would view the conspiracy literature as paranoid claims of the alienated right-wing extremist groups in Turkey. Certainly, this would not explain why they pick on the Dönmes and why the theories become popular in different periods. On the other hand, even though the cultural approach focuses on the social and cultural backgrounds that facilitate conspiracy theories, it does not pay much attention to their historical significance and political impacts. In the Dönme case, the cultural perspective would be most likely to look at the social and cultural changes in the 1990s in Turkey and how they might have led people to believe in or create the conspiracy literature. This would not only ignore the historical build-up of the conspiracy literature since the early twentieth century, but it would also avoid explaining how political movements use the conspiracy literature. Last, both perspectives lack empirical studies to understand the socio-political significance of conspiracy theories.

This study addresses these problems while analysing the significance of secrecy in the creation and the belief in the conspiracy literature on the Dönmes. It outlines the historical evolution of the conspiracy accounts and discusses questions such as what kind of events preceded the creation of the conspiracy accounts, what role secrecy played in the production and propagation of conspiracy theories, and which political groups used and believed those accounts. Moreover, through interviews, the research looks empirically at how contemporary political parties approach the issue of secrecy in the conspiracy theories. It considers secrecy not only as a natural, objective element of the Dönme identity but also as a perception or social construction of the general public. Indeed, the conspiracy theories about the community are a way of perceiving or conceptualising the Dönme secrecy. Needless to say, the study does not pathologise conspiracy thinking like the classical perspective but investigates its place among political groups.

The paper particularly focuses on the secrecy of the Dönme community. As will be discussed below, the Dönmes constitute a secret society whose members pretend to be Muslims in daily life while keeping their Judaic beliefs – they hide their real identity from the public. One of the few works that examine the social significance of secrecy is Georg Simmel's seminal piece called "The Sociology of Secrecy and Secret Societies", where he argues that secret societies are social units that are characterised by the secret they keep.[5]

---

[5] Cf. Georg Simmel, "The Sociology of Secrecy and Secret Societies", in: *American Journal of Sociology*, 11/1906, 4, pp. 441–498.

He adds that secret societies constitute an alternative community, because they form an exclusive group segregated from the rest of the society.[6] Moreover, secret societies provide an area of freedom for their members by creating a space veiled from the public gaze. Simmel suggests that secret societies demand full confidentiality and devotion in return, because they cannot exist without protecting their secrecy.[7] According to Simmel, secret societies create suspicion among the public because of their concealment: "the secret society, purely on the ground of its secrecy, appears dangerously related to conspiracy against existing powers".[8] This seems to be an important reason for the creation of conspiracy theories about secret societies. A secret society ignites conspiracy views by being a perfect example of what Pipes called "the hidden hand mentality", a group that conceals its identity for its sinister ends.

In parallel, Zygmunt Bauman suggests that one of the reasons of anti-Semitism was that Jews represented a stranger figure in a sociological sense: Jews were uncanny and in-between figures, who were neither insiders nor outsiders of the societies they habituated.[9] From this point of view, anti-Semitism is an ideology that opposes and problematises this ambivalent stranger character of the Jewish community. Bauman's theory is in line with Simmel's view, as secret societies represent a stranger figure because they are neither fully insiders nor outsiders. For example, the Dönme community has an ambivalent stranger identity because it is a secret group that is neither inside nor outside the Turkish society. Therefore, this paper suggests that the identity of the Dönmes as a secret society plays a significant role in the production and dissemination of the conspiracy theories about the community.

3. Dönmes, Secrecy, and Conspiracy Theories

History of the Dönme Community and Its Secrecy

Dönme in Turkish means convert, and the name of the community comes from their conversion from Judaism to Islam in the seventeenth century. The Dönme community consists of the followers of an acclaimed Jewish messiah, Sabbatai Sevi (1626–1676), who was educated to become a rabbi and

---

6 Cf. Simmel, "Sociology of Secrecy", p. 470.
7 Cf. Simmel, "Sociology of Secrecy", p. 474.
8 Simmel, "Sociology of Secrecy", p. 498.
9 Zygmunt Bauman, *Modernity and Ambivalence*, Cambridge 1991, p. 53.

studied the Talmud and Halakha (Jewish law).[10] Isaac Luria's (1534–1572) mystical interpretation of Judaism and teachings of Kabbalah influenced Sevi. In 1665, his follower Nathan of Gaza declared that Sevi was the messiah of the Jews, and that he was the prophet of Sevi.[11] Sevi's message quickly gained acceptance. Millenarian Christian movements thus spread Sevi's message because they believed that this would produce the conditions necessary for the second coming of Jesus.[12] Sevi became an important religious figure in the seventeenth century, whose message was spread throughout the European, African, Asian, and Northern American continents.

The growing impact of Sabbatai Sevi concerned the Orthodox Jewish community, and they requested the Ottoman Emperor to take action. The Ottoman authorities forced Sevi to convert to Islam.[13] After his conversion, his name was changed to Aziz Mehmed Efendi, and he was employed by the Emperor. According to Cengiz Şişman, this demonstrates that the Ottoman ruler was sympathetic to Sevi.[14] However, doubts about the genuineness of his conversion to Islam led the authorities to take him to court. Eventually, he was sent to a small town called Ülgün in today's Albania, where he stayed until the end of his life.[15]

Most of Sevi's believers were disappointed with the conversion, and they ceased following him. Only several hundred families kept their faith in him and converted to Islam. These people constitute the origins of the Dönme community. They appeared as Muslims in public, but they practiced Sevi's version of messianic Judaism in private.[16] The Dönmes had prohibitions against marrying outsiders and therefore existed as a secret and closed community. Regardless, their existence as a secret community was known in the Ottoman Empire and remained an "open secret".[17] In other words, during the Ottoman period, the Dönmes were identified and perceived as a secret society, and their secrecy was tolerated by the public. As will be mentioned below, this attitude altered during the Turkish Republic era.

---

10 Cf. Gershom Scholem, *Sabbatai Sevi: The Mystical Messiah*, Princeton 1971, p. 23.

11 Cf. Scholem, *Sabbatai Sevi*, p. 25.

12 Cf. Cengiz Şişman, "Sabetaycılığın Osmanlı ve Türkiye Serüveni", in: *Tarih ve Toplum*, 223/2002, pp. 4–6.

13 Cf. Cengiz Şişman, *Sabatay Sevi ve Sabataycılar: Mitler ve Gerçekler*, İstanbul 2008, p. 65.

14 Cf. Şişman, *Sabatay Sevi*, p. 68.

15 Cf. Şişman, *Sabatay Sevi*, p. 36.

16 Cf. Marc Baer, *The Dönme: Jewish Converts, Muslim Revolutionaries, and Secular Turks*, Stanford 2010, p. 4.

17 Baer, *The Dönme*, p. 30.

Due to disputes about who incarnated Sevi's spirit, there were divisions within the community. It was divided into sub-sects, called Karakaşlı, Kapancı, and Yakubi.[18] Some members of the community believed that Jacob Querido, Sabatai Sevi's brother-in-law, was the incarnation of Sevi, and they formed the Yakubi (Jacobite) group in 1683. Later on, the remaining followers argued whether Baruchya Russo (Osman Baba) incarnated Sevi's spirit. Russo's believers formed the Karakaşlı sect, whereas the Dönmes who continued to believe only in Sevi are called the Kapancı group. These three communities specialised in different trades and avoided marrying each other. The division thus shaped the basic structure of the Dönme community.

In the late nineteenth century, the Dönmes were influenced by the modernisation movements in Europe. They were seen as cosmopolitan figures in the Ottoman Empire. Indeed, most of them lived in Salonika at the time, a city hosting the modernisation movement of the Ottoman Empire, the Committee of Union and Progress (CUP). Some members of the community played important roles in the CUP. For example, Mehmed Cavid Bey acted as the minister of finance in 1908 when the CUP was in government.[19] When the Ottoman Empire collapsed and the modern Turkish Republic was established in 1923, most of the Dönmes were living outside the Turkish borders in Salonika, which was a part of Greece. In 1924, there was a population exchange between Muslim Turks in Greece, excluding the Western Thrace, and the Orthodox Greeks in Turkey, excluding Istanbul. With the exchange, the Dönmes, seen as Muslim Turks by the authorities, came to Turkey. Although the Dönmes were thought to be concealed among Turks and they kept their identity secret, the Turkish state could still identify some families. The Capital Levy of 1942, which imposed heavy taxes on non-Muslim minorities, included lists of Dönme families in the non-Muslim category. Afterwards, the community was not the subject of any state policy or public interest. Until the 1990s, the Dönmes were mainly mentioned in the right-wing and Islamist political literature, some of which included conspiracy accounts about them. The community has attracted public attention in the 1990s especially through the works of Ilgaz Zorlu. His book *Yes I am a Salonikan*[20] and his media appearances amplified the interest in the Dönmes.

---

18 Cf. Baer, *The Dönme*, p. 6.

19 Cf. Leyla Neyzi, "Remembering to Forget: Sabbateanism, National Identity and Subjectivity in Turkey", in: *Comparative Studies in Society and History*, 44/2002, 1, pp. 137–158, p. 145.

20 Cf. Ilgaz Zorlu, *Evet Ben Selanik'liyim: Türkiye Sabetaycılığı*, Istanbul 1998.

The historical record suggests that the Dönme community is a secret society and has been perceived by the public as such. It is general knowledge in Turkey that the community exists, but the Turkish public only knows about a few prominent Dönme families like the Bezmens and İpekçis or about a few community members who unveiled their identity such as Ilgaz Zorlu.[21] This seems to have three important implications: (1) most of the claims about the Dönmes are speculations; (2) there is a suspicion about the deeds of the community that gives rise to conspiracy theories; (3) the conspiracy theories about the Dönmes remain unchallenged because of the community's silence. The following section analyses the influence of the Dönme secrecy on the conspiracy theories.

History of the Conspiracy Theories about the Dönmes

The conspiracy rhetoric focusing on the Dönmes emerged at the beginning of the twentieth century, while the objective existence of the community dates back to the seventeenth century. The Dönme involvement in the CUP proved to be a source for the conspiracy theories. The opponents of the Young Turk movement framed the CUP as a part of a Jewish conspiracy. There were two historical incidences that seeded the conspiracy rhetoric. First, Theodor Herzl, the head of the World Zionist Organisation, visited Istanbul in 1899 to buy Palestine for Jews to establish a state, but the Ottoman ruler Sultan Abdulhamid II did not grant the request.[22] Second, when Abdulhamid II was toppled by a CUP-organized *coup d'etat* in 1908,[23] some conspiratorial lines claimed that this was a response to his refusal to sell Palestine. They used the Dönme Mehmed Cavid Bey and the Jewish Freemason Emmanuel Carosso's involvement in the *coup d'etat* as an indicator of a Jewish conspiracy.

Afterwards, the conspiracy theories about the Dönmes became widespread among the Turkish public in three distinct periods: the single-party period (1923–1950), the multi-party democracy period (1950–1990), and the post-1990 period.[24] To start with, the conspiracy accounts in the single-party period emerged after Karakaşzade Rüşdü, a self-acclaimed member of the group, submitted a petition to the Turkish parliament about the immigration

---

21 Cf. Rifat Bali, *A Scapegoat for All Seasons: The Dönmes or Crypto-Jews of Turkey*, Istanbul 2008, p. 38.

22 Cf. Bali, *Scapegoat*, p. 17.

23 The 1908 Young Turk revolution ended the rule of Sultan Abdulhamid II.

24 Türkay Salim Nefes, "The History of the Social Constructions of Dönmes", in: *Journal of Historical Sociology*, 25/2012, 3, pp. 413–439.

of Dönmes in 1924. He argued that the Dönmes had always avoided mixing with Turks, and therefore their deportation from Greece to Turkey should only be authorized if they were willing to assimilate into the Turkish society.[25] This led to a heated discussion about the Dönmes in the Turkish media, which lasted a few weeks. Rüşdü was forced to retreat from the discussion because of the immense hostility shown against the group, which also marked the end of the media debate. Subsequently, there were not many printed conspiracy theories about the Dönmes due to the single-party censorship on political publications.

After the end of the single-party regime in 1950, the state censorship of political groups decreased. In this context, Nazif Özge, who claimed to have a Dönme wife, accused the community of having attempted to rape his wife for religious reasons.[26] Although they stated that they did not trust the mental state of Özge, some right-wing journals and newspapers, such as *Sebülreşşad* and *Büyük Doğu*, published his claims in 1952. This was followed by other conspiracy theories published in right-wing sources. Until the 1990s, only right-wing and Islamist extremist groups circulated the conspiracy theories about the Dönmes. Some of these theories accompanied violence against some well-known members of the Turkish society who were known to be Dönmes. For example, Ahmed Emin Yalman was attacked on November 22, 1952 by a right-wing Islamist.

There was a change in the nature of the published material on Dönmes beginning in the 1990s. This period started after Ilgaz Zorlu, another self-acclaimed member of the community, began to give interviews and write about the Dönmes. Prominent Islamist intellectuals, such as Abdurrahman Dilipak and Mehmet Şevket Eygi, engaged in debates with Ilgaz Zorlu on the Dönmes. The Dönme discussion eventually became widespread through a variety of publications ranging from newspaper articles to alleged lists of Dönmes on the Internet. The conspiracy theories about the Dönmes were not only propagated by right-wing and Islamist groups but extended to left-wing and Kurdish groups after the 1990s. Yalçın Küçük, a well-known Marxist professor, and Soner Yalçın, a well-known left-wing journalist whose *Efendi* series became a best-seller in Turkey, wrote on the topic.[27] The

---

[25] Cf. Paul Bessemer, "Who is a Crypto-Jew? A Historical Survey of the Sabbatean Debate in Turkey", in: *Kabbalah: Journal for the Study of Jewish Mystical Texts*, 9/2003, pp. 109–152, pp. 121–122.

[26] Cf. Rıfat Bali, "Dönmenin Hikayesi: Nazif Ozge Kimdir?", in: *Tarih ve Toplum*, 38/2002, 223, pp. 15–21, p. 19.

[27] Cf. Soner Yalçın, *Efendi: Beyaz Türklerin Büyük Sırrı*, Istanbul 2004; Soner Yalçın, *Efendi 2: Beyaz Müslümanların Büyük Sırrı*, Istanbul 2006.

left-wing theories use a more scientific rhetoric compared to the ideologically-biased, pejorative language of the right-wing theories, and they seem to make the Dönme issue a popular debate in Turkey as they have reached a variety of audiences.[28] The conspiracy theories were also visited by some Kurdish nationalists such as Musa Anter and Abdülmelik Fırat, who accused a member of parliament, Coşkun Kırca, of being a Dönme and trying to throw Kurds out of the country. Kırca's Turkish nationalist stance played an important role in the conspiratorial claims of the Kurdish activists. Both Anter and Fırat associated Kırca with state oppression of the Kurdish minority and ridiculed him for not being Turkish but imposing Turkish nationalism.[29]

There are significant differences between these three periods. The first period was initiated by the fear of incoming Dönmes, but the conspiracy theories did not become widespread because of the state censorship in the single-party era. In the second period, right-wing extremist groups produced anti-Semitic accounts about the Dönmes, claiming that they were secretly powerful. In the third period, members of other political groups, such as left-wing intellectuals and Kurdish politicians, contributed to the conspiratorial views of the community with similar accusations. Through a variety of publications and media attention, the issue entered the mainstream culture, which marked a change from the second period, when the conspiracy literature was only a part of the right-wing extremist rhetoric in Turkey. Nonetheless, the Dönme question was not addressed in political parties' speeches and debates in the Turkish Parliament or elsewhere and did not cause any anti-Dönme movements in the 1990s. It rather remained an intellectually eccentric issue in popular culture.

There are recurrent themes in these three seasons of the conspiratorial literature. These could be listed as follows:

- The Dönme community is a secret and closed group like Freemasons.
- The Dönmes are secretly in control of the media, politics, and higher positions.
- They are secretly behind the establishment of the Turkish Republic in 1923.
- They secretly cause moral decay.
- They are secretly allied with foreign powers against the well-being of the country.[30]

---

28 Cf. Türkay Salim Nefes, *Towards a Sociology of Conspiracy Theories: An Investigation into Conspiratorial Thinking on Dönmes*, Diss. University of Kent, 2010.

29 Cf. Bali, *Scapegoat*, p. 176.

30 Cf. Nefes, *Towards a Sociology*, p. 95.

The most persistent aspect of these themes is the secrecy of the Dönme community, which is at the centre of the problematisation of the group. Second, the three periods were all started by an alleged insider of the community, whose confessions claimed to unveil some hidden aspects of the Dönme life. Karakaşzade Rüşdü, Nazif Özge, and Ilgaz Zorlu did not promote the conspiracy theories about the community, but they talked about the necessity for the community to dissolve into the Turkish society (Karakaşzade) or into the Jewish community (Zorlu). Whatever their real motivations were, they reminded the Turkish public about the secret existence of the group and stirred up conspiratorial discussions. It could be argued that the secret character of the community creates an anxiety among the public about the deeds of the group, and therefore, whenever the secrecy of the community is exposed by acclaimed insiders, this anxiety is expressed via conspiracy accounts. In other words, the confessions trigger the anxieties about a secret society that is a perfect example of "the hidden hand mentality".

This could help us to understand the different treatment of the community in the Ottoman Empire and the Turkish Republic. The Dönmes' secrecy was tolerated during the Ottoman period, but not in the Turkish Republic. Indeed, the conspiracy accounts began to circulate mainly after the establishment of the Republic. Elsewhere I have explained this shift in conception as a result of the ontological insecurities of Turkish politics.[31] I argue that Turkish state ideology was suspicious of minority identities, as the Ottoman Empire collapsed because of the minority independence movements.[32] The Turkish Republic found it dangerous to promote different identities and attempted to assimilate the minorities. Indeed, the above-mentioned population exchange between Turkey and Greece could be seen as a product of this fear. In this context, the Dönme identity as a secret society represented a community that could not be assimilated into the Turkish society, and therefore created an anxiety about its deeds.[33]

Overall, the historical analysis demonstrates that the perception of the secret character of the community predisposes and facilitates the creation and communication of the conspiracy theories. The interviews with the political parties which are presented in the next section bring another insight to the discussion on the significance of secrecy in the conspiracy theories. As mentioned in the introduction, the academic literature on conspiracy

---

31 Cf. Nefes, *Towards a Sociology*, p. 102.
32 Cf. Nefes, *Towards a Sociology*, p. 104.
33 Cf. Nefes, *Towards a Sociology*, p. 105.

accounts lacks empirical analyses. Therefore, the next section not only provides further evidence to the argument about the conspiracy theories on the Dönmes but also fills this gap in the literature.

4. Political Parties' Approaches to the Secrecy of Dönmes

This section outlines the data obtained from semi-structured interviews conducted in December 2008 with members of four political parties representing major ideological views in Turkey:[34] the Nationalist Action Party (Milliyetçi Hareket Partisi, MHP) with a Turkish nationalist view, the Islamist Felicity Party (Saadet Partisi, SP), the liberal-conservative Justice and Development Party (Adalet ve Kalkınma Partisi, AKP), and the Kurdish/leftist Democratic Society Party (Demokratik Toplum Partisi, DTP). It also discusses the reasons for the Kemalist Republican People's Party's (Cumhuriyet Halk Partisi, CHP) refusal of giving interviews on the topic.

The interviews were conducted with one member from each political party except the CHP. In order to find party members, who could provide better insights into their parties' reflections, all interviewees were chosen from the central headquarters of their parties in Ankara. They regularly attended the party assemblies and were aware of the official party approaches at the time of the interviews. All respondents were prominent members of their political parties: respondent A from the SP was one of the founding members of the party, who had spent thirty-five years in the movement. Respondent B from the MHP was a member of parliament and a co-chairman of the party. Respondent C from the AKP was a former foreign minister and a founding member of the party. Respondent D from the DTP was a member of the party assembly. The interviews, which took between forty and one hundred minutes, intended to assess the general party approaches on the Dönmes and the conspiracy accounts. The respondents were thus asked whether they agreed with those accounts or not, and how they would describe the Dönme community. They were given the choice for the location, which was either the party offices in the Turkish parliament or the party headquarters.

The analysis focuses on the ways in which these political parties approach the secrecy of the Dönme community in the conspiracy accounts. First, it mentions the reasons CHP gave for rejecting the interview request. Then, it groups the data from the interviews into two: the political parties rejecting the conspiracy theories and the parties accepting the theories. It exam-

---

34 These conversations were in Turkish, and all citations from them are my translations from the Turkish original.

ines how the secrecy of the Dönme community was mentioned in both approaches.

4.1 The Republican People's Party's Refusal of the Interview Request

Indeed, the research aimed to interview representatives of five political parties, but the Kemalist Republican People's Party (CHP) refused the interview request. The party secretaries who assisted me in searching for someone to interview stated that party members did not want to give interviews on the topic, because they did not take the conspiracy theories seriously. They saw these theories as political pathologies and did not think that they were worth an interview. This is interesting as the representatives of the two other political parties who did not agree with the conspiracy literature on the Dönmes either nevertheless talked about their reflections.

Moreover, the party itself did not distance itself from conspiracy narratives at the time of the interviews in 2008. After a party member's talk within the headquarters had been published by the Islamist newspaper *Vakit*, the party accused the AKP government of spying on them with new technological devices in a manner similar to the Watergate scandal.[35] In the end, it turned out to be a mistake on the part of the CHP member, who had not turned off his mobile telephone after speaking to a reporter from the newspaper. This shows that while the party is not unwilling to propagate conspiracy theories, it does not find the conspiracy accounts about a minority important enough to give an interview.

4.2 The Political Parties That Accept the Conspiracy Theories

The representatives of the Felicity Party (SP) and the Nationalist Action Party (MHP) were convinced of the conspiratorial views of the Dönmes. The ideological orientation of the SP is political Islam. The party is a product of the historical tradition of Islamist politics and the *Milli Görüs* (National Vision) movement in Turkey. From its founding in the 1960s onwards, this movement was represented in the parliament under different political parties, such as the National Order Party and Welfare Party.[36] The SP is the last

---

[35] Cf. Tolga Şardan, "Vakit Önder Sav'ı 44 Dakika Dinlemiş", in: *Milliyet*, May 31, 2008, http://www.milliyet.com.tr/default.aspx?aType=HaberDetay&ArticleID=761223 (accessed March 17, 2009).

[36] Cf. Birol Yeşilada, "The Virtue Party", in: *Turkish Studies*, 3/2002, 1, pp. 62–81, pp. 64–70.

party of the movement as the former incarnations of the movement have been successively dissolved by the Turkish state. The MHP is also a right-wing political party, which represents an ultra-nationalist stance. Burak Arıkan classifies the party as a part of the European extreme-right tradition.[37] Both the MHP and SP have historically been linked to the right-wing movements which have embraced the conspiracy theories.

The representatives of the MHP and SP view the secret character of the Dönme community as a proof of the conspiracy theories. They formulate their suspicions about the community by condemning their secret character. To start with, respondent A from the SP describes the Dönmes as Jews who fake conversion to be able to conspire against Turks:

> During the fall of the Ottoman Empire, when the ambassadors felt ashamed in foreign countries as representatives of a losing country, the Jews suggested that they could be ambassadors [...] The Ottomans rejected the request, as they were not Muslims. Then, they replied: 'We will become Muslims!' [repeated three times in a Jewish accent] Unfortunately, they just appeared to be Muslims. In their hearts, they kept their former belief. These people are called Dönmes, and Sabbatai Sevi led them this way.

Respondent A of the SP conceptualises the secrecy of the Dönme community as an expression of the deceitful political style of Zionism. His hostility towards the Dönmes stems from his perception that the Dönmes are aligned with Zionism. He argues that he is not against all Jews, because "not all Jews are Zionists; there are some Jews against Zionism". The respondent links the Dönmes to Zionism and the conspiracy theories due to the secret nature of the community. In other words, the secrecy of the community allows the respondent to see the group as a part of Zionist treachery. For instance, he claims that the current AKP government is deceived by Zionists. He argues that the Turkish Prime Minister Recep Tayyip Erdoğan came to power with the help of Zionists, and one of the ways he returns the favour is by becoming a co-chairman of the Greater Middle East Initiative (Büyük Ortadoğu Projesi-BOP),[38] which is an aspect of the Zionist project to control the Islamic world.

In parallel, respondent B from the MHP sees the secrecy of the Dönme community as an indication that they engage in conspiratorial activities:

---

[37] Cf. Burak Arıkan, "Turkish Ultra-Nationalists Under Review: A Study of the Nationalist Action Party", in: *Nations and Nationalism*, 8/2002, 1, pp. 357–375, p. 358.

[38] The Greater Middle East Initiative, initiated by George W. Bush during the G8 summit of 2004, is an attempt to transform the region politically and economically.

"Dönmes, the sacred light, represent a thought, which hides real ideas and feelings with a false appearance. This is a political style". Like respondent A, he claims that he is not against Jews but against the Dönmes, because the community's secret identity represents a political treachery:

> Dönmeism is a system of thought of someone who changes his/her religious identity. If s/he is not really wholeheartedly converted and trying to alter the new belief system that they were converted to, s/he is a Dönme. I believe that the Dönme belief system is not right. If someone changes his/her convictions, there is no problem. The trouble starts when they serve the previous belief [...] Consequently, if the Dönme thought is dominant in Turkey, it means that Turkey is governed towards different targets than its own.

Respondent B links the conspiratorial style of the Dönmes to the AKP's politics by claiming that the AKP also hides its real motives: "the same approach that AKP and Dönmes share: to hide their real motives and to convince society to hidden policies. AKP appears to be conservative, but it undermines the traditional values. The Dönme view is effective in that political style". While respondent B's rhetoric is quite similar to that of the SP representative, he differentiates their approaches by arguing that the others (meaning the SP) think that everything is a Jewish plot, but the MHP does not start from such an *a priori* stance. Instead, the MHP "realistically analyses where the plots are coming from".

Overall, the representatives of both political parties legitimise their use of the conspiracy theories by equating the secret nature of the Dönme identity to conspiratorial politics. The secrecy of the community enables them to assume the conspiracy theories to be true. While doing so, they pragmatically formulate their opposition against the AKP government by connecting them to the conspiracy theories in different ways.

4.3 The Political Parties That Reject the Conspiracy Theories

The representatives of the Justice and Development Party (AKP) and the Democratic Society Party (DTP) do not agree with the conspiratorial rhetoric about the Dönmes. The AKP's ideological orientation is a synthesis of conservatism and neo-liberalism. Menderes Çınar proposes that the AKP has an Islam-sensitive political stance with a "comprehensive and consistent language of democracy and human rights".[39] The party is more liberal than

---

[39] Menderes Çınar, "Turkey's Transformation Under the AKP Rule", in: *The Muslim World*, 96/2006, 3, pp. 469–486, p. 474.

the traditional Islamist *Milli Görüs*.[40] The AKP has recently been targeted in conspiracy theories about the Dönmes, traces of which could be seen in the interviews presented above. The DTP is a left-wing oriented political party associated with the Kurdish minority movement. Because of its strong ties with the Kurdish movement, it was seen as a mouthpiece of the Kurdish terrorist group PKK.[41] The party has a democratic vision of Turkey with more freedoms for minorities.

While rejecting the conspiracy theories about the Dönmes, respondent C from the AKP claims that the small group must be assimilated into the Turkish society. The respondent believes that the silence of the community is not linked to its secrecy or conspiracies but to the assimilation of the Dönmes. He proposes that it is really difficult to comply with the religious dogma of the Dönme community in the twenty-first century: "How many people can read prayers a couple of times a day, and how can they avoid marrying Muslims? Therefore, I think that the Dönme belief is diluted today". Moreover, he believes that the conspiracy theories emerge because the public is jealous of the success of the members of the Dönme minority. He adds that in Turkey different groups co-exist in politics without a hegemonic relationship. Hence, even if there are some Dönmes in politics and high-ranking positions, this is an aspect of Turkish meritocracy, not a conspiracy: "if successful people collaborate, we should see it as legitimate [...] as a part of Turkish meritocracy".

In parallel, respondent D of the DTP claims that the small community of the Dönmes cannot be powerful in Turkish politics due to the conservative nature of the country:

> Kurds constitute forty percent of Turkey's population and have the fourth greatest party in the parliament [...] While such a powerful political movement does not have little influence on government policies, [...] it is really absurd to claim that the representatives of two hundred families have extraordinary powers.

Like the AKP respondent, he suggests that the conspiracy theories show the jealousy of the good qualities and success of the Dönmes: "all moderate liberals and Islamists basically argue that the Ottoman Empire collapsed due to Dönme conspiracies, because this group had the capacity to understand the

---

40 Cf. Hasan Turunç, "Islamist or Democratic? The AKP's Search for Identity in Turkish Politics", in: *Journal of Contemporary European Studies*, 15/2007, 1, pp. 79–91, p. 81.

41 Cf. Nicole Watts, "Allies and Enemies: Pro-Kurdish Parties in Turkish Politics, 1990–94", in: *International Journal of Middle East Studies*, 31/1999, 4, pp. 631–656, p. 631.

bourgeois culture". He explains the conspiracy theories as a part of the political scapegoating mechanism that functions to protect the Turkish state ideology: "to blame all these political failures of the state, military interventions, cultural degradation, poverty, and stupidity on the Dönmes is nothing but an attempt to defend the state tradition". In this sense, he sympathises with the minority status of the community and rejects the conspiracy accounts as an aspect of the state ideology that oppresses all minorities such as the Kurds.

Neither the AKP nor the DTP representative criticises the secret character of the Dönme community. Instead, both representatives appreciate the success of some of the community's members. In their rhetoric the secrecy of the community is used to affirm that the Dönmes either are assimilated into Turkish society or remain an insignificant small group. For example, respondent D ignores the secret nature of the Dönme identity in stating: "why would such a powerful Judaist tradition hide itself? Actually, this shows the limits of the Dönme power. Otherwise, they would have established a cultural and political hegemony". The DTP and AKP representatives pragmatically confirm their own ideological views (despite being utterly opposite) in their rejection of the conspiracy theories: the DTP respondent criticises the state oppression of minorities, and respondent C of the AKP underlines his vision of a meritocratic Turkey, where different identities co-exist in a non-hierarchical political context.

5. Conclusion

The evidence gathered from the historical analysis of the conspiracy theories and the interviews with the political parties support the main premise that the secrecy of the Dönme community, as perceived by outsiders, plays a significant role in the production and dissemination of the conspiracy theories. The conspiracy rhetoric used to describe the community is legitimised because the group's secrecy is viewed as a proof of the existence of their conspiracies. The historical record of the Dönme society demonstrates that its secrecy is the most repeated theme in the conspiracy literature. Moreover, the three distinct periods of the conspiracy literature were initiated by alleged insiders of the community, which seems to suggest that Karakaşzade Rüşdü, Nazif Özge, and Ilgaz Zorlu reminded the Turkish public about the existence of a secret society and therefore triggered the public anxiety that led to the proliferation of conspiracy theories about the group. In other words, the alleged insiders reminded the public about the secrecy of the Dönme community, which was seen as a proof of the politically treacherous style of the community and ignited the conspiratorial rhetoric. Furthermore, the interviews show that the political party representatives that accepted the conspiracy theories legitimise their conspiratorial views by perceiving the secret nature of the Dönme identity as a conspiratorial political style. Respondent A from the SP saw the group's secrecy as an aspect of Zionism while the MHP respondent perceived it as a treacherous political style. The political parties that rejected the conspiracy theories understand the silence and secrecy surrounding the Dönme community not as a conspiracy but as a proof of the insignificance of the community. All political party representatives accept or reject the conspiracy theories pragmatically to verify their own political stances. For example, although the AKP and DTP respondents had opposing views on Turkish politics and society, they found support for their standpoints in their rejections of the conspiracy literature.

The evidence shows that Simmel is right to suggest that secret societies cause suspicion among the public. In the Dönme case, the conspiratorial view is facilitated by the misgivings about the secret community. Bauman's view of ambivalence is also relevant for understanding the stranger status of the Dönme community, which is neither an insider nor an outsider of the Turkish society. This in-between character of the community caused by its secrecy seems to have created the misgivings about their loyalty. In this regard, the conspiracy theories are very likely to appear in the future as well, because whenever there is publicity about the Dönmes, it usually echoes already existing questions and suspicions that characterise the conspiracy literature. Even if the community unveils itself fully to the Turkish society, this may not stop the attribution of secrecy to the community. The seventeenth-century crypto-Jews of Spain, the *conversos*, provide a very good example to this point. Following their conversion to Christianity, there was a suspicion that the Jews secretly continued their religious practice in private. Like in the Dönme case, it was a socially constructed suspicion about the community's secrecy. This led to the emergence of conspiracy theories about the Jewish converts and reinforced blood purity laws.[42] Hence, even the attribution of secrecy is enough to trigger the propagation of conspiracy literature. In addition, the Dönme case demonstrates that if the attributions are supported by alleged confessors from the group, they seem to prevail more easily.

While the conspiracy literature about the community is quite representative of the global anti-Semitic rhetoric, this research is solely confined to the Dönme case in Turkey, and it might not be realistic to generalise all of its

---

[42] Marc Shell, "Marranos (Pigs), or from Coexistence to Toleration", in: *Critical Inquiry*, 17/1991, 2, pp. 306–335, p. 309.

conclusions. Nevertheless, secrecy is an indispensable element of conspiracy theories, and future studies could investigate its significance in different contexts to test the main arguments of this study. Last, this paper also draws attention to the lack of empirical studies on the socio-political impacts of conspiracy theories. Future research could fill this lacuna and develop an understanding of the reasons of ethnic and religious conflicts that are initiated by and communicated through conspiracy theories.

Stephan Schmid (Beirut)

Hizbullah between Pan-Islamic Ideology and Domestic Politics: Conspiracy Theories as Medium for Political Mobilization and Integration

With the release of its political manifesto on February 16, 1985, the Lebanese Shiite radical resistance movement Hizbullah (the Party of God) started its endeavor to become one of the major political players and opinion-makers in the Lebanese as well as the regional political scene. As the following excerpt from the so-called *Open Letter* illustrates, the reference to conspiracy theories was from the start an integral part of Hizbullah's ideological framework and political strategy:

> Be aware of the malignant colonial discord (*fitna*) that aims at rupturing your unity in order to spread sedition among you and enflame Sunni-Shiʿa sectarian feelings. [...] The colonizers left this mission of spreading dissention among the Muslims to their collaborators, be it the governing elite, the corrupt Muslim religious scholars (state jurists), or the feudal leaders (*zuʿama*). God is with the unity of the Muslims [...] It is the rock that breaks all the conspiracies of the oppressors; it is the hammer that crushes the evil schemes of the oppressors.[1]

Many observers and analysts have described this phenomenon of conspiracy rhetoric, if at all aware of it, as an expression of an irrational, fundamentalist, and paranoid outlook, which allegedly constituted an integral part not only of Hizbullah's ideology but also of the social and political life in the entire Middle East. Equally, whether explicitly or implicitly, they inferred that this reference to conspiracy theories by Middle Eastern political actors was an expression of their inferior status in international power relations.[2]

---

1 Hizbullah, "Section 22: God is with the unity of the Muslims", in: Joseph Alagha (ed. and trans.), *Hizbullah's Documents: From the 1985 Open Letter to the 2009 Manifesto*, Amsterdam 2011, p. 53.

2 Cf. Daniel Pipes, *The Hidden Hand: Middle East Fears of Conspiracy*, New York 1996. His entire study is dedicated to exhibit this alleged inferiority as expressed by the conspiracy theories. Cf. also Amal Saad-Ghorayeb, *Hizbu'llah: Politics and Religion*, London 2002, pp. 90–93. Studies on Hizbullah are dominantly focusing on the movement's origins, its political and ideological development, or its relationship to other powers in the Middle East, notably Syria and Iran. The party's conspiracy rhetoric often remains a marginal aspect at best. Cf., for example, Augustus Nor-

Acknowledging the discrepancy between Hizbullah's often rational analysis of political developments and adoption of pragmatic propagandistic tactics on the one hand, and the explanation of the party's use of conspiracy theories as a paranoid excess of its fundamentalist view that the West and the Islamic world are incompatible on the other one, this paper aims at a revision of this often echoed reductionist interpretation of Hizbullah's conspiracy rhetoric by illustrating and analyzing the background of this phenomenon.[3] In so doing, I argue that the articulation of such theories by Hizbullah officials today, though born out of an ideology based on the dichotomy of an Islamic movement resisting against an allegedly continuously conspiring Zionist or western enemy, are not the reflection of a bizarre, irrational, and intransigent anti-western and anti-Zionist outlook. Rather, they function as a very rational medium of propaganda and political maneuvering adopted by the Party of God in the course of its changing role in the domestic and regional political arena. It is a fairly remarkable and still little recognized fact that conspiracy rhetoric was not exclusively used by Hizbullah as a tool for inciting strive but, on certain occasions, also as a means to absorb the negative domestic repercussions of the sometimes violent preservation, if not extension, of the party's political power and privileges. As I will illustrate, for the purpose of covering up the party's attempts to undermine state authority and recklessly strive for domestic dominance, Hizbullah officials have presented the party more than once over the past decades as a guardian against foreign conspiracies allegedly responsible for sectarian tensions in Lebanon as well as for denouncing Hizbullah's image of a legitimate resistance movement. In this function, the Party of God sought support from all political and religious camps.

---

ton, *Hezbollah: A Short History*, Princeton, N.J. 2007; Walid Charara/Frederic Domont, *Le Hezbollah: un mouvement islamo-nationaliste*, Paris 2004; Hala Jaber, *Hezbollah: Born With a Vengeance*, New York 1997.

3 Although Saad-Ghorayeb describes this seemingly paradox display of rationalism and paranoia, she was not able to give a satisfying explanation for it (cf. *Hizbu'llah*, pp. 88–111).

1. The "Paranoid Style" Interpretation of Conspiracism and Its Flaws

The term "conspiracy", in the meaning of political conspiracy,[4] involves "three analytically distinct but interrelated characteristics: secrecy; vulnerability to defeat by exposure; and one or a combination of illegality, deception, betrayal of legitimate purposes of an authorized activity, and contradiction of generally accepted moral codes of behavior".[5] Whereas the third criterion distinguishes conspiracies from other kinds of secret collaboration, the question of what distinguishes a conspiracy from a conspiracy theory is much more difficult to determine.

Though I agree with Daniel Pipes's basic working definition that a conspiracy theory is "the nonexistent version of a conspiracy",[6] in many, if not in most, cases related to Hizbullah's use of the term, the question whether a conspiracy is really existent or non-existent is very difficult to discern. In fact, none of the conspiracies that Hizbullah officials talk of today are founded on baseless assumptions but are in one way or another linked to facts, though interpreted on the basis of particular ideological and sociopolitical considerations.

We do not gain much from defining a conspiracy theorist as someone who "discerns malignant forces at work wherever something displeases him; plots serve as his first method for explaining the world around him".[7] If conspiracism was nothing more than such a paranoid-style "hidden-hand mentality" – with the power to affect the course of the Middle East's history –, Hizbullah's leading cadres and the larger part of the Arab-Muslim society would have to consult a host of psychiatrists to treat their paranoia and reinvigorate their sense of rationality and reality.

---

4 Under political conspiracies I understand conspiracies which are characterized by an enemy outside the state with potential supporters inside the state. We may contrast these to social conspiracies which focus on domestic issues and mostly on the relationship between the rich and the poor. It is dominantly the former to which Hizbullah is continuously referring today. Although the Arabic term which is usually used for conspiracy is *mu'amara*, Hizbullah officials also often refer to the term *istikbar* when speaking about conspiracies. The latter term means literally "arrogance of power" and clearly indicates that the conspirators are seen as being powerful but morally inferior.

5 Daniel Hellinger, "Paranoia, Conspiracy, and Hegemony in American Politics", in: Harry G. West/Todd Sanders (eds.), *Transparency and Conspiracy: Ethnographies of Suspicion in the New World Order*, Durham, NC 2003, pp. 204–233, p. 209.

6 Pipes, *The Hidden Hand*, p. 10.

7 Pipes, *The Hidden Hand*, p. 10.

Deeming conspiracy theories the result of an inherently irrational world view and a pathologically paranoid outlook not only turns a blind eye to the many dimensions such theories and their promoters may display, but it also foils any closer understanding of how and under which circumstances conspiracy theories emerge, why they are propagated, and how they may influence the course of history.[8] The consideration of the circumstances in which a political actor like Hizbullah is referring to conspiracy theories, the framework in which such theories are articulated, and the identification of the intended audience are crucial parameters for the understanding of conspiracy rhetoric.[9] This applies even more in the face of the assumption that Hizbullah's conspiracy rhetoric has been used for dominantly pragmatic political purposes. Consequently, it is necessary to change the perspective when analyzing the phenomenon of conspiracism. Rather than aiming to discern how truthful the conspiracies are which Hizbullah or any other political actor is propagating, it appears to be of much more importance – just as it promises to provide much more insights into the dynamics of conspiracy rhetoric – to elaborate on the question *why* certain political parties or groups are disseminating particular conspiracy theories. I shall illustrate the necessity of reconsidering the "paranoid style" interpretation by referring to a prominent example related to the Middle East, namely the claim that an Israeli policy exists to create a "Greater Israel," a controversial expression and idea with changing biblical and political meanings over time.[10]

After presenting a selection of statements made by leading political figures from major Middle Eastern states in which they express their concerns

---

8 In particular, political science literature is inclined to interpret conspiracy rhetoric as a paranoid style. Richard Hofstadter thus called conspiracy theories a "paranoid leap into fantasy" ("The Paranoid Style in American Politics", in: *Harper's Magazine*, 11/1964, pp. 77–86, p.78); Jeffrey Ostler labeled them as being "bizarre and irrational" ("The Rhetoric of Conspiracy and the Formation of Kansas Populism", in: *Agricultural History*, 69/1995, 1, pp. 1–27, p. 25). Brian L. Keeley's judgment that the general omission of conspiracy theories in academic literature is rooted in the fact that most academics simply find conspiracy theories "to be silly and without merits", is probably correct ("Of Conspiracy Theories", in: *Journal of Philosophy*, 96/1999, 3, pp. 109–126, p. 109, n.1).

9 For the still understudied rhetorical dimensions of conspiracy theories, cf. Michael William Pfau, *The Political Style of Conspiracy: Chase, Sumner, and Lincoln*, East Lansing 2005.

10 The term Greater Israel, indicating the alleged Jewish or Zionist dream to create an empire spanning from the Nile valley to the Euphrates, became, in particular in anti-Semitic circles, a common reference for "proving" the Jews' aim to rule the world or at least a large part of it.

about Israel aiming to establish a so-called Greater Israel, Pipes comes to the conclusion that this idea was a baseless Arab fantasy, void of any historical or rational considerations. He emphasizes:

> [The b]elief in Israel's plan to expand from the Nile to the Euphrates, and perhaps beyond, makes the Jewish state's very existence a threat to the entire Middle East and increases the already substantial paranoia in the Middle East to even higher levels. [...] The Greater Israel myth also justifies anti-Israel behavior as a defensive act.[11]

Although I agree with the claim that with the dissemination of the Greater Israel conspiracy theory the Arab world's inclination to see Israel as an entity to be wiped out becomes even more cemented in the public discourse as well as in political decision-making, two important remarks need to be made about Pipes's argumentation.

First, conspiracy theories such as the one referring to a Greater Israel are not the reason *why* Arabs oppose Israel. They are rather an expression of existing fears on the popular level and a vehicle to catalyze mobilization and decisions on the political level. This simple relationship between matter and cause has been turned upside down in many academic accounts on conspiracism in the Middle East, and their research methods have enshrouded the mechanisms and functions of conspiracy theories in the region's societies. By restricting their studies only to collecting and ridiculing statements of Arab political actors in which they accused Israel of secretly following the policy of extensive expansionism, the direct and broader context of these statements has been entirely neglected. As I will show, a contextualized analysis of the articulation of conspiracy theories reveals that very often quite rational considerations lay at the heart of such statements.

Second, fears of Israeli expansionism seem to be by far not as "extravagant" as Pipes contends if we consider the matter from an Arab-Muslim point of view that is shaped by the experience of Israel's ongoing military operations and aggressive settlement policy in the Palestinian territories, Israel's twenty-year-long occupation of Lebanese territory (while the Shebaa farms and the Golan Heights remain under Israeli occupation until today), and the enormous and costly efforts to arm and drill the Israeli military forces with almost unrestricted help of the U.S. In view of this political reality, Arab-Muslim "conspiracy believers [...] have good reasons to suspect he-

---

11 Pipes, *The Hidden Hand*, pp. 68–69. For the entire line of argumentation, cf. Pipes, *The Hidden Hand*, pp. 49–73.

gemonic powers," even if specific accusations may not be true.[12] Just as U.S. foreign policy since World War II is replete with operations undertaken behind a screen of secrecy and deception, so is Israel's regional policy since its foundation based on secret operations and hidden activities to expand or consolidate its regional hegemony.[13]

Undeniably, Arab states also conspired against Israel, but it is Israel that proved to be militarily stronger and thus triggered the suspicion of a hidden hand being behind its power. Since the facts seem to fit the theory, the exaggerated belief in a Greater Israel conspiracy seems not to be as irrational as Pipes assumed.[14] In other words, truth and imagination, fears and reality become frequently mingled in a way that they appear indistinguishable and a matter of attitude rather than fact, or a matter of interpretation of the facts. Consequently, little is gained from the attempt to answer the question whether a certain alleged conspiracy is in fact true or whether it is fiction.

The following reference by Hizbullah's current secretary general, Hassan Nasrallah, to the idea of an alleged secret Zionist plan to establish a Greater Israel illustrates that it is untenable to interpret conspiracy theories in the Middle Eastern context as expressions of a paranoid style. On February 16, 2000, in an interview with Egypt's *al-Ahram*, Nasrallah stated:

> Israel will remain, in our minds and plans, an illegitimate, illegal, aberrant, and cancerous entity, which we therefore cannot recognize. We will instead work with others to combat normalization with it, because fighting normalization will impede its development into a regional superpower. Just as the wars of 1973 and 1982, the impact of the Lebanese resistance and of Israel's failure to occupy Leb-

---

12 Todd Sanders/Harry G. West, "Power Revealed and Concealed in the New World Order", in: West/Sanders (eds.), *Transparency and Conspiracy*, pp. 1–37, p. 25.

13 One may just recall Israel's hidden nuclear program in Dimona, or secret liquidation operations such as that of Abu Jihad, one of the PLO's major planners of terrorist operations, in Tunis in 1988, or the killing of Mahmud al-Mabhuh, a high Hamas official, in Dubai in 2010. For further details cf. Yoel Cohen, *Whistleblowers and the Bomb; Vanunu, Israel and Nuclear Secrecy*, London 2005, pp. 243–245; Said K. Aburish, *Arafat: From Defender to Dictator*, New York 1998, pp. 203–210; and Robert F. Worth, "United Arab Emirates: Police Chief Accuses Israeli Spy Agency of Threats", in: *New York Times*, Oct. 1, 2010, p. 7.

14 For the relationship between facts and conspiracism, cf. Charles Pigden, "Popper Revisited, or, What is Wrong with Conspiracy Theories?", in: *Philosophy of the Social Sciences*, 25/1993, 1, pp. 3–34. Israeli politicians themselves increased these fears by referring from time to time to the idea of a Greater Israel, without specifying what they meant exactly. Equally, the existence of Israeli groups like the *Movement for Greater Israel* provided in the past much ground for Arabs to fear such an imagined entity (cf. Yaacov Bar-Siman-Tov, *Israel and the Peace Process, 1977–1982: In Search of Legitimacy for Peace*, Albany, NY 1994, pp. 74–77, 93–95, 150).

> anon [have together led] to the demise of the military aspect of the Greater Israel plan, combating normalization would lead to the demise of the political, economic, and cultural aspects of the Greater Israel plan.[15]

Such stances have often been interpreted as an expression of Hizbullah's paranoid, diehard ideological enmity toward Israel. Without denying that this enmity and the reference to conspiracism is indeed an integral part of Hizbullah's ideology, such a reductionist interpretation obscures the complex and often very rational motives behind the articulation of conspiracy theories.

The pretext of Nasrallah's conspiracy rhetoric was neither a true fear of Israeli expansionism nor an expression of the party's seemingly irrational belief in an Israeli enemy constantly secretly conspiring against the Arab-Muslim world. Rather, the reference to an ongoing conspiratorial Israeli expansionism by non-military means was based on the very real challenge that Hizbullah as a resistance movement faced with the predicted end of a direct confrontation with Israeli forces in South Lebanon only three months later (May 26, 2000) as well as with the ensuing possibility of a lasting peace settlement between Israel and all Arab states. Although Hizbullah celebrated the Israeli withdrawal as a major victory that boosted the party's reputation beyond sectarian borders, its leaders were aware that such a development could severely jeopardize the *raison d'être* of Hizbullah, its fight against occupation. Thus, the conspiracy theory of an ongoing hidden Israeli economic, political, and cultural expansionism – though deprived of its military dimension – was disseminated to emphasize the necessity of an undiminished resistance toward Israel spearheaded by the Party of God. It was also propagated to curb any rise of popular support for a normalization of the relations with Israel which would have enormously jeopardized Hizbullah's position as a political party within Lebanon and the region. In particular on the popular level, such a rational propagandistic instrumentalization of conspiracy theories could draw on already widespread fears of "Zionist expansion" among large parts of the Arab society which could be easily fomented at any time.[16]

---

15 Nicholas Noe (ed.), *Voice of Hezbollah: The Statements of Sayyed Hassan Nasrallah*, New York 2007, p. 221.

16 A survey among Arabs in 1999 revealed that more than 50 % of the interviewees were worried about Israeli policies (cf. Hilal Khashan, *Arab Attitudes Toward Israel and Peace*, Washington, D.C. 2000, p. 20, table 3). Whereas Arabs with a high socio-economic status were more confident of Israel's intentions to live in peace with the Arabs (26.4 %) and consequently less receptive to conspiracy theories concerning Israeli's expansionist policies, Arabs with low socio-economic status (78.3 %) showed a strong inclination towards a belief in Israel's hunger for land.

2. From Grand to Operational Conspiracy Theories

Hizbullah's affinity to conspiracy theories originated doubtlessly from a blend of the party's anti-western Islamic ideology, its Iranian-style revolutionary Shiite dogma, and its attempt to re-construct past and present according to the party's *raison d'être*, the struggle against Israel.[17] However, we can observe a strong tendency toward a more pragmatic use of conspiracy theories from about the mid-1990s on, when Hizbullah had already been well on the way to integrate itself into the Lebanese political system. Part of this pragmatism was a more pronounced distinction between grand and operational conspiracy theories by Hizbullah officials, depending very much on the audience and occasion. Whereas the former type of conspiracy theory "usually stretch[es] the bounds of plausibility and [...] [is] not regarded by believers as falsifiable",[18] the latter tends to be much more rational and plausible. Operational conspiracy theories are generally seeking

> to prevent or encourage a political outcome promoting or discouraging a significant shift in power among political actors – individuals, groups, or states. They involve a secret combination of political operatives or officials pursuing their goals through illegal or covert means (usually both). They seek to hide such outcomes and the means to achieve them from public view for fear of widespread reproach, defeat in constitutional or democratic arenas, or political (possible criminal) sanction.[19]

---

17 *Shiism* shows historically a certain affinity toward conspiracism. According to the Shiite tradition, all Shiite imams became victims of conspiracies. Equally, the development of the principle of *taqiyya* (disguise) in the wake of Sunni persecution throughout many regions and periods in Islamic history displays a strong tendency to conspiracy thinking within the Shiite community. In combination with the apocalyptical hope for the return of the *mahdi*, who will free the world from injustice, *taqiyya* may be seen as an expression of distrust in an environment that has already so often in history plotted against the Shiite community. Conspiracism has been a determining constant within the modern political Shiite community of Lebanon as well. The disappearance of its leader Imam Musa al-Sadr in August 1978 was widely claimed to be a Libyan plot. For a comprehensive account of *Shiism*, cf. Paul Luft/Colin Turner, *Shi'ism*, London 2008. For an example of how Hizbullah mingled from time to time Shiite history and conspiracy theories, cf. Nasrallah, in: *al-Manar TV*, May 7, 1998. For a translation into English, cf. Noe (ed.), *Voice of Hezbollah*, p. 192: "This struggle is our religion, prayer, fasting, pilgrimage and life. It is our Hussein and Zeinab, and our infants. [...] Like Hussein, we call on the traitors, the agents, and those led astray [...] to repent".

18 Hellinger, "Paranoia, Conspiracy, and Hegemony", p. 210.

19 Hellinger, "Paranoia, Conspiracy, and Hegemony", p. 210. World conspiracies, in contrast, can be defined as consisting of three elements: "a powerful, evil, and clandestine group that aspires to global hegemony; dupes and agents who extend

Though world conspiracy theories, which dominated Hizbullah's rhetoric during the 1980s and early 1990s, remained a valid medium of partisan mobilization and ideological cohesion in particular when addressing a rather homogenous Shiite or anti-western audience, Hizbullah's move to increasingly propagate operational conspiracy theories for political and propagandistic purposes reflects the party's attempts to become a more rational political actor in the changing domestic and regional environment during the 1990s. Such operational conspiracy theories could revolve around very diverse topics and events, such as alleged espionage attempts, plots to assassinate party officials or other Lebanese or Arab public figures, campaigns to bring the image of the party into discredit, or – most famously – the so-called "strife-project" according to which the eruption of sectarian strife in the Arab-Muslim world was incited by an outside power, Israel or the U.S., in order to create division among Arabs.[20]

To illustrate this shift I will briefly exhibit Hizbullah's articulation of grand conspiracy theories during the first decade of its existence. Reflecting the movement's Islamic ideology, the *Open Letter* of 1985 is replete with the articulation of grand conspiracy schemes against the Muslim world allegedly masterminded by the evil colonizers (the West) and its henchmen (Israel, corrupt Muslim regimes, etc.). Already in this early document we encounter the mentioned "strife-project" conspiracy theory, then articulated within the framework of a larger anti-Islamic world conspiracy which placed any Shiite-Sunni discord into the context of the western world's historical struggle and plotting against the Muslim world. The excerpt cited in the Introduction is only one example of such grand conspiracy schemes articulated by Hizbullah during the 1980s. Though less rational than operational conspiracy theories, even such a grand conspiracy rhetoric does not belong to the realm of para-

---

the group's influence around the world so it is on the verge of succeeding; and a valiant but embattled group that urgently needs to help stave off catastrophe" (Pipes, *The Hidden Hand*, pp. 21–22). Pfau makes a similar distinction between these two types of conspiracy theories in the context of the Slave Conspiracy Theory in the U.S. during the mid-nineteenth century (cf. *The Political Syle*). He emphasizes that certain irrational aspects of conspiracy theories were toned down when addressing a broader audience, and thus explains the transition of a conspiracy theory from periphery to mainstream thinking. Several parallels can be drawn between Pfau's observations and Hizbullah's use of conspiracy rhetoric.

20 Hizbullah's "strife-project" conspiracy theory is illustrated in the following statement by Nasrallah made on Apr. 22, 2003, in which he referred to the U.S. invasion of Iraq in March 2003: "Bush's Zionist administration was planning to turn Iraq into a Christian-Muslim war [... and foment] sectarian sedition among Muslims [Sunni and Shia]" (Noe [ed.], *Voice of Hezbollah*, pp. 295–296).

noia but fulfills rather important socio-political functions. For instance, it gives an easily understandable explanation for the Muslim world's decade-long subjugation to foreign rule as well as for the long marginalization of Shiites in Lebanon, and provides a common basis for the numerous and highly fragmented Islamic groups active during the Lebanese civil war.[21] In this sense, grand conspiracy theories helped Hizbullah to muster broad Muslim support and to justify its political goals, the fight against Israel and the West in order to liberate Lebanon as a prelude to the liberation of Palestine and the establishment of an Islamic state in and beyond Lebanon, thus emulating the Iranian model of *wilayat al-faqih* (guardianship of the Islamic jurist).[22]

Unlike operational conspiracy theories, which were dominantly used for political instrumentalization in a later period, grand conspiracy theories were integral parts of Hizbullah's ideological framework strongly influenced by the religio-political teachings of Ayatollah Khomeini.[23] As such, grand conspiracy schemes constituted the benchmark for political action during the movement's early existence and gave its concrete local *jihad* against occupation an international dimension.[24] They were deeply imbedded into the traditional Islamic division of the world into good and evil, the world of war (*Dar al-Harb*) and the desirable world of peace (*Dar al-Islam*) which Hizbullah

---

21 Cf. Matthew Gray, "Explaining Conspiracy Theories in Modern Arab Middle Eastern Political Discourse: Some Problems and Limitations of the Literature", in: *Critique: Critical Middle Eastern Studies*, 17/2008, 2, pp. 55–174, p. 164.

22 *Wilayat al-faqih* is a Shiite religio-political concept that since the revolution of 1979 forms the basis of the constitution of the Islamic Republic of Iran. It stipulates that an Islamic jurist has to serve as the Supreme Leader of the government, whose duty it is to see to it that state institutions and all parts of society strictly abide to the religious laws of the prophet Muhammad and the Shiite imams (cf. Hizbullah, "Section 1: Who are we, and what is our identity?"; and "Section 7: Our objectives in Lebanon", in: Alagha, *Hizbullah's Documents*, pp. 40–41, 43–44). For details on Hizbullah's attitude toward the concept of *wilayat al-faqih*, cf. Saad-Ghorayeb, *Hizbu'llah*, pp. 59–68.

23 Cf. Magnus Ranstorp, *Hizb'allah in Lebanon: The Politics of the Western Hostage Crisis*, Hampshire 1997, p. 34. The Iranian Revolutionary Guard played a pivotal role in bringing Hizbullah into existence and in forming its ideology.

24 The term *jihad* literally means "struggle". It is usually used to describe the religious duty of a Muslim or a Muslim's act of striving in the way of God (*al-jihad fi sabilallah*), respectively. In a political context, *jihad* can also take on the meaning of an armed and violent struggle against the enemies of Islam. For an extended discussion of this concept, cf. David Cook, *Understanding Jihad*, Berkeley, CA 2005.

pursued to establish.[25] This conspiratorial pan-Islamic ideological outlook, in which the Muslim world was under continuous attack by and in continuous struggle with an evil West plotting against Islamic unity, was an integral part of Hizbullah's *raison d'être* during the 1980s and early 1990s.[26] According to one of Hizbullah's major grand conspiracy narratives, which may be called the oppressor-colonizer's conspiracy scheme,[27] it was this evil West that started to engage in conspiratorial activities to pursue its goals after the era of colonialism, the subjugation of the Islamic world. The following excerpt from Hizbullah's 1985 *Open Letter* illustrates this point:

> Through its local collaborators, the US has tried to persuade the people, that those who crushed their arrogance in Lebanon and frustrated their conspiracy against the oppressed (*mustad'afin*) were nothing but a bunch of bigots and terrorists who have nothing to do except detonate liquor stores, gambling venues, instruments of diversion, and the like.[28]

3. The Period of Infitah: Rationalizing and Instrumentalizing Conspiracy Rhetoric

The often repeated simplistic categorization of Hizbullah today as a religious fundamentalist group, which expresses its Manichean division of the world into good and evil through a grand conspiracy rhetoric in the way as illustrated above, needs to be seriously questioned in light of the fact that over the last two decades that followed the end of the civil war in 1990, the Party of God has developed into a quite pragmatically acting political party, which gradually adapted to the political realities in Lebanon. Part of this shift was the reconfiguration of Hizbullah's perception and articulation of its conflict

---

25 Ridwan al-Sayyid discusses this traditional Islamic worldview, which basically stipulates that the ignorant non-Muslim world, which is doomed to remain in continuous warfare, needs to be incorporated into the world of Islam, marked by justice and peace (cf. "*Dāral-ḥarb* and *Dāral-islām*: Traditions and Interpretations", in: Thomas Scheffler [ed.], *Religion between Violence and Reconciliation*, Beirut 2002, pp. 123–133).

26 Stanley Reed, "Why They Hate Us", in: *Nation*, Feb. 14, 1987, p. 168. Also cf. Hizbullah, "Section 22: God is with the unity of the Muslims", in: Alagha, *Hizbullah's Documents*, p. 53. Therein Hizbullah proclaimed: "America, France and their allies must leave Lebanon once and for all […] We are for dealing with evil at its roots and its roots are in America".

27 Alagha, *Hizbullah's Documents*, p. 20.

28 Hizbullah, "Section 2", in: Alagha, *Hizbullah's Documents*, p. 41.

with its enemies – Israel and the U.S.[29] The previously global ideological struggle had become more pragmatic and was increasingly seen in regional and local terms. Accordingly, during the 1990s, Hizbullah officials gradually replaced the articulation of world conspiracies by the use of operational conspiracy theories, which became detached from or were only superficially linked to the party's universal Islamic ideology. Such operational conspiracy theories fulfilled new functions in domestic politics as they were instrumentalized by Hizbullah officials. Rather than guiding the process of political decision-making as grand conspiracy theories did to some extent, operational conspiracy theories were applied as rhetorical means for political mobilization. On the following pages, I will elaborate in more detail on this shift in the usage of operational conspiracy theories and its link to Hizbullah's integration into the domestic political system.

Hizbullah came into being as an Iranian-inspired Shiite movement with an Islamic ideology that was able to weld together the independent Shiite groups in Lebanon. However, already in the *Open Letter*, the Party of God compromised its radical Shiism to some extent by emphasizing the importance of bridging of intra-Muslim differences.[30] Nevertheless, it was only with the end of the civil war that the special conditions in Lebanon, in particular the country's multi-confessional and multi-ethnical society, necessitated a serious deviation from the example of the Iranian ideology. After almost a decade of radicalism, Hizbullah started a process of gradual integration into the Lebanese political system, which included the endorsement of inter-religious reconciliation and cooperation. Born out of the need to thwart political isolation, this still ongoing process, which started with the party's decision to enter the parliament elections in 1992, is commonly referred to as *infitah* (opening).[31]

---

29 Hizbullah's statements are contradictive regarding the question of who of the two enemies is controlling the other. For a discussion of the background of the Arab world's enmity toward both Israel and the U.S., cf. Ussama Makdisi, "'Anti-Americanism' in the Arab World: An Interpretation of a Brief History", in: *Journal of American History*, 89/2002, 2, pp. 552–556.

30 To assuage rising Sunni-Shiite animosities became an urgent matter with the increase in Sunni extremist groups in Lebanon in the last years, in particular the *salafists*, who were inciting Muslims to fight Shiites by accusing them of *takfir*, i.e. charging somebody with being an apostate. For an account of recent *salafist* activities in Lebanon, cf. *Lebanese Salafism; Between Global Jihad and Syrian Manipulation*, 2008, http://www.nowlebanon.com/Library/Files/EnglishDocumentation/Other%20Documents/salafist%20english1.pdf (accessed Sept. 24, 2011).

31 The elections sent a clear signal that Hizbullah was on the way to change its radical course and attempting instead to enhance its legitimacy as a mainstream party

The Party of God's conspiracy rhetoric followed this political shift and was adapted to the post-civil war situation in Lebanon. Hizbullah more and more tried to win political and popular support not just by its traditional Shiite clientele, because the party realized that the political rationality of a confessional democracy necessitated the cooperation of candidates of different faiths to win the elections. By toning down its Islamic fundamentalist ideology and stressing instead its patriotic resistance against Israeli occupation, Hizbullah started to display a strong ideological ambiguity, "a technique that would [...] be applied whenever the public or its political representatives were the intended recipients of messages conveyed by the Party of God".[32] Into this context of ambiguity we also have to place the articulation of the two mentioned forms of conspiracy theories. While the familiar Iranian revolutionary-style grand conspiracy rhetoric, with all its implicit socio-political functions, was still used when a homogenous Shiite or Muslim audience was addressed,[33] operational conspiracy theories were articulated by Hizbullah officials when, as happened more and more, addressing a multi-confessional audience, whether on the political or popular level. Concretely, this propagation of operational conspiracy theories from the early 1990s on shows a significant alteration regarding the argumentation and underlying purpose of Hizbullah's conspiracy rhetoric.

On a very broad level, operational conspiracy theories has become one of the party's tools to implement its *infitah* policy, aiming at transforming Hizbullah from an Iranian-inspired Shiite fundamentalist elite militia, as which it came into existence during the early 1980s, to, on the one hand, a distinctly Lebanese, more popular political party, integrated in and reconciled with the Lebanese state, and, on the other one, to a broader and supra-confessional, non-sectarian resistance movement with a more pragmatic political program

---

with a resistance wing. For a discussion of Hizbullah's motivation to participate in the parliament elections in the years 1992, 1996, and 2000, cf. Shiho Yasunobu Sakai, *Political Adaptation of Hezbollah*, Beirut 2005, pp. 74–97.

32 Harik, *Hezbollah*, p. 66.

33 For example, in the program of Hizbullah's satellite broadcast channel *al-Manar*, which addresses dominantly the party's faithful Shiite partisans and other Muslim supporters, grand conspiracy theories veiled in Islamic terminology remained prominent. Avi Jorisch's *Beacon of Hatred: Inside Hizballah's al-Manar Television* (Washington, D.C. 2004) does not raise the question of purpose behind the dissemination of such seemingly "irrational" conspiracy statements. Furthermore, the author remains unaware of the fact that when addressing more diversified audiences Hizbullah applied an altered conspiracy rhetoric, toning down in particular Islamic fundamentalist ideas.

and outlook.[34] Conspiracy theories have been articulated and applied in particular to legitimate Hizbullah's very existence as an armed resistance movement within the Lebanese political system and to boost the support for its cause. At times, the party went so far as to imply that the refusal to support the resistance equaled siding with the conspirators. Furthermore, conspiracy theories aimed at dealing a blow to the international stigmatization of Hizbullah as an extremist and fanatic Shiite militia, which was feared to have negative repercussions on the party's domestic status. For this purpose, the allegations of terrorism were constantly labeled as being a part of a U.S.-Zionist conspiracy scheme intended to distort Hizbullah's "true" face – a respected Lebanese resistance movement with a broad multi-sectarian basis – and to isolate the party domestically, regionally, and internationally.

Hizbullah's conspiracy rhetoric represented an outreach to all Lebanese political parties and religious communities to support the resistance in its struggle against the alleged conspirators. Hizbullah officials hoped that this would contribute to reduce *religious* animosities of non-Shiite political actors toward Hizbullah's political projects as well as convince these groups of Hizbullah's *political* legitimacy as a national resistance movement. At the same time, they made remarkable concessions to, if not completely abandoned, one of the party's most uncompromising political objectives: the establishment of an Islamic state in Lebanon imitating the Iranian model of *wilayat al-faqih*. In other words, conspiracy rhetoric was employed as a propagandistic and political medium to enhance Hizbullah's image as a promoter of sectarian reconciliation and domestic political cohesion.[35]

The often highlighted negative dimension of conspiracy rhetoric, the admittedly existing profound hatred of an outside enemy – in the case of Hizbullah, the U.S. and Israel –, often overshadows the "positive" effects this political and propagandistic medium has for those applying it. It is another remarkable fact that conspiracy theories have been very rarely, if at all,

---

[34] Harik, *Hezbollah*, p. 73. This shift in policy was initiated by Hezbollah's second General Secretary al-Sayyid Abbas al-Mussawi (1989–1992), whose introduction of a politically inclusive and conciliatory discourse stood in sharp contrast to the party's first General Secretary Shaykh Subhi al-Tufayli's (1985–1989) politically exclusive and intolerant tone. Hassan Nasrallah, who succeeded al-Mussawi after his assassination by Israel in 1992, followed the new course and accentuated the themes of Christian-Muslim reconciliation and co-existence in a politically pluralist society, though remaining unabatedly opposed to Israel and the U.S. policy in the Middle East.

[35] This duality of inclusion (all those who are targeted by a conspiracy) and exclusion (the conspirators) is, in fact, inherent in any conspiracy theory.

used by Hizbullah in the recent past to escalate domestic political tensions, even though conspiracy theories could be just as easily used for this purpose as for the preservation of domestic peace, in particular in such a fragile political environment as Lebanon.

The need for upholding the image of a dangerous, continuously conspiring outside enemy became finally of imminent importance for Hizbullah when, as already mentioned above, in May 2000 the Israeli army withdrew from Southern Lebanese territory. Hizbullah was very concerned about the possible political consequences which the end of the occupation and the disappearance of its *raison d'être* might have for the party's status as a resistance movement. Thus, the Party of God was very quick to emphasize its dedication to the liberation of Palestine and to frequently reiterate its conviction that Israel and the U.S. had not given up their evil schemes for Lebanon but had only changed tactics from open confrontation to hidden conspiratorial activities.[36]

Within this problematic mechanism, which required Hizbullah to continue its struggle against its enemies while simultaneously preventing the end of this confrontation (that is, to avoid to reach victory or be defeated), conspiracy theories were a crucial instrument to maintain the political *status quo* which guaranteed the Party of God's existence and its powerful position within the Lebanese political system. Conspiracy rhetoric was used to keep the danger of the enemy alive, in particular in times of relaxation of political and military tensions, as well as to avoid any direct physical confrontation with the enemy, and to avert the eventual danger of defeat in light of Israel's dominating military capability.[37]

That this strategy was a tightrope walk is illustrated by the outbreak of the July War 2006, when, for one or another reason, Hizbullah considered it to be necessary to prove its military power or its determination to fight Israel through an abduction attempt on the Israeli-Lebanese border. According to Nasrallah, however, there is no reason to doubt that if he had known that this operation would have led to an all-out war with Israel it would have been aborted.[38]

---

36 Cf. Nasrallah's interview with the Kuwaiti newspaper *al-Ra'y al-'Amm* on Nov. 16, 2001. For a translation into English, cf. Noe (ed.), *The Voice of Hezbollah*, pp. 256–266.

37 One may also consider Hizbullah's amassment of weaponry since July 2006 as an admittedly dangerous strategy to keep its struggle alive and extend its position as the only capable power in Lebanon to defend the country in the event of an Israeli attack.

38 Cf. Nasrallah's interview with *New TV* on Aug. 27, 2006. For a translation into English, cf. Noe (ed.), *Voice of Hezbollah*, p. 394.

4. Politics and Ideology: Hizbullah's Conspiracy Rhetoric during the Last Decade, 2000–2010

The following examples shall illustrate how Hizbullah pursued its conspiracy rhetoric strategy over the last decade and how this instrumentalization was guided by the changing political and propagandistic challenges the party was facing rather than by any static ideological considerations.

When in the aftermath of the July War Hizbullah came under domestic pressure due to the vast destruction which this confrontation had brought upon Lebanon, Hassan Nasrallah countered that the U.S. administration and Israel's leadership had decided for a war on Lebanon already months before Hizbullah's operation. He also claimed that the current campaign against Hizbullah's privilege of keeping weapons was another subtle Israeli conspiracy, initiated by the July War, which attempted to weaken the party's support among the Lebanese population and to implement Israel's rule over Lebanon "within the framework of the New Middle East".[39] Thus, once more, Hizbullah used conspiracy rhetoric to head off domestic pressure from the party, which makes it necessary to revise the common explanation of the party's articulation of conspiracy theories as expressions of an irreconcilable irrational and ideological hate and paranoia toward an allegedly continuously conspiring Israeli aggressor. The uncovering of dozens of Israeli spies in Lebanon over the last years contributed enormously to the credibility of Hizbullah's conspiracy rhetoric, even among some of its political opponents.[40]

Another occasion on which Hizbullah conveniently applied its conspiracy rhetoric strategy to ease political pressure was the looming indictment of several high-ranking Hizbullah members by the Special Tribunal for Lebanon (STL) for the assassination of former Sunni prime-minister Rafiq Ha-

---

39 Noe (ed.), *Voice of Hezbollah*, p. 401. Some hints exist that Nasrallah's claim might have been indeed true (cf. Seymour Hersh, "Watching Lebanon", in: *New Yorker*, Aug. 21, 2006, http://www.newyorker.com/fact/content/articles/060821fa_fact [accessed Sept. 24, 2011]; and *PM 'says Israel pre-planned war'*, in: *BBC News*, Mar. 8, 2007, http://news.bbc.co.uk/go/pr/fr/-/2/hi/middle_east/6431637.stm [accessed Sept. 24, 2011]).

40 After the spectacular shift from an outspoken critique of Hizbullah and Syria to an open ally of the Party of God, the leader of the Druze community in Lebanon, Walid Jumblat, endorsed in an interview with *al-Safir* on Sept. 2, 2010 Hizbullah's point of view that there was an U.S.-Israeli plan at work to destabilize the region and in particular Lebanon. This example illustrates how the re-iteration of Hizbullah's conspiracy rhetoric became a marker of political alliance with the Party of God. For an English summary of Jumblat's interview, cf. "Lebanese press round-up", in: *NOW Lebanon*, Sept. 2, 2010, http://www.nowlebanon.com/NewsArchiveDetails.aspx?ID=198474 (accessed Sept. 24, 2011).

riri on February 14, 2005.[41] Initially, Syria was regarded as the perpetrator, leading to the withdrawal of the Syrian army from Lebanese soil only weeks after Hariri's death. However, rumors spread and were finally confirmed by the STL indictment in mid-2011 that four high-ranking Hizbullah cadres had had a leading role in the assassination of Hariri.[42]

When in mid-2009 the first hints of Hizbullah's involvement in the assassination reached the public, the Party of God was very aware that an indictment of high-ranking Hizbullah members might bring the party into a precarious situation. Alerted by the possible harm the STL might cause to Hizbullah's carefully established status as a supra-sectarian Lebanese resistance party, Hizbullah officials felt urged to prevent or at least to diminish the expected negative repercussions of such an event. Since the goal was in particular to avoid the risk of any lasting domestic isolation, while simultaneously preventing the eruption of Sunni-Shiite violence in the event of an indictment, the Party of God needed to choose a non-violent strategy to cope with this matter. Thus, once more, an elaborated conspiracy theory was developed, according to which Hizbullah was the victim, not the perpetrator.[43]

In order to turn the tide in Hizbullah's favor, the party's all-out media campaign to discredit the possible outcome of the STL investigation reached its first climax between July and August 2010. Hassan Nasrallah delivered a number of speeches in which he presented a conspiratorial counter-narrative to exculpate the Party of God from the charges made against it. A brief excerpt of Nasrallah's three-hour-long speech on August 9, 2010 shall illustrate the core narrative of this conspiracy theory:

---

41 The Lebanese government, in consensus with all Lebanese political parties, requested on Dec. 13, 2005 the United Nations to establish a tribunal of an international character, the Special Tribunal for Lebanon, to try all those who were allegedly responsible for the assassination of Hariri. For more information and key documents cf. *Special Tribunal for Lebanon*, 2010–2012, http://www.stl-tsl.org/ (accessed Sept. 24, 2011).

42 Already two months after the STL commenced its work on Mar. 1, 2009, an article in the international edition of the German magazine *Spiegel* accused Hizbullah of having being responsible for Hariri's assassination by referring to sources close to the Special Tribunal (cf. Erich Follath, "New Evidence Points to Hezbollah in Hariri Murder", in: *Spiegel Online*, May 23, 2009, http://www.spiegel.de/international/world/0,1518,626412,00.html [accessed Sept. 24, 2011]).

43 It may appear paradoxical that Hizbullah on the one hand fervently tried to prevent the eruption of inter-sectarian strife while – if the indictment proves to be true – the party was provoking it on the other. However, this fits perfectly into the party's strategy to increase its political influence, also with the threat and use of violence, while simultaneously appearing as a fervent defender of all Lebanese beyond sectarian borders.

> The "Israeli" enemy has the capacity and the opportunity to carry out such a sophisticated assassination operation [referring of course to the assassination of Hariri]. Today it is being revealed that the enemy has many collaborators in various specializations. That means that in any field they want, there are collaborators in Lebanon. This is what has been revealed so far, and what is not revealed yet is even greater. […] The assassination operation came in the framework of a political scheme which started in 2000 and which is related to the whole region: Lebanon, Syria and Palestine were but chains in this great political scheme which led to the invasion of countries (Iraq and Afghanistan) and led to wars and also led to assassination operations as important as the assassination of PM Hariri. […] The "Israeli" enemy is interested in benefiting from any military or security or internal chance to exterminate the resistance or to disarm it at least.[44]

In short, Nasrallah's basic message was that Hariri had been assassinated by Israel under the pretext of pressuring the Lebanese government to establish the STL in order to harm the resistance by accusing it of being responsible for Hariri's death. Conveniently drawing on the ongoing uncovering of Israeli spies and spying devices by the Lebanese security apparatus and their infiltration of the Lebanese telecommunication sector, Nasrallah constructed a more or less convincing narrative aimed to solve the serious challenge to the party's domestic integrity. Though Hizbullah's conspiracy campaign did not succeed in bringing about the dissolution of the STL, it has substantially discredited the STL among large parts of the Lebanese population and among political leaders. It has even led most political camps to come to an agreement on how to handle a possible indictment of Hizbullah members, namely to consider them as individuals not acting on behalf of the Party of God.[45]

5. Conclusion

Although to expose conspiracism as a pragmatic propagandistic instrument for political ends does not provide an exhaustive explanation for this very complex phenomenon in the Middle Eastern context, it illustrates that we urgently need to revise the still prevalent interpretation of conspiracy rhet-

---

44 "Full Text of Hizbullah SG Press Conference on Evidence of Former PM Hariri Assassination", *Islamic Resistance in Lebanon*, 2010, http://www.english.moqawama.org/essaydetailsf.php?eid=11988&fid=11 (accessed Sept. 24, 2011).

45 For example, former Labor Minister Boutros Harb warned that disagreements among Lebanese political figures might invite successful conspiracies against Lebanon (cf. "Harb: Conspiracies Against Lebanon Will Succeed if there are Lebanese Disagreements", in: *NOW Lebanon*, Aug. 7, 2010, http://www.nowlebanon.com/NewsArchiveDetails.aspx?ID=192340 [accessed Sept. 24, 2011]).

oric as a paranoid style, in particular if articulated by political actors. As I have illustrated, in the case of Hizbullah, conspiracy theories, as simple and easily understandable explanations for a complex reality, became an important means to translate the party's political and ideological struggle into a currency utile for a consolidation of the party's domestic position.

Furthermore, Hizbullah's conspiracy rhetoric has proven to be closely linked to the Party of God's dual status as a political party on the one hand and as a militia and resistance movement on the other, which constantly resulted in dilemmas in daily political life. Whenever political developments occurred which challenged the party and forced it to take a clear stance regarding its identity, Hizbullah used conspiracy theories to prevent any change in its *status quo*. Concretely, the party claimed that conspiracies were at work either when its special status as a militant resistance movement fighting against Israel was questioned, or when sometimes violent rifts between Hizbullah and other Lebanese groups and parties occurred which endangered the Party of God's broader public support as a distinct Lebanese political party. In other words, the party has repeatedly applied conspiracy rhetoric to mend its dual identity.

A final word may be suited regarding scope and limitations of the instrumentalization of operational conspiracy theories by Hizbullah. Whereas Hizbullah's application of conspiracy rhetoric serves dominantly short-range purposes, that is, a specific conspiracy theory is articulated to reach a quick propagandistic result or to directly influence decision-makers concerning a certain matter, it also serves, though less reliable and controllable in outcome, long-run purposes. By articulating a specific conspiracy scheme, such as the "strife-project" conspiracy theory,[46] the party seems to try as well to shape the broader public discourse on political matters in Hizbullah's favor. Furthermore, conspiracy rhetoric, as one of Hizbullah's modern political techniques to consolidate and expand its reach in many domains of national life, suiting the psychological needs of the varying constituencies

---

46 The frequency of mentioning this so-called "strife-project conspiracy" is staggering. This statement which Sheikh Nabil Qaouk, deputy head of Hizbullah's Executive Council, made only days after the formation of a Hizbullah-led Lebanese cabinet in early July 2011, is exemplary for this conspiracy theory scheme: "We are today in a new stage able to save Lebanon from the sectarian project and the U.S.-Israeli conspiracy which comes at the expense of Lebanon's unity" (cf. "Resistance is stronger, more popular: Hezbollah", in: *Daily Star*, July 10, 2011, http://www.dailystar.com.lb/News/Politics/2011/Jul-10/Resistance-is-stronger-more-popular-Hezbollah.ashx?searchText=conspiracy#ixzz1V50gFjZe [accessed Sept. 24, 2011]).

Hizbullah wished to mobilize, is basically a broadly applicable tool.[47] Nevertheless, as several examples in the past have shown, conspiracy rhetoric was obviously only of limited use when political fronts were hardened and conspiracy theories expected to fall on deaf ears. This suggests that the success of this propagandistic tool depends to a large extent on the broader dynamics of political bargain and compromise. Being part of these dynamics, the articulation of conspiracy theories may be seen as a kind of political offer made to other political actors in order to solve a crisis or as a last warning before escalating the situation by violent means should the conspiracy theory not be endorsed. Of course, much more research is still needed to comprehend the political instrumentalization of conspiracy theories and to estimate their real impact on political decision-making. However, several examples related to Hizbullah show that conspiracy rhetoric fails to achieve the anticipated results in particular if the addressed political actors consider too high the political costs of believing in a certain conspiracy theory, or if conspiracy rhetoric does not go hand in hand with other means to manipulate the process of political decision-making.

[47] Cf. Harik, *Hezbollah*, p. 4.

III. The Promises of Conspiracy Theory

Sebastian M. Herrmann (Leipzig)

Narrating the 'Crisis of Representation': The Cultural Work of Conspiracy in Larry Beinhart's Novels on the Bush Presidencies

1. 'Epistemic Panic' and the U.S. Presidency

U.S. fiction author Larry Beinhart has written one novel for each of the two Bush presidencies, *American Hero* (1993) and *The Librarian* (2004).[1] Both books, among many other similarities, imagine conspiracies aimed at deceiving the American public and at securing their respective incumbents' reelections. In the following, I will read these two novels for how they narrativize broader concerns about 'knowability' by imagining large-scale deceptions on behalf of the U.S. president. The differences between these two novels, I will argue, are indicative both of the different cultural moments they were written in and written for and of a shift in the model they draw on to narrate deception.

In doing so, my reading will take two important cues from Timothy Melley's *Empire of Conspiracy*. Melley reads conspiracy theories as "crude theories [...] – crude not, because they are wholly mistaken", but because they imagine "a mysterious and magical process".[2] Crude theories, in this sense, are forms of popular theorizing that mark the broader circulation of discussions usually associated with expert discourses (psychology, philosophy, sociology, etc).[3] Indeed, my primary texts are deeply indebted to such expert discourses: in explaining the conspiracies and deceptions they narrate, they gesture towards concepts taken from, among others, psychology, political

---

1 Cf. Larry Beinhart, *American Hero*, New York 1994; *The Librarian*, New York 2004. *American Hero* inspired the successful 1997 feature film *Wag the Dog*.

2 Timothy Melley, *Empire of Conspiracy: The Culture of Paranoia in Postwar America*, Ithaca, NY 2000, p. 5.

3 Melley's take here, of course, mirrors other readings of conspiracy theory as forms of 'crude' theorizing, such as, for example, Fredric Jameson's famous notion of a "poor person's cognitive mapping" ("Cognitive Mapping", in: Cary Nelson/Lawrence Grossberg (eds.), *Marxism and the Interpretation of Culture*, Urbana 1988, pp. 347–57, p. 356). Melley's approach, however, seems particularly invested in examining how philosophical discourses impact the parameters of such theorizing, an operation crucial to my interests in this paper.

science, media studies, and semiotics. In effect, they participate in and contribute to popularized forms of expert discourse, most prominently of postmodern epistemological debate.

Melley, secondly, sees "crude" theorizing not as triggered by specific historic events (Watergate, the Kennedy assassination/s, the Gulf of Tonkin, etc.), but, inversely, reads such specific historic events – in the (hi)stories they generate – as indicative of how a culture negotiates more abstract and more fundamental crises. Using a term by Jane Tompkins, one could say that he is interested in the "cultural work" these theories do. Along these lines, I read Beinhart's two novels not as triggered by specific historic events (the two wars in Iraq, the first of which was widely perceived as 'unreal', the second of which was declared for 'unreal' reasons), but as indicative of an 'epistemic panic', a widespread cultural anxiety about the limitations of knowledge and the elusiveness of the 'real' as a fundamental social category, a popular form of epistemological debate, of which the public interest in the wars and their presumed 'unrealness' is one indication.

This reading of Beinhart's two novels for 'epistemic panic' is part of a larger project that investigates how and in how far American culture uses the U.S. presidency as a "focal point of [...] cultural angst"[4] to express and work through a more fundamental, broadly perceived "crisis of representation" usually associated with postmodernism.[5] In such a reading, politics, and the U.S. presidency in particular, emerge as privileged sites for expressing and discussing a more general distrust in signification and in the limits of representing 'reality' altogether. Indeed, political scientist Diane Rubenstein has noted how the "category of the 'real' and its putative erasure or endangerment [...] has increasingly become an object of concern in our political culture today",[6] and I read this worry, whether it is circulated in fiction or in non-fiction 'texts', as an incarnation of this broadening discourse on a presumed significatory crisis. This "concern", then, can be traced to the late 1960s at least, when, in his *The Selling of the President 1968*, Joe McGinniss used Daniel Boorstin's *The Image*, along with Marshall McLuhan's writings and an existing anti-advertising discourse, to tie together the presumed "unreality"[7]

---

4 Trevor Parry-Giles/Sean J. Parry-Giles, *The Prime-Time Presidency: The West Wing and U.S. Nationalism*, Urbana 2006, p. 2.

5 Frederic Jameson, "Foreword", in: *The Postmodern Condition: A Report on Knowledge*, Geoff Bennington/Brian Massumi (trans.), Minneapolis 1984.

6 Diane Rubenstein, *This Is Not a President: Sense, Nonsense, and the American Political Imaginary*, New York 2008, p. 11.

7 Daniel J. Boorstin, *The Image: A Guide to Pseudo-Events in America*, New York 1992, p. 3.

of the president with a more fundamental form of "iconoclast" (or: iconophobic) cultural critique.[8] Iconoclasm, the critique of the presumed power of images to obscure or obliterate 'substance', in fact, remains a dominant paradigm in discussing the alleged demise of the 'real'. It has, however, been amended by other paradigms since. For instance, the George W. Bush presidency, that, surprisingly, embraced epistemic uncertainty rhetorically (think of Donald Rumsfeld's famous "known unknowns"),[9] was marked by a distinct public concern for 'facts' and 'truth' as categories of the 'real'. Here, most clearly, a new paradigm structured public discussions: Stephen Colbert's "truthiness",[10] Ron Suskind's fear for the "reality-based community",[11] and Michael Moore's Academy Awards speech on a "fictitious president"[12] give ample evidence both of the ongoing concern for the 'real' in American politics and of a shift towards truth, fact, and narrative, rather than image and substance, as key terms within this discourse. Bringing together Rubenstein's observation on politics as one site in which a culture obsesses about the "the real as a semiotic category"[13] and Melley's take on conspiracy theory as crude theorizing will allow me to read Beinhart's novels for how they indicate shifts in the way (a part of) the American public utilizes the signifiers of politics (and the U.S. presidency) to discuss a perceived postmodern crisis of signification.

---

[8] Jon Simons, "Popular Culture and Mediated Politics: Intellectuals, Elites and Democracy", in: John Corner/Dick Pels (eds.), *Media and the Restyling of Politics: Consumerism, Celebrity and Cynicism*, London 2003, pp. 99–116. Cf. also W.J.T. Mitchell, *Iconology: Image, Text, Ideology,* Chicago 1987. For a reading of this particular dynamic in McGinniss's book, cf. Sebastian Herrmann, "Something New and Undefined", in: Herrmann et al. (eds.), *Participating Audiences, Imagined Public Spheres,* Leipzig 2012, pp. 131–156.

[9] Donald Rumsfeld, *DoD News Briefing – Secretary Rumsfeld and Gen. Myers, Tuesday, Feb. 12, 2002 – 11:31 a.m. EST,* http://www.defenselink.mil/transcripts/2002/t02122002_t212sdv2.html (accessed Apr. 9, 2012). Also cf. Hillary Profita, "Known Knowns, Known Unknowns and Unknown Unknowns: A Retrospective", in: *CBS News,* Nov. 9, 2006, http://www.cbsnews.com/8301-500486_162-2165872-500486.html (accessed Apr. 9, 2012).

[10] The term was coined by comedian Stephen Colbert in 2005. For an academic discussion of the concept cf. e.g. Jeffrey P. Jones, "Believable Fictions: Redactional Culture and the Will to Truthiness", in: Barbie Zelizer (ed.), *The Changing Faces of Journalism: Tabloidization, Technology and Truthiness,* New York 2009, pp. 127–143.

[11] Ron Suskind, "Without a Doubt", in: *New York Times Magazine,* Oct. 17, 2004, p. 44.

[12] "Moore Fires Oscar Anti-War Salvo", in: *BBC News,* Mar. 24 2003, http://news.bbc.co.uk/2/hi/entertainment/2879857.stm (accessed Apr. 9, 2012).

[13] Rubenstein, *This Is Not a President,* p. 11.

2. Heroes and Librarians: Larry Beinhart's Two Novels on the Bush Presidencies

Larry Beinhart's novel featuring George Herbert Walker Bush, *American Hero*, published in 1993, imagines that the Gulf War did not take place as a regular war triggered by actual hostilities,[14] but as a media event organized and coordinated by a Hollywood producer, with the fighting soldiers of both sides working (and dying) as extras in a play they themselves do not understand.[15] In the novel, fictional Hollywood director John Lincoln Beagle is hired to produce the fake war for President Bush. After he cancels a film project with movie star Magdalena Lazlo to focus on the war, she hires private investigator Joe Broz to find out the reasons for the cancellation. Hard-boiled Broz moves in with Lazlo as her chauffeur/bodyguard to perform background investigation. Finding out that Lazlo's house has been bugged by Broz's regular employer, security company U.Sec., the two simulate a love affair to confuse their observers. After considerable spying and killing, Lazlo and Broz begin to understand the background situation. Together with a few ex-Marine friends, Broz manages to steal a memo from Beagle outlining the project. When he returns, U.Sec. has kidnapped Lazlo, and Broz ends up trading her for the memo. All parties agree to a truce, but at a film gig in Mexico, U.Sec. moves unilaterally, killing Lazlo and a stranger they mistake for Broz, leaving Broz (heart-)broken. He turns to drinking and eventually knocks at the fictional author's door to tell his story.[16]

Beinhart's second fictional exploration of a Bush presidency, the 2004 *The Librarian*, features a fictional George W. Bush stand-in by the name of Augustus W. Scott. Here, the rich, old real estate tycoon Alan Carston Stowe collaborates with former Marine Jack Morgan, the Rove-Cheney-mashup Secretary of State Hoagland, and a Supreme Court Justice to manufacture Scott's second term in the (2000/2004ish) presidential election. Expecting a close election, the conspirators plan to use Stowe's economic power to blackmail members of the electoral college of crucial swing states to vote for Scott even if their state should go to Democratic contender Anne Lynn

---

14 Cf., of course, Jean Baudrillard's famous essay of this title, subsequently published as a book, together with his two other essays on the topic (*The Gulf War Did Not Take Place*, Paul Patton (trans.), Bloomington 1995). Note, however, that in Beinhart's novel the war *did* take place as a real, albeit staged, event jointly organized by Iraq and the U.S.

15 Iraq is not mentioned in the body of the book but heavily referenced in the extradiegetic parts of it.

16 This final turn is absent from the German 1994 Kiepenheuer und Witsch edition. The missing chapters are present in my 1994 Ballantine edition.

Murphy. A series of fake terror attacks, attributed to Islamic fundamentalists presumably threatening more attacks if the U.S. were to elect a woman, is meant to provide cover for the electors' purported change of mind. The novel's protagonist and first-person narrator, librarian David Goldberg, is drawn into this plot by chance. Intent on gaining immor(t)al post-mortem fame as the man who rigged the election, Stowe needs a professional librarian to archive his files and to thus make sure that his library will reveal his deeds to later generations of researchers. His co-conspirators naturally are worried by this plan. They also fear that David, unsuspectingly working Stowe's library, might actually be a spy hired by Murphy. When they move to eliminate David, he (faultily) believes that his only chance for survival is to find out what secret he could have discovered. He is helped by his former co-librarians, as well as by Jack's beautiful wife Niobe who turns out to be Murphy's spy and with whom David falls in love. In a final showdown in Stowe's library during which Niobe is fatally shot, the librarian's team finds the relevant documents and hands them over to the police, leaving open what impact they will have on the election.

Several continuities between the two books suggest reading *The Librarian* as an attempt to retell (and update) the same basic idea as *American Hero.* To name but a few similarities, both novels are about a large-scale deception meant to alter a presidential election in favor of the sitting (Republican, Bush-like) presidents. Both identify the unreliability of reality as the precondition for the conspirators' success. Both hold the distinct appeal of semi-fictional writing, making unmistakable gestures to their readers' reality while enjoying all the liberties that fiction grants.[17] Both begin with an act of conspiracy to then switch over to an unsuspecting hero, both then interweave first-person chapters narrated by this hero and third-person narration of the

---

17 Reviewing *The Librarian* along with a number of other semi-fictional pieces, Caryn James has described this position: "Like many other current political fictions, these take a skewed approach to realities too fraught to face head-on" ("Laughing Instead of Screaming", in: *The New York Times*, Sept. 24, 2004, http://www.nytimes.com/2004/09/24/books/24JAME.html [accessed Apr. 9, 2012]). This semi-fictional appeal, at the same time, is overdetermined by the lineage of "political fiction" (Hans J. Kleinsteuber, "Tom Wolfe und der Mythos vom New Journalism", in: Joan Kristin Bleicher/Bernhard Pörksen (eds.), *Grenzgänger: Formen des New Journalism*, Wiesbaden 2004, p. 211) and the "political scenario novel" (J. E. Vacha, "It Could Happen Here: The Rise of the Political Scenario Novel", in: *American Quarterly*, 29/1977, 2, pp. 194–206), as well as by the inherent "melding of fact and fiction" of the "conspiracy narrative" (Mark Fenster, *Conspiracy Theories: Secrecy and Power in American Culture*, Minneapolis 2008, p. 120).

evildoers' plotting. In both, the first-person narration is focalized through the male main character. In both, the plot is advanced by this character's love affair with a woman whose power lies in her ability of "making weak men strong and strong men weak",[18] and in both books, the main plot ends after this woman is killed while the narrator is spared, left to tell the story.

At the same time, the two books are remarkably different, and their differences are indicative of the distinct cultural moments they were written at (and for). Most practically, *The Librarian* faces an upcoming presidential election and, other than *American Hero*, does not enjoy the safety of the retrospective. It also responds to a presidency that, to many contemporaries, was much more radical and aggressively conservative than the earlier Bush, Sr. term. Where *American Hero* could thus indulge in playful what-if fantasies, the shivers of an imagined fake war that would almost have led to a second term by George Bush, Sr., *The Librarian* confronts an ongoing political situation and the very concrete, very pressing danger of a second George W. Bush term. On all levels, I argue, the book is shaped by the resulting feeling of crisis on behalf of its intended readership, and it is almost impossible not to read it as an attempt to engage its immediate political environment. This political environment, beginning with the Florida election results and peaking in the decision to attack Iraq under unsubstantiated claims of alleged weapons of mass destruction, was marked by a particularly bitter distrust between political camps, and the aftermath of the terrorist attacks of 9/11, with conspiracy theories beginning to gain a broader audience around the time of the novel's publication,[19] might have further discouraged a more playful approach to the conventions of the conspiracy narrative. Other differences between the two novels, however, cannot simply be attributed to the sense of panic felt by progressive intellectuals around the 2004 election or the 'paranoid' climate of the second Bush presidency. These differences are indicative of a shift in the philosophical model used to think about the "putative erasure or endangerment" of the 'real',[20] which, in the 2000s, came to be conceptualized less as a consequence of the image's power to hide or

---

18 Beinhart, *American Hero*, p. 10.

19 Cf. Peter Knight's assessment that "[b]y 2004 conspiracy theories had begun to gain ground in the United States [...] with the mainstream media finally taking note of the increasing popularity of the theories". Knight specifically names Michael Moore's *Fahrenheit 9/11* and several "sophisticated homemade videos" as particularly influential in spreading these theories ("Outrageous Conspiracy Theories: Popular and Official Responses to 9/11 in Germany and the United States", in: *New German Critique*, 35/2008, pp. 165–193, pp. 169–170).

20 Rubenstein, *This Is not a President*, p. 11.

eclipse the 'real' than as an indicator of the power of narratives and narrative framings to create realities.

All these factors, I argue, come together in the way that *The Librarian* opts out of the more "experimental" mode of its predecessor and instead tells a more "classical conspiracy narrative".[21] In the following, I will read the two novels' narrative setup, the setting and atmosphere they utilize to tell their story, and the epistemic frameworks they evoke in narrating the threats to the 'real' to trace differences between these two cultural moments and the kinds of narratives they have invited.

3. Flirting with Disaster: *American Hero*'s Textual Performance and the End of Reality

American Hero sports a highly complex narrative setup. Its core narrative is framed and amended by different pseudo-paratextual additions, texts that pretend to stand outside of the narrative proper while being openly written for effect and as part of the narration. Between the acknowledgments and title page, a very short preface insists that the novel was "a work of fiction" and consisted of "figments of the author's imagination except where supported by public record". It ends asserting that "[t]here are those who feel that fact and fiction are significantly less distinguishable than they used to seem to be" and quotes from an ABC show on 'Operation Desert Storm' that tells viewers that "no distinction is made among these elements". Remarkably, it does not explain how these – multiply couched – lines relate to the novel's own storytelling project. On its other end the novel is terminated by a twelve-page treatise on "Conspiracy", including a list of thirty-nine questions aimed at destabilizing the credibility of the official story of the 1991 Gulf War. This already complex diegetic setup is further complicated by the embedding of the main plot in a frame narrative in which the novel's protagonist relates the story to a fictional version of Larry Beinhart. Yet further complication comes in the form of the more than one-hundred footnotes that serve different (and conflicting) functions, at times pointing at extradiegetic texts (such as newspaper reports on Bush, Sr.), at times cross-referencing within the text, and at times commenting on the writing process of the novel. While these textual strategies, at first glance, seem to evoke (pseudo-)documentary realism, they turn out to be textual games the novel self-consciously indulges in. These games do not so much authenticate the narrative as truthful as they serve to destabilize the notion of authentic, truthful narration altogether.

---

21 Fenster, *Conspiracy Theories*, p. 153.

Agendas similarly askew are at work in the novel's setting and atmosphere. To narrate the power of media-generated images over reality, *American Hero* chooses a canonical setting, California, and taps into the established tradition of Hollywood Fiction. This allows it to pit its own "authentic American hero"[22] against a highly narcissistic, highly unreal "facile place filled with facile people",[23] a move that straightforwardly implements the model of iconoclast cultural critique: it aligns film, image, and popular culture, in short: 'surface', in an opposition to 'substance' and 'realness'. Indeed, the fakery of Hollywood that enables the large-scale deception of the Iraq War is contrasted with a more 'real' American heartland where detective Joe Broz comes from. A stereotypical mapping on gender categories – the authentic, masculine "real man" Broz versus the actress Magdalena Lazlo – supports the dichotomy, again drawing credibility from established, canonical roles of hard-boiled/Hollywood fiction. At the same time, this model gets complicated by the textual games the novel plays. To a large extent, Broz's masculinity, guarantor of his realness, turns out to be a performance he skillfully and self-consciously stages, and both the unreal Hollywood and the real American heartland turn out to be projections by the novel's characters – cultural myths rather than actual presences in the (novel's fictional) world. Broz, moreover, actually enjoys trading his reality for a life 'in film': as he observes early on, "[i]t's like [Lazlo]'s taking me inside her movie. Which is an A picture, with a top cinematographer and director, the best Hollywood has to offer",[24] an evaluation he comes back to again and again. Becoming part of her real-life film, her co-star, turns out to be quite appealing, not least because he describes their sex as "cinematic".[25] The image-substance dichotomy of the iconoclast model that the setting evokes, then, remains in place only to some extent. The power of media-generated images is still the precondition for the faking of the Gulf War, but it is not threatening enough to keep the novel from playing with it to a point at which the novel's textual performances undermine it.

In thus playing with iconoclasm as a dominant paradigm of theorizing a crisis of representation, *American Hero*'s narrative project subscribes to, but clearly also goes beyond simply affirming, the dangers of a presumed rise of the image. In the process, the novel, positively and programmatically, draws

---

22 Beinhart, *American Hero*, p. 7.

23 Greg Jericho, *Hollywood Dreaming: Satires of Hollywood 1930–2003*, Diss. James Cook University, 2004, p. 97.

24 Beinhart, *American Hero*, p. 20.

25 Beinhart, *American Hero*, p. 375.

on the epistemic and narrative model of gossip.[26] On the level of plot, this becomes most evident in the joy the book takes in relating Hollywood rumors, mostly through the conversations Broz, in his role as Lazlo's chauffeur, has with other servants and mostly in the footnotes. Imagining a rumor according to which a fictional Jacqueline Conroy has slept with "Patrick Swayze, Kevin Costner, and Madonna – [indicating] a strong upwardly mobile orientation", a footnote adds: "We remind the reader, and the attorneys, that Jacqueline Conroy is a fictional person. The suggestion that a famous person had, or has, fictional sex with a non-existent person should not, in the normal course of things, be libelous",[27] an implicit comment, of course, on the question whether the suggestion that a real president has staged a war with the help of fictional movie producers could be considered libelous. More openly tying Hollywood gossiping to its own imaginative work, the novel comments on the rumor that Jon Peters had slept with Nancy Reagan, a rumor, a footnote explains, that is so improbable that it "didn't even show up in Kitty Kelley's scandal-mongering biography of Mrs. Reagan. However, it is so exactly symptomatic of Hollywood gossip that *it would be hard to imagine it not being said* in this conversation".[28] Playing with rumors, then, allows the book to playfully comment on its own gestures of disclosure.

Beyond such open references, gossip is central to the novel's own narrative design. While the narrative setup described above – the inside narrator who hears the story 'authentically' from Broz himself – seems to bolster the narrative's credibility, it actually also alludes to a pseudo-ghostwriting setup. This does not only reference Hollywood-style celebrity writing. More significantly, it turns all of the story into a friend-of-a-friend story, a piece of gossip, or, taking this logic one step further, into gossipy slander, an insinuation, if you will, of a scandalous fraud perpetrated by the president of the USA. Accordingly, the multiple disclaimers in which the novel denies claiming truth-value for its own story and emphasizes its fictional nature end up being not so much a legal safeguard but rather the novelistic equivalent of 'I'm just saying', a textual gesture meant to evoke the narrative mode of gossiping.[29] In

---

26 Cf. Clare Birchall for more on gossip as "illegitimate knowledge" (*Knowledge Goes Pop: From Conspiracy Theory to Gossip*, Oxford 2006, p. 121).

27 Beinhart, *American Hero*, p. 228.

28 Beinhart, *American Hero*, p. 76; emphasis added.

29 Stacy Olster, in one of the very few scholarly reactions to the novel, notes the repetition of Beinhart's "disclaimer about his book being a work of fiction" and "the heightened rhetoric" that insists on the book's fictional nature. She notes that "more is at work here than mere authorial ingenuousness" (*The Trash Phenomenon:*

fact, the questions at the end of the book work in a similar fashion. They do not so much claim to know the true story of the Gulf War, they simply raise suspicion.

American Hero, in my reading, is a highly complex, highly meta-fictionally aware novel that is hard to pin down. One of its undeniable projects is to destabilize solid, 'official' knowledge. It affirms a crisis of representation, a cultural context in which it is possible to medially stage an entire war, but it boasts a narrative voice strong enough to flirt with the opportunities and dangers the "putative erasure" of the 'real' allows for. In the process, it destabilizes all kinds of knowledge, among them the medial, image-generated official story of the 1991 Iraq war as well as the image-substance dichotomy of iconoclast cultural criticism that makes its story tellable.

4. Post-Enlightenment Blues: The Disenchanted Librarian and the Power of Narrative

The games that *American Hero* so vigorously plays are absent from Beinhart's second Bush-themed novel, *The Librarian*, which features a narrative setup that is mostly disenchanted. There are no more games with different diegetic layers, no footnotes, and no toying with the performative power of language. Instead, the novel is narrated in straight first- and third-person narration (with quite a bit of philosophical background explanation), and only one transgression of these conventional perspectives occurs. Close to the end, the narrator directly addresses the readers, demands that they get involved, and makes a halfhearted gesture at questioning his own narrative by explaining that there will be another version, a courtroom version that "will not be this one. It will be the one that [my attorney] guides me to. It will be limited to what I have firsthand knowledge of, what is relevant to the case, [...] and what the judge permits".[30] Apart from this one weak gesture that asserts that the narrator has just told more than "what [he has] firsthand knowledge of", *The Librarian* avoids messing with its own project of representation. Rather than playing games, it aims at giving a transparent, sober account, an ultimately didactic story,[31] and this unwillingness to risk more is indicative of the urgent sense of panic the book is written from.

Contemporary Literature, Popular Culture, and the Making of the American Century, Athens 2003, p. 68), but never comes back to explaining what is at work exactly.

30 Beinhart, *The Librarian*, p. 431.

31 In fact, Beinhart ended up publishing a non-fiction treatise explaining the philosophical background of the novel under the title *Fog Facts: Searching for Truth in the Land of Spin* (New York 2005).

This unwillingness to play games is reflected in the setting and atmosphere as well: This time, the story is not set in a presumably unreal, yet enchanting, Hollywood, there are no gaudy games with the novel's ability to represent reality, there is no gossip and no cinematic sex. The main plot line opens to the protagonist, head of library services at a college, having to fire a subordinate librarian, feeling as if he was breaking "some delicate flower, snapp[ing] its stalk, and crush[ing] its petals".[32] He has to fire her because "the national budget [is] designed to destroy government services" and the president has "deliberately set out to destroy public education".[33] The librarian he fires is described as an out-of-time relic, a naïve, childlike, and innocent idealist who "loved books and presumed they would love her back", who became a librarian because she "wanted to serve humanity", and who, in dress and style, seems outdated: "She wore large glasses and had large curls that were always clean and always brushed and never styled. She lived like a nun on her meager starting salary in a room she rented from a retired professor and his elderly wife, empty because their own children had grown up and gone west".[34] The protagonist, in turn, refers to himself as the "keeper of the flame",[35] someone who preserves a sacred fire during an age of darkness. In total, the way that *The Librarian* portrays libraries, readers, and librarians is rich with overtones of a culture on the verge of total extinction, or surviving as a marginalized underground culture only.

In this "desert of the real"[36] far beyond the "graphosphere",[37] facts have become a problematic concept. To make this tellable, the novel introduces "Fog Facts", facts that are known but do not have the impact one would expect. They are introduced in reference to President Scott's lack of military experience. Like W. Bush, Scott had found a way to get into the national guard to avoid deployment to Vietnam, a fact that

> was not a secret. It was known. But it was not known. That is, if you asked a knowledgeable journalist [...], they knew about it. If you yourself went and checked the record, you could find out. But if you asked the man in the street [...], they wouldn't have a clue, and, unless they were anti-Scott already, they wouldn't believe it.[38]

---

32 Beinhart, *The Librarian*, p. 4.
33 Beinhart, *The Librarian*, p. 5.
34 Beinhart, *The Librarian*, p. 4.
35 Beinhart, *The Librarian*, p. 42.
36 Jean Baudrillard, *Simulacra and Simulation*, Sheila Faria Glaser (trans.), Michigan 1994.
37 Debray qtd. in Simon, "Popular Culture", p. 173.
38 Beinhart, *The Librarian,* pp. 63.

The novel attributes this elusiveness of facts to their overabundance: "In the information age there is so much information that sorting and focus and giving the appropriate weight to anything have become incredibly difficult". In effect, the 'wrong' facts sometimes get too much attention, while the important information "nobody seems able to focus on any more than they can focus on a single droplet in the mist".[39] In this model, facts fail to be simply pieces of evident, true information. In *The Librarian*, the worry over reality is decidedly not about the presumed power of media-generated images cloaking or distorting an underlying reality. Rather, it is about the arbitrariness with which reality emerges from its smallest entity, the fact, and it is a worry urgent enough to disallow any games with it.

In light of these fog facts, the novel assigns a crucial role to narrative. By embedding Scott's lack of combat experience in a story of her own service as a nurse in Vietnam, Democratic candidate Murphy surprisingly manages to solidify facts into reality:

> by framing it in a charge of cowardice and attaching it to his conduct as president, it had already, in that moment, emerged from the mist and was solid and whole and the lighting crews were already running cable to set up spotlights on it and every commentator and pundit in America would walk up to it [...].[40]

This power of narrative over facts, however, creates further difficulties: if narrative validates facts, not the other way around, what constitutes a true, right story? The novel engages this question by telling two alternative stories of how Scott became president in the first place. In one, he "was an attractive, vigorous, young politician, elected to the Senate on his first try", who, once elected, "pursued the policies that he and [Hoagland's friends], synchronistically, believed in". The narrator then presents "an alternative narrative using the same characters and events"[41] in which Hoagland and his peers "needed a president" and picked "a relatively undistinguished senator" as a puppet.[42] Having established that facts are not a reliable basis for judging the truth-value of either story, the narrator needs another way of authenticating one version over the other and introduces the concept of the "things that Must Be So But Can't Be Stated". The concept remains very unclear, introduced as residing "[i]n the misty realms – outpast Fog Facts" but never

---

39 Beinhart, *The Librarian*, pp. 63–64.

40 Beinhart, *The Librarian*, p. 98.

41 Beinhart, *The Librarian*, p. 160.

42 Beinhart, *The Librarian*, p. 161. Note how the project of "an alternative narrative using the same characters and events" resonates with both novels' storytelling project.

fleshed out. Rather than insisting on empirical evidence, the narrator asks his readers to "[think] things through", and, when he reaches an impasse in authenticating one of the two versions, he resorts to a metaphor: "[i]t's just that if there is fruit, somewhere there must be a tree".[43] His explanation ends up moving the truth-value of narratives closer to what Jerome Bruner, in his seminal essay on narrative, has termed "narrative necessity". "Narratives", Bruner writes, "are a version of reality whose acceptability is governed by convention and 'narrative necessity' rather than by empirical verification and logical requiredness".[44]

Indeed, getting the narrative right becomes a central problem in the novel and makes a strong appearance on two very different levels: in David Goldberg's difficulty in assessing his own situation and adapting his behavior accordingly, and in Beinhart's difficulty in telling the story he wants to tell. In the novel, Goldberg's struggle to understand what he got into is framed in terms of 'narrative' early on. Flirting with Niobe and trying to address their relationship, Goldberg remarks that the situation made him "[think] of a couple of movie scenes", to which Niobe replies: "Oh, what movie are we in?" Goldberg, it turns out, imagines himself being "in a Woody Allen movie" and reads her warnings that he did not "know what you are getting into here" as a warning about romantic entanglements,[45] a serious misreading: the meeting has been prearranged by the villains, and Niobe has been sent by Jack to spy on him.[46] Simultaneously, in her secret role as a spy for Murphy, she hopes to learn from him what the Republicans are up to, deceiving him and her husband at the same time. As Goldberg corrects his assessment later on: "I'm in the wrong movie. I thought it was a Woody Allen film, a neurotic love story, but then it turned into a crazy thriller, with sadists chasing me".[47] Goldberg's struggle with genre returns in Beinhart's difficulties in telling the story right. He sets out to narrate how a librarian, a member of the "graphosphere" with the skills necessary to find truth in the fog of facts, stops a massive conspiracy. This project, however, gets hijacked by the genre of the spy thriller. As Goldberg has to "throw [himself] into James Bonding" and do "all those silly things" that a spy would do rather than doing what "logic and reason" would demand,[48] Beinhart looses his message. Gold-

43 Beinhart, *The Librarian*, p. 160.
44 Jerome Bruner, "The Narrative Construction of Reality", in: *Critical Inquiry*, 18/1991, 1, pp. 1–21, p. 5.
45 Beinhart, *The Librarian*, p. 75.
46 Beinhart, *The Librarian*, pp. 303–304.
47 Beinhart, *The Librarian*, p. 189.
48 Beinhart, *The Librarian*, p. 261.

berg's librarian's skills end up playing hardly any role, and what really saves the country are his unexpected (and not entirely plausible) skills as secret agent.

Regardless of whether one reads Goldberg's more average cognitive skills or his unexpectedly well-developed physical skills as crucial to propelling the narrative forward, the novel's central idea that only a librarian's 'typographic' skills can form the right story from the fog of facts collapses. Somewhere in between kidnapping a taxi at gunpoint,[49] killing one of his adversaries,[50] burning a car that could reveal his fingerprints,[51] and blackmailing a supreme court justice in order to save the incriminating documents,[52] Goldberg just happens to overhear one of the conspirators' names on the radio and remembers seeing this name in Stowe's files. Neither his cataloging nor his indexing of Stowe's files play any role in the process; no additional research, no index, and not a single book make the difference.[53] He merely recalls seeing a statement of debt when going through Stowe's files, mostly feeding them into his scanner for automatic classification and mostly attending to the "physical" problems of feeding the documents into the machine.[54] Proving the conspiracy, then, also does not follow any particularly bibliophile strategy: Goldberg and his friends simply break into Stowe's mansion to retrieve the original documents. Whether read as conspiracy fiction or as action thriller, these later parts of the book fail to capitalize on Goldberg's function as a member of the graphosphere.

In effect, *The Librarian* is a largely disenchanted piece of fiction. It works hard to provide a theory of the crisis of representation, of the obliteration of the 'real', that does not draw its plausibility from the iconoclast model with its elitist overtones and that resonates more harmoniously with a style of thinking prevalent at the time of its writing. Its appeal to narrative as a fundamental category in the creation of (social) reality indeed is in sync with much of the political punditry at the time, as is its agonizing over the low

---

[49] Cf. Beinhart, *The Librarian*, p. 283.

[50] Cf. Beinhart, *The Librarian*, p. 386.

[51] Cf. Beinhart, *The Librarian*, p. 393.

[52] Cf. Beinhart, *The Librarian*, p. 429.

[53] In fact, he attempts to do research from his hiding place, but, as he notes himself, he does not have time for the kind of research "any serious librarian or biographer or scholar would have wanted" and accordingly only makes some "very rough judgments" (Beinhart, *The Librarian*, p. 232). More importantly, this 'research' does not lead to any results, and when he finally understands the conspiracy his apprehension is not related to the research he has done.

[54] Beinhart, *The Librarian*, pp. 34–35.

impact of facts. As a piece of fiction, however, it falls short of *American Hero*'s qualities, and the narrative difficulties it encounters may well be indicative of the difficulties of theorizing political deception without resorting to the notion of a substance of reality. After all, if there is no substance to reality, one can hardly be deceived, and any notion of deception, in return, presumes and thus implicitly affirms the knowability of 'reality', something that the novel tries to suspend.

V. Conclusion

I read *American Hero* and *The Librarian*, Larry Beinhart's two novels on the two Bush presidencies, as two different attempts to tell the same story of how the president of the USA attempts to exploit the postmodern elusiveness of the 'real' for political gain. In this, both novels are products of – and participants in – a larger 'epistemic panic', a social panic that interprets a widely perceived 'crisis of representation' as ultimately threatening to politics and, by implication, to society. They use different models to conceptualize this crisis. *American Hero* taps into a tradition of iconoclasm that reads 'image' as the fundamental threat to the 'real', whereas *The Librarian* works along a model organized around the power of narrative to forge facts into reality. They also have different agendas. The former plays with the appeal of 'illegitimate' knowledge and questions official narratives, the latter tries to save 'fact' on the eve of its presumed obliteration by the George W. Bush presidency. Written at different historic and cultural moments, both books thus testify to a broadening discourse on the crisis of representation and to the changes in the way that parts of the American public have theorized (and narrated) the threat such a presumed postmodern obliteration of the 'real' poses to society.

Christoph Herzog (Bamberg)

Small and Large Scale Conspiracy Theories and Their Problems: An Example from Turkey

The trouble with conspiracy theories is that they are like an iceberg. The tip is easily visible from afar, but its visible parts conceal its true dimensions. The easily visible part of conspiracy theory is the literary genre that, in its modern form, was invented at the end of the eighteenth century.[1] Although the genre had its origin in clerical anti-enlightenment circles, it has been convincingly argued that, as a mode of thinking, it was not limited to what has been traditionally regarded as the political right.[2]

Used mostly in a derogatory way, the term "conspiracy theory" includes a twofold dispraise. Even though Charles Pigden in his reappraisal of Karl Popper's classical ideas on conspiracy theory allows for a positive use of the term conspiracy, the phenomenon is commonly regarded as a vice. The term "conspiracy theory" is not used as a term of the social sciences like "criminological theory" (for instance, the "Broken Windows Theory") but as a derogatory expression to express strong epistemological disapproval and moral reprobation. The derogatory use has been legitimized because the term targets some of the more obviously politically dangerous and historiographically absurd literature of the sort of the infamous *Protocols of the Elders of Zion*. However, it might not be superfluous in this context to note that in Great Britain at the time of its publication the *Protocols* was object of a serious public debate as to its authenticity.[3] This points to the fact that what is regarded as plausible is dependent on social context, and that networks of trust

---

1 Cf. Johannes Rogalla von Bieberstein, "Zur Geschichte der Verschwörungstheorien", in: Helmut Reinalter (ed.), *Verschwörungstheorien: Theorie, Geschichte, Wirkung*, Innsbruck 2002, pp. 15–29.

2 Cf. Pierre-André Bois, "Vom 'Jesuitendolch und -gift' zum 'Jakobiner-' bzw. 'Aristokratenkomplott': Das Verschwörungsmotiv als Strukturelement eines neuen politischen Diskurses", in: Reinalter (ed.), *Verschwörungstheorien*, pp. 121–132; Karl Popper, *The Open Society and Its Enemies*, vol. 2, New York 1995, p. 111.

3 Cf. Michael Hagemeister, "The Protocols of the Elders of Zion: Between History and Fiction", in *New German Critique*, 35/2008, 1, pp. 83–95, p. 89.

rather than immediate verifiability play the central role in assessing the plausibility of data people encounter.[4]

Browsing the increasing academic literature on conspiracy theory one cannot help but notice an interesting paradox. On the one hand, writers seem to be both critical and dismissive of conspiracy theories when referring to those that freely mingle Templars, Zionists, Communists, and Freemasons into stories of large-scale plotting. On the other hand, a considerable amount of the academic research conducted since the last decade or so has raised doubts whether Popper's epistemological verdict against conspiracy theory has done sufficient justice to the complexity of the case. The fact that much of the theoretical effort has focused exclusively on the context of the European and North American dimensions of the phenomenon while much of the research in the Near Eastern context has been more empirically oriented seems to have created an imbalance in the discussion of the phenomenon. I think that on closer inspection the iceberg of conspiracy theory will turn out to be even larger as hitherto believed.

Offering a summary and partial translation of two examples of conspiracy theory from Turkey, this paper discusses some epistemic issues on the basis of these examples and proposes a simple distinction between small- and large-scope conspiracy theories according to their conspiratorial scopes. By "conspirational scope" I do not simply mean the either local or global perspectives on the alleged conspiracy that a given conspiracy theory purports to uncover but whether the explanation offered could be verified in principle – even if not necessarily in practice. I will argue that the challenges faced by researchers when assessing the plausibility of certain conspiracy theories may be different in each of the two scopes with large-scope conspiracy theories being typically beyond verifiability.

***

In the absence of systematic research about the production and consumption of conspiracy theory in Turkey, any assessment of the spread and importance of the phenomenon there will remain rather speculative. However, there can be no doubt that conspiracy theories occupy an important place in the Turkish mainstream media, and that they are not an exclusive domain of any extremist political camp. Many, but not all of them, seem to belong to the

4 Cf. Michael Baurmann, "Rational Fundamentalism? An Explanatory Model of Fundamentalist Beliefs", in: *Episteme: A Journal of Social Epistemology*, 4/2007, 2, pp. 150–166.

type of anti-Semitism that mingles anti-Freemasonry and anti-Zionism, claiming that the Jews' ultimate goal is to plot for world domination using both capitalist imperialism and Communism as their tools.[5] A variant of this literary tradition of anti-Semitic conspiracy theory characteristic of Turkey is the preoccupation with the *Dönme*, converted followers of the seventeenth-century rabbi Sabatai Zevi. There is a tendency to describe them as Crypto-Jews – incorrectly so, because they were not accepted by their alleged Jewish co-religionists as Jews, nor did they regard themselves as such[6] – or even to simply conflate Jews and Dönme altogether. The idea that the Republic of Turkey was essentially founded and run by members of the Dönme community has seen broad coverage in the Turkish media during the last decade.[7] It would be misleading, however, to assume that conspiracist thinking in Turkey has been limited to these "classical" themes. There are other – and, epistemologically speaking, perhaps more interesting – examples of what may be termed conspiracy theories in Turkey. In addition to nationalism, anti-imperialism has thus played a tremendously important role in Turkish conspiracy theorizing.

In what follows, two examples by Erol Mütercimler, a contemporary and relatively well-known self-confessed proponent of conspiracy theory in Turkey, are presented. Erol Mütercimler (b. 1954) is a journalist teaching strategic studies at several private universities in Istanbul (İstanbul Ticaret Üniversitesi, Doğuş Üniversitesi, and Yeditepe Üniversitesi). He was the editor of the journal *Komplo Teorileri* and produced several TV series about the topic. He approaches conspiracy theories in the framework of strategic studies as a phenomenon of political reality that has to be discussed in order to uncover real conspiracies. It is his contention that the history of Turkey is especially rich in conspiracies.[8] In 2005 he published a book which he declared to be a

---

5 Cf. Süleyman Yeşilyurt, *Türkiye'nin Büyük Masonları*, Ankara 2001. In the introduction, the author states flatly that Freemasonry was a "way of Zionist administration" ("Siyonist idare tarzıdır"), that Jews remained Jews pursuing Jewish goals no matter whether they changed religion or not (p. 13). Yeşilyurt also identifies a number of well-known Turks, including Ziya Gökalp, as alleged Freemasons. For a commentary on another book by the same author cf. Murat Belge, ""Tonlar'dan Bazıları", in: *Radikal*, Dec. 13, 2003, http://www.radikal.com.tr/haber.php?haberno=98691 (accessed Sept. 28, 2010).

6 Cf. Marc David Baer, *The Dönme: Jewish Converts, Muslim Revolutionaries, and Secular Turks*, Stanford, CA 2010.

7 For a thorough discussion of this phenomenon cf. Rıfat N. Bali, *A Scapegoat for all Seasons: The Dönmes or Crypto-Jews of Turkey*, Istanbul 2008.

8 Cf. Erol Mütercimler, *Komplo Teorileri: Aynanın Ardında Kalan Gerçekler*, Istanbul 2005, p. xiv.

collection of 73 conspiracy theories entitled: *Komplo Teorileri: Aynanın Ardında Kalan Gerçekler.* The title of this book (*Conspiracy Theories: The Reality Behind the Mirror*)[9] also figured prominently on his webpage.[10]

It should be noted that the conspiracies dealt with in the book are not strictly restricted to alleged conspiracies in and against Turkey, although these are the main focus. The conspiracies discussed also include some of those that are familiar to conspiracy theorists outside Turkey, like the assassination of John F. Kennedy, the Oklahoma bombing, the September 11 attacks, or the assassination of Mohammad Baqir al-Hakim in Najaf in 2003. In addition, the book contains some excursions into Ottoman history, for instance the execution of Çandarlı Halil Paşa after the conquest of Constantinople in 1453. The book's underlying historiographic pattern clearly reveals the author's affiliation with Kemalist ideological positions. Moreover, the overall picture emerging from the volume is that of a global and globalizing conspiracy of western capitalists. At the same time, the book has a certain affinity to the mentioned anti-Freemason, anti-Zionist tradition. At times, this affinity comes close to being explicit, for instance when the author introduces the former Secretary-General of the UN, Kofi Annan, looking for the secret force that helped him to attain this position ("Kofi Annan ve arkasındaki gizli güç"), "the son of a freemasonic African clan leader who gained the support of the Jewish lobby and global capitalism through his wife".[11] The reason why Mütercimler takes issue with Kofi Annan is obviously the Annan Plan for Cyprus, and the question he poses at the end of this chapter is a rhetoric one: "Would you entrust the fate of Cyprus and Turkey to the decision of such a man?"[12] It could therefore appear as if Mütercimler's book was just another variant of the "classical" anti-Semitic conspiracy theories. But although the book certainly draws some inspiration from that literary tradition (if one may call it that) I will argue that the wholesale dismissal of all of its conspiracy theorizing could be hardly justified on rational grounds. While his treatment of Annan may convince us that Mütercimler holds an anti-Semitic worldview, it does not automatically disprove other arguments he makes in his book. We still would have to apply the hermeneutic principle to assume the most solid version of argumentation the text we are taking issue with is offering us.

---

9 Unless indicated otherwise, all translations are my own.

10 As of Feb. 26, 2012 his website is not available anymore (http://www.erolmutercimler.com/ [accessed Sept. 28, 2010]).

11 Mütercimler, *Komplo Teorileri*, p. 415.

12 Mütercimler, *Komplo Teorileri*, pp. 415, 419.

Under the heading "Orgeneral Eşref Bitlis Cinayeti" ("The Crime against Army General Eşref Bitlis"),[13] Erol Mütercimler insinuates that the commander of the Turkish Gendarmery, Eşref Bitlis, who died in a plane crash in Ankara on February 17, 1993, was killed by an act of sabotage. Bitlis, he claims, was a thoughtful specialist in the Kurdish question who was unpopular with the Americans because he had criticized their politics towards the Kurds as aiming at the creation of an independent Kurdish polity. In support of his thesis Mütercimler claims:

- that the expert opinion by the American manufacturer of the Beechcraft B300 heard in court had ruled out an ordinary technical defect;
- that Turkish military experts used the term "probably" when declaring that the crash had been brought about by wing icing;
- that the weather report of the day in question spoke of "thaw";
- that a soldier on guard on the airfield reported an unidentified officer who had known the password and visited the location the night before the crash;
- that this incident has not been investigated;
- that a commission of aerial experts from the Technical University of Istanbul had ruled out icing and human failure as possible causes of the crash;
- that two Turkish politicians, Necmettin Erbakan and a member of the CHP, Mahmut Işık, declared that Eşref had been assassinated;
- that the sister of one of the crashed aircraft's pilots claimed that the judge of the trial had confessed to her that he, together with several witnesses, had been put under pressure by certain "dark forces" ("karanlık güçler");
- that the son of Eşref Bitlis filed a lawsuit claiming that his father's death had been the result of an act of sabotage.

In addition, Mütercimler refers to an article in the Turkish mainstream newspaper *Sabah* from September 16, 2002 where a colleague of Eşref Bitlis, Army General Necati Özgen, reported about an incident that had happened in 1992, the year before the deadly plane crash of Bitlis. According to Mütercimler's summary of the article, Özgen had accompanyied Bitlis on a special mission on a flight in a Sykorsky helicopter from Şirnak to the headquarters of Masud Barzani in Northern Iraq. During the flight two American F-15 fighters had approached the helicopter and had twice tried to intercept and bring down the helicopter by risky flight maneuvers. Özgen claimed that, contrary to usual practice, they had not been informed by the American mili-

[13] Mütercimler, *Komplo Teorileri*, pp. 16–22.

tary air control for North Iraq about the two fighters. He also added that Bitlis had managed to practically clear the region of PKK fighters killing more than 4,500 of them. It should be noted that Erol Mütercimler's dealing with the issue does not include any investigations of his own but is based on a discussion that forms almost its own small branch within the Turkish conspiracy literature.[14]

Politically motivated assassination, to be sure, is not a rare incident in recent Turkish history. Murders include a considerable number of controversial journalists, writers, and academicians. Until today, most cases have remained unresolved. Among these unresolved murders are also a number of pensioned high-ranking generals,[15] and doubt has been cast on the deaths of some military officers connected to Eşref Bitlis.[16] Conspiracy theories abound in the media and in public discourse. They group around two key notions that are basically incompatible to each other: *dış mihraklar* ("outward factors") and *derin devlet* ("deep state"). While the first reflects the idea of a perpetual colonialist-imperialist threat to Turkey's sovereignty, the second describes the Turkish state as a conglomerate of secretive groups and organizations using every legal and illegal means in pursuit of their ends. The difference between the two basic foci of conspiracy theory in Turkey is also a political one, although its ideological demarcation is not always clear.

The notion of the deep state is symbolized by the famous traffic accident of Susurluk. On November 3, 1996 a Mercedes Benz crashed into a truck in the province of Balıkesir, leaving the four people in the car dead or wounded and exposing a connection between the government, the armed forces, right-wing militias, and organized crime. When a militia leader and a contract

---

14 Cf. Cüneyt Özdemir, *Komutanın Şüpheli Ölümü: Eşref Bitlis Olayı*, Istanbul 1998; Adnan Akfırat, *Belgelerle Eşref Bitlis Suikastı*, Istanbul 1997. There are also numerous articles in journals and newspapers on this topic.

15 In 1991 and 1992, a number of pensioned generals were allegedly killed by the leftist terrorist organization Dev-Sol: Hulusi Sayın, Memduh Ünlütürk, İsmail Selen, and Kemal Kayacan.

16 In November 1993 Major Ahmed Cem Ersever was found shot in the head in Ankara, his hands bound on his back; he had leaked information to the media. Brigadier-general Bahtiyar Aydın was killed in action in 1993 in Lice; he was allegedly shot by a sniper. Kazım Çillioğlu was found dead in his house in 1994; his death was publicly ruled a suicide. In 1995 Colonel Rıdvan Özden was killed in action while serving in Mardin; his wife and reports in several media doubted the official version (cf. Akfırat, *Eşref Bitlis Suikastı*, pp. 18–19; Özdemir, *Şüpheli Ölümü*, pp. 117–118; "Bitlis'in Kadrosu Öldürüldü", in: *Star*, Aug. 16, 2009, http://www.stargazete.com/politika/-bitlis-in-kadrosu-olduruldu-haber-207836.htm [accessed Nov. 4, 2010]).

killer, red-listed by Interpol (Abdullah Çatlı), a member of parliament (Sedat Edip Bucak, who survived), the director of a police academy (Hüseyin Kocadağ), and a former beauty queen (Gonca Us) are found in a car together with forged documents, drugs, and guns there can be little doubt of a conspiracy. The scandal led to the resignation of the minister of the interior, Ahmet Ağar, and several investigations which, however, did not result in uncovering its full scope.

This incident – and some lesser known cases such as the events around the bombing of a Kurdish bookshop in the Turkish town of Şemdinli in 2005 – has convinced many people that the notion of Turkey as a deep state reflects reality. Yet, it does not explain who is ultimately pulling the strings in the background. The book on the NATO's secret "stay-behind" armies by the Swiss historian Daniele Ganser[17] was translated into Turkish in the year of its initial publication in English,[18] opening a new perspective on the NATO involvement in terrorist acts especially in Italy and Turkey. In 2008 the so-called Ergenekon lawsuit began. It comprised the hearings of over one hundred people, among them generals, politicians, and journalists, who were allegedly involved in plotting against the government and preparing a *coup d'état*. Although it remains unclear whether there existed any connection between the "Counter-Guerilla" (as the secret NATO operation Gladio was called in Turkey) and Ergenekon, such a connection seems a natural option for all those trying to combine the deep state with the idea of a colonialist-imperialist threat to Turkey.

Given this political background – that quite naturally refueled the discussion about the death of Eşref Bitlis –,[19] it seems out of question for the time being to verify or to falsify the claims that the crash of Bitlis' plane in 1993 had been the result of sabotage. Taking the generally confusing and complicated structure of the Turkish political theater into account, both options seem possible. Likewise, the American factor in the incident can be neither confirmed nor ruled out. The problem here is quite simply the lack of reliable sources of information combined with the considerable personal risks that anyone looking into such conspiracy theories is facing (not only) in Turkey.

---

17 Daniele Ganser, *NATO's Secret Armies: Operation Gladio and Terrorism in Western Europe*, London 2005.

18 Cf. Daniele Ganser, *Nato'nun Gizli Orduları Gladio Operasyonları: Terörizm ve Avrupa Güvenlik İlkeleri*, Gülşah Karadağ (trans.), Istanbul 2005.

19 The official investigation was re-opened in September 2010 by the solicitor general in Ankara (cf. "Eşref Bitlis'in Ölümüne İlişkin Soruşturma Başlatıldı", in: *Yeni Şafak*, Sept. 30, 2010, http://yenisafak.com.tr/Gundem/?t=30.09.2010&i=280908 [accessed Oct. 10, 2010]).

Whether the Ergenekon lawsuit and connected lawsuits will bring light to this issue and, if so, whether the insights will be convincing remains to be seen.

However, it is certainly not rare that we find ourselves in a position where it seems impossible to obtain sufficient evidence that allows us to prove or disprove the factuality of a given conspiracy theory. It is obvious that the crucial point in such cases becomes the question of probability which itself hinges on the problem of plausibility. Given the circumstances briefly sketched above, it nevertheless seems not unreasonable to assume that *if* Bitlis' death was the result of a conspiracy, this conspiracy might be part of a larger plot. In other words, while the explanation offered by Mütercimler and others on the reason why the plane crashed is in itself a small-scale conspiracy theory, the plane crash might be part of a larger conspiracy to be uncovered by some kind of medium or large-scale conspiracy theory.

Erol Mütercimler's book offers such a narrative. A chapter entitled "Brüksel Asker Istemiyor!" ("Brussels Doesn't Want the Soldiers!") deals – albeit extremely cursory – with Turkish history and international relations since the 1950s. It offers a useful summary of a conspiratorial trend of thought that is certainly not uncommon in Turkey:

> Because of the fear of communism that had spread in the Western world during the Stalin era the Turkish armed forces within the NATO framework were strengthened in order to defend especially Greece and the oil of Mesopotamia against the Soviets. But as soon as Stalin died in 1953, an armistice was achieved in Korea, and Turkey was confronted with not having obtained the loans for industrial development it had hoped to get in exchange for its military support of America in this war and with the fact that Cyprus was given to Greece. When the leaders of the *Demokrat Parti*, who had brought Turkey to the NATO in 1952, did not renounce Cyprus completely and even thought of demanding the credits for industrialization from the Soviet Union, if necessary, they were removed from power by the NATO military *coup d'état* on May 27 [1960]. Prime Minister Adnan Menderes, Foreign Minister Fatih Rüştü Zorlu and Minister of Economy Hasan Polatkan were executed and paid with their lives for having offered resistance [to the designs of the West]. Regardless of this warning of the West which showed what would happen to people who did not march in the prescribed direction, Turkey neither gave up industrialization nor Cyprus. The heads of the armed forces and of the government changed, but the threatening letters sent by President Johnson did not bring about these changes. With the operation of 1974 Turkey solved the question of Cyprus on its own.
>
> To punish this behavior the West brought to stage the [Armenian] terror organization ASALA under the pretext of the 'Armenian Genocide' and paved the way for the murdering of Turkish diplomats. Films like *Midnight Express* appeared. While America imposed an arms embargo on the one hand, the 'Kurdish Question' was set up on the other hand. It was not enough. From May 1, 1977 onwards it was tried to trap Turkey in a conflict that from the outside looked like a clash between leftists and rightists.

> While Turkey, despite all the pressure that had been put on it, refused to show the obedience that was expected from it, something unexpected happened in Iran. The black-cloaked women sent to the streets by Khomeini and the apparently Muslim-turned Iranian Communists managed to overturn the Shah and make him flee abroad. When a Mollah regime that declared America "the great Satan" came to power in Iran and entered a fierce war with Saddam Hussein, who had been made to attack them, it was unclear in which direction the domestic disturbances would drag Turkey. However, within a week, anarchy and terror in Turkey were put to an end by the military coup of September 12, 1980. While its neighbors were fighting to death, Turkey came to a state of peace and quietness.
>
> A flow of money began, unprecedented in the history of the Republic of Turkey, especially from the oil-producing Arab countries to Turkey (of course with American consent). With Iran and Iraq having closed down their sea transportation routes, the only windows open to the world were the harbors of Iskenderun and Mersin in Turkey.
>
> Endless convoys of commercial transportation units moved from these harbors to the gates of Iran and Iraq. The Southeast [of Turkey] flourished. Moreover, Turkey decided to use its own resources to build the Atatürk Dam for the Southeastern Anatolia Project (GAP) without raising foreign credits. These were developments of a sort which the West would not easily accept, but the fear of Iran preponderated.[20]

In much the same way Mütercimler then goes on to interpret the political role of Turgut Özal, who was Prime Minister of Turkey from 1983 to 1989 and President of Turkey from 1989 until his death in 1993. Özal is characterized as one of the Turkish naifs who believed in the West. As had happened after the Korean War, Turkey was not rewarded for its contributions to the Cold War – on the contrary. western support for the PKK and the assault on the Turkish destroyer *Muavenet* by a ship-to-ship missile during a NATO exercise in 1992 made even Özal become aware of the situation, and shortly before his death he began to re-orient Turkish politics to the East. As to the cause of his death in office in 1993, Mütercimler cites rumors that the President, who had a heart condition, might have been assassinated. He continues:

> The leaders who sided with America against the Soviets were vanishing at the moment when it was time to pay them. Who in Turkey remembered the President of Pakistan, Ziya-ul-Haq, who provided the most important support for the Soviet defeat in Afghanistan and died in a mysterious plane crash? Or, let's not think of Zia-ul-Haq. Is it implausible to think of a conspiracy theory that claims a link between the death of the military commander against the PKK, Eşref Bitlis, who died in another crashed plane, and the death of Özal?[21]

---

20 Mütercimler, *Komplo Teorileri*, pp. 24–25.
21 Mütercimler, *Komplo Teorileri*, pp. 24–25.

It is from this perspective, too, that Mütercimler views the question of Turkey's EU membership as a neo-colonialist enterprise in the spirit of the infamous Treaty of Sèvres and the Turkish armed forces as the last obstacle to a western-dominated Turkey whose social fabric has been ruined and torn apart by neo-liberalism.

Our second example is a conspiracy theory of the rather large-scale, almost global, type, even if its focus on the side of the victims is largely limited to Turkey. An essential characteristic of the second example of conspiracy theory is that it is comprised of a chain of many instances of (comparatively) small-scale conspiracy, our first example of the alleged plane sabotage being just one of them. Thus, we may distinguish here two levels of conspiracy theories: a low, first-order or small-scale level that forms the building material for the other second-order or large-scale level that forms a master narrative out of the narratives of its components. Despite their interdependence the two levels co-exist in relative independence from one another. Above it has been argued that it is difficult to obtain the factual evidence for either proving or disproving the alleged manipulation of Eşref Bitlis's aircraft. The difficulty of proving or disproving would probably be comparable in each single instance of small-scale conspiracy contained in our second example of a large-scale conspiracy theory by Mütercimler. Even if the majority of the small-scale conspiracy theories could be proven wrong, this would still not be enough to disprove the existence of Mütercimler's large-scale conspiracy. Furthermore, it would be difficult to give a percentage of first-order conspiracy theories which have to be disproved in order to finally unmask the second-order conspiracy theory they are part of. We might even argue that the refutation of all first-order claims of conspiracy would be needed for that purpose. It might therefore seem reasonable to begin at the other end and try to deconstruct the master narrative. However, it would be certainly too naïve to argue that Turkey and the U.S. were both members of the NATO and that therefore any undercover action by the U.S. against Turkish individuals or institutions detrimental to perceived western interests was out of question. On the other hand, one could take issue with Mütercimler's contention that it had been long-standing western politics to keep Turkey underdeveloped and weak. In either case, taking issue with Mütercimler's second-order conspiracy theory would not automatically affect all the small-scale conspiracy theories it comprises. The plane crash could still be claimed to have been the outcome of some conspiracy, and to disestablish that contention would require separate work.

In considering these and other possible arguments it becomes evident that the requirements for dealing with the claims of this large-scale conspiracy theory are qualitatively different from those of small-scale theories. While a conspiracy involving a plane crash caused by technical manipulation can be uncovered in principle (although it might not be in practice), a long-term and large-scale conspiracy as presented in our second example cannot, at least not in the same way. This difference in verifiability and falsifiability is the result of the differences in scope and abstraction of the two levels of conspiracy narratives. In itself this difference is not specific to conspiracy theory but can arise in any historiogaphical context. The question whether Elvis Presley faked his own death in 1977 is basically not different from the questions when Sultan Mehmed II was born and what the original identity of his mother was or whether Martin Luther really nailed his 95 theses on the door of the All-Saints' Church in Wittenberg in 1517 or whether this has been a myth. All these questions are of a nature that requires answers which leave no room for interpretation because they refer to simple facts. If we do not have the answers the reason is simply a lack of data, as is the case with the causes for the crash of Eşref Bitlis' aircraft. On the other hand, Mütercimler's narrative of the role of the West in recent Turkish history evades verifiability, as does any hypothesis that tries to determine the ultimate reasons for the outbreak of World War I in German politics. It is not only that we lack the data to prove or disprove every single conspiracy theory that Mütercimler links together in his historical *tour de force*, but the fact that he weaves them into a master narrative of a scope as large as "the West against Turkey". Ultimately, the master narrative cannot be reduced to the question whether the conspiracies it links together are real.

***

But perhaps the master narrative of "the West against Turkey" does not qualify as a conspiracy theory? Let us consider the definition of conspiracy theory given by David Coady that revises formulations proposed by Brian L. Keely and Steve Clarke:

> A conspiracy theory is a proposed explanation of an historical event, in which conspiracy (i.e., agents acting secretly in concert) has a significant causal role. Furthermore, the conspiracy postulated by the proposed explanation must be a conspiracy to bring about the historical event which it purports to explain. Finally, the proposed explanation must conflict with an "official" explanation of the same historical event.[22]

---

[22] David Coady, "Conspiracy Theories and Official Stories", in: *International Journal of Applied Philosophy*, 17/2003, 2, pp. 199–211, p. 201.

Mütercimler's narrative of "the West against Turkey" seems to miss already the first part of Coady's definition. *Prima facie*, it appears to be difficult to reduce "the West" to a group of actors. The second part of the definition is equally problematic: a conspiracy theory is expected to deal with successful conspiracies; failed conspiracies do not qualify for conspiracy theories. While in the case of ours the sub-conspiracies are claimed to have been successful, the course of history is not determined entirely by them. The West is depicted as acting under the conditions of the Cold War, and at least the Iranian Revolution is presented as an unforeseen and unplanned event that forced the West to modify its policy towards Turkey. But is this policy a conspiracy? Do many small conspiracies add up to a big one? The conflict between the West and Turkey depicted in Mütercimler's second-order narrative could also be read as a long-standing conflict of interests with one party being considerably more powerful. In the last instance this problem is again related to our first, the question of authorship or, more exactly, whether a reification of the West as an actor meets the definition of conspiracy theory. Consider the footnote that Popper put in the context of his own discussion of conspiracy theory:

> In the discussion which followed the lecture, I was criticized for rejecting the conspiracy theory, and it was asserted that Karl Marx had revealed the tremendous importance of the capitalist conspiracy for the understanding of society. In my reply I said that I should have mentioned my indebtedness to Marx, *who was one of the first critics of the conspiracy theory*, and one of the first to analyze the unintended consequences of the voluntary actions of people acting in certain social situations. Marx said quite definitely and clearly that the capitalist is as much caught in the network of the social situation (or the 'social system') as is the worker; that the capitalist cannot help acting in the way he does: he is as unfree as the worker, and the results of his actions are largely unintended. But the truly scientific (though in my opinion too deterministic) approach of Marx has been forgotten by his latter-day followers, the Vulgar Marxists, who have put forward a popular conspiracy theory of society which is no better than the myth of the Learned Elders of Zion.[23]

I believe that a similar argument can be used regarding Mütercimler's view of history. It may be considered a nationalist vulgarization that is ultimately derived from the Marxist theoretical debate on imperialism and reinforced by the popularization of the Huntington thesis of "the clash of civilizations". Ultimately, it may be categorized as a leftist Kemalist position. It should be noted, however, that this position is not without academic acclaim in Turkey

---

23 Karl Popper, *Conjectures and Refutations: The Growth of Scientific Knowledge*, London 2002, p. 167, n. 3; italics in the original. Cf. also Popper, *Open Society*, p. 111.

and that the notion of contemporary western imperialism is an essential part of it.[24]

In Mütercimler's narrative, regardless of the Turkish debate on the "deep state", it is only the more powerful western side that uses conspiracy as a regular tool of politics. Also, his rhetoric points to a dichotomy of good and evil, or at least of justified and unjustified claims. As is well known, Popper was not only critical of Vulgar Marxists but also of Marx himself, yet for different reasons. He accused him of having subscribed in his views on history to the theoretical fallacies of what Popper characterized as "historicism". It is interesting to note, however, that Popper seems to have believed that historicism was closely related to conspiracy theory.[25] Indeed, for all practical political purposes it seems irrelevant whether the actions of the capitalist and, for that matter, of the western imperialist are determined by class affiliation or by psychology (as Popper claimed Vulgar Marxists believed).[26] The Marxist political application of the theory of class consciousness was to blame individuals because, ultimately, individual people form the only tangible targets for political action. The idea of class consciousness, an abstract concept which holds that the political action of individuals is determined by their class status, could only be concretized by being translated into an ethical categorization of individual intent that formed the basis of political orientation and action. In other words, the moment Marxist theory was put into political practice (which was its explicit philosophical program), it became irrelevant whether undesired political attitudes had emerged from class consciousness or from bad intentions. At least from the perspective of the victims of this politics who were liquidated or put in the Gulags this differentiation was of limited interest.

For the question of plausibility of conspiracy theories the differentiation between structural or systemic forces and personal agency may therefore be of less relevance than the definition by David Coady, providing for "agents acting secretly in concert", seems to suggest. The element of secrecy in the definition is equally of less significance than one may surmise at a first glance. Any concerted action taken in situations of perceived antagonistic group interests (in a zero-sum situation) will probably not be announced – and therefore secret.

---

[24] Cf. Faruk Alpkaya, "Bir 20: Yüzyıl Akımı: 'Sol Kemalizm'", in: Murat Belge (ed.), *Modern Türkiye'de Siyasî Düşünce*, vol. 2, Istanbul 2001, pp. 477–500.

[25] Popper, *Open Society*, p. 104.

[26] Popper, *Open Society*, p. 122.

As we have seen, the notion of the "imperialist West" does not necessarily rely on the presupposition of an omnipotent group of evil actors, although it easily may degenerate into that depiction. In a way, Mütercimler's narrative leaves a lacuna at this point that is open to further specification. His opaque version of "the West" might easily be developed into a vision where the West is directed by, for instance, a conspiratorial group of Zionists or Freemasons. His depiction of Kofi Annan's relation to the "Jewish lobby" demonstrates that Mütercimler elsewhere in his book moves closer to this type of conspiracist thinking than in the two chapters discussed here.

I believe that the apparent similarities between (Vulgar) Marxist theory and conspiracy theory can also be viewed from a hermeneutic perspective. Paul Ricœur differentiates two basic approaches to hermeneutics. The "hermeneutics of trust", that aims at the reconstruction of meaning, and the "hermeneutics of suspicion", that attempts to decode meaning that is hidden or disguised. He famously counted Marx along with Freud and Nietzsche as one of the "three masters of suspicion" and emphasized that suspicion in this context did not mean skepticism.[27]

If the hermeneutics of suspicion is chosen as the fundamental strategy of historical interpretation, conspiracy theory (in the widest sense) becomes a valid option as a tool of explanation. As such, it is neither irrational nor reproachable but an indispensable and powerful tool for social and cultural critique. It is, however, metaphorically speaking, a rather dangerous tool, much like a sharp knife that can easily cause thinking to lapse into irresponsibility or absurdism. In other words, striving to uncover the hidden meaning behind what seems to be the obvious is a shared concern of both conspiracy theory and the hermeneutics of suspicion. The difference between them is that conspiracy theory seeks for "the truth" while the hermeneutics of suspicion in Ricœur's reading needs to remain conscious of the ambivalent and provisional character of any attempt to understand. But as in the cases of Vulgar Marxism and Marxism the difference may be less important in hermeneutic practice than in hermeneutic theory. Thus, Marx's contention in what may be described as his application of the hermeneutics of suspicion was that he had discovered the law of motion of the capitalist society.

Looking at the examples of conspiracy theory that I have presented, I would argue that while it may be useful to classify some historical texts as "conspiracy theories" this classification by itself does not help to assess the validity of the explanations offered. Even Brian Keeley in his noted article of

---

27 Paul Ricœur, *Die Interpretation: Ein Versuch über Freud*, Eva Moldenhauer (trans.), Frankfurt 1999, pp. 45–47.

1999, in which he set out to establish a catalog of distinctions between warranted and unwarranted conspiracy theories (of which he abbreviated the latter to UCT), admits that it is difficult to give a definition of conspiracy theories and to carve out a class of unwarranted conspiracy theories one would be able to exclude from assent by definition.[28]

Although Keeley emphasizes that his essay is epistemological, not sociological,[29] his notion of "errant data", which he believes to be the key tool of conspiracy theories, is based on a sociological approach. Errant data, according to Keeley's definition, is evidence that is either contradictory or neglected in the received or official accounts.[30] Relying on errant data, UCT offer a surplus amount of explanation in contrast to the official or received explanation. This strength, however, comes at the cost of a hidden weakness that lies in the underlying assumption that the official explanation is purposely hiding something. Therefore, errant data is implicitly more important than the data given by the official explanation. Nevertheless, the existence of errant data, as Keeley argues, does not necessarily indicate that a theory is wrong: "the existence of errant data alone is not a significant problem with a theory. Given the imperfect nature of our human understanding of the world, we should expect even the best possible theory would not explain *all* the available data".[31]

Although Keeley does not draw on this parallel, his argument seems to reflect the concept of paradigm shift offered by Thomas S. Kuhn in the context of scientific revolutions. Kuhn claims that "anomalies" and "discrepancies" (which would be his equivalents to Keeley's "errant data") always occur and do not necessarily lead to a shift of paradigms.[32] It can be easily seen that Keeley's notion of "errant data" is wholly dependent on another characteristic he believes to be typical of a UCT: "[a] UCT is an explanation that runs

---

28 Brian L. Keeley, "Of Conspiracy Theories", in: *The Journal of Philosophy*, 96/1999, 3, pp. 109–126, p. 111: "The definition conspiracy theory poses unexpected difficulties. There seems to exist a strong, common intuition that it is possible to delineate a set of explanations – let us call them unwarranted (UCTs). It is thought that this class of explanation can be distinguished analytically from those theories which deserve our assent. The idea is that we can do with conspiracy theories what David Hume did with miracles: show that there is a class of explanations to which we should not assent, *by definition*. One clear moral of the present essay is that this task is not as simple as we might have heretofore imagined."

29 Keeley, "Of Conspiracy Theories", p. 110.

30 Keeley, "Of Conspiracy Theories", p. 118.

31 Keeley, "Of Conspiracy Theories", p. 120.

32 Thomas S. Kuhn, *The Structure of Scientific Revolutions*, Chicago 1996, p. 81.

counter to some received, official, or 'obvious' account".[33] In that context, Coady's contention that Keeley's definition is missing "the requirement that a conspiracy theory conflict with an official explanation of the event in question" seems somewhat unfounded.[34]

Moreover, the dichotomy of official explanation and conspiracy theory is not very helpful in transnational or intercultural contexts. As Coady rightly observes, "quite often the official version of events is just as conspiratorial as its rivals".[35] There are cases like the question of the Armenian Genocide in 1915 where there might be even two "official" versions. Also, as in the Turkish case, an official version might be heavily contested so that its characteristic of "being official" is of less value for epistemological considerations. To put it more bluntly: in a political culture where the notion of "deep state" is common coin, and is so not without solid reason, the idea that a conspiracy theory should be defined by opposing an official explanation would appear rather problematic. In a scenario of information warfare it would seem extremely difficult even to distinguish "official" and "officially leaked" information. It is thus illustrative that some of the leading cadres of the leftist-nationalist Turkish Worker's Party (*İşçi Partisi*) have been arrested in the context of the Ergenekon lawsuit. The party's journal *Aydınlık* has been among the foremost print media uncovering alleged conspiracies, blaming them generally on western imperialists and their Turkish collaborators.[36] *Aydınlık* has frequently made use of allegedly leaked state documents.[37]

From a general perspective, conspiracy theories account for the fact that conspiracies do exist. Moreover, they tend to assume that conspiracies rarely come alone. Mostly, they seem to link a whole series of conspiracies and explain them in a master narrative. The differentiation of conspiracy theories according to their scale accounts for this fact. It does not, however, solve the problem that the labeling of an explanation as a conspiracy theory on whatever grounds does not say anything about its plausibility or its factuality.

---

33 Keeley, "Of Conspiracy Theories", pp. 116–117.

34 Coady, "Conspiracy Theories", p. 201.

35 Coady, "Conspiracy Theories", p. 208.

36 Among the arrested was Adnan Akfirat who had contributed several articles in *Aydınlık* and the book mentioned above on the subject of the alleged murder of General Bitlis (cf. "Perinçek tutuklandı, 'Ergenekon terör örgütü' yöneticiliği ile suçlanıyor", in: *Zaman*, Mar. 24, 2008, http://www.zaman.com.tr/haber.do?haberno=668504 [accessed Nov. 4, 2010]).

37 For a more recent example of a document that, according to *Aydınlık*, was classified as "very secret" ("çok gizli"), cf. Nusret Senem, "Eşref Bitlis 'Ergenekon' Lideri", in: *Aydınlık*, Oct. 10, 2010, p. 7.

Both have to be assessed on a case-by-case basis. Large-scale conspiracy theories pose basically different epistemological problems than small-scale ones do. Small-scale conspiracy theories can be verified or falsified in principle, even if in practice they may not. In the latter case, however, the reason is not of an epistemological nature but is based on the unavailability of reliable data.

It appears that Popper would have agreed that conspiracies happen and that trying to uncover them is an epistemologically legitimate undertaking. Nevertheless, he would have objected against large-scale conspiracy theories which bind together many "individual" conspiracies into a master narrative of grand conspiracy. He argued that large-scale conspiracy theories seem to assume that a small group of conspirators is able to control almost everything, which he deemed to be impossible. One might re-phrase his argument of scale by saying that the problem with large-scale conspiracy theory is the two implausible underlying assumptions that (1) small-scale conspiracies are part of large-scale conspiracies and that (2) large-scale conspiracies function exactly like small-scale ones.

However, looking at the Turkish experience and the two examples taken from Erol Mütercimler's book demonstrates that both objections, although not totally unfounded, are too vague to be useful. For example, the cases of politically motivated murder in Turkey during the 1980s and 1990s were so frequent and pointed into such a direction that it would be rather implausible *not* to assume they were part of one larger-scale conspiracy – in other words, the existence of the "deep state" suggested itself. On the other hand, the assumption of the existence and historical effectuality of "western imperialism" that has impregnated the leftist Kemalist discourse inherits the hermeneutics of suspicion with its Marxist theoretical roots. In addition, Turkey's peculiar political position vis-à-vis the West and the fact that there is no "official" western politics of imperialism against Turkey contributes to the transformation of this explanatory concept into conspiracy theory. In a sense, the concept of western imperialism in the leftist Kemalist discourse is very close to what Popper criticized as "Vulgar Marxism". This however, should not lead critics of vulgarization to believe that by refuting the vulgarized theory one can also tackle the original. Reading Mütercimler's large-scale conspiracy theory as a vulgarized interpretation of western hegemony over Turkey, therefore, does not refute the assumption of the existence of western imperialism nor does it disprove the suspicion that elements of the deep state in Turkey were being controlled from outside and serving foreign interests.

Whether a plane crashes accidentally or for reasons of technical sabotage is a historical question of a different epistemological quality than the historical question of western imperialism. Both, I have argued, qualify for conspiracy theories, yet on different levels of scope. While their factuality may be difficult or even impossible to establish, a certain plausibility of small-scale conspiracies like the alleged sabotage of General Eşref Bitlis' plane cannot be denied out of hand. As this type of alleged small-scale conspiracies forms part of the large-scale conspiracy theory of western imperialism in Turkey both cannot be treated independently from one another. Approaching the large-scale conspiracy theory of western imperialism from this side makes it look different – and arguably more plausible – than approaching it without paying attention to the many examples of potential small-scale conspiracies that have happened during the past few decades of Turkish history. We may still disagree with Mütercimler's explanation and we may still conclude that western imperialism did not play a significant role in Turkish politics. But it seems reasonable to admit that the frequency and the circumstances of political murder and similar incidents in Turkey were pointing towards the existence of a larger conspiracy and that the question of foreign involvement was a natural one to ask in this context.

Again, that does not prove Mütercimler's vision of grand conspiracy to be correct but approaching it from the side of small-scale conspiracy theories adds to its plausibility even if one may conclude it to contain exaggeration and trivialization or even myth making. As with rumors, the production costs of conspiracy theories tend to be much lower than the efforts required to prove or disprove them in a, scholarly speaking, satisfactory manner. It seems that there is no way to avoid these efforts.

Annika Rabo (Stockholm)

"It Has All Been Planned": Talking about *Us* and Powerful Others in Contemporary Syria

1. Preamble

After weeks of public unrest Syrian president Bashar al-Assad made his first public appearance on March 30, 2011 by giving a speech in the Syrian parliament. Demonstrations had been met with brutal armed interventions on the part of the regime. While acknowledging the enormous changes which had taken place in the region in the last months, he underlined the correct path of the Syrian state and the need to protect the country against the conspiracy it was facing: "We have not yet discovered the whole structure of this conspiracy. We have discovered part of it but it is highly organized. There are support groups in more than one governorate linked to some countries abroad".[1] Throughout the spring and summer, Syrian officials and supporters of the regime reiterated again and again the rhetoric of a conspiracy against the country.

This article is about everyday talk of evil planning and conspiracies by powerful others in contemporary Syria. It is based on material collected during a number of anthropological fieldwork trips in various parts of the country since the late 1970s. My last visit to Syria was from February to March 2011, after the downfall of the presidents in Tunisia and Egypt, just at the beginning of the civil war in Libya, but before the real turmoil started in Syria. During my travels in the country I was surprised by the disappearance of "it-has-all-been-planned" talk. Of the many people I met in the spring only a young trader in Aleppo asked me: "Is it really possible to believe that the revolutions have spread from Tunisia, to Egypt, to Libya and across the Arab peninsula without outside help?" But he offered no answer as to who might be behind this chain of events, and he winked and smiled as he posed the question. In sharp contrast to the talk of foreign agents and nefarious plots broadcast by political leaders in various Arab countries, the "ordinary" Syrians I met were conspicuously silent. This novel silence, to which I will re-

---

1 The English translation of Bashar al-Assad's speech could be found on al-bab.com (www.al-bab.com/arab/docs/syria/bashar_assad_speech_1103 [accessed Aug. 14, 2011]).

turn in the end of this article, marks a crucial alteration in the perception of political action among many Syrians. This article can be read as a background to this historically important shift.

In the late 1980s, Rim, a woman in her thirties and living in Damascus, remarked: "They knead us like dough, you know. They get us just where they have planned. We spend all our time thinking about how to run our households, how to find this and that and not thinking about how to change society for the better".[2] The pronoun "they" refers to the Syrian regime – variously talked about as *an-nizam* ("the system") or *as-sulta* ("the authorities"/"powers-that-be"). Her comments are very similar to many others I have heard in the Middle East since the early 1970s as a student, an activist, and later on as a fieldworker.

In much of the "everything-is-planned" talk in the region, focusing on regional or international "big" politics, the USA or Israel are implicated, for very obvious reasons. However, there is hardly any incident with political implications that does not seem to point at the involvement, or the behind-the-scenes-presence, of these two countries, a generic West, or their own *nizam* (or a combination of all of them). The calculations and planning of immoral others extend beyond simple political subjugation. Deplorable social evils coming from abroad – like pornography on television – can be explained by the planning of distant, but also near, enemies, including the regime.

It is exceedingly difficult to argue against a reasoning in which everything has been planned and anything can be accounted for. I have had many heated and uncomfortable arguments in Syria, not about the importance of foreign or domestic interests in trying to influence, divide, or rule the country, but about linking this to a single-minded ability to plan, control, and execute a complicated chain of events on the part of named actors, regimes, or whole countries. My discomfort is partly related to my own background. As a student in, and of, the Middle East – particularly Lebanon and Syria since the early 1970s – I was heavily exposed to conspiracy theories. In many ways I lived with and through talking about conspiracies. But in the late 1970s, when I started doing anthropological fieldwork, I became bored with such talk and my own conspiracy theorizing. When I did my first long-term research in Syria between 1978 and 1980 I often closed my ears to talk about the regime as kneading the pliable dough, that is, the Syrian people.[3] Thus I

---

2 This is not an exact translation from the statement in Arabic, but it captures and encapsulates the speech.

3 Dough and clay are typical metaphors Syrians use when describing how *as-sulta* treats them.

missed the opportunity to try and analytically link conspiracies, conspiracy theories, and conspiracy talk, and it was only in the late 1990s when doing fieldwork among traders in Aleppo that I began to more systematically collect material on this topic.[4]

The first part of this paper will provide examples of conspiracy – and "it-has-all-been-planned" – talk related to international and regional politics by using material collected mainly between 1997 and 2010. In this article, I deliberately use the term *conspiracy talk* rather than *conspiracy theory* or *conspiracism* in order to underline that views and opinions in Syria are seldom consistent or elaborately organized. The second part of the paper will provide examples of how local and national debates about bribes and corruption are discussed in Syria and how such discussions can be linked to local understandings of global relations. In the third section, I will put forward different interpretations of Syrian conspiracy talk. Finally, I will briefly return to the disappearance of conspiracy talk mentioned above.

2. Talking about Regional and International Politics

In Syria, the perceived lack of stability in the region they inhabit forms a backdrop to the everyday lives of citizens. This was certainly noticeable during the fieldwork I started in Aleppo in the late 1990s. But although regional political crises and instability were constants to be counted on, they were not all perceived as similar in terms of intensity or danger. In the fall of 1998, for example, Turkish-Syrian relations became very strained as Turkey accused Syria of harbouring and supporting Abdallah Öcalan, the leader of the Kurdish PKK party. Turkey also demanded that Syria recognize the 1939 border.[5] Syria countered by claiming that Öcalan was not in Syria and that it would not recognize this border. Troops were massed close to the border, and the propaganda war in the Syrian media was quite intense. Despite Aleppo's proximity to the Turkish border, my informants in Aleppo, however, did

---

[4] Much of the empirical material in this paper has been used in my book *A Shop of One's Own: Independence and Reputation among Traders in Aleppo*, London 2005. I am very grateful for the opportunity to learn from conspiracy theorists during the conference organized by Michael Butter and Maurus Reinkowski in Freiburg in January 2011.

[5] During the French mandate between World War I and II the Iskanderoun province (Hatay in Turkish) was ceded to Turkey. This was not accepted by the Syrians, and on all Syrian maps this province is still inside Syrian territory. For a detailed analysis of Syrian policies toward Iskanderoun, cf. Emma Lundgren Jörum, *Beyond the Border: Syrian Policies towards Territories Lost*, Uppsala 2011, especially pp. 137–161.

not seem excessively perturbed. The international highway between Syria and Turkey was still open and merchandise could get through. Flights operated between the two countries, and the Turkish consulate in Aleppo remained open. At the end of October, a security agreement was signed after the mediation of the Egyptian and Iranian presidents. Many of my informants argued that Turkey was not acting as an aggressor on its own, but that Israel and the United States had an interest in keeping Syria in threat of an armed conflict and busy along its northern border.

In December 1998, just before the start of Ramadan, Britain and the United States, in the name of the UN alliance, resumed air bombardment over Iraq, causing fury in the media and among most of my informants.[6] The next day, to my great surprise, there were demonstrations in the centre of Aleppo. The participants, carrying the Syrian flag, the flag of the Ba'th party, pictures of Hafez al Assad and his dead son Basel, shouted "with our spirits, with our blood, we redeem you, oh Iraq". Somebody called "eat shit Clinton" and somebody else "*allahu akbar*". This was an unusual event – a demonstration concerned with foreign politics rather than a manifestation lauding the Syrian regime or the president. It was obvious that people had been allowed – even encouraged – to show their anger and frustration. In Damascus, the U.S. and British embassies were attacked by demonstrators. In Aleppo, the British consulate was attacked, and a café with *American* in its name was forced to close (and quickly changed its name before reopening). I was also told that boys, imitating the "popular" demonstrations, had staged one of their own in a residential quarter of the city. But instead of hailing Iraq, they had hailed Saddam Hussein, an old enemy of the regime, causing fear of reprisals among the bystanders.

Many in the Aleppo bazaar thought that these demonstrations and attacks were childish and silly and only orchestrated – planned – to appease public opinion. But traders and customers in the market were also venting their anger at the USA and Britain. Later that day the Syrian regime officially declared its opposition to the bombings and said that it supported the Iraqi (sister) people. The bombings continued throughout Ramadan and were a common starting point for political analyses of the international and regional systems. Many of my informants – in the bazaar and outside – insisted that the current situation in Iraq had been orchestrated by the USA. Saddam Hussein, many claimed, was a victim of American (and/or Israeli) planning. He had been, according to many, lured to invade Kuwait in 1991 in order for the Americans to wage war against the only economically strong and well-

6 Those supporting the bombing were Kurds.

armed Arab state and the only country which, in the long run, could pose a threat to Israel.[7] When discussing such a scenario, or variations of this theme, it was futile to highlight the atrocities committed by Saddam Hussein. These could always be explained away by his relations with some foreign power, and the outcome of any given event could always be accounted for. Saddam Hussein was still in power in Iraq, not because the Americans (with their allies, including Arabs) had failed, but because he was meant to stay in power, as an excuse for continued warfare against the country and its people. The continuation of the bombings served not only to crush Iraq but also as a warning and deterrent to all other Arabs. "We are supposed to be like clay to be shaped and formed as they like", some of my informants would say. Despite such bleak visions, all my informants in the bazaar, apart from one, fervently hoped for the end of the bombings. He, instead, hoped for more, so that eventually all Arabs and Muslims would rise up in anger.

In March 1999, NATO waged war on Serbia, which continued until June. Syrians had followed the events in former Yugoslavia for a decade. Many had initially been surprised by the large number of native Muslims in the Balkans, and the Syrian Greek Orthodox community was also made much more aware of co-religionists in that region.[8] Middle Eastern Muslims organized medical and humanitarian support for Bosnia in the early 1990s. During my fieldwork, traders in the bazaar told me that they had been urged to marry Kosovo-Albanian women. There had been announcements in the mosques that 4,000 women were coming to Syria as refugees from Kosovo and that good Muslims should marry them to give them safe homes and the dignity of matrimony.[9] The ethnic and religious affiliations of people in Central and Eastern Europe and the former Republics of the Soviet Union became more apparent and were discussed more vehemently in Syria after the fall of the socialist and communist regimes. While some of my informants in various locations in Syria voiced the opinion that these affiliations actually caused conflict,

---

[7] The view that Saddam Hussein had been conned to invade Kuwait was very prevalent all over the Arab world. The fact that this made him and the Iraqi regime appear incredibly gullible did not seem to bother the propagators of this view (and they were certainly not only of the so-called "Arab street").

[8] The Greek Orthodox community is the largest Christian community in Syria, followed by the Armenian Orthodox. All in all, the Christians make up perhaps 10–12% of the Syrian population, and they are divided into eleven recognized sects.

[9] Interestingly, nobody thought it strange that only women were to be "saved" as married refugees. The whole issue of these marriages passed, and I never heard that anybody had actually married female refugees from Kosovo.

others rather saw them as being manipulated through conflicts in which other issues were also involved. Whereas many in the Aleppo bazaar argued that only strong, or authoritarian, regimes could hold together a country where different religious and ethnic groups reside, pointing to Syria as an example, others actually argued differently.

The 1999 NATO bombings in Serbia were typically seen as the instrument of American policy and interests. They were strongly condemned by most of my informants. Some claimed that Milošević, like Saddam Hussein, was an agent of the West; his task had been to break up Yugoslavia and open up this militarily strong country to foreign influence. Analogous to the situation in Iraq, the USA wanted war in Europe so that the Europeans would stay weak, divided, and in need of American help. "World peace is threatened", one trader in Aleppo agonized: "Russia, with its Orthodox people, cannot silently watch this war. They will have to react and there might be a clash with America". Christian traders not only voiced their anger against the USA but also supported Milošević as a co-religionist and claimed that the Albanians in Kosovo were "recent settlers, much like the Jews in Palestine". One trader – a devout Muslim – was against Milošević, against the bombing, but also against the aspirations of the Kosovo-Albanians. He said they were at fault to want a country for themselves at any cost: "According to Islam, life is more dear than anything else. You are even allowed to hide your religion if that can save your life".[10]

In Aleppo, as elsewhere in Syria, the conflict between Israelis and Palestinians was uniformly seen as the basis of regional instability and as a core issue that had to be resolved. Syrians had different analyses as to its development or solution, but all agreed about its repercussions on the lives of every person in the Middle East. I had just arrived in Aleppo at the end of March 2002 when the Israeli army "reoccupied" most of the limited territory under the Palestinian Authority in the West Bank. Despite media censorship by the Israelis, there was ample coverage of the West Bank by the large Arab satellite television stations. People were glued to their TV sets and hardly spoke of anything else. Many of my informants argued that hopes of a peaceful and just settlement, both for themselves and for the Palestinians, were being crushed. Many were in a state of shock after having seen close-ups of demolished cities and swollen corpses. The siege of the Church of the Nativity and the humiliation of the Palestinian leadership, surrounded by Israeli tanks in Ramallah, underlined their sense of powerlessness. Although many con-

---

10 This informant was a Sunni Muslim, although such a notion is more associated with Shiʿa theology.

demned Palestinian suicide bombings, and many more disliked the politics of Yassir Arafat, the plight of the Palestinian people overshadowed everything else. One man said: "They call Arabs terrorists, but now we see the face of real terrorism. The Israelis have no mercy, they will not be satisfied until every Palestinian is dead. That is their final solution". The lack of support and help from the Arab world and the silence from their own political leadership underlined, for all to debate, the perceived Arab and Syrian impotence.

The Israeli military operation in the spring of 2002 marked a new media era in modern Syria. For the first time, Syrians were daily and closely exposed to media violence. They felt well-informed by Arab media and listened to a myriad of arguments by Arab intellectuals and political commentators.[11] But there was no just, or even clear, solution in sight. People talked, debated, or wept, but all to no purpose. Resentment centred not only on Israel and the United States; all Arab regimes were implicated as well. Everybody in Aleppo spoke of the link between the current events in Palestine and the attacks in New York and against the Pentagon on September 11, 2001. Many in the Aleppo market drew the conclusion that "it was all part of the plan". If Osama bin Laden and al-Qa'ida were behind the attacks, then they were American/Israeli agents. Such a conviction was used to explain why bin Laden had not yet been found and how he was being used to smear the image of Islam: "This is not the work of real Muslims". One young trader earnestly told me that no Arab could ever plan such a detailed and complicated terrorist attack: "They would have bungled the whole thing". According to the bazaar consensus, the September 11 attack had been carried out to provide the Israelis with the excuse to find a "final solution" to their problems of territory and security. Arab regimes, including the Palestinian Authority, were implicated because the regional instability provided them with an excuse not to grant their citizens more freedom.[12]

---

11 It became clear, after some time, that the sense of being well-informed was not so well-founded.

12 This line of reasoning was of course not confined to Aleppo or Syria but found all over the Arab world as well as outside (cf. Stephen Marmura, "Tales of 9/11: What Conspiracy Theories in Egypt and the United States Tell Us about 'Media Effects'", in: *Arab Media & Society*, 11/2010, http://www.arabmediasociety.com/?article=752 [accessed Aug. 14, 2011]).

3. Linking the Local and the Global

The vast majority of the Syrians I have met and talked to complain about the malfunctioning public sector. In the 1990s, such complaints were voiced much more openly and publicly compared to the 1970s and 1980s. When I did fieldwork among Aleppo traders, no topic – apart from marriage, family life, and religion – was brought up as much by my informants as that of the perceived malfunction of the public sector. The complaints did not surprise me since traders were dependent on employees in the public sector for a variety of papers and permissions. They faced a great deal of uncertainty and inconvenience in their daily dealings with representatives of the public sector. Rules and regulations were, they thus claimed, deliberately left unclear, applied in a haphazard way, or subject to change.[13]

Syrians commonly link the problems of the public sector to corruption in the country and to the prevalence of bribes. I heard an endless number of stories and witnessed many incidents where money changed hands between a citizen and a public employee. Over the decades I have often heard that "everything" in Syria is infused with bribes because "everybody" wants their cut. The ubiquity of graft and bribes, however, never stopped people from complaining or from expressing anger or shame. Everyday petty corruption is typically attributed to the low salaries of Syrian public employees. After Bashar al-Assad's succession as President of Syria in the summer of 2000, Syrians hoped, in vain, for a substantial increase in the salaries of public employees. "This country will remain corrupt as long as salaries are so low", many informants reiterated again and again.[14]

Syrians typically express the view that the prevalence of bribes leads to widespread corruption in Syria. In principle, bribes are abhorred by people working in both the private and the public sector, but are often excused when offered, or accepted, by themselves or others close to them. In Aleppo, for example, from the traders' point of view, they had certain rights and could use means – considered illegal by Syrian law – to demand those rights, since the employees of the state did not grant them their rights without a bribe. Bribes in Syria are always a matter of hard cash, while corruption is perceived as a structural disease prevailing in the public sector, with reper-

---

[13] One way to hedge against the risks in such encounters is to use mediation (*wasta*). For an analysis of mediation as well as bribes and corruption in Syria, cf. Annika Rabo, *Change on the Euphrates*, Stockholm 1986; and *A Shop of One's Own*.

[14] "Who loves his *watan* (homeland) on three thousand lira [US$ 60] a month?" a woman in Aleppo asked me rhetorically when we were debating whether bribe-taking was unpatriotic.

cussions in the private sector. My informants in the private sector in Aleppo defended their own practices of bribes as a necessary evil to get their job done or to be granted their rights and did not implicate themselves in the corruption of the country.

The process whereby bribery has become more and more common in Syria, or at least perceived as more and more common, is obviously very complex. It is partly connected to the relationship between the private and the public sectors – between entrepreneurs and public employees, and between citizens at large and the public sector. Citizens are increasingly tied to public bureaucracy in many different ways. The need for voting cards, identity cards, passports, and a myriad of permissions to travel, to build, to marry, and to be employed increase the intensity of contacts between citizens and the public authorities. The "opportunity structure" for petty bribes has grown because Syrian authorities are still approached through face-to-face interaction. Citizens cannot call by telephone or write in for papers or permits or to pay their taxes or fees; they have to appear in person or enlist the help of a mediator.

Although my informants did not implicate themselves in the spread of corruption, they commonly expressed shame and anguish over the general corruption in Syria. Sometimes this led to holding others, further away, responsible. In Aleppo, my informants in the bazaar often claimed that Damascene traders had intimate and close contacts with politicians and those in power. They insisted that Aleppo traders had to pay bribes because they were disadvantaged compared with Damascene traders. In such a line of reasoning, they were deliberately kept on short rein by private and public actors in the capital. Similar stories blaming "national others" close to the *nizam* or part of the *sulta* were heard all over Syria.

In Iraq and in Kosovo, most of my informants could see the obvious presence of Americans and assess this in terms of policy and interests. In Palestine, the Bush administration was just as heavily implicated. Everything of possible political importance was interpreted as instigated by the USA or Israel. "Why do the Americans defend Kosovo-Albanians but not Kurds or Palestinians?" one informant in the Aleppo bazaar exclaimed and went on to say: "Because it has all been planned and calculated". He told me that the CIA had killed President Kennedy as well as the Swedish Prime Minister Olof Palme because the two of them had been too peaceful. Yeltsin had been paid by the Americans in order to finally dissolve the only other superpower able to confront the USA. Mu'ammar Qaddafi was an American agent, and the Lockerbie explosion had been planned as an excuse for American aggression against Libya in order to control Libyan gas and petroleum resources.

In Syria, the calculations and planning of wilful others commonly extended beyond simple political subjugation. A deplorable, social evil coming from abroad could be explained by the planning of distant or near enemies. European TV channels showed pornography on satellite channels, one Aleppo trader earnestly told me, in order to corrupt Arab men and prevent them from doing honest work. It thus contributed to the underdevelopment of the region. Arabs were unable to fight against this evil, he claimed, because the sexual repression of society made men unable to resist watching. He complained: "And the governments do not mind. They want docile people more interested in pornography than politics". In Aleppo, only one trader brought out a detailed far-reaching analysis on a number of occasions. When discussing the World Trade Organization, he told me that it planned to create a region of recreation for western tourists in Syria, Lebanon, and Jordan, so that these countries would never compete industrially with the West.

Although most of my informants did not explain Syria's lack of industrial development as having been planned from the outside, many linked current difficulties to their historical heritage. "Turkish colonialism" or "five hundred years of Turkish rule" has until recently been brought forward as an explanation for perceived underdevelopment (*takhallouf*) in Syria and the Middle East. This argument is part of the ideological underpinnings of Arab nationalism and is propagated by parties of the left and the ruling Ba'th party. It holds that "Turks" exploited "Arabs" and that "Arabs" have a historical mission to liberate themselves.[15] Another time the trader with the detailed far-reaching analysis told me that the Americans have planned to bring Syria down economically since the 1950s:

> Syria was on its way to really develop. Our industry did not lag much behind that of Belgium. Then they forced the union with Egypt on us. You do know that Gamal Abdel Nasser was an American agent? Don't you remember that the Americans helped him in 1956 against Israel, France and Britain! And that was the beginning of the nationalization of industry. Then they brought in the Ba'th party and socialism of the worst kind. They wanted to crush religion in the country, because when people lose their religion they lose their sense of right and wrong.

---

[15] Cf. Inga Brandell/Annika Rabo, "Arab Nations and Nationalism: Dangers and Virtues of Transgressing Disciplines", in: *Orientalia Suecana*, LI–LII/2002–2003, pp. 35–46; Annika Rabo, "Trade across Borders: Views from Aleppo", in: Inga Brandell (ed.), *Borders, Boundaries and Transgressions*, London 2005, pp. 54–74. For an analysis of the importance of "Turkish occupation" for the development of Greek nationalism, cf. Michael Herzfeld, *The Social Production of Indifference: Exploring the Symbolic Roots of Western Bureaucracy*, Oxford 1992.

4. Interpreting Conspiracy Talk in Syria

A lot of research has been done on the topic of "a paranoid style in politics" and conspiracy theories.[16] The concern over and interest in conspiracies is also echoed in much of western popular culture. Conspiracies seem to be the theme of the year in American television series, a columnist recently noted in a large Swedish newspaper and cited *Rubicon* and *The Event* as examples.[17] But although conspiracy talk, as discussed above, is very prevalent in Syria, its content and concerns are much less "exotic" than in Europe and especially in the USA. Many contemporary conspiracies discussed in scholarly literature deal with western and notably American fears about aliens as well as plots and conspiracies related to new technologies.[18] Ideas and talk about conspiracy are clearly different in Syria. Summarizing the conspiracy talk discussed above, a few points stand out.

First of all, in the "it-has-all-been-planned" talk the topics are often quite prosaic and deal with very concrete and tangible threats. There is, second, seldom any consistency as to the details or the internal order of the analyses. The "it-has-all-been-planned" talk could in any given conversation range from rage over corruption in Syria to insisting that electricity cuts are made in order to fill the thoughts of citizens with unimportant worries, and to an exegesis of why Jews "throughout history have been distrusted because they have tried to dominate the world".[19] Third, most of my informants, disagree with the "facts" of others. There is consensus only on the far-reaching influence and capability of Israel and the USA. Fourth, sifting through my empirical data I can clearly see that men engage in conspiracy talk more often than women, and that more educated people are perhaps more prone to "it-has-all-been-planned" talk than people with little or no education. Although there is no single explanation for conspiracy talk in Syria,[20] it clearly speaks to questions of power and influence, subjectivities, personhood, and responsibility and blame.

---

16 Richard Hofstadter's essay from the early 1960s – "The Paranoid Style in American Politics" – discusses how certain right-wing American politicians see the world and express themselves. It has inspired scores of comments and reformulations and influenced work also outside the USA.

17 Cf. Hanna Fahl, in: *Svenska Dagbladet*, Sept. 24, 2010.

18 Cf. Jane Parish/Martin Parker (eds.), *The Age of Anxiety: Conspiracy Theory and the Human Sciences*, Oxford 2001.

19 I find no analytical value of dividing conspiracies into grand and petty as Daniel Pipes does (cf. *The Hidden Hand: Middle East Fears of Conspiracy*, Houndmills 1996, p. 9). On the contrary, it is important to analyse connections between them if we are to grasp everyday conspiracy talk in Syria.

20 Cf. Matthew Gray, *Conspiracy Theories in the Arab World*, London 2010, p. 3.

Finally, and on a different note, I would like to underline that conspiracy talk in Syria concomitantly gives opportunities for individuals to assert their creativity or persuasiveness.[21] Such talk not only consists of repeated plots but often of new and unique elements, added by the speaker. It is important, I think, to see that there is a tension between the need to list the usual suspects – e.g. the regime, the USA, Israel – in order to credibly frame the narrative, and the need to make a creative contribution within this overarching discourse. Hence, conspiracy talk in Syria can also be analysed as a form of entertainment or as a way to "elevate" trivial incidents.[22] Men more than women, and the educated more than the illiterate, have the time and the cultural resources to cultivate the creative aspect of conspiracy talk.[23] But it is equally important to underline that such talk is not entertainment only. After all, conspiracies do exist – in Syria and elsewhere.

Conspiracies, as noted by Coward and Swann, were normal and widespread in, for example, early modern Europe and "an integral part of politics, the principal means by which rules were deposed".[24] Such conspiracies and plotting have until today also been the "normal" way of regime change in much of the modern Middle East. Experiences of such plotting in large part account for how politics are perceived in Syria. Cubitt makes a distinction between *conspiracy theory* and an analysis in which conspiracies are regarded "as a normal and widespread activity".[25] Propagators of conspiracy theories, according to Cubitt, in contrast to those seeing conspiracies as normal, attribute events in the past and present to human volition.[26] They sharply differentiate between good and evil, and they see a difference between a superficial and a hidden reality. These aspects may be more or less pronounced in the individual conspiracy theories.

---

21 Cf. Mark Fenster, *Conspiracy Theories: Secrecy and Power in American Culture*, Minneapolis 1999, pp 79–80, 210.

22 "Elevating" incidents to a conspiracy is probably common in many places. In Sweden, for example, the murder of Prime Minister Olof Palme on a Stockholm street in 1986 is still widely believed to have been the product of a conspiracy. That way, the murder becomes more important and "meaningful" than if Palme was simply shot by a "common criminal".

23 This is a huge and important topic which I have only recently begun to think about. I would very much like to see some comparative research on the topic of class, gender, and conspiracy talk.

24 Barry Coward/Julian Swann, "Introduction", in: Coward/Swann (eds.), *Conspiracies and Conspiracy Theory in Early Modern Europe*, Aldershot 2004, pp. 1–11, p. 2.

25 Geoffrey Cubitt, *The Jesuit Myth: Conspiracy Theory and Politics in Nineteenth-Century France*, Oxford 1993, p. 1.

26 Cf. Cubitt, *Jesuit Myth*, p. 2.

Cubitt's distinction is enlightening but also rather problematic since hidden or "unseen" realities are perfectly normal in societies where, for example, the presence of witches is considered mundane and taken for granted. Many anthropologists have noted the similarities between beliefs in witchcraft and beliefs in conspiracies. Both can be understood as ways to causally link events and to decide on blame and – or – responsibility. In Evans-Pritchard's classical account of the Azande, witchcraft is an idiom that allows to assign the ultimate blame or responsibility for bad events.[27] The Azande do not believe in coincidences. Evans-Pritchard explains that if a granary collapses just when a man is resting under it the Azande put it down to witchcraft. It is not that they cannot accept that the granary collapses. They acknowledge, for example, that termites may have weakened the structure. But the fact that it collapsed at that particular moment when that particular man was resting under it can only be attributed to the work of a witch.[28] Bad things happening to people are thus caused by witchcraft, even though witches may be unaware of their own powers. For the Azande, witchcraft is thus both normal and widespread but also part of a hidden reality which literally cannot be seen. Witches are responsible for their acts, but they cannot really be blamed.

Questions of "causality, responsibility, and culpability" are, as noted by Shaver, part of wider cultural values.[29] To blame someone, he stresses, is to take part in "a particular sort of social explanation".[30] Like the Azande described by Evans-Pritchard, my Syrian informants do not believe in coincidences. But unlike the Azande witches, conspirators are, as my informants underline, evil because they are fully aware of what they are doing. Somebody causes men to watch pornography – to be kneaded like dough – rather than to work productively, pray, or act politically. Somebody is to blame; somebody is responsible.

As noted, my Syrians informants see contemporary national or international political plotting as normal in the sense that it is perceived to be prevalent and frequent. But they are not happy about this normality and demand accountability and transparency instead. West and Sanders point out that such buzz words can be analytically linked to conspiracy talk and feelings of suspicion. The more these buzz words are seeping into our vocabu-

---

27 Cf. E. E. Evans-Pritchard, *Witchcraft, Oracles and Magic among Azande*, Oxford 1976.

28 Cf. Evans-Pritchard, *Witchcraft*, p. 22.

29 Kelly G. Shaver, *The Attribution of Blame: Causality, Responsibility, and Blameworthiness*, New York 1985, p. 2.

30 Shaver, *Attribution of Blame*, p. 4.

lary, the more elusive they have become.[31] People in many parts of the world have a feeling that "something is not as it is said to be".[32] This "something" easily feeds into theories or elaborations of hidden meanings in the world. Conspiracy theories, like any strong belief, are obviously tautological and self-referential where the proof is in the pudding.[33] Even if conspiracy theories are wrong, they might, as noted by Fenster, be "on to something".[34]

When we discuss or write about conspiracy theories or conspiracy talk we often get stuck in the details of each plot or plan. We clearly need details in order to compare the different contexts in which these theories or this talk occurs. But by paying closer attention to ideas of personhood and responsibility among our informants, rather than to the elements of the plots, we should be able to arrive at more comparative analyses.

Another way of interpreting conspiracy talk in Syria is to compare it to the way modern anthropology understands rituals as both "doing" and "saying" something, and that these two aspects mutually reinforce each other. Clearly, conspiracy reasoning can be seen as a desperate expression of the weak. Such predictable, yet flexible, analyses as those in the Aleppo market and elsewhere in Syria provide a comforting predictability, as well as meaning and order, to events perceived to be beyond one's influence. This is the "doing" of conspiracy reasoning; the "saying" is more ambiguous. On the one hand, it squarely puts blame and responsibility on distant, and not so distant, others. But on the other hand, conspiracy talk in many instances involves verbal self-flagellation.[35] Just as many of my informants stressed that almost everything of political importance is planned by cunning agents, they also,

---

31 In *Transparency and Conspiracy*, the volume edited by West and Sanders, anthropologists show how the world is seemingly becoming less transparent, how corruption is spreading, and that good governance is a chimera (cf. Harry G. West/ Todd Sanders (eds.), *Transparency and Conspiracy: Ethnographies of Suspicion in the New World Order*, Durham, NC 2003).

32 West/Sanders, *Transparency and Conspiracy*, p. 2.

33 Brian L. Keeley argues that by studying conspiracy theories we can learn about theoretical explanations more generally (cf. "Of Conspiracy Theories", in: *Journal of Philosophy, Inc.*, 96/1999, 3, pp. 109–126). Steve Clarke, on the other hand, claims that although such a project is important, Keeley has gone about it "in the wrong way" ("Conspiracy Theories and Conspiracy Theorizing", in: *Philosophy of the Social Sciences*, 32/2002, pp. 131–150, p. 133). Both are philosophers, and both take conspiracy reasoning very seriously.

34 Fenster, *Conspiracy Theories*, p. 67.

35 For an account of blame and self-accusation in Greece, cf. Michael Herzfeld, *The Social Production of Indifference: Exploring the Symbolic Roots of Western Bureaucracy*, Chicago 1992, pp. 134–135. This is the only other example of self-flagellation I have come across.

again and again, argued that they do not really deserve anything better. "We have the rulers we deserve", they said, or: "We are so divided and so unorganised, we will never be better". After the massive Israeli incursion into the West Bank in 2002, I visited a trader in Aleppo who complained about the behaviour of his market neighbours, saying that they put garbage outside his shop and claiming that this was due to jealousy and a lack of affection. He continued: "The problem of the bazaar is the problem of the Arab world. There is too much jealousy and no affection between us. That is why we are divided and why Israel and the USA have power over everything". By saying that that they did not deserve better rulers, Syrians implied that others had the benign power holders they deserve. Through global links and connections Syrians are made aware of the world order in which there are two types of nations. In the first type, citizens enjoy democratic rights, freedom of expression, and free and fair elections. In those nations, citizens have governments (rather than having a *nizam*) which have the interests of their citizens at heart because they need those citizens. There is the rule of law and the accountability of public servants. The second type of nations lacks all this. Nations of the first type are economically strong and commonly use that strength as an instrument to dominate nations of the second type, both politically and economically. Syrian informants constantly underlined the "second-class" status of Syria, thereby often idealizing the "first-class" status of other nations. Through comparisons, a political order of inclusion and exclusion is both manifested and created, and the boundaries of "us" and "them" are contextually fixed.

The "we-get-what we-deserve" reasoning in Syria may seem like a contemporary version of fatalism, commonly associated in the West with Islam.[36] But it is, I would argue, far from the case. The "it-is-written" fatalism in contemporary Syria is a reminder of the need to accept and embrace the power of God to both initiate and terminate the life of every single human being. Such fatalism is hence an equalizer focused on the individual: we come into this world with nothing, and we leave with nothing, regardless of riches or misfortunes. Such fatalism does not preclude Syrians from engaging in very earthly pursuits. "Fatalism" can and does co-exist with the reasoning of "it-has-all-been-planned" and "we-get-what we-deserve".

But the "saying" of conspiracy talk simultaneously reaffirms that the speakers actually deserve better. The persuasive power of conspiratorial rea-

---

[36] Pipes claims that the paranoid mentality in the Middle East impedes modernization (cf. *Hidden Hand*, p. 13). I would rather argue that it is intimately linked to modernization.

soning in Syria is totally different from an acceptance of humanity's equal fate. It rests on contrasts and differences, and it is grounded in the comparative experience of people propagating them. My informants can clearly sense that what they lack – justice, the rule of law, economic and political development (or, more concretely, riches and power over other nations) – is precisely what important others guard, protect, and monopolize. Inequalities and differences in political power, wealth, and resources cry out for an explanation in the modern world, because, through global connections and national state-building, Syrians, like other people, have been taught to expect a better life and a better world. Thus I argue that blaming "us" is the flip side of blaming "them" – one cannot exist without the other.

5. The New Silence and the New Voices

> Isn't it fantastic! The Tunisian regime has fallen. Mubarak is gone and here in Syria people are starting to protest. And it is the young people who are bringing it all about. We used to say that the young generation is spoiled and selfish and has no political consciousness. But we were wrong. The young have the courage we do not have. I am very very optimistic.

These euphoric words expressed by my friend Rim in Damascus in March 2011 stand in sharp contrast to how she expressed frustration over being "kneaded like dough" in the beginning of this article. Although not all people I met in Syria in the spring were so outspokenly optimistic, there was – as noted earlier – a noticeable disappearance of "it-has-all-been-planned" talk. It was as if the recent events in the region where regimes were overthrown and truths about their corrupt practices were openly voiced made "it-has-all-been planned" talk superfluous. It seemed clear to most Syrians I met that these events had not, in fact, been planned at all. They happened because people – especially young people – acted rather than blamed distant others or victimized themselves.

The outcome of the so-called Arab spring for the region as a whole in general, and for Syria in particular, is still not clear. Conspiracy talk has not disappeared. In particular, it flourishes among supporters and representatives of the regime. They blame enemies inside and outside the country for undermining the integrity of the country. But even if the Assad regime is able to hang on to power for a number of years in Syria, I think that the new silence and the new voices are here to stay. A point of no return has been reached so that everyday politics will be differently performed in the future.

IV. Travelling Theories

Andrew McKenzie-McHarg (Gotha)

The Transfer of Anti-Illuminati Conspiracy Theories to the United States in the Late Eighteenth Century

1. Conspiracism as a Reading Experience

In late eighteenth-century America, a confrontation with an act of political violence was not the only experience which might turn thoughts to notions of conspiracy. In some cases, it sufficed to visit a bookstore. On a visit to Philadelphia in April 1798, Jedidiah Morse, the pastor at the First Church in Charlestown, purchased a copy of a work which had recently caused some excitement in Europe.[1] This volume bore the title "Proofs of a Conspiracy against all the Religions and Governments of Europe". Its author, the Scottish scientist John Robison, claimed with this book to unveil the real cause of the French Revolution.[2] In Robison's mind, the French Revolution represented only the fruition of a preliminary stage in the anti-royalist and anti-clerical plans of an originally German secret society known as the Illuminati.

Eight years earlier, in the fall of 1790, Morse had been in another bookstore, this time in Boston, when he stumbled across a recent edition of religious songs. It caught his attention that the author had purged the songs of all references to Christ's divine nature. The rest of the episode is recounted by Morse's biographer, Richard Moss: "Alarmed, Morse wrote the *Boston Centinel* in order to alert the public of the presence of this dangerous book. He argued that if such alterations in children's books passed unchallenged, whoever was responsible would grow bolder and 'every sacred truth of the Holy Bible may be in danger'".[3]

Such an experience was undoubtedly one of many whose cumulative effect was to convince men such as Morse that traditional Christian faith was being eroded. Elusive and perplexing remained, however, the causes of this trend. But it is not implausible to assert that Morse's visit to the bookstore in

---

1 Cf. Vernon Stauffer, *New England and the Bavarian Illuminati*, New York 1918, p. 233.

2 John Robison, *Proofs of a Conspiracy against all the Religions and Governments of Europe, Carried on in the Secret Meetings of Free Masons, Illuminati and Reading Societies: Collected from Good Authorities*, London 1798.

3 Richard J. Moss, *The Life of Jedidiah Morse: A Station of Peculiar Exposure*, Knoxville 1995, p. 56.

Philadelphia provided an answer to the nagging questions posed by the visit he had made eight years earlier to the Boston bookstore. In revealing the insidious operations of the Illuminati, Robison submitted an explanation which could find application well beyond the context of revolutionary events in France. Furthermore, his account of events seemed to receive additional corroboration from a French ex-Jesuit, Augustin Barruel, who had published a massive four-volume work detailing the pre-meditated overthrow of the *ancien régime*.[4] The English translation of this work arrived in the colonies in June 1799. Once more, the Illuminati figured prominently.

The Illuminati actually existed. Contrary to widespread and persistent opinion, the society did not begin as a sub-branch of Freemasonry, even if it later became linked to the lodges as a result of its subsequent expansion. Rather, its founding occurred in 1776 within the student milieu of the University of Ingolstadt in Bavaria. The initiative came from the Professor of Canonical Law, Adam Weishaupt. 1776 was, of course, also an important year in American history, but none of the sources indicate that there was anything to this other than mere coincidence.[5] There were in any case never any branches of the Illuminati in America nor was there any polemical tradition in the young Republic which targeted this secret society. One can only presume that, until the arrival of Robison's book, the Illuminati were a virtual unknown for Americans.

In view of the blank expressions which mention of the Illuminati must have drawn from most Americans and in view of the relative paucity of references to America contained within Robison's volume, it is somewhat surprising that his ideas would resonate in the mind of a New England Calvinist preacher like Morse. But resonate they obviously did, primarily because the

---

[4] Cf. Augustin Barruel, *Mémoires pour servir à l'histoire du Jacobinisme*, London 1797–1798. Translated by Robert Clifford into English as: *Memoirs, Illustrating the history of Jacobinism*, London 1797–1798.

[5] It hardly need be said that conspiracy theorists are instinctively suspicious of any appeal to chance or coincidence. Thus, there have been attempts to construe some deeper meaning behind this coincidence (cf. George Johnson, *Architects of Fear: Conspiracy Theories and Paranoia in American Politics*, Los Angeles 1983, p. 76). In one of the first works which treated the tradition of conspiracism as a serious object of academic inquiry Johannes Rogalla von Bieberstein claimed that the rebel colonialists on the further side of the Atlantic were a source of inspiration for the group of students who gathered around Adam Weishaupt, the society's founder, in Ingolstadt (cf. *Die These von der Verschwörung 1776–1945: Philosophen, Freimaurer, Juden, Liberale und Sozialisten als Verschwörer gegen die Sozialordnung*, Flensburg 1992, p. 49). He however does not provide any evidence of this and I have not been able to find any in the Illuminati documents.

notion of a conspiracy itself seemed to throw light onto trends within American society. If few had heard of the Illuminati before the publication of Robison's work, then this only attested to their skill in cloaking their actions in secrecy.[6]

In the course of the following year, Jedidiah Morse held three sermons, all subsequently published, which aimed to alert his audience to the presence of the Illuminati on the North American Continent.[7] Other clergymen in America willingly affirmed the view that American society had been developing in a direction which betrayed the signature of Illuminati influence. David Tappan, a professor of theology at Harvard, conveyed to the university's departing senior class of 1798 the sense of crisis exacerbated by signs of Illuminati infiltration.[8] And the president of Yale, Timothy Dwight, submitted his dire assessment in a lecture delivered some weeks later on July 4.[9]

Furthermore, through acquaintances who served in the Cabinet, Morse attempted to alert President John Adams to the danger threatening America. Adams himself was at the time in an apprehensive frame of mind – he had issued a call for a national day of fasting in an attempt to instil a sense of common destiny in his fellow countrymen. This day fell on May 9, 1798 and served as the first occasion on which Morse elaborated from the pulpit upon the infiltration of the Illuminati into America. There is the possibility that Adams was influenced by the spectre of conspiracy invoked by Morse – his call for a second day of fasting and prayer in 1799 was tinged with the darker tone of a conspiracist interpretation. But Adams was circumspect in a way that Morse had not been. There was after all an egregious dearth of hard evidence which might substantiate Morse's claims. When the highly critical assessments issued by a number of European commentators on the allegations made by Robison and Barruel reached America, they served to deflate much of the overblown anxiety which Morse and his cohorts had generated.

---

6 Conspiracists in general frequently appeal to this argument. For its specific deployment by Morse, cf. Stauffer, *New England*, p. 259.

7 Jedidiah Morse, *A Sermon delivered at the New North Church, in the morning, and at the afternoon in Charlestown, May 9th, 1798*, Boston 1798; *A Sermon preached at Charlestown, Nov 1798, on the anniversary thanksgiving in Massachusetts*, Boston 1798–1799; *A Sermon, exhibiting the present dangers, and the consequent duties of the citizens of the United States in America: Delivered at Charlestown, April 25, 1799*, Charlestown 1799.

8 David Tappan, *A Discourse delivered in the Chapel of Harvard College, June 19, 1798, Occasioned by the Approaching Departure of the Senior Class from the University*, Boston 1798.

9 Timothy Dwight, *The Duty of Americans in the Present Crisis. Illustrated in a Discourse, Preached on the Fourth of July, 1798*, New Haven 1798.

This was, however, only the initial phase in the remarkable American career of the Illuminati and, more particularly, Adam Weishaupt. This career has for the most part unfolded in narratives cultivated on the right-wing fringes of the American political scene. The first bout of anti-Illuminati conspiracist anxiety which gripped the young nation at the end of the eighteenth century was, however, anything but a fringe phenomenon. It found its spokesmen among prominent clerics who could be numbered among the Establishment elite. In part, it reflected genuine insecurities about their own social standing, but it found a wider compass in the international troubles which beset the young republic and seemed to threaten its sovereignty.

The American historian Vernon Stauffer outlined the ebb and flow of these conspiracist fears in a dissertation published in 1918 and entitled "New England and the Bavarian Illuminati". Stauffer's work demonstrates how sound judgement and comprehensive familiarity with the relevant sources can produce historical scholarship of enduring value. It would seem that there is little to add, and nothing which would impose upon us the need of revising Stauffer's essential findings. But a few details not known to Stauffer have the potential of enhancing our understanding of this episode and teasing out its relevance for the more general phenomenon of conspiracism.

2. Conspiracism: A Natural Tendency or an "Acquired Taste"?

One such detail can be addressed already at this juncture because it corroborates Stauffer's own judgement while touching upon an aspect of conspiracism around which many of the following observations revolve. With the term "conspiracism", I employ a concept first introduced by the American academic Frank Mintz in a book which examined the ideology of the extreme right wing in American political culture. According to Mintz, conspiracism is a "belief in the primacy of conspiracies in the unfolding of history".[10] Conspiracism manifests itself in what are popularly known as "conspiracy

---

10 Frank P. Mintz, *The Liberty Lobby and the American Right: Race, Conspiracy and Culture*, Westport 1985, p. 4. In the discussion of the extreme right in America the term has found repeated usage. Thus Chip Berlet and Matthew Lyons provide the following definition: "Conspiracism is a particular narrative form of scapegoating that frames the enemy as part of a vast insidious plot against the common good, while it valorizes the scapegoater as a hero for sounding the alarm" (*Right Wing Populism in America: Too Close for Comfort*, New York 2000, p. 11). Michael Barkun provides a somewhat more concise definition when he speaks of conspiracism as "the belief that powerful, hidden, evil forces control human destinies" (*A Culture of Conspiracy: Apocalyptic Visions in Contemporary America*, Berkeley 2003, p. 2).

theories" – a term of relatively recent origin which, as I will argue later, is somewhat misleading.

In a landmark essay first published in 1964, conspiracism was identified by Richard Hofstadter as a recurrent feature in the history of American politics.[11] Instead of using the term "conspiracism", Hofstadter subsumed the propensity to project conspiracies under the heading of the "paranoid style". The term was suggestive of a treatment which psychologized and marginalized the particular mentality it denoted. This tendency was countered by the historian Gordon Wood – at least as it applied to the eighteenth century. His essay represents a milestone in the understanding of eighteenth-century conspiracism due to its persuasive argument that such an interpretation of history was entirely consonant with the premises which informed the intellectual culture of this period.[12] Wood speaks of the "underlying metaphysics" or of the "grammar and vocabulary" in which the thought of the age was expressed.[13] Whereas Hofstadter thus describes a recurring trait threading its way through the history of American political culture, Wood's emphasis is less diachronic and more synchronic. His interest lies in what might in Foucauldian terms be seen as an aspect of the *episteme* of eighteenth-century thought (even if Wood never references Foucault). More specifically, Wood argued that a form of causality linking events and trends with human actions could only be sustained in the face of increasing social and historical complexity by assigning these human actions an intentionally covert character. There was thus nothing original about positing intrigue and conspiracy – it rather reflected the general predicament experienced by a view of the world which had abandoned the recourse to supernaturalism but had not

---

11 Richard Hofstadter, *The Paranoid Style in American Politics and Other Essays*, London 1966.

12 Gordon Wood, "Conspiracy and the Paranoid Style: Causality and Deceit in the Eighteenth Century", in: *The William and Mary Quarterly*, 39/1982, 3, pp. 402–441. Due to his focus upon the eighteenth century, Wood does not address the issue of how we are then to treat conspiracism when it is no longer sustained by the dominant epistemological culture. Presumably, the epistemological naiveties of the eighteenth century survive in some form on the fringes, and this in turn explains why conspiracism moves from being a mainstream to a fringe phenomenon in the course of time. Consideration needs to be given to the time-frame for this process – if one concurs with Daniel Walker Howe then at the very least the "conspiracy paradigm", as he calls it, held sway over the minds of men through a good portion of the nineteenth century (cf. Howe, *The Political Culture of the American Whigs*, Chicago 1979, pp. 79–81).

13 Wood, *The Paranoid Style*, pp. 407, 422.

yet fully developed and inculcated a sociological vocabulary equipped to deal with historical processes and societal change.

However, this raises an important question in the historical analysis of conspiracism: are we dealing with a pattern of interpretation which, as Wood seems to suggest, coalesced naturally and more or less involuntarily in the minds of eighteenth-century actors on the basis of the presumptions they held about the way the world worked? Or should we rather describe conspiracism in the eighteenth century as an idea that could be treated as the original creation of its specific intellectual progenitor who then planted it in the mind of another actor before it was then further passed onto others? In actual fact, the either-or configuration suggested by these alternatives is misleading. Both can be seen as complementary. Eighteenth-century intellectual culture represented fertile ground for the idea of conspiracy, but the specific seed still needed to be planted. In this sense, Wood's work can only function as starting point for more detailed reconstructions of the efflorescence of conspiracism.

Of course, this combination of generalized receptiveness and specific instantiation can be found in virtually all intellectual history. We might celebrate the achievements of great minds, but the fact that these minds are not working from scratch becomes obvious in those instances where the same discovery is made independently. Thus, both Newton and Leibniz worked out the details of infinitesimal calculus without collaborating and, in a similar manner, Darwin and Wallace both developed theories of natural selection as a result of independent inquiry. If we step down a significant number of rungs on the ladder of intellectual achievement, it might seem at first that we can assert the same fact for Robison and Barruel, the two literary purveyors of the legend that the Illuminati had concocted a conspiracy which, by implication of its global nature, extended across the Atlantic to America's shores. Their essential agreement regarding the explanation for recent historical events was all the more remarkable in view of their wildly contrasting biographies. The Abbé Barruel was an ex-Jesuit who had become involved in anti-Enlightenment circles of publicists after the Society of Jesus was dissolved.[14] Robison was a Scottish scientist who, among other things, invented the siren, a curiously apposite detail in view of the alarmist character of his conspiracist ideas.

---

14 For a discussion of conspiracism in this context, cf. Amos Hoffmann, *Anatomy of a Conspiracy: The Origins of the Theory of the Philosophe Conspiracy 1750–1789*, Diss. University of Michigan, 1986, pp. 149–205.

It is hardly surprising that this alignment in the historical interpretation of Barruel and Robison was not seen by eighteenth-century observers as an indicator that their world-views – despite all the other differences in their respective intellectual backgrounds – were informed by the same epistemological presumptions. Rather, to these observers the independent nature of the discoveries made by Barruel and Robison attested to the empirical truth of their claims. Stauffer wrote of the "precious conceit" cherished by the adherents of this version of history, namely "that the two 'great' European writers on the subject of Illuminism, Robison and Barruel, while working independently had unearthed the same set of facts and arrived at the same conclusion as to their import".[15] Thus, in a volume which appeared in 1802 when the waves of agitation had all but subsided in America, Seth Payson, a pastor at the Congregational Church in Rindge, New Hampshire, wrote: "It is obvious that the testimony of these writers is greatly strengthened by its remarkable coincidence".[16] His conclusion was that "a greater degree of harmony could not be expected from any two historians relating events of equal magnitude".[17]

But there is an explanation for this convergence in the views of Robison and Barruel which lies not just in the underlying metaphysical assumptions shared by diverse participants in the political discourse of the eighteenth century. Rather, it is to be found in a process of transfer. We can appreciate this by turning our attention to a small German university town in the Duchy of Hessen-Darmstadt. It was in Gießen that the local director of government, Ludwig Adolf Christian Grolman, made mostly anonymous contributions to a journal bearing the title "Die neuesten Religions-Begebenheiten" (roughly translatable as: "The Most Recent Events in Religion").[18] Grolman had at one stage been a member of the Illuminati. He had, however, grown disenchanted at being denied the advancement to the higher grades for which he believed he qualified. After the suppression of the society he had retained in his possession material which he would later publish in order to perpetuate the myth that the Illuminati had survived its persecution and unleashed the French Revolution. Indeed, in his contributions to the Gießen journal Grol-

---

15 Stauffer, *New England*, p. 311.

16 Seth Payson, *Proofs of the Real Existence and Dangerous Tendency of Illuminism*, Charlestown 1802, p. 18.

17 Payson, *Proofs*, p. 19.

18 The best treatment of Grolman's life is to be found in Rolf Haaser, *Spätaufklärung und Gegenaufklärung: Bedingungen und Auswirkungen der religiösen, politischen und ästhetischen Streitkultur in Gießen zwischen 1770 und 1830*, Darmstadt 1997, pp. 58–138.

man had outlined an elaborate conspiracy theory.[19] Some issues of this German journal made their way to the country house of one of Robison's friends where, upon reading them, Robison's eyes were opened to the real but secret history of recent events. In addition to this, Grolman, together with the theologian Johann August Starck, was involved in supplying Barruel with material for his work.[20]

Thus, even if both Barruel and Robison were living in a time marked by a heightened receptiveness to the general notion of a conspiracy, this detail also reveals that in their invocation of a specifically Illuminati contribution to the subversion of the old order they were drawing upon a common source. Both were taking their cues from Grolman. This allows us to see that when it comes to reconstructing the genesis of the vision of conspiracy expounded by Barruel and Robison, the specific way in which ideas could be channelled and transferred was just as important as the more generalized propensities induced by the epistemological presumptions of late eighteenth-century thought. Indeed, if we cross to the other side of the Atlantic, there are no grounds for believing that conspiracism was introduced with the arrival of the volumes penned by Robison and Barruel. Rather, we can find earlier manifestations of conspiracism in the tense atmosphere of mutual mistrust precluding the wars of independence and in even earlier fears of uprisings among the slaves.[21] But obviously the more specific fear generated by the spectre of an Illuminati conspiracy was for American readers a foreign imported ware. As we have seen for the particular case of Morse, he first absorbed it after purchasing Robison's volume in the Philadelphia bookstore in 1798. In what follows I want to look more closely at what happened to the notion of an Illuminati conspiracy as a result of its transfer across the Atlantic.

---

[19] The contributions dedicated to the exposure of the conspiracy were then collated and printed anonymously as *Nachrichten von einem großen aber unsichtbaren Bunde gegen die christliche Religion und die monarchischen Staaten*, 1795.

[20] Haaser, *Spätaufklärung und Gegenaufklärung*, p. 65. Starck would go on to produce a German re-working of the same myth in his *Triumph der Philosophie im achtzehnten Jahrhunderte*, 1803.

[21] For the prevalence of concepts of conspiracy in the discourse at the time of the Revolutionary Wars, cf. Bernard Bailyn, *The Ideological Origins of the American Revolution*, Cambridge, MA 1992, pp. 144–159.

3. Transfer and Speech Acts

The academic interest in transfer is a relatively recent phenomenon, but, as is often the case, its occurrence has long been observed and described in a different and more naive terminology. Thus, eighteenth-century conspiracy theorists were highly aware of the "transfer" of ideas and ideologies, even if they tended to interpret it more as infiltration and to falsely concretize it in terms of human agency. The process of transfer differs from a simpler process corresponding to the spread or dispersion of an idea. Transfer involves the crossing of a boundary, be that boundary linguistic, cultural, or political in nature. Crossing the boundary has, however, an impact upon the character of the ideas that are transferred. In this sense, transfer can be a process of creative adaptation in a way that dispersion is not. New aspects accrue and enrich and possibly distort the original idea while at the same time old aspects of the original idea are shed.

It firstly needs to be asked in what sense the passage of Robison's and Barruel's notion of a conspiracy across the Atlantic corresponds to a transfer, and, more particularly, what the nature of the border was across which the transfer occurred. Essentially, the border was political – but less in the narrow geographical sense and more in accordance with a cultural and ideological meaning. Robison and Barruel were monarchists devoted to what their respective countries had inherited from the past. America represented a bold attempt to realize a republican form of government on a geographically unprecedented scale. The innovation was not lost on Morse who also hoped that his fellow citizens would "be impressed by the high importance of the experiment we are now making for the world".[22]

The gulf separating the proto-reactionary stance of European conspiracy theorists from the political mindset of their American readers can be most effectively thrown into profile by quoting the opening words of Barruel's version of events: "At an early period of the French Revolution, there appeared a sect calling itself Jacobin, and teaching that *all men were equal and free*! In the name of their equality and disorganizing liberty, they trampled under foot the altar and the throne; they stimulated all nations to rebellion, and aimed at plunging them ultimately into the horrors of anarchy".[23] The cumulative effect of the following 1295 pages aimed to demonstrate why the principle that *all men were equal and free*! should induce indignation in the reader. However, the prospects that Barruel's work might provoke outrage in the

---

22 Morse, *November 1798*, p. 15.
23 Barruel, *Memoirs I*, p. i; italics in the original.

American reader had to be queried in view of the fact that this reader was a citizen of a nation which had claimed its independence by declaring the "self-evident" truths: "that all men are created equal, that they are endowed by their Creator with certain inalienable Rights, that among these are Life, Liberty and the pursuit of Happiness".[24]

Admittedly, the juxtaposition of these words against those of Barruel has been contrived to starkly highlight the feats of adaptation confronting Morse – and in view of this, two qualifications should be mentioned. Firstly, Morse's political views had a greater congruence to those of Robison rather than those of the more reactionary Barruel. Secondly, invoking an "American reader" falsely insinuates a consensus in America about how the ideas expressed in the Declaration of Independence were to be translated into the political culture. In actual fact, this consensus did not exist, and much of the bitter party-wrangling was ultimately rooted in a clash of political visions. Morse's sentiments were aligned with traditional notions of a social order based on distinction and deference. This also implied a vehement opposition towards those alternative conceptions of society whose precepts were more radically egalitarian.[25]

---

24 *In Congress, July 4, 1776. The unanimous declaration of the thirteen United States of America*, Baltimore 1776, http://hdl.loc.gov/loc.rbc/bdsdcc.02101 (accessed Jan. 15, 2012).

25 Obviously, critical issues are being intimated here which deserve a more probing and nuanced investigation but which would represent a deviation away from the more conceptual issues addressed in this paper. Suffice to say, I have discussed with colleagues whether the conspiracism espoused by Morse and the other representatives of the New England clergy can be subsumed under the "conspiracy paradigm" which Daniel Walker Howe identified as a defining characteristic of American politics in the nineteenth century. Howe saw this paradigm as the "logical corollary" to republican ideals (cf. Howe, *Political Culture*, p. 81). I tend to think that these ideals were first fully installed into American political culture with the victory of the Jeffersonian party in 1800. For an eloquent analysis of this decisive development in American political culture, cf. Joyce Appelby, *Capitalism and a New Social Order: The Republican Vision of the 1790s*, New York 1984. Morse's conspiracist apprehensions were actually rooted in a dire prognosis of the social ramifications of that political culture which in turn would generate its own specifically republican "conspiracy paradigm". Appelby has also described the contentiousness surrounding the issues of how the principle of equality was to be realized and reflected in the political realities of the young republic. Adams believed that any system which did not make allowances for a natural propensity in human societies to generate an aristocracy was doomed to fail. He envisaged a government capable of taming the aristocratic impulse instead of denying its permanent imprint upon human nature. Jefferson was far more disdainful of attempts to accommodate an aristocracy. For an analysis of how Adams went against the tide of popular sentiment and championed a system that attempted to harness the ambitions of an

But if this might have predisposed Morse and other members of the New England clergy to a more sympathetic hearing of the jeremiads issued by Old World defenders of the old order, it does not change the basic fact that considerable feats of adaptation were required to then make this message palatable for an American audience. In an attempt to more precisely grasp what the transfer of the anti-Illuminati conspiracy narrative actually entailed, I would like to explore a complex of ideas which can remind us of a general and oft-overlooked aspect of conspiracism. In his seminal series of lectures "How to Do Things with Words", the Oxford philosopher J. L. Austin drew a distinction between performative and constative utterances. Austin claimed that "for too long the assumption of philosophers [had been] that the business of a 'statement' can only be to 'describe' some state of affairs, or to 'state some fact' which it must do either truly of falsely".[26] Philosophy had thus exhibited a bias for examining constative utterances. But as Austin pointed out, many utterances could only be understood in view of their performative function. An example often cited by Austin was a promise which as a statement could not be evaluated in terms of being true or false. To clarify the first distinction between performative and constative utterances, Austin introduced the further distinction between locutionary and illocutionary acts. Any speech act can be analytically decomposed into these two acts. The locutionary act is the act by which a meaningful statement is articulated, while the illocutionary act embeds this in the context provided by some convention. Constative utterances are those in which the locutionary act takes centre stage, while with a performative utterance the focus shifts to the illocutionary act.[27]

The relevance of Austin's ideas for the phenomenon of conspiracism requires us to abandon the focus upon individual statements and use his terms in the looser sense which allows us to apply the terms "locutionary" and "illocutionary" to aggregates of statements, such as those that make up a "theory". Two points can then be made. Firstly, conspiracism emerges from

---

elite, cf. Appelby's *Liberalism and Republicanism in the Historical Imagination*, Cambridge, MA 1996, pp. 188–209 (Chapter 7: "John Adams and the New Republican Synthesis").

26 J. L. Austin, *How to Do Things with Words*, Oxford 1975, p. 1.

27 Of course, the application of Austin's ideas for intellectual history has generated an extensive discussion. I point simply to Quentin Skinner's essay "Interpretation and the Understanding of Speech Acts" (in: Skinner, *Visions of Politics, Vol. 1: Regarding Method*, Cambridge, MA 2002, pp. 103–127), and add that there are complexities lurking here which I naively skirt, confident that simply introducing the distinction between the illocutionary and locutionary dimensions of language will in itself prove fruitful enough for further discussion.

a polemical context in which statements are essentially accusations. An accusation is a form of statement which tightly coils within itself both a locutionary and illocutionary dimension. In making an accusation, one performs the act of identifying and denouncing the accused, but of course the accusation, in order to be effective, is dependent upon the adherence of the locutionary act to the criteria of truth. After all, I cannot accuse a person I dislike of any random transgression but only of transgressions where a plausible case can be made for this person having committed them.

This might seem to be splitting hairs, but it is nevertheless important simply because to attain a correct historical and sociological understanding of "conspiracy theories" it is necessary to relinquish at the outset any naive notion that "conspiracy theories" are theories in the strict sense of a disinterested attempt to explain some historical phenomenon or history itself. What later takes on the name "conspiracy theory" actually has its origins in the denunciations made by one group attempting to delegitimize and disqualify another group with opposing ideas and interests.[28]

Thus, Austin's distillation of two dimensions to language adds another important way in which we can move beyond the analysis offered by Wood. Conspiracism emerges not just as a result of a dispassionate attempt to understand historical events and trends. Rather, it is generated in a context of accusation and denunciation – "speech acts", in which the performative and the constative are tightly interwoven. We thus need to note that conspiracism, like language in general, has a dual nature – it is an instrument deployed both to understand the world and to change and influence it.

Indeed, conspiracy theorists are themselves often highly attuned to the illocutionary dimension of language and are apprehensive of the manner in which performative intents can hide behind apparently earnest and sincere constative statements. Thus, Barruel writes:

> Of all the arts put into practice by the conspirators, none has succeeded better with them, than that perpetual appeal in all their writings to toleration, reason and humanity [...] it would be useless for the reader to seek the definition of each of these high-sounding words imposed upon the public, when their private and real sentiments are to be seen in their continued cry of *Crush religion*.[29]

---

[28] It is interesting in this regard that within the academic system the actual term "conspiracy theory" is mostly deployed to achieve these same illocutionary ends. To describe a set of ideas or assertions as constituting a "conspiracy theory" is to effectively delegetimize them. As Jack Bratich has stated: "Conspiracy theories exist as a category not just of description but of disqualification" (*Conspiracy Panics: Political Rationality and Popular Culture*, Albany 2008, p. 3).

[29] Barruel, *Memoirs I*, 154; italics in the original.

The intolerance manifest in the antipathy towards Christianity as expressed by the Enlightenment philosophers is for Barruel evidence of the insincerity in their call for tolerance.

It is at this point that we can return to the concept of transfer. If a statement such as an accusation is to be understood in terms of both its locutionary and illocutionary dimensions, then it is also necessary to see how the illocutionary dimension ties the statement to a specific context. Austin sums up this insight with the following words:

> for some years we have been realizing more and more clearly that the occasion of an utterance matters seriously, and that the words used are to some extent to be 'explained' by the 'context' in which they are designed to be or have actually been spoken in a linguistic interchange.[30]

It is precisely this context which is disregarded as a result of the process of transfer. Transfer uproots a statement from the context in which it is embedded. The transfer of a statement has then the effect of distilling the locutionary dimension so that the statement takes on the notions of an idea to be judged according to whether it is true or false.

4. The Trans-Atlantic Transfer of Conspiracism

In the published version of his first sermon, Morse conceded that Robison's reflections "are peculiarly applicable to the people of Great Britain, for whose immediate benefit the book was written".[31] Indeed, *Proofs of a Conspiracy* contained passages which presumably sat uneasily with an American reader. Thus, Robison reminds his readers that "Our excellent Sovereign at his accession to the throne, declared to his Parliament that HE GLORIED IN HAVING BEEN BORN A BRITON. – Would to God that all and each of his subjects had entertained the same lofty notions of this good fortune!"[32] Read within its context, such a passage was not necessarily a jibe directed at ungrateful American insurrectionists. But other passages in which Robison's eulogizes the British Constitution must have begged the questions about the work's relevance for Americans who had so recently severed their relationship to this Constitution and embarked on their own course of constitutional experimentation.[33]

---

30 Austin, *How to Do Things*, p. 100.

31 Morse, *May 9th, 1798*, p. 25.

32 Robison, *Proofs*, p. 496.

33 Cf., for example, the extended passage with its conspicuously Burkean tone in Robison, *Proofs*, pp. 444–446.

Obviously, Robison's *Proofs of a Conspiracy* and Barruel's more reactionary volumes dramatized the narrative by extending and generalizing the range of entities which could fall prey to a conspiracy. Conspiracies were not just political affairs. They could also target religion and civil order. It was this broadened notion of an anti-religious and anti-social conspiracy which invested the work of monarchists with an ominous resonance for a portion of the readership in a country which had so recently divested itself of the impositions of monarchy. A passing phrase employed by Theodore Dwight, the brother to Yale's president, makes it possible to observe the way the imported message was reframed in being transferred to the American context. The French Revolution, he assured his readers, "was planned by a set of men whose avowed object was the overthrow of Altars and Thrones, that is the destruction of all Religion and Government".[34] There might be no king sitting upon a throne in America, and the altars in the nation's churches might have had a more modest and simpler appearance than those in Catholic Churches in the Old World. But based on a broad reading of the conspiracist message, American political and religious institutions were no less susceptible to subversion.

Indeed, in his second sermon, Morse provided a list of symptoms indicating that American society already suffered from a debilitated constitution. The catalogue included the infusion of a "selfish spirit" into many areas of American life, it extended to "the spread of infidel or atheistical principles", and was then enlarged by the state of internal disunion which had proven so fatal for the ancient Greeks. How much of this was to be attributed to the clandestine influence of hostile forces?

Reading Morse's sermons and the public pronouncements of other figures at this time, it becomes obvious that conspiracism vied with other alternative and indeed opposing modes of explanation. As much as the conspiracist narrative in its locutionary aspect might have offered a suggestive explanation of lamentable developments in American society, it competed with an older pattern of self-chastisement and contrition. At the end of his first sermon Morse had enjoined each member of his audience to "inspect his own heart and conduct, and repent of, and correct, what he finds amiss".[35] In his last sermon, Morse pointed out that

> our pious ancestors saw the hand of GOD in every thing, more especially in all signal events, such as pestilence, famine, earthquakes, war and other calamities. But it has become fashionable of late to ascribe these things to the uncontrolled operations of natural *causes*, and to keep out of view the Divine agency.

---

34 Qtd. in Stauffer, *New England*, p. 253.

35 Morse, *May 9th, 1798*, p. 28.

He went on to claim, however, that, regardless of how

> attentive and careful we may be to remove *natural causes*, which ought by no means to be omitted, yet we can have no good reason to expect that this calamity will cease from among us, till the *moral causes* be removed, till we acknowledge the righteous hand of GOD in it, and are truly humble for our sins and reform our lives.[36]

Although Morse thus conveyed this last message in accordance with a notion of the Deity imposing rightful retribution for sinfulness – and thus in opposition to the "scape-goating" scheme of attribution prescribed by conspiracism –, on a deeper level it also becomes apparent why those who were traditionally predisposed to discern in the events of the world the workings of God and who had long cultivated a conceptual vocabulary centred around notions of Providence, divine design and plan, were also susceptible to the allures of conspiracism. Indeed, this points to the crux of the issue: Morse and numerous other observers who were similarly attuned to the rise of a commercial society and the ascendancy of a scientific view of the world seized upon conspiracism as an explanation for what might be very generally called secularization. In seeing in this trend no longer a divine but rather a diabolical plan, and in suspecting no longer the presence of a supernatural and beneficent Deity but the operations of an earth-bound and inimical agency, conspiracism was just as much a symptom of secularization as it was a diagnosis of it.

There were more immediate reasons why the imported conspiracist mode of explanation could appear instructive when transplanted to an American context. In 1795 President Washington had denounced "self-created societies". These societies often tapped into a substratum of grievances occasioned by a sense of disappointment with the merely surface changes wrought in the constitution of American society by the emancipation from colonial rule. It was therefore not surprising that they also became a forum in which enthusiasm for the French Revolution was articulated.[37] A series of uprisings known as the Whiskey Rebellions afforded the authorities the opportunity to suppress the movement and established in the collective political consciousness a link between voluntary, pseudo-secret societies and a breakdown of public order.

---

36 Morse, *April 25 1799*, pp. 12–13.

37 Matthew Schoenbachler, "Republicanism in the Age of Democratic Revolution: The Democratic-Republican Societies of the 1790s", in: *Journal of the Early Republic*, 18/1988, 2, pp. 237–261.

Furthermore, deep uncertainties created by the international situation contributed to the sense of crisis. The young nation was trying to navigate a course on the choppy seas thrown up by the conflict between Britain and France. The American government attempted to preserve its neutrality and assert its sovereignty, but as its office-holders hoped for re-election, the course they steered had to take account of a public opinion which oscillated between outpourings of anti-British and anti-French sentiment. Thus, the Jay Treaty, negotiated by John Jay in his capacity as Minister Extraordinary to Great Britain and ratified by Washington in 1796, aroused the anti-British rancour of numerous observers who perceived in its articles a spirit of obsequiousness suited to a colony but not to a sovereign nation. Then the pendulum swung in the other direction in 1798 with the XYZ affair, in which the letters X, Y, and Z stood for the French negotiators who had given their American counterparts a singularly sordid reception when the latter had travelled on a diplomatic mission to France. Now the pro-British, anti-French party had the opportunity to vent their spleen.

The details of these diplomatic entanglements need not overly concern us here. More important was simply the fact that the alternative policies associated with closer allegiances with either the British or the French acted as a powerful stimulant upon the bifurcation of political opinion and party organization. In thus linking attitudes toward these powers with party politics in America the focus shifts from the locutionary to the illocutionary. The arresting and improbable element in the original story of Illuminati subversion – that a secret society originally founded among students by a Professor in the Bavarian town of Ingolstadt would thirteen years later topple the *ancien régime* in France – fell by the wayside as the Illuminati were re-fashioned both into a cipher for covert French intrusion and into a weapon against the pro-French party grouped around Jefferson.[38]

The political sympathies of the New England clergy lay with the Federalist Party and the tendency among preachers to use the pulpit as a platform

---

[38] Thus, in his history of American Freemasonry, Steven C. Bullock writes: "When Jedidiah Morse had first raised American fears of the Illuminati in May 1798, he meant more to awaken people to the dangers of the Francophile Jeffersonian party than to attack the American fraternity" (*Revolutionary Brotherhood: Freemasonry and the Transformation of the American Social Order 1730–1840*, Chapel Hill 1996, p. 174). Indeed, cajoling the masons, who could point to Washington as one of their members, became one of the rearguard actions Morse was forced to undertake in an attempt to assuage the offence felt by way of association with the Illuminati.

for political sermonizing was noted and criticized.[39] As a result of sharply focusing the gist of this sermonizing into an accusation of subversion, a dynamic began to unfold which can be observed in other cases of conspiracism and which can be explained by the way the locutionary and illocutionary dimensions dovetail into one another – the locutionary assertion that a conspiracy existed was dismissed as a dissembling illocutionary ploy designed to distract attention from the real conspiracy. Thus John Cosens Ogden flung the charge of "Illuminism" back in the Federalist direction from which it had come. According to Ogden, the New England clergy were the Illuminati, a "self-created" society headed by the President of Yale, Doctor Dwight, whose aim was to promote "party, bigotry and error".[40] Measured in intermediate steps of transfer and reception, Ingolstadt was, by this stage, a long way away.

5. Perlocutionary Effects

Late eighteenth-century America was witness to the emergence of party divisions rooted in questions of ideological preference.[41] This was a development which occurred largely in spite of the anti-party sentiments which constitute a point of consensus in the writings of figures otherwise as bitterly opposed to each other as Morse and Ogden. Indeed, the birth of the party system could actually be promoted precisely by anti-party sentiments. The days of fasting and prayer decreed by Adams were calculated to promote a sense of community and common destiny in the face of perilous times. Morse's sermons picked up on this theme – dangers internal and external imposed on the nation the duty to close ranks. This meant rallying behind the President and, more specifically, the Federalist cause. Of course, the actual course of events veered away from the illocutionary intent, as was evident by the hostile reactions expressed by Ogden and others.

Ironically, Morse himself had revealed a perceptive sense of judgement in prognosticating the real effects of such polemic when in June 1798 he addressed Freemasons who felt slighted by the anti-masonic implications of his conspiracist scare-mongering: "This imputation of selfish and sinister designs, produces acrimony, begets hatred and divisions, and is followed by

39 Stauffer, *New England*, p. 94.

40 Ogden, *A view of the New England Illuminati; who are indefatigably engaged in destroying the religion and the government of the United States*, Philadelphia 1799, pp. 12, 17.

41 "By 1800 two coherent but opposing conceptions of society had emerged to polarize the voters' sympathies" (Appelby, *Capitalism and a New Social Order*, p. 6).

many serious evils to the community".[42] By virtue of its illocutionary force as a form of accusation, conspiracism seeks to weld a community together by invoking the common task of combating the internal enemy. Of course, the presumption is that there will be a consensus about the existence of this internal enemy and the threat it represents. When this consensus does not emerge, the *effet pervers* is to exacerbate those divisions for which conspiracism feigned to provide the elixir.[43]

To explain this we can return a last time to Austin. Austin's primary interest was in the illocutionary act which bestowed upon an utterance its performative impulse. But in isolating this illocutionary act, Austin had to distinguish it not just from the locutionary but also from the perlocutionary act, the latter which has not yet been mentioned. Its definition can be best supplied by Austin himself:

> The perlocutionary act may be either the achievement of a perlocutionary object (convince, persuade) or the production of a perlocutionary sequel. Thus the act of warning may achieve its perlocutionary sequel of alarming, and an argument against a view may fail to achieve its object but have the perlocutionary sequel of convincing our opponent of its truth ("I only succeeded in convincing him").[44]

The last clause reminds us that Austin was aware that even at this micro-level of the singular speech act a discrepancy can open up between the intent and the effect, between the "object" and the "sequel" of a speech act. This is compounded on the macro-level to produce a history whose course runs obliquely to the direction of the intentions pursued by its human actors. In-

---

42 Jedidiah Morse, *A Sermon Delivered before the Grand Lodge of Free and Accepted Masons of the Commonwealth of Masachusetts*, Leominster, MA 1798, p. 10. The phenomenon discussed here where an opposition to parties or factions ends up promoting their emergence was also noted by Hofstadter: "the whole tradition of anti-party writing is full of the works of men who were strong partisans: this tradition is, in very large party, the work of partisan writers and political leaders who are actually appealing to a general distrust of the idea of party in order to subvert some particular part or to advance the interest of another party whose greatest claim to glory is that is will surmount and eliminate the party battle itself" (*The Idea of a Party System: The Rise of Legitimate Opposition in the United States, 1780–1840*, Berkley 1970, pp. 17–18).

43 Interestingly enough, even Morse espies the possibility of a modern society which can exist and indeed profit from its pluralism of values and opinions: "From the different organization of the human mind and the structure of civil society, it was doubtless intended by the Creator and Governor of the world, that there should exist a variety of opinions" (Morse, *A Sermon Delivered before the Grand Lodge of Free and Accepted Masons*, p.10).

44 Austin, *How to Do Things*, p. 118.

deed, the course might even run counter to the direction of these intentions, thus bestowing upon the episode a certain ironic quality.

Conspiracism in its locutionary content represents in some ways a resistance to this insight. Even within the work of a conspiracy theorist such as Robison, it is possible to find passages which, at least for the reader, are tinged with irony. Thus, at one point in his narrative, Robison lends some credence to the notion that the catalyst for the French Revolution came not from the clandestine operations of the German Illuminati in the East, but rather from the experiment in republicanism being carried out to the West. The passage, one of only two in the work which directly reference America, deserves to be quoted in full:

> In this attempt to ruin Britain, even the court of France was obliged to preach the doctrines of Liberty, and to take its chance that Frenchmen would consent to be the only slaves. But their officers and soldiers who returned from America, imported the American principles, and in every company found hearers who listened with delight and regret to their fascinating tale of American independence. During the war, the Minister, who had too confidently pledged himself for the destruction of Britain, was obliged to allow the Parisians to amuse themselves with theatrical entertainments, where English law was represented as oppression, and every fretful extravagance of the Americans was applauded as a noble struggle for native freedom. All wished for a taste of that liberty and equality which they were allowed to applaud on the stage; but as soon as they came from the theatre into the street, they found themselves under all their former restraints. The sweet charm had found its way into their hearts, and all the luxuries of France became as dull as common life does to a fond girl when she lays down her novel.[45]

This passage is all the more telling because it does not adhere to the conspiracist logic which otherwise informs Robison's account. Nowhere is there the suggestion that this infusion of American ideals into French social life was steered and directed by shadowy forces. Robison appeals to the French enthusiasm for America as one of the unexpected ramifications of French intercession in America's revolutionary struggle – a ramification whose irony is first appreciated when it is understood how it pushed France in the direction of revolution.

In summary: when Morse originally perused Robison's volume in the Philadelphia bookstore, it is unlikely that his initial response was: "I can use this against the Jeffersonian party". The idea of a conspiracy spoke to him on the very general level as an explanation for perplexing trends of secularization and pluralization. It was therefore the locutionary element which ensured the transfer of conspiracism across the Atlantic. However, conspiracy

---

[45] Robison, *Proofs of a Conspiracy*, pp. 210–211.

theories are not just explanations but also implicitly accusations. When Morse took to the pulpit to deliver his sermon, the narrative had been fitted out with an illocutionary intent hostile to the Jeffersonian party. All the same, Morse was not a cynic. Everything indicates that, in a locutionary sense, he entertained little doubt about the reality of the subversive elements. There is also little reason to doubt the sincerity of his hope that his declarations of conspiracy would bolster the cohesive solidarity within American society. In a perlocutionary sense, he could not foresee that his search for the American Illuminati would end up having the opposite effect.

Of course, there never were any American Illuminati. At most, there were groups whose ideas and programs had some highly mediated affinity with the Illuminati of historical reality. It is worth noting, however, that in the summer of 1780 a number of Illuminati in Munich had genuinely formed the idea of establishing an American colony. To this end they had, under the cover of a pseudonym, written a letter of inquiry to an American then officiating as a diplomat in Paris. His name was John Adams. Adams wrote a cordial response to their inquiry, obviously in total ignorance of the real character of the *société réquerante* who had sent the letter.[46] The work undertaken by the editors of the Illuminati correspondence has thus been able to shed light on the identity of the society in question. We therefore now know that, slumbering in the archived correspondence of John Adams, a document existed which attests to the actual existence of the historical Illuminati. One can only imagine the excitement which would have been generated in 1798 or 1799 if this information had come to light. Jedidiah Morse, who spent these years clutching at straws in the attempt to substantiate his alarming reports of subversion, would have doubtless seen in this letter the infallible proof to support his claim of an Illuminati presence on the North American continent. In the old question about whether the historical reality or the human imagination writes the best stories, it might be conceded that the conspiracy theorists give history a good run for its money. Such an anecdote, however, affirms the old finding that, when all is said and done, history still comes out on top.

---

[46] *The Papers of John Adams*, vol. 9, Cambridge, MA 1996, p. 296. I am indebted to Reinhard Markner and Hermann Schüttler for this intriguing detail. Reinhard Markner is in the process of preparing a paper which will more closely examine this exchange. For a few details about the colony project, cf. Stephan Gregory, *Wissen und Geheimnis: Das Experiment des Illuminatenordens*, Frankfurt a. M. 2009, pp. 31–36.

Barbara De Poli (Venice)

The Judeo-Masonic Conspiracy: The Path from the Cemetery of Prague to Arab Anti-Zionist Propaganda

The success of the myth of a Judeo-Masonic conspiracy, which reached its literary zenith with the *Protocols of the Learned Elders of Zion*, built on some indispensable ingredients: Jews, Freemasons, the need to or usefulness of pointing a finger at an enemy who had almost diabolical features and aims, as well as a popular tendency – because of influence, ignorance, or interest – to believe in it. The paranoia of some may be a basic starting point of the phenomenon, but it is not a necessary premise for the phenomenon to last and take root. If we consider Augustin Barruel to be the founder of the genre,[1] the myth has fed anti-Jewish and anti-Masonic campaigns and pogroms through over two hundred years of history and, last but not least, contributed to motivating the Nazi genocide of the Jews.

Having lost credit in Europe which was trying to come to terms with the Shoah after World War II, the conspiracy myth did not disappear but found new channels to spread in Latin America, Asia (especially in Japan), and above all in the Middle East.[2] In the Arab countries, a particular historical coincidence favoured the return of this conspiracy myth. Jews were an important element in those societies, and Freemasonry was widespread at a time when an enemy was insinuating itself which lent itself perfectly to this kind of accusation: Zionism. In this context, the social and political environment which had been shaped by regional events provided a fertile ground for the tradition which pointed at Jews and Masons as one of the most subtle and evil threats in the history of mankind and which prospered in the shadow of the Arab-Israeli conflict.

---

1 Cf. Augustin Barruel, *Mémoire pour servir à l'histoire du jacobinisme*, Hamburg 1798–1799.

2 The myth of the Jewish-Masonic conspiracy has also spread in Turkey and has met with success in today's Iran. Here I refer exclusively to the production of the myth in the Arabic language.

1. Freemasons and Jews in the Near East

In the Muslim Arab world, Jews and Freemasons have a specific history, which they have only partly and occasionally shared for a very short and recent stretch of time. Jews were a structural component of Islamic societies until the mid-twentieth century; they were spread along the southern coast of the Mediterranean, and their communities were significant both in terms of population and economics. In compliance with the Islamic legal tradition, Jews in the Near East, like Christians, for centuries had enjoyed the special status of *ḏimma* (literally "protection"), reserved for monotheists belonging to revealed religions. Until this status was abolished and replaced by a model of citizenship along the lines of European law between the nineteenth and twentieth centuries,[3] Jews could live in Muslim territories only if they acknowledged Islamic political authority and accepted having to pay a poll tax. Though subject to a discriminatory status of inferiority, their lives and belongings as well as their right to practice their faith were protected. Scholars disagree about the treatment of religious minorities, which varied from region to region, epoch to epoch, and dynasty to dynasty, times of crisis alternating with times of prosperity, but there is no doubt that all told, conditions were more favourable for religious minorities in the Muslim territories than for those in the Christian West.[4] Not only did they not suffer the systematic persecution they underwent in Europe,[5] but they often held high-ranking positions in the administrations of Islamic governments.[6]

In the Near East, the situation of non-Islamic minorities took a turn for the worse starting in the nineteenth century, when European imperialism

---

[3] The system changed from one of religion-based discrimination to one, at least in theory, based on equal rights for all citizens. In a majority of Muslim countries, recognized minorities continued to have different family laws (governing marriage, divorce, and inheritance), which were still based on confessional law.

[4] Cf. M. R. Cohen, *Under Crescent and Cross: The Jews in the Middle Ages*, Princeton 1994.

[5] The massacre committed in 1066 in Granada by Muslims, when three or four thousand Jews were murdered, is one of few such episodes. Forty years before, fifty thousand had been killed in Prague by the Crusaders on their way to the Holy Land. In Germany, one hundred thousand Jews were killed in 1298, because of the supposed profanation of a host (cf. Arno J. Mayer, *Soluzione finale: lo sterminio degli ebrei nella storia europea*, Milan 1990, pp. 1–38).

[6] Cf. B. Lewis, *The Jews of Islam*, London 1984; N. A. Stillman, *The Jews of Arab Lands: A History and Source Book*, Philadelphia 1979; and Y. Friedmann, *Tolerance and Coercion in Islam*, Cambridge 2003.

also began to operate by causing intercommunal tensions,[7] and it further aggravated with the rise of radical Islamic movements.[8] There is no doubt, however, that, in the overall context, the security of Jews was finally compromised by the foundation of Israel. The conflict between the Jewish state and the neighbouring Arab states created, in Muslim countries of the Mediterranean, a "Jewish Question" which had not existed at all before. It should be remembered that, until political tensions grew unbearable, Zionism had had no particular interest in the native Jews in the region, since they mostly continued living safely in their countries. Nevertheless, the progressive identification of Zionism with Judaism led to general hostility against the Jewish minorities, causing them to emigrate, especially after 1948 – but also because of pressure from Israel. Until then, more than 75,000 Jews had lived in Egypt, 135,000 in Iraq, about 10,000 in Lebanon, and maybe 30,000 in Syria.[9] The hundred or so Jews living in all these countries together today give an idea of the profound social change and the human drama which has stricken those regions.

The presence of Freemasonry in the Levant dates back to more recent times.[10] Masonic infiltration began in 1738, at the hands of Europeans who

---

7 An example would be Lebanon, but intercommunal tensions increased all over the Muslim countries (cf. O. Bengio/G. Ben-Dor [eds.], *Minorieties and State in the Arab World*, London 1999; A. H. Hourani, *Minorities in the Arab World*, London 1947; and, for a more specific example, S. A. Aldeeb Abu-Sahlieh, *L'impact de la religion sur l'ordre juridique: Cas de l'Egypte: Non-musulmans en pays d'Islam*, Fribourg 1979).

8 The Islamic radicals (that originated in Egypt in the 1920s and spread in the Islamic countries from the 1970s onwards), advocate a project of society founded on Islamic ideals, often using a restrictive and backward-looking interpretation of the religious texts. In that way, they may show more or less hostility towards non-Muslims but also towards those Muslims who do not adhere to their personal vision of Islam (cf. G. Kepel, *Le Prophète et Pharaon: Aux sources des mouvements islamistes*, Paris 1993; Y. M. Choueiri, *Islamic Fundamentalism*, London 1990).

9 Figures are necessarily approximate and also diverge considerably depending on the sources (cf. for instance: Hourani, *Minorities*, pp. 12–13; A. Aharoni, *The Forced Migration of Jews from Arab Countries and Peace*, Aug. 2002, http://www.hsje.org/forcedmigration.htm [accessed Feb. 18, 2012]; and the tables in: *Jewish Exodus from Arab and Muslim Countries*, http://en.wikipedia.org/wiki/Jewish_exodus_from_Arab_and_Muslim_countries [accessed Feb. 18 2012]).

10 No in-depth general work covers the history of Freemasonry in the Near East. In Western languages, there is the excellent volume by T. Zarcone on Freemasonry in Turkey (*Mystiques, philosophes et francs-maçons en Islam*, Paris 1993). Concerning Freemasonry in general, there is a useful article by Jacob M. Landau, "Farmāsūniyya", in: *Encyclopédie de l'Islam*, Leiden/Paris, pp. 295–296. In Arabic, important works include: J. Zaydān, *Tārīḫ al-Māsūniyya al-'ām* [*Universal History of Freemasonry*], Cairo 1889; and Š. Makāriyūs, *Al-ādāb al-māsūniyya* [*Masonic Principles*], Cairo 1890. For the contemporary period, cf. the works by H. A. Hamāda, *Al-Māsūniyya wa-al-Mā-*

founded lodges in the Syrian and Anatolian areas (in Izmir, Aleppo, and Corfu), in Istanbul around 1768, and in Egypt during Napoleon's campaign. Until the mid-nineteenth century, these were often ephemeral events, animated by foreign merchants and diplomats, who recruited local Christians (Greeks and Armenians), Jews, and – rarely – Muslims. It was only during the second half of the nineteenth century that the latter began to join the organizations. Especially in Egypt, Freemasonry saw a rapid growth with the foundation of the Egyptian National Lodge in 1876 by Egyptians and with branches in other Near Eastern countries, especially in the Syrian area.[11]

Leaving aside the initiatic contents of Freemasonry, the organisation was certainly not aloof from the political, social, and cultural issues of the time. Foreign and native Freemasons were often directly involved in political events, especially in Egypt, from the government of Ismā'īl (1863–1879) to Zaġlūl's (1859–1927) nationalist struggles,[12] and in Turkey, where Italian Freemasons provided logistical support for the Young Turks.[13] Freemasonry

---

sūniyyūn fī al-Watan al-'Arabī [*Freemasonry and Masons in the Arab Countries*], Damascus 1989; and *Al-Adabiyyāt al-māsūniyya* [*Masonic Literatures*], Damascus 1995. Despite their anti-Masonic and anti-Jewish nature, they provide interesting information.

11 In 1929 there were 52 lodges, with about 7,500 active members. Concerning Egypt, the most detailed study is still that of Barbara De Poli, *La Massoneria in Egitto*, Diss. University of Venice, 1993; and – in Arabic – the two volumes by 'Alī Šalaš, *Al-Yahūd wa-l-māsūn fī Misr* [*Jews and Freemasons in Egypt*], Cairo 1986; and *Al-māsūn fī Misr* [*Freemasons in Egypt*"], Cairo 1993.

12 In 1864, the Khedive Ismā'īl accused the Italians of plotting against the throne together with Prince Halīm, who was later driven into exile. Freemasonry also experienced an important split during the nationalist uprising in 1882, when it was divided into a nationalist and a pro-British faction. Generally speaking, Freemasonry took the side of Zaġūl (a member of the Grand Lodge) during the independence struggle of 1919.

13 In order to escape persecution by Sultan Abdülhamit II, the Committee of Union and Progress (CUP), a fraction of the Ottoman Freedom Society, used the *Macedonia Risorta* lodge of Salonika, out of bounds since it belonged to a foreign organization, to store the archive of the movement. The contributions of Italian Freemasons to the clandestine struggle did not only cover logistical matters: the Young Ottomans and later on the CUP and the Young Turks drew their inspiration from the Carbonari system in organizing their groups, copying their expressions, ceremonies, and oaths. Between 1901 and 1908, 188 people joined the *Macedonia Risorta* lodge, including 23 high-ranking Turkish army officers (cf. Zarcone, *Mystiques*, pp. 210–211; Zarcone, *Secret et sociétés secrètes en Islam*, Milan 2002, pp. 25–30; Hamāda, *Al-Adabiyyāt*, pp. 320–322; E. Ferrari, "La Massoneria italiana e la rivoluzione turca", in *Acacia*, 2/1910, pp. 21–131; A. Iacovella, *Il triangolo e la mezzaluna: I Giovani Turchi e la massoneria italiana*, Istanbul 1997).

certainly did not decide the course of events, but it surely took an active part, especially through some of its members. Also and above all, Freemasonry was a vehicle for the spread of enlightened and liberal thought and nationalist principles, at first propagated in particular by Italian veterans of the *Risorgimento* who had immigrated to those countries.

Another significant aspect for the Near East of those days was the multicultural nature of Freemasonry, which took in members belonging to various religious and linguistic minorities. Europeans, Muslims, Jews, and Oriental Christians with a more progressive mentality often stood side by side in the lodges. Jews were never the dominant element in the lodges, but they often played leading roles.[14]

This fact was of no secondary importance for the rise of anti-Masonic feelings. In Arab countries, the foundation of Israel was a turning point both for Jews and for Freemasonry, leading to a crisis in the Brotherhood under the blows of a conspiracy-minded propaganda, until many lodges were closed down or outlawed in the early 1960s.[15] The myth of the Jewish-Masonic conspiracy, which united Zionists and Masons and was sometimes nourished by political ingenuity on the part of the lodges,[16] was for the Jews an unpleasant collateral damage in a context of open hostility, while their fate was already leading them away from the Muslims. However, it turned out to be fatal for Freemasonry, which is still struggling to regain credibility in those regions.[17]

---

14 In 1929, eight of the 52 lodges of the Grand National Lodge of Egypt had a Jew as Grand Master, and the directors of three important Egyptian Masonic reviews were Jews (cf. Šalaš, *Al-Yahūd*, pp. 238–239).

15 It survived with difficulties only in Turkey (the Turkish lodges, however, were shut down between 1935 and 1948), Lebanon, and Jordan.

16 For example, the pro-Zionist appeal published by the Grand National Lodge of Egypt in 1922.

17 The Regular Grand Lodge of the Middle East, founded in 2005 and recognized by the Grand Lodge of the United Kingdom, inaugurated lodges in Lebanon and Egypt in 2007 (cf. *The Masonic High Council the Mother High Council*, 2005, http://www.rgle.org.uk; and Masonic High Council, *Regular Grand Lodge of the Middle East*, 2009, http://vimeo.com/844565 [both accessed Sept. 18, 2011]).

2. From Europe to the Levant: Matrix and Path of an Invented Conspiracy

The myth of the Jewish-Masonic conspiracy has European roots and origins which have largely been identified.[18] It draws on the anti-Jewish tradition in Christian Europe since the twelfth century, when the belief in a secret Jewish government plotting against Christianity was widespread.[19] However, the forerunner of the modern form of the Jewish-Masonic world conspiracy myth may be considered the five-volume work by the French Jesuit *abbé* Augustin Barruel, *Mémoire pour servir à l'histoire du jacobinisme*, published in 1797. The author upheld the idea that the French revolution was the outcome of a centuries-old conspiracy, organized by a secret society which was the direct heir of the Templars and the secret force directing Freemasonry.[20] In his *Mémoire*, the *abbé* barely mentioned the Jews, but in 1806 he claimed he had received from a certain J. B. Simonini of Florence a letter underlining that the "Jewish sect" was paving the way for the Antichrist. Before dying, he confided to Father Grivel how the sect had founded the orders of the Freemasons and the Illuminati, had even infiltrated the ecclesiastical hierarchy, and intended to dominate the world in less than a century.[21] Barruel thus managed to transform his own personal obsession into the lasting myth of a Jewish-Masonic conspiracy, which the Jesuits continued to believe and tried to foil by fighting Masonry always and everywhere – we shall see that this, too, played a key role in spreading this myth in the Near East.

The conspiracy theme was taken up in the second half of the nineteenth century in other European countries: in Germany, with August Rohling's *Der Talmudjude* [*The Talmudic Jew*] (1871), followed by the famous *Rabbi's Speech*;[22]

---

[18] Cf. Norman Cohn, *Warrant for Genocide: The Myth of the Jewish World-Conspiracy and the Protocols of the Elders of Zion*, London 1967; Pierre André Taguieff (ed.), *Les Protocoles des Sages de Sion*, Paris 1992; Taguieff, *Les Protocoles des Sages de Sion: Faux et usages d'un faux*, Paris 2004; Taguieff, *L'imaginaire du complot mondial*, Paris 2010.

[19] Cf. Léon Poliakov, *Histoire de l'antisémitisme I: Du Christ aux Juifs de Cour*, Paris 1955; S. Almog, *Antisemitism Through the Ages*, Oxford 1988.

[20] The Papacy had openly condemned Freemasonry already in 1738, of course without accusing the Freemasons of international conspiracies.

[21] "Souvenirs du P. Grivel sur les P. P. Barruel et Feller", in: *Le Contemporain*, July 1878, p. 62.

[22] Published in many reviews and journals as the authentic speech of a Great Rabbi made during a meeting of Jews, the *Speech* spread widely through the Austrian Empire and in Russia. It outlined a plot for world domination involving every level of politics and society, undermining the economy and religion, and manipulating the press and social movements. Of course, no mention was made of the fact that it was a rehash of a chapter of the novel *Biarritz*, titled "In the Jewish Cemetery of

in France, with *Le juif, le judaisme et la judaisasion des peuples chrétiens* (1869) written by the far-right Catholic Gougenot des Mousseaux, or the 600-page book called *Les francs-maçons et les juifs* (1881) by *abbé* Chabauty. In Italy, the struggle against Freemasonry undertaken by Leo XIII found ample expression in the Jesuit magazine *La civiltà cattolica*, while in Russia, propaganda based on the Jewish conspiracy was also spread by state officials, who published works like the *Rabbi's Speech*, not to mention domestic products such as *Jewish, Local and Universal Brotherhoods*, written in 1888 by Jacob Brafmann, or *Conquest of the World by the Jews*, written by the (supposed) Serbian Osman-Bey.

These are some of the texts which formed the cultural substrate on which the key work of anti-Jewish conspiracy thinking drew: the *Protocols of the Elders of Zion*.[23] The famous forgery, that became a long success story even after the Court of Bern had established its falsehood in 1935, represented the ideal confirmation of all the webs of the Jewish plot that had been hinted at from Barruel onwards, certifying the existence of a worldwide conspiracy led by the "representative of Zion, of the 33rd Degree".[24] As is well known, the *Protocols* were also a propaganda tool for Nazi ideology, whose anti-Semitism led to the most dramatic genocide in European history. Following the event, traumatic for the conscience of the West, anti-Semitic hatred in general became anathema or was at least censored. Conspiracy theories – with few and stigmatized returns – were buried under the horrors of the Shoah.[25]

Prague", published in Berlin in 1868 by Hermann Goedsche under the pseudonym of Sir John Retcliffe (cf. Cohn, *Warrant*, pp. 13–19, 221–224).

23 Presented as the outcome of the First Zionist Congress in Basel held in 1897, the *Protocols* were already circulating in French in 1884. Probably a product of the Russian-French espionage and counter-espionage, they are basically an at least partial plagiarism of a satirical work about Napoleon III, written and printed in Geneva in 1864 by a certain Maurice Joly. Besides the volumes by Cohn (*Warrant)* and Taguieff (*Les Protocoles* and *L'Imaginarie*) mentioned above, reference may be made to Hadassa Ben-Itto, *The Lie That Wouldn't Die: The Protocols of the Elders of Zion*, London 2005; and Cesare de Michelis, *Il manoscritto inesistente: I 'Protocolli dei Savi di Sion'*, Venice 2004.

24 As stated the signature at the bottom of the document.

25 In 1995 the French philosopher Roger Garaudy published *Les mythes fondateurs de la politique israélienne*, where he did not refer to the *Protocols* but claimed the existence of a Zionist plot which had supposedly invented the holocaust to lend legitimacy to the foundation and expansionist politics of Israel. For this thesis, charged with defamation and instigation to racial hatred, the author was condemned to six months in prison and numerous fines. Holocaust denial is also a recurring theme in Islamic anti-Zionist propaganda and especially a leitmotif of the Iranian president, Ahmadinejad. There was, for instance, the international convention on this topic in Tehran in December 2006 organized by the Iranian Foreign Ministry.

However, the dramatic outcome of a propaganda that had been based on a literary invention was not enough to remove all traces of the myth. As I said above, for reasons quite different from those which originated the myth of the Judeo-Masonic conspiracy in Europe, it is the Arab world which seems to have inherited a genre which in its homeland had finally run out of its motivations and creative verve.

In the Near East, one can identify two distinct (but converging) channels of diffusion of the conspiracy myth: the first, a Christian one, Jesuit and Maronite – therefore, in line with Barruel's anti-Masonic and anti-Semitic thinking –, dates back at least to the second half of the nineteenth century; the second emerged because of Nazi propaganda, already operating in the Middle East in the 1920s, and focuses more specifically on the *Protocols.*

Actually, in the Ottoman Empire, Christian religious authorities had opposed Freemasonry ever since it began to spread, especially when the Papal Bull of 1738 condemned it. Clement XII's text circulated in the churches of the Levant and was followed not only by Catholics but also by Greek Orthodox and Armenians. The Christian authorities engaged in preventing the spread of Freemasonry among Muslims as well, and even asked Sultan Mahmut I in 1748 to take steps against the lodges of Istanbul. Jean Claude Flachat, in the account of his journeys, writes that at the time of the Empire, "Chrétiens, Juifs, Idolatres" were tolerated and allowed to practise their religion as long as they did not offend the Qur'an and did not proselytize, but:

> *Les franc-maçons sont les seuls qu'on ne tolère pas: ils passent pour des infâmes et des magiciens, que le libertinage et l'avarice conduisent aux assemblées. Le peuple était convaincu qu'ils se servaient des ténèbres de la nuit pour cacher leurs débordements.*[26]

At the time, however, there were no conspiracy theories which associated Masons and Jews. These only began to proliferate later on, in the wake of Barruelian propaganda. It is well known that in the late nineteenth century, especially in Christian-Catholic Lebanon, the anti-Jewish campaign, nourished by Arabic translations of works like *Der Talmudjude*, was accompanied by an anti-Masonic campaign. In the early 1880s, several Syro-Lebanese intellectuals emigrated to Egypt, fleeing on the one hand from the repressive regime of the Ottoman Sultan Abdülhamit II and on the other one from

---

[26] *Observations sur le commerce et les arts d'une partie de l'Europe de l'Asia et de l'Afrique, et même des Indes orientales*, Lyon 1756, pp. 418–420, qtd. in Zarcone, *Mystiques*, pp. 191–192; italics in the original.

the anti-Masonic propaganda promoted by the Lebanese Jesuit Lūys Šayḫū,[27] among other author of *The Masonic Secret in the Sect of Freemasons.*[28] The Christians Šāhīn Makāryūs (1853–1910), Ya'qūb Sarrūf (1858–1927), and Fāris Nimr (1857–1951), besides being accused of unfaith by the local religious authorities for having adopted evolutionist ideas in the pages of the magazine *al-Muqatataf* ("The Anthology"), were also accused of belonging to the association *The Sun of the Benefactor*, which Šayḫū considered to be a Masonic association.

It is significant that, at the time, such anti-Masonic and anti-Jewish positions did not enjoy much popularity outside the Arab Catholic milieu, since – as has been said – Freemasonry prospered between the nineteenth and twentieth centuries not only among Christian and Jewish minorities but also among Muslims throughout the Near East. In fact, in the Arab Islamic world and especially in Egypt, anti-Jewish and anti-Masonic propaganda did not take root until Zionism took on the proportions of a regional conflict. Catholic propaganda, Jesuit and Maronite, thus sowed the seeds for a plant which bore its fruits only decades later, laying the "doctrinal" foundations for the conspiracy literature which was later re-developed.

For example, in Egypt, attacks in the Egyptian press against Egyptian Freemasonry increased after 1922, when the National Grand Lodge of Egypt exposed, and doubtlessly compromised itself, through an appeal to the Palestinians which was substantially in favour of the Zionist cause.[29] The general political (anti-Zionist) rather than religious (anti-Jewish) nature of its polemics, following the intensification of Zionist colonization in Palestine, seems to be confirmed by the fact that the appeal appeared in publications of an Islamic tendency,[30] such as the review *al-Manār* [*The Minaret*], but also in

---

27 Cf. Zaydān, *Tārīḫ*, p. 142. He is another Lebanese Christian intellectual, who emigrated to Egypt shortly after his colleagues and was a celebrated man of letters and Freemasonry of his days.

28 Cf. Lūys Šayḫū, *Al-Sirr al-masūn fī šī'at al-farmāsūn* [*The Masonic Secret of Freemasonry*], Beirut 1909–1911.

29 On April 2, 1922 the National Grand Lodge of Egypt published an appeal calling on "Palestinian organizations and on everyone, men and women, to multiply their efforts of achieve peace, understanding and tolerance, in the project of a united nation". In line with the typical Zionist propaganda of the time, the idea of a "shared homeland" was repeatedly stressed, while the issue of a national Jewish home was only implicitly mentioned. It immediately triggered reactions in the national press and also by Freemasons who heavily criticized the organization for this initiative, seeing it as shameful (cf. Šalaš, *Al-Yahūd*, pp. 334–338).

30 We are not speaking here of radical Islamists but of a traditional Islamic milieu. For further detail, cf. B. Etienne, *L'islamismo radicale*, Milan 1988, pp. 169–216.

liberal ones, such as *al-Siyāsa al-Usbū'iyya* [*The Weekly Politics*], where conspiracy theses began to appear.[31]

There is, however, no doubt that the most influential product of this specifically anti-Jewish and anti-Masonic trend was the work of the Maronite and self-avowed former Freemason 'Awād al-H̱ūrī, titled "Asl al-Māsūniyya" ["The Origin of Freemasonry"] and published in Beirut in 1929,[32] which in Arab countries became the prime source for much of later anti-Masonic literature. According to the information provided by al-H̱ūrī himself, he was born in Beirut in January 1871. First a teacher of Arabic and French in Lebanon, then a businessman in Paris, he finally sought his fortune in Brazil, where he met then president Prudente de Morais Barros, who assigned him with the task of recording the private matters of the presidency from February 1896 to September 1897.[33] It was in those circumstances that he met "the owner of this History".[34]

In his text – which we shall describe in detail later on –, al-H̱ūrī brought up the history of the plot promoted by the Jews since biblical times, through a cult called the "Mysterious Force", and of the creation of Freemasonry – among other secret entities – as a smokescreen for the cult's activities. To the long list of anti-Jewish and anti-Masonic fiction, he thus added an original variant of the myth of international conspiracy, developed on the basis of previous literature of Catholic origin. Using the *topos* of this genre, al-H̱ūrī, in the foreword to what he calls a "translation", maintains that he came into possession of the original document by pure chance:

---

31 For example, in July 1928, *al-Siyāsa al-Usbū'iyya* published an article by Muhammad 'Abd Allāh 'Anān, titled "Al-hatar al-Yahūdī" ("The Jewish Peril"), where the author expressly referred to the danger the Jews posed within the Semitic race, consisting in the secret and organized attempt, under the cover of Masonry, to dominate the world and abolish any non-Jewish religion. The following week, the same weekly published a comment entitled "Al-hatar al-Yahūdī aydan: al-Bināya al-hurra fī Misr" ("Another Jewish Peril: Freemasonry in Egypt"), where a certain Muhammad Kāmil Hasan from Zaqaziq confirmed the threat posed by the Jews and their connection to Masonry: he claimed he had been a member of the organisation for about five years, but had not found those humanitarian qualities so aptly depicted in the Jewish propaganda – quite the contrary.

32 We will refer here to the English version of the text, *Dissipation of the Darkness*, taken from the following website: http://heygeorge5.tripod.com/id10.htm (accessed Aug. 25, 2011; as of Mar. 21, 2012, the site is no longer available).

33 Cf. Al-H̱urī, *Dissipation*, p. 6.

34 Al-H̱urī, *Dissipation*, p. 6.

And one day, providentially, I met Mr. Lawrence, son of George, son of Samuel, son of Jonas, son of Samuel Lawrence, thanks be to God and to Dr. Prudente de Moraes, President of Brazil, who introduced him to me. Mr. Lawrence is the owner of this History (the Hebrew manuscript) that I present to the reader translated into Arabic, and he is, at the same time, the last heir of one of the nine founders of the association (The Mysterious Force), as will be seen later.

[...] My intentions are: [...] To dissipate the darkness that, for nineteen centuries has enveloped a humanity that is wavering in doubt. To reveal this mystery to the eyes of men to alert them before this cruel danger.

I must point out, as well, that I was inspired by the exclusively Christian intentions of de Moraes, in accord with one of his declarations that states thus: "With this action of ours we extend to the Christian religion a great benefit, eliminating the forces of evil that attack it, from this fantasy encrusted by the absurd. And you, especially, with your task in the Turkish Empire, will extend another great service to the Muslim religion".[35]

This line of conspiracy thought with its epicentre in Lebanon met in the 1920s with another one. In Cairo, the presence of cells of the German National Socialist Party, already active since 1926–1927 on the initiative of Rudolf Hess' brother Alfred, probably instigated the publication of the first Egyptian edition of the *The Protocols of the Elders of Zion*,[36] until then mainly translated into Arabic by Arab Catholics and Maronites.[37] At the time, the impact which anti-Semitic propaganda had on Egyptian Muslims, outside of radical circles, was substantially irrelevant, but after the creation of the State of Israel Egyptians became aware of the importance of the new situation in the region, and the Nazi-based conspiracy production once again became influential.

In Egypt alone, by 1948, about twenty-five books about Masonry had come out, but only one of these attacked it, dealing in a general fashion with the history of secret societies and subversive movements.[38] In the 1950s, however, two more came out which targeted Freemasonry, confirming the

---

35 Al-Ḫurī, *Dissipation*, p. 7.

36 On the use of the *Protocols* in Arab countries, cf. Taguieff, *Les Protocols*, pp. 207–253; Taguieff, *L'imaginaire*, pp. 142–178; Yehoshafat Harkabi, "Les Protocols dans l'antisemitisme arabe", in: Taguieff (ed.), *Les Protocols*, pp. 325–340.

37 An Arabic edition was mentioned in Damascus in 1920 or 1921 (cf. Taguieff, *Les Protocols*, p. 239). Bernard Lewis believes that the Protocols were first mentioned in polemical Arabic writings tying Zionism to Bolshevism in 1920 and were published on January 15, 1926, in *Raqib Sahyùn*, a magazine of the Catholic community of Jerusalem. A couple of years later, an edition came out in Cairo, translated from French by a Christian Arab (cf. Bernard Lewis, *Semites et antisemites*, Paris 1987, pp. 235–236; Daphne Tsimoni, "The Arab Christians and the Palestinian Arab National Movement during the Formative Stage", in: Gabriel Ben-Dor [ed.], *The Palestinians and the Middle East Conflict*, Ramat Gran 1978, p. 79).

38 M. 'Abd Allāh 'Anān, *Tārīḫ al-jam'iyyāt al-sirriyya* [*History of Secret Societies*], Cairo 1954.

trend reversal: *Zionism and Freemasonry* and *The Masonic Society: Its Truths and Mysteries.*[39] Even magazines which until the 1930s had regarded Masonry with open favour began to ignore the phenomenon (like *al-Muqattam*) or to spread decidedly hostile propaganda. Among the latter, *al-Muqtataf*, founded by the same Syro-Lebanese who had fled from anti-Masonic propaganda in Lebanon in 1882, changed its pro-Masonic profile suddenly and unexpectedly in March 1950, when it published an unsigned article with the eloquent title "The Moral Superiority of Freemasonry: Non-liberty, non-fraternity, non-equality",[40] where the journalist mentioned the *Protocols* as a clear revelation of an ongoing Judeo-Masonic conspiracy.

From then on, the plots of the *Elders of Zion* became the centrepiece of every conspiracy argument. The 1927 edition of the *Protocols* seems to have been the only one published before 1951, when the first Arabic translation by a Muslim appeared in Cairo, with a long introduction by Muhammad Halifa al-Tunsī. From then on, new editions came out with increasing regularity and in close succession, until the latest, published by Aẖbār al-Yawm in 2002.[41] As will be shown in greater detail in the following paragraph, the arguments drawn from Nazi propaganda writings, which often serve as an introduction to the various editions, leave no doubt as to the direct source of such material.

3. The Themes of Arab Conspiracy Propaganda

In its Arab variant, this genre focusing on the myth of the Judeo-Masonic conspiracy reached its peak in the 1980s and 1990s with the publication of at least twenty works, mostly published in Beirut, Damascus, and Cairo. All of them, with marginal differences, work with the same ingredients: the ancient Judaic origins of the conspiracy, its slow, occult, but constant evolution through time to an international scale, aiming at achieving the ultimate goal – world domination. The irrefutable proof of this thesis is "precise", and quotes are taken from two main works: al-H̱ūrī's *The Origin of Freemasonry* and *The Protocols of the Learned Elders of Zion.* Not only are the political activities of Masonry taken as the most obvious evidence of its Jewish nature, but the origins, history, and symbols of the Masonic organization, concealed by an

39 'Abd al-Rahmān Sāmī Ismat, *Al-sahyūniyya wa-l-māsūniyya* [*Zionism and Freemasonry*], Alexandria 1950; Ahmad Galūš, *Al-jam'iyya al-māsūniyya* [*The Freemasonry Association*], Cairo n.d.

40 Šalaš, *Al-yahūd*, p. 284.

41 Cf. Taguieff, *Les Protocols*, pp. 293–294.

ambiguous facade, are alleged to hide a reality, which gives value to and proves this essential outlook.

Publications which came out in the 1980s[42] are of interest precisely because they confirm the validity of the arguments against Masonry even in places where the organization had long been outlawed, such as Egypt and Syria.[43] The "history" of Masonry, when told alongside the usual anti-Masonic arguments, takes up a considerable space in the books, about one third or little less of the total. Considering the quality and huge extent of their arguments, reference can be made to such texts as *Freemasonry* by Sa'yid al-Jazā'irī, *Masonry, That Unknown World* by Sābir Ta'īma, and *The Masonic Plans* by Muhammad Ahmad Dayāb almost without distinguishing between them, since they are set up in a quite similar manner and deal with the same topics and reach the same conclusions.

According to these authors, both Masonic mythology and the historical works which locate the roots of Masonry in the medieval guilds attempt to falsify and hide the true essence of Masonry, its intrinsically Jewish nature. The various conflicting traditions which see it, from time to time, as originating from Egypt, transmitted by King Æthelstan,[44] or arising from the professional guilds of the Middle Ages,[45] only serve to confirm this hypothesis, their contradictions and inconsistency merely revealing the deliberate inten-

---

42 Following is an indicative but by no means complete sample of this kind of work: 'Ābid Mansūr 'Ābid, *Al-māsūniyya al-ālamiyya* [*World Freemasonry*], Cairo 1988; Sābir Ta'īma, *Al-māsūniyya ḏalika al-'ālam al-majhūl* [*Freemasonry, That Unknown World*], Beirut 1986; Abū Islām Ahmad 'Abd Allāh, *Al-asābī' al-ḫafiyya* [*Invisible Fingers*], Cairo 1989; Muhammad Ahmad Dayāb, *Al-muḫattatāt al-māsūniyya* [*Masonic Plans*], Cairo 1989; Sa'yid al-Jazā'irī, *Al-māsūniyya* [*Freemasonry*], Beirut 1990; As'ad al-Sahmarānī, *Al-māsūniyya* [*Freemasonry*], Beirut 1988; Mahmūd 'Abd al-Hamīd al-Kafrī, *Al-'alaqāt al-sirriyya bayna al-yahūdiyya wa-l-māsūniyya wa-l-suhyūniyya* [*The Secret Relations between Judaism, Freemasonry and Zionism*], Damascus 2002; 'Abd al-Majīd Hammū, *Al-māsūniyya wa-l-munaẓẓamāt al-sirriyya* [*Freemasonry and Secret Organizations*], Damascus 2003.

43 In these countries, the lodges gradually disappeared between the 1950s and 1960s.

44 King Æthelstan was the King of England from 924 to 939 and is often recalled by the Masonic mythology as the one who introduced Freemasonry in York (cf., for instance, the *Cooke Manuscript [1430–1440]*, qtd. in Eugenio Bonvicini, *Massoneria antica*, Rome 1989, pp. 156–163).

45 Even if the historical origins of Freemasonry are still disputed, it is ascertained that it is the product of the fusion of hermetical currents of the seventeenth century and the Masonic crafts (cf. Robert Freke Gould, *History of Freemasonry*, London 1882–1887; Harry Carr, "600 years of Craft Ritual", in: *Ars Quatuor Coronatorum*, 81/1968, pp. 153–205; *Harry Carr's World of Freemasonry*, London 1984; and David Stevenson, *The Origins of Freemasonry*, Cambridge 1988).

tion of hiding Freemasonry's true origin and aims. Anti-Masonic authors date the roots of the ideological and political thinking of Masonry back to the first millennium BC, when it emerged in rabbinical milieus at the time when the Talmud was compiled. More precisely, the birth of the movement supposedly dates back to the building of Solomon's Temple, the evident symbolism of which is still the foundation for the lodges.[46] The work bearing witness to this version of the conspiracy myth is al-H̲ūrī's *The origin of Freemasonry*.[47]

The events described by al-H̲ūrī (and later on repeated by other anti-Masonic authors) supposedly took place as follows: in the year 37 AD, nine Jews founded the organization Mysterious Force in Jerusalem to destroy Christianity and wipe out the Christians. After seven years of preparatory work, they officially set up their activity, which was of course equally directed against Islam when it arose. Thus, the first Masonic temple, called Jerusalem, was founded. The list of nine founders included the names of Herod II and Hiram Abiud, as well as that of Moab Levi, the ancestor of Lawrence. The history of this episode is rich in details, reporting even the dates of the meetings and the main events which took place in those early years, such as the speeches made by Herod,[48] or the frightful oath which bound the members of the society together and whereby they swore to eliminate the Gentiles, using all available means including murder.[49]

Nine meetings were held before the death of Herod in 44 AD; his successor Hiram continued the work of destruction of Christianity with even greater violence. Each of the nine members of the board of the organisation, before dying, handed down his secret to a close descendant, thus ensuring that the mission would continue through the ages. During the following five hundred years, the Mysterious Force grew stronger, founding new temples and gathering ever more disciples, especially in Rome. But the followers of Christianity increased as well, and a new religion also appeared – Islam – which made the triumph of Judaism more difficult, forcing it to fight on two

---

46 Of course the *Talmud* does not date back to the first millennium BC, but these publications contain many such "inaccuracies" (cf. Ta'īma, *Al-māsūniyya*, pp. 11–33; al-Jazā'irī, *Al-māsūniyya*, pp. 21–38; Dayāb, *Al-muḫattatāt*, pp. 10–29; 'Ābid, *Al-māsūniyya*, pp. 17–28; Hammū, *Al-māsūniyya*, pp. 15–25).

47 All those books devote several chapters to H̲ūrī's account: for instance, Hammū, *Al-māsūniyya*, chs. 1–27 of the second section, pp. 26–78; Ta'īma, *Al-māsūniyya*, chs. 1–3, pp. 9–125; al-Jazā'irī, *Al-māsūniyya*, chs. 1–2, pp. 26–149.

48 Cf. Al-H̲urī, *Dissipation*, pp. 29–35.

49 Cf. Al-H̲urī, *Dissipation*, pp. 34–36.

fronts.[50] Of course, the followers of the Mysterious Force did not lose heart, and in the eighth century, the temple of Rome reached its peak, expanding its activities against the Gentiles. At that time, descendants of the founders were sent to spread the organisation abroad, founding temples in Russia, France, and Germany, each depending hierarchically on a mother temple and in the last instance on the Central Temple of Jerusalem.[51] This went on until 1166, when the Rome temple – on which most of the European offices depended – had become more important than the one in Jerusalem, so that the heads of the Central Temple set up the supreme head of all western temples. The members of the temple were obliged to meet exclusively underground, painting their faces black to pretend they were coal miners.[52]

In this manner, Herod's ideal survived through the centuries until in London, Joseph Levi (1665–1717) decided to renovate the Mysterious Force organisation which had lost its vitality, contacting two Englishmen to this end, Desaguliers and George.[53] They decided to call it Masonry because this was the name Italian stonemasons of the thirteenth century used, and the guilds of free stonemasons had a system of symbols similar to those employed in the Mysterious Force, including the "building symbols" invented by Hiram. Furthermore, the stonemasons' guilds were still active in the eighteenth century, so it appeared easy to blend in with these structures and maintaining the cover while altering their purposes and main motivations. All this made it possible to keep the true story of the foundation of the Mysterious Force a secret. On March 10, 1717, a meeting of masons was called, led by James Anderson, a friend of Desaguliers. After long discussions, they decided to carry out their project setting a great meeting for June 24, 1717, the starting date of modern Masonry.[54] Practically speaking, from then on, while believing that they were still faithful to the tradition of the old guilds, Freemasons became unsuspecting followers of the plots of the Mysterious Force.

Al-H̱ūrī's version, given here in its essential outline, would doubtless fit in well in a showcase of similar texts, next to works by Barruel, Chabauty, or Mausseaux. For Arab anti-Masonic authors, however, any interpretation of Masonry which contradicts al-H̱ūrī's narrative is not worthy of any consider-

---

50 Cf. Al-H̱urī, *Dissipation*, p. 64.
51 Cf. Al-H̱urī, *Dissipation*, p. 65.
52 Cf. Al-H̱urī, *Dissipation*, p. 65. The reference is clearly to "very ancient" predecessors of the Italian *carbonari*.
53 Rev. Dr. Desaguliers, who was actually of French origin, played an important role in the foundation of speculative Freemasonry; we are not told who George was.
54 Cf. Al-H̱urī, *Dissipation*, p. 67.

ation and viewed as another proof of the extraordinary skills of Masonry and the Jews in hiding their plots behind credible smokescreens.

Nevertheless, not all anti-Masonic authors refer to the testimony of al-H̱ūrī. Some only make a quick mention and then concentrate on the main theme: the *Protocols of the Learned Elders of Zion*. The document is still not only regarded as the strongest "evidence" in the excursions through history which intend to uncover the Jews as secretly plotting for world domination, but also consulted to explain the basic reasons for the crisis which contemporary society is going through.[55] A crisis brought about by the constant political threat posed by Israel, but also by the corruption, the demolition of values, and the religious vacuum which the Jews have supposedly deliberately and systematically imposed on the current world's societies.

There are at least nine different complete translations of the Protocols in Arabic (from French, English, and German), besides many books of commentaries.[56] The official edition published in Cairo by the Information Services of the United Arab Republic (UAR), on behalf of the Ministry of National Guidance on April 13, 1956, was presented as the "most important Zionist secret".[57] The text was introduced by a series of quotations and "evidences", dealing with the sources of the document and the issue of its authenticity. Paradoxically, while admitting that the text was plagiarized from Jolie's *Dialogue aux Infers*, the publishers did not rule out that it could be a Jewish document. To support the authenticity of the text, the edition quoted the arguments made by the Nazi publisher Ulrich Fleischhauer – described as an expert on Jewish matters –,[58] according to which the Jews had been unable to prove the falsehood of the text. Finally, the "conclusive evidence" of their guilt was provided by the actions of the Jews themselves, which fitted perfectly the descriptions in the *Protocols*. A similar deduction made by the racist expert Alfred Rosenberg was also quoted in the intro-

---

55 Cf. Dayāb, *Al-muẖattatāt*, pp. 61–72; Al-Kafrī, *Al-'alaqāt*, pp. 86–103, 'Ābid, *Al-māsūniyya*, pp. 211–237; Ta'īma, *Al-māsūniyya*, pp. 232–273.

56 Cf. Y. Harkabi, *Arab Attitudes to Israel*, Jerusalem 1972, pp. 229–241; Y. Harkabi, "Les Protocols", pp. 325–340.

57 Harkabi, "Les Protocols", p. 231.

58 Ulrich Fleischhauer was an anti-Semitic publisher of books and news articles spreading the myth of the Judeo-Masonic conspiracy and member of the *Deutschnationale Volkspartei*. In 1933 he founded the *Weltdienst*, an international anti-Semitic news agency, and in 1935 participated at the Berne Trial on *The Protocols* as a key defence coordinator.

duction.[59] The following passage is especially indicative of this line of argument: "In these circumstances, an investigation of the identity of the author of the Protocols in of secondary importance, for the text of the documents is sufficient to prove that is beyond the power of *any Aryan mind* in the world to draw up such a program".[60] Considering the numerous quotations from German, the references made to anti-Semitic Nazi propagandists and to an 'Aryan mind', Yehoshafat Harkabi infers that this introduction was written by a German or was translated from German – which is perhaps the reason why it was not signed.[61] Nevertheless, the UAR was not alone in spreading the *Protocols*: the governments of Egypt, Iraq, and the PLO played a key role, too.[62]

Concerning Freemasonry, we have already seen how anti-Zionism motivated the attacks on this association since the publication of the first anti-Masonic literature in Egypt. However, from the 1950s onward, every criticism of Freemasonry focused on the international Judeo-Masonic conspiracy myth, making it inseparable from the *Protocols* and from Zionism. For example, Sābir Ta'īma, who among the authors mentioned so far is the one who dedicates the most space to the *Protocols*, quoting the full text of chapters fourteen through twenty,[63] does not hesitate to provide the full introduction by Nilus to the text published in 1905 in order to explain as accurately as possible the true nature of the document.[64] Thus, the ambiguous Nilus himself becomes the most authoritative voice on the authenticity of the *Protocols*.[65]

---

59 Alfred Rosenberg, official thinker of the National Socialist Party, was originally the main propagandist of the myth. Between 1919 and 1923, besides countless articles, he wrote a whole volume of comments on the *Protocols* and five booklets on the Jewish world plot which were strongly influential.

60 Harkabi, *Arab Attitudes*, p. 232; italics in the original.

61 Cf. Harkabi, *Arab Attitudes*, p. 233.

62 According to Harkabi, besides the United Arab Republic, which continued to publish them in Arabic and in other tongues, the President of Iraq, Aref, expressed in 1967 his appreciation for the essay on the *Protocols* by the historian 'Ajjāj Nuwayhid; the PLO seems to have bought a thousand copies, while President Nasser, in an interview with the publisher Russi K. Karanjia in September 1958, said that the *Protocols* proved beyond any doubt that three hundred Zionists decided the fate of the European continent, electing their heirs among their own group (cf. Harkabi, *Arab Attitudes*, p. 235).

63 Cf. Ta'īma, *Al-māsūniyya*, pp. 249–273.

64 Cf. Ta'īma, *Al-māsūniyya*, pp. 234–236.

65 Cohn draws a thorough and disquieting portrait of Nilus: a former magistrate, with a degree from the University of Moscow, he converted to Orthodox Christianity because of financial problems and became a supporter of the Tsarist autocracy. He appears to have been a fanatic who sincerely believed in the terrible prophecies of the Elders of Zion (cf. Cohn, *Warrant*, p. 65).

As in the case of some other authors, Ta'īma supports his views by tautological arguments, which are often presented in a confused and abstruse fashion, such as the following: "The Jews claim the *Protocols* are false, but the Terrible War is no falsehood. The Elders of Zion were already predicting it in 1901".[66] Applying this tautology, the existence of the dark project is proven but also its gradual and inexorable realization, as is shown by the strikes, revolts, and assassinations which took place afterward, according to their orders: one example is the fate of Russia when it fell into the hands of Communism.[67] This way, it becomes easily possible to attribute all the evils of the world to the Elders of Zion, since their program of domination includes every aspect of society.

To illustrate the projects of the Judeo-Masons, Sābir Ta'īma provides more than four pages of quotations from the *Protocols*.[68] Ta'īma also tells us about a further compact between Masonry and the Jewish representatives of the secret plot, which was negotiated during a meeting held in the Jewish cemetery of Prague in front of the tomb of the rabbi Shimon ben Yehuda.[69] This episode is clearly taken from the *Rabbi's Speech*, one of the main sources which laid the foundations for the *Protocols*, although it is not explicitly mentioned as a source – these texts often lack bibliographical references. There is even a mention – as usual without explicit quotation – of Rathenau's statement,[70] to which Nasser had referred in 1958, which shows the use of typical arguments of Nazi anti-Jewish propaganda.

---

66 Ta'īma, *Al-Māsūniyya*, p. 234.

67 Another version of the Judeo-Masonic conspiracy, following the Russian Revolution of 1917, is the International Communist-Judeo-Masonic conspiracy, involving a secret coalition of Jews, Freemasons, and Communists.

68 For example, he quotes from the Fourth Protocol: "Gentile masonry blindly serves as a screen for us and our objects, but the plan of action of our force, even its very abiding-place, remains for the whole people an unknown mystery". (Ta'īma, *Al-Māsūniyya*, pp. 238–242). For an English version of the *Protocols*, cf. Jew Watch, http://www.jewwatch.com/jew-references-protocols-full-text-folder.html (accessed Aug. 19, 2011).

69 Cf. Ta'īima, *Al-Māsūniyya*, p. 209.

70 In June 1922, the German foreign minister Walter Rathenau – a Jew – was killed by a group of young right-wing fanatics, who saw in him an agent of the Elders of Zion because of a statement he had made in 1922 in his book *Zur Kritik der Zeit*: "Three hundred men, all of whom know each other, guide the economic destiny of the continent and choose their successors among their disciples". The sentence appeared in a context which dealt with economic issues and with the fact that industry and finance were almost entirely in the hands of a hereditary oligarchy, but the right managed to quickly manipulate the unfortunate expression.

> Those who deal with Jewish issues also know that there are, among the Jewish organizations in the world, three hundred men who know each other well – actively and in terms of organization – who have particular skills and great powers enabling them to carry out this activity in these secret governments. When one of them dies or is eliminated, another is immediately appointed to the same role in the secret movement, with the same title.[71]

In his large volume, Ta'īma – though in a disorderly and incongruous fashion – in fact repeats the main stages of western anti-Semitic literature; other authors are less prodigal of their references and do not deal in such detail with the *Protocols*, only quoting extensively from it. However, the constant element in all these cases is the central role that the plots of the *Elders of Zion* played, from which the main anti-Masonic and anti-Jewish arguments descend, whose truthfulness is proven by the *Protocols* themselves.

4. Conclusion: Why an Imaginary Conspiracy Meets with Success

So far, we have shown how the convergence of a conspiracy narrative of European (Jesuit and Nazi) origin gave rise in the Near East to a new inner-Arab thread of the myth of the Judeo-Masonic conspiracy – a myth as successful as it was fatal. Nevertheless, this literature, though dating back to the nineteenth century for the Jesuit branch and to the 1920s for the Nazi one, long remained marginal in public debates and only began to gain in importance from the 1950s onwards, following the foundation of the State of Israel. This clearly shows that the anti-Jewish and anti-Masonic ideology which marked the conspiracy myth did not find fertile ground in the Islamic world, since the social and cultural context was not particularly susceptible to these topics.[72] However, the myth spread and took root for political reasons after

---

71 Ta'īma, *Al-Māsūniyya*, p. 210.

72 The conspiracy theories failed to take root not only due to the record of Muslims and Jews living together in the Near East. In the 1920s, especially in Egypt, Masonry was at the peak of its popularity, counting on dozens of lodges and thousands of Muslim, Jewish, and Christian members, including some renowned politicians who held high positions at the top of the organization (cf. Šalaš, *Al-yahūd*, pp. 247–249). We may also point out that the Jewish communities in the Near East were not, at the time, especially receptive to Zionism. In Egypt, for example, the Zionist movement initiated by Joseph Marco Barukh at the end of the nineteenth century, especially with the foundation of the Bar-Kochba Zionist Society, met with no special success among the composite Jewish community of Egypt (about 65,000 individuals in 1928), both because of the political indifference of Egyptian Jews and the relative prosperity and safety they enjoyed under the British domination (cf. Thomas Mayer, *Egypt and the Palestine Question*, Berlin 1983; Jacob M. Landau, *Jews in Nineteenth-Century Egypt*, New York 1969,

the first Arab-Israeli war, when the Arab governments (in the first place, nationalist Egyptian, Syrian, Iraqi, and Palestinian leaders, as well as Wahhabi-oriented Saudi Arabia) realized its propaganda potential against Zionism and directly promoted its dissemination.

It is equally clear that the myth of the Judeo-Masonic conspiracy spread mainly through publications which were explicitly anti-Masonic but implicitly anti-Jewish. The central theme of anti-Masonic propaganda revolved essentially, if not exclusively, around the conspiratorial nature of Freemasonry, which was supposed to be a Jewish organization both by origin and by nature. That the real object of the attacks was not Masonry also clearly emerges from the fact that the conspiracy myth became most widespread long after Freemasonry had been outlawed in many countries of the region.

That the Arab governments lent credibility to and promoted the conspiracy myth shows the state involvement in anti-Zionist propaganda, probably also due to failure in defeating an enemy of ridiculous size when compared to its neighbours;[73] a useful expedient above all for the regimes which had been humiliated by the wars with Israel. One may argue that the Arab regimes saw the *Protocols* – or al-H̱ūrī's tale – not so much as a useful tool for attributing to the Jews wickedness, perfidy, and all those detestable traits which have been assigned to them through history, but rather as an explanation of the recent historical events in the Middle East which located Israel at the heart of the problems: they were not simply fighting an enemy state but an intangible secret worldwide organization. Zionism and the establishment of Israel were not a mere product of international and regional political developments but the diabolical outcome of a subterranean plot carried on for thousands of years by the Mysterious Force. Such an outlook gives, from a populist and demagogic point of view, a new balance to the relationships of force between the actors in the conflict.

The use of a conspiracy myth born abroad for such a purpose shows its peculiar nature when we take into account that in this propaganda, the specifically Islamic anti-Jewish tradition – which would seem much more handy to use – normally only plays a marginal role.[74] According to the vision of the

---

pp. 115–125, 327–329; Anna Scarantino, "La comunità ebraica in Egitto fra le due guerre mondiali", in: *Storia contemporanea*, 6/1986, pp. 1033–1082).

[73] In terms of territorial extent, not, of course, of military power.

[74] This is not the case for radical Islamic material, which may at most mention the *Protocols* as a confirmation of the unreliable nature of the Jews, but which focuses on more political and religious arguments (cf. Ronald N. Nettler, *Past Trials and Present Tribulations: A Muslim Fundamentalist's View of the Jews*, Oxford 1887; Olivier Carré, *Mystique et politique: Lecture révolutionnaire du Coran par Sayyid Qutb, Frère musul-*

Qur'an, Jews are Muslims' worst enemies, falsifiers – together with the Christians – of divine truth, those who disobeyed the prophets sent by God;[75] yet, such arguments are subordinate to the conspiracy fantasies of an extra-Islamic kind. At most, they are used as further confirmation of the existence of a Judeo-Masonic conspiracy and the danger it poses, since the Jews are alleged to have worked against Islam from the start, for the same reasons for which they put obstacles in the path of every non-Jewish religion.

The same holds true for the anti-Masonic contents of the myth. Muslims who join Masonry are not, for example, accused of apostasy or misbelief, for following a non-Islamic, hermetic path of initiation and enlightenment;[76] nor is Masonry, as a western fabrication, accused of being a subtle tool of European imperialist policies since the nineteenth century[77] – obvious arguments, which would have been potentially more credible for any audience. Yet, the only anti-Masonic argument made is that Freemasonry is an agent of the international Jewish conspiracy, and based on this premise all the other more or less abstruse issues are usually dealt with.

The ability of such a grotesque myth to reproduce itself in such culturally different milieus can be explained by its ductility and functionality. Whether it legitimates an irrational, centuries-old aversion (as in the case of the Jesuit thread), motivates a plan of extermination (as in the case of the Nazi thread), or absorbs humiliating political failures (as in the case of the Arab regimes), in the outlook of those who use it – even when their relations of power compared to the "enemy" are extremely different –, the myth of the Judeo-Masonic conspiracy serves a single purpose: to justify what common sense, reason, and logic are unable to justify.

---

man radical, Paris 1984; Carré, *L'Utopie islamique dans le monde arabe*, Paris 1991; Kepel, *Le Prophète*; Michael Curtis [ed.], *Antisemitism in the Contemporary World*, London 1986).

75 *Qur'an*, VII, pp. 163–171; IX, p. 30; XVII, pp. 4–8.

76 As was the case in the early days of Masonic infiltration in the Levant. For example, around 1800, a soldier of the Sultan who "had studied Masonry, magic and alchemy in Europe" was accused of having failed to conform to Islam and behaving like a "heretic, without faith" (Zarcone, *Mystiques*, p. 196). However, in 1978 the court of law of Casablanca declared that the Qur'an and Masonic rules were compatible (cf. Georges Odo, *La Franc-maçonnerie en Afrique*, Paris 2000, p. 102).

77 Cf. the introductory part.

Matthew Gray (Canberra)

Western Theories about Conspiracy Theories and the Middle Eastern Context: The Scope and Limits of Explanatory Transpositions

While there is an expanding corpus of explanatory literature on conspiracy theories available to scholars, this is truer in the case of the United States – in terms both of the U.S. as the society under study and the domicile of the scholars writing on the topic – than it is of the Middle East. The topic is a growing one of interest in the Middle East, especially in popular contexts such as the mass media, but scholarship seeking to focus on Middle Eastern conspiracy theories is incomplete without significant references to the U.S. literature. It is the purpose of this paper to evaluate the transferability of U.S. conspiracy theory literature to the Middle Eastern context. In that process four questions are specifically covered:

- How can the literature on U.S. conspiracy theories be categorized?
- What do these bodies of theory argue?
- What is the scope for the transmission of explanations from a U.S. to a Middle Eastern context, including any intellectual risks of such?
- What ultimately are the limits – and why – of this transmissibility?

There is, in short, some scope for literature on the U.S. to be transposed to an explanation of the Middle East, especially where some similarities can be discerned in the political origins or motivations of the conspiracy theorist(s). However, beyond this, caution is required in so doing. There are risks in trans-regionally transposing theoretical explanations too readily: the hazard of falling into cultural reductionism or over-simplification, of course, but also constraints in comparing the two political structures or their political and social dynamics, and the problem of very dissimilar historical experiences between the U.S. and the Middle East and important developmental variations between the two.

1. The State of the U.S. Literature on Conspiracy Theories

The literature on U.S. conspiracy theories is well-developed. Many date its emergence to the publication of Richard Hofstadter's essay *The Paranoid Style in American Politics*,[1] but the interest in conspiracy theories accelerated, especially in the 1990s and 2000s, to encompass a broader range of explanatory approaches and frameworks. In contestation is not that there is a preponderance of conspiracy theorizing in the U.S., but rather the source(s) of it, and in entering this debate, scholars vary greatly in approach and style. Broadly, the theories now proffered about conspiracy theories in the U.S. (and for that matter, about conspiracy theories in most western cultures) fall into three broad categories, which may be labelled as: 'cultural deterministic' explanations, societal- or group-centric explanations, and external- or exogenous-centric explanations. To this, some might argue that there should be added a category on the state and its leadership as narrators of conspiracy theories, however, that is to confuse the messenger for the source of the message, as will be discussed later.

The 'cultural deterministic' explanations were among the first schools of thought on U.S. conspiracy theories – Hofstadter's essay is a case in point. By 'cultural deterministic' is meant that conspiracy theories are part of the cultural pathology of certain societies,[2] dictated by history perhaps, but set in cultural stone by intergenerational transmission. At its worst, it is a 'mentality', as Daniel Pipes has in effect argued.[3] Hofstadter, and some of this contemporaries such as Brion Davis,[4] focused on conspiracy theories as a way

---

1 Cf. Richard Hofstadter, *The Paranoid Style in American Politics and Other Essays*, New York 1965. This is an extended version of the seminal article that originally was published as Richard Hofstadter, "The Paranoid Style in American Politics", in: *Harper's Magazine*, 11/1964, pp. 77–86, which can also be found online: http://karws.gso.uri.edu/jfk/conspiracy_theory/the_paranoid_mentality/the_paranoid_style.html (accessed June 21, 2010).

2 Previously I have used the term 'pathological' instead of 'cultural deterministic', but mean essentially the same thing: convenient and often-reductionist attempts to explain conspiracy theorizing as a cultural trait that is difficult if not impossible to change. On the 'pathological' idea cf. for example Matthew Gray, *Conspiracy Theories in the Arab World: Sources and Politics*, Abingdon/New York 2010, pp. 21–24; Matthew Gray, "Explaining Conspiracy Theories in Modern Arab Middle Eastern Political Discourse: Some Problems and Limitations of the Literature", in: *Critique: Critical Middle Eastern Studies*, 17/2008, 2, pp. 161–162.

3 Cf. Daniel Pipes, *Conspiracy: How the Paranoid Style Flourishes and Where It Comes From*, New York 1997, p. 7.

4 Cf. for example David Brion Davis (ed.), *The Fear of Conspiracy: Images of Un-American Subversion from the Revolution to the Present*, Ithaca 1971; David Brion Davis,

for American individuals to reaffirm the dominant principles of the U.S. and to enhance social cohesion by attacking small groups that were isolated from mainstream opinion. Many later works explaining conspiracy theories drew heavily on Hofstadter: Pipes' works on it is a case in point. In *Conspiracy: How the Paranoid Style Flourishes and Where It Comes From*,[5] Pipes outlines a history of conspiracy thinking and Othering, in particular by Westerners and especially targeting Jews and Masons.[6] Like his earlier *The Hidden Hand*[7] the book is useful for some outlines of conspiracy theories and in pointing out the longevity of certain paranoias (especially anti-Semitism) in the West, but ultimately it essentially implies that such fears have been virtually ingrained into people's thinking in western societies.

This approach also is linked to the psychological explanations for conspiracy thinking, for the obvious reason that psychology is concerned with the behavioural dynamics of people and most often individuals. While group cohesion is important in many respects, it may also be genetically in the individual interest to act deceptively: thus Robins and Post argue that "cheaters *do* prosper", and nature, through natural selection, will favour those who are more attuned to the psychology of others.[8] People are hardwired to be deceptive, but also hardwired to fear the enemy.[9]

The second category, 'societal-centric' or 'group-centric' explanations, arguably currently are the most common. This category is about conspiracy theories that seem to draw from societal dynamics and especially inter- and intra-group relationships. They fall into several bodies of literature. Perhaps the most obvious are those seeking to explain majority and minority discourses about other groups. The majority discourses are essentially about how in-groups frame their worldviews and develop group identity by differentiating themselves from others, while minority conspiracy theories come from a sense of marginalization, alienation, or discrimination. Bale suggests

"Some Themes of Counter-Subversion: An Analysis of Anti-Masonic, Anti-Catholic, and Anti-Mormon Literature", in: *The Mississippi Valley Historical Review*, 47/1960, 2, pp. 205–224.

5 Cf. Pipes, *Conspiracy*.

6 Cf. Sam Tanenhaus's review of Pipes's book: "Plots and Counterplots", in: *Partisan Review*, 63/1998, 4, pp. 658–664.

7 Cf. Daniel Pipes, *The Hidden Hand: Middle East Fears of Conspiracy*, London 1996.

8 Robert S. Robins/Jerrold M. Post, *Political Paranoia: The Psychopolitics of Hatred*, New Haven 1997, p. 71; italics in the original.

9 Cf. Robins/Post, *Political Paranoia*, p. 74.

three main sources of conspiracism,[10] and while he is focused on minority discourses, his arguments are also valid for some majorities who feel uncertain or threatened by change. The first is that it is an attempt to make events and affairs more understandable through reductionism and oversimplification.[11] His other reasons are that conspiracism is an attempt to locate and identify a source of misery and injustice in the world – a way of "explaining why bad things are happening to good people or vice versa"[12] – and finally that by creating a conspiracy narrative construct, a person is able to personify a source that they see as evil, threatening, or dangerous, by which they might "paradoxically [...] reaffirm their own potential ability to control the course of future historical developments".[13] Other authors have made similar points: a paper by Abalakina-Paap et al. is consistent with Bale's latter two points.[14]

Further, as Putnam and others have pointed out, a decline in social trust (not to be confused with trust in government, which arguably has also declined in the same period) has occurred at local and community level,[15] although some areas of community interaction, such as memberships of social movements and internet groups, has conversely risen.[16] Such groups – especially internet communities but also groups of like-minded individuals, whether from minorities or part of a majority – are a key mechanism through which conspiracy ideas and arguments are shared and debated. Paradoxically, the internet provides its own conspiracy fears by people suspicious of viruses or a hidden control of online space,[17] but it also is a very effective and popular tool for conspiracy discourse. The internet can spread conspiracy theories "almost effortlessly"[18] and with few if any of the normal constraints

---

10 Cf. Jeffrey M. Bale, "'Conspiracy Theories' and Clandestine Politics", in: *Lobster: The Journal of Parapolitics*, 29/1995, http://www.lobster-magazine.co.uk/articles/l29consp.htm (accessed Jan. 20, 2006).

11 Cf. Bale, "'Conspiracy Theories'".

12 Bale, "'Conspiracy Theories'".

13 Bale, "'Conspiracy Theories'".

14 Cf. Marina Abalakina-Paap et al., "Beliefs in Conspiracies", in: *Political Psychology*, 20/1999, 3, pp. 637–647.

15 Cf. Robert D. Putnam, *Bowling Alone: The Collapse and Revival of American Community*, New York 2000. A similar point is made in Francis Fukuyama, *Trust: The Social Virtues and the Creation of Prosperity*, London 1995.

16 Cf. Putnam, *Bowling Alone*, especially ch. 9.

17 Cf. Peter Knight, *Conspiracy Culture: From Kennedy to* The X-Files, London 2000, pp. 209–216.

18 Laurent Belsie, "UFOs? Secret Agents? On the Net, Conspiracy Theories Abound", in: *The Christian Science Monitor*, 1997, p. 12.

to publishing books, magazine articles, or other printed matter. The internet also allows for direct web links to (supposedly) supporting evidence, and the inclusion of multimedia evidence such as voice or video files to support an argument.[19] Conspiracy theorists can be, and often are, from sub-groups which they feel to be marginalised or excluded by a mainstream, but need not always be.

The idea of conspiracy theorizing as (attempted) self-empowerment is an important one, again for both majorities and minorities. One view is of conspiracy theorizing as "naïve deconstructive history."[20] Floyd Rudmin gives popular conspiracy theories a somewhat academic basis by explaining them as something that people uneducated in academic history nonetheless create with much the same goal in mind as the professional historian. Conspiracy theories thus are an attempt at a hypothesis about opaque events: they are 'history' because they seek to explain events that have happened, and 'deconstructive history' specifically because they counter official accounts or the orthodox position on the event.[21] The validity of naïvely deconstructed conspiracy theorizing may be undermined by its lacking falsifiability and thus the scientific methodology expected with professional scholarly history. Popular conspiracy theorizing is open to the usual failings of intellectual explanation (Rudmin gives the example of confirmation bias),[22] but as an explanation of the social origins of conspiracy theorizing it has merit, especially in approaching conspiracy theories in a way other than a negative or delusional one. Another, somewhat related way of seeing conspiracy theorizing as empowerment is in the view that it plays a role as a check on the power and transparency of political actors and institutions. One is conspiracy theorizing as 'coded social critique', where it is:

> an underlying message that critiques various social, political, or economic institutions and actors. In other words, the point of dispute in the competing theories and [official/orthodox] accounts is equally over the different institutions' ethos and legitimacy as it is over the facts.[23]

This could be as true of the Middle East as of the U.S., if not more so – the limited scope for criticism of authoritarian leaderships in the Middle East

---

19 Cf. Shane Miller, "Conspiracy Theories: Public Arguments as Coded Social Critiques: A Rhetorical Analysis of the TWA Flight 800 Conspiracy Theories", in: *Argumentation and Advocacy*, 39/2002, 1, p. 46.

20 Floyd Rudmin, *Conspiracy Theory as Naïve Deconstructive History*, 2003, http://www.newdemocracyworld.org/old/conspiracy.htm (accessed Mar. 11, 2005).

21 Cf. Rudmin, *Conspiracy Theory.*

22 Cf. Rudmin, *Conspiracy Theory.*

23 Miller, "Conspiracy Theories: Public Arguments", p. 41.

make conspiracy theorizing, along with political humour, rumouring, and other indirect commentary, appealing.[24]

Finally, the third category of literature, focused on 'external-' or 'exogenous-centric' explanations, is about how external variables create an impetus or propensity (and of course also act as a target) for conspiracy theories. Broad societal changes from globalization and postmodernism are perhaps the best examples, to which might be added theories about the state or political elite which is or are seen as opaque, out of touch, and acting in their own interests rather than society's or the nation's.

Globalization is important in several ways. The first is that state sovereignty, and thus the power of the state as perceived by its citizens, has diminished with globalization, creating a sense that the community is under threat from external powers and dynamics that even the state cannot protect against. In some cases it may also encourage or reinforce a retreat to sub-state social units that use a prism of 'self' and 'other' in constructing their identity. Second, globalization has an impact on conspiracy theories and thinking by virtue of its economic and technological characteristics. This is not always separate to the decline of state sovereignty: many of the corporate symbols of economic globalisation (such as McDonald's, Coca-Cola, or Nike) have grown stronger both in relative power and as symbols of increased multinational corporate power at the expense of state economic power. Such symbols send a message of cultural penetration and economic weakness and make economic threats more symbolized and identifiable. On a related level and as a third point, the advances in technology and transportation that have accompanied globalisation have had an impact of disjointing and displacing some people from traditional territory or from long-established social units and societies. This is a key point made by Olivier Roy when examining Muslim communities in the West and the impact of globalisation on Islam. He holds that the removal of religion from old geographic boundaries and the erosion of old patterns of leadership within Islam, as a direct outcome of globalisation, migration, and technological change, has "globalised" Islam, made it increasingly rootless, and changed the way the idea of *'ummah* ("community") is understood.[25] Such an argument helps explain things that would otherwise seem paradoxical: for example, where conspiracy theorists use technologies such as the Internet or online chat rooms to denounce the impacts of globalization and westernization.

---

24 Cf. Gray, *Conspiracy Theories in the Arab World*, pp. 103–104.

25 Olivier Roy, *Globalised Islam: The Search for a New Ummah*, London 2004.

Related to both globalization and the earlier empowerment idea is the argument that conspiracy theories provide a context or local authority to groups or societies that are being dislocated or impacted by changes at a global level. From this approach, conspiracism is less about delusion or paranoia and more a response that gives a local relevance or importance to events that are global in nature or at least which transcend the local:

> people do not simply listen to, and assess, the ideas conveyed in global ideoscapes. In their quest for meaningful modernity, people create and convey their own terms and images, producing and sustaining ideoscapes that cohabit the world along with those of global dimensions.[26]

Not surprisingly in the U.S. and western context, such arguments about meaning and truth and how these are perceived, at times stray into a debate about postmodernism. Postmodernists often cite, as characteristics of postmodernity, societal structures and dynamics that could contribute to conspiracy theorizing by alienating or disorientating the individual. The relativising effect on knowledge and scientific method that is typically given as signifier of postmodernism could be construed as encouraging conspiracist discourse as it undermines the need, according to the orthodoxy of the modernist period, for falsifiability in explanation.[27] The multiculturalization characteristic of postmodernity is also crucial, both because it reinforces the relativisation of knowledge among different groups and individuals in society, thus presumably offering new discursive legitimacy to alternative or other voices, and because it creates separate corpuses of knowledge among different groups that could conceivably create friction or misunderstanding between them.[28] From yet another angle, conspiracy theories constitute a legitimisation of many aspects and symptoms of postmodernism: the "collapse of distinction between the literal and the metaphorical, the factual and the fictional, the paranoid and the persecuted, the diagnosis and the symptom, the personal and the political, the trivial and the worthwhile, the plausible and the incredible".[29] The result

---

[26] Harry G. West/Todd Sanders, "Power Revealed and Concealed in the New World Order", in: Harry G. West/Todd Sanders (eds.), *Transparency and Conspiracy: Ethnographies of Suspicion in the New World Order*, Durham, NC 2003, p. 12.

[27] Cf. Jonathan Friedman, "The Implosion of Modernity", in: Michael J. Shapiro/Hayward R. Alker (eds.), *Challenging Boundaries: Global Flows, Territorial Identities*, Minneapolis 1996, p. 250.

[28] For more details on multiculturalisation cf. Friedman, "Implosion of Modernity", p. 250.

[29] Alasdair Spark, "Conspiracy Thinking and Conspiracy Studying", in: *Centre for Conspiracy Culture*, http://www2.winchester.ac.uk/ccc/resources/essays/thinkstudy.htm (accessed Jan. 15, 2012).

of this has been not only to "disable traditional outlooks and politics", but also to obscure the difference between "conspiracy as legitimate revelation or deluded mystification".[30]

2. Non-Western Approaches and Issues with Conspiracy Theories

Beyond the quite advanced theoretical literature on the U.S. and some other western states, there is some, albeit less, material on non-western states and societies as well. Some is directly and explicitly about the development and articulation of conspiracy theories in non-western societies, and other material is more focused on related areas such as the roles of spiritual medicine, xenophobia (justified or not), metaphysical explanations for strange events, and the role of exaggeration or misinformation in inter-cultural and intra-cultural conflict, to name just a few foci and angles of approach.[31] Important here, though, is the fact that conspiracy theorizing is part of political discourse in various states and regions and not a unique feature of the U.S., or the Middle East, or any other region – even if its frequency and specifics vary quite considerably.

In general terms, literature on non-western conspiracy theories tends to vary by disciplinary approach – anthropological, sociological, political science – and by the degree to which the author is sympathetic or antipathetic towards the subjects of inquiry and the place and role of conspiracy theories. This is similar to the scholarly approaches towards conspiracism in the U.S., but with a couple of notable exceptions and differentiations. One is that scholarship on the U.S. is commonly coming from U.S. scholars or other scholars in the West, while much of the material on non-western cases is the product of western observers, which carries with it the problems of inter-cultural interpretation and differences in how ideas are structured as logical and internally consistent. At its worst, work by, say, a scholar who is hostile towards the subjects of study and their beliefs can lead to scholarship that enlarges rather than lessens a breach in understanding between the two cultures. There is a corpus of literature on the politics and 'culture' of the Middle East that is of this style, the reductionist (neo-)Orientalist type, while

---

30 Spark, "Conspiracy Thinking".

31 As just a few examples of these, cf. Leslie Butt, "'Lipstick Girls' and 'Fallen Women': AIDS and Conspiratorial Thinking in Papua, Indonesia", in: *Cultural Anthropology*, 20/2005, 3, pp. 412–441; Jane Parish, "The Dynamics of Witchcraft and Indigenous Shrines among the Akan", in: *Africa*, 69/1999, 3, pp. 426–447; as well as several of the case study chapters in the already-cited edited work West/Sanders (eds.), *Transparency and Conspiracy*.

less menacing but still important is simply the problem of interpretation across cultures. Most western scholars will bring their own methodologies and tools of analysis in such study, which also has risks if the contrasting worldviews and logical approaches of others are not sufficiently taken into account.

The way in which past western actions are translated into a discourse with contemporary relevance in the non-western worlds is often through the development of popular memories and mythologies, in which past events are recreated and re-narrated, usually with a particular focus or selectively, and usually with history framed as a linear excursion in which the present can be directly and clearly linked back to the past. Mythologies are "narratives that shape collective consciousness and national-cultural identity and that seek to anchor the present in the past",[32] and collective memories, while sometimes similar to mythologies or shaped by them, are shared group recollections, both real and constructed, that define a current worldview or which feed into social narratives.

However, this is not to over-state the role of mythology, because the nature of non-western conspiracy theorizing also varies from the U.S. case because of variations in societal structures. Traditional kinship patterns, class structures, social hierarchies, and group autonomy all affect conspiracy theories in non-western societies. All can promote and represent suspicion about other groups or invite a group to develop narratives that will strengthen its cohesion and seek to pre-empt forces or actors that might undermine it. Such discourses, moreover, can derive from mythology and collective memory, or can be a genuine attempt at self-identification in response to an actual threat. As in the U.S., the manifestation of this may be a majority conspiracy theory about a minority, or a minority's about a majority, or in more fragmented societies, a minority's view of another minority. Yet further but importantly in settings outside the U.S., it may include a conspiracy theory targeting alleged conspirators in another country, especially because of the power and financial imbalances between the developed and the developing worlds.

Finally but crucially, a key dynamic that separates US conspiracy theorizing from much else of the world – not least of all the Middle East – is the role of the state as a narrator or supporter of conspiracy explanations. The most overt examples come from authoritarian systems of government – authoritarians (not to mention totalitarians) obviously have greater direct controls

---

32 Robert Bowker, *Palestinian Refugees: Mythology, Identity and the Search for Peace*, London 2003, p. 12.

over mass media and the debates that occur in the public sphere.[33] The literature about state conspiracy rhetoric in the Soviet Union makes several arguments that are relevant more broadly about the goals of state-narrated conspiracy theories: the characteristics of conspiracist rhetoric allow for a "false dilemma" (creating a false image to the public that only two stark options are available to those in power),[34] for example, and conspiracy theories use a power of inference that turns weak internal consistency into fact or near-fact, again empowering the narrator (in this case, of course, the state).[35]

This said, conspiracy theories are also a feature of softer regimes than the Soviet one. The rhetoric used by former Malaysian Prime Minister Dr. Mahathir Mohamad is illustrative, for example, when in 1997, during the Asian financial crisis, he blamed a fall in the Malaysian currency and the country's heavy debt on a conspiracy by international Jewish financiers: "We are Muslims and the Jews are not happy to see Muslims' progress. [...] If viewed from Palestine, the Jews have robbed Palestinians of everything but they cannot do this in Malaysia, so they do this [i.e. undermine Malaysia's economy]".[36] South African President Thabo Mbeki's assertion that AIDS could not possibly develop from the human immunodeficiency virus[37] and that its growth can be attributed to a conspiracy by U.S. pharmaceutical firms is another case in point.[38] These are likely either genuinely-believed theories or, otherwise, attempts to distract or confuse the public and deflect criticism from the regime and the leader. More on this issue of state conspiracy theorizing, in the specific Middle East context, follows below.

This does not preclude social dynamics from informing, sustaining, or relating to the state's use of conspiracist political language. The state may not simply (or too simply) adopt a conspiracy theory as explanation for the pur-

---

33 On Nazi language, but with some ideas more widely applicable, cf. John Wesley Young, *Totalitarian Language: Orwell's Newspeak and its Nazi and Communist Antecedents*, Charlottesville, VA 1991, pp. 76–103.

34 Marilyn J. Young/Michael K. Launer, *Flights of Fancy, Flights of Doom: KAL007 and Soviet-American Rhetoric*, Lanham, MD 1988, p. 223.

35 Cf. Young/Launer, *Flights of Fancy*, pp. 223–224.

36 Qtd. in "Mahathir in his Own Words", in: *BBC News*, Jan. 27, 2006, http://news.bbc.co.uk/2/hi/asia-pacific/3198105.stm (accessed Apr. 18, 2007).

37 Cf. "Mbeki Digs in on AIDS", in: *BBC News*, Sept. 20, 2000, http://news.bbc.co.uk/2/hi/africa/934435.stm (accessed July 12, 2006). Mbeki is not alone in this argument; the AIDS Reappraisal Movement in the Western world is a minority, but not insignificant, movement making exactly the same argument.

38 Cf. Carol Paton/Carmel Rickard, "Mbeki Links AIDS to US Drug Conspiracy", in: *Sunday Times* (South Africa), Oct. 1, 2000, http://www.suntimes.co.za/2000/10/01/news/news03.htm (accessed July 12, 2006).

poses of deceiving or confusing the public. Instead or additionally, leaders sometimes repeat or reinforce a conspiracy theory that came originally from a societal source. Such discourse may aim to reinforce a leader's legitimacy or perceived relevance to the public or a constituency within it or send a message to the audience that the state is cognizant of their concerns. Specifically, that societal explanations are often framed in simple language and with only basic frameworks means also that, by copying or engaging with such discourse and its idioms, and being seen to share in ordinary societal concerns, the state or a leader is able to imply a bond with society, or at least an understanding of, or even affinity with, everyday life and perspectives.

A pertinent and recent example is the willingness of local political figures in Egypt in late-2010 to join with popular explanations for a spate of shark attacks in the Sinai. What began as a societal conspiracy theory – blaming Israel, and in particular its external intelligence agency Mossad, for several shark attacks near Sharm el-Sheikh – was reinforced by the Governor of the South Sinai in a media interview on December 6, 2010, in which he claimed that "what is being said about the Mossad throwing the deadly shark in the sea to hit tourism in Egypt is not out of the question".[39] By repeating the conspiracy in such a context, he was able to demonstrate an affiliation with popular political language and a common public explanation, while reiterating what to many people was the key concern – namely that the attacks would undermine Egypt's and the Sinai's economic base, heavily reliant as it has long been on (wealthy, western) tourists. This language also fits well with critical theory arguments, especially anti-positivist approaches such as postmodernism, to explaining conspiracism, more on which later.

3. The Scope and Limits of Transmissibility

How universally applicable, therefore, are theories about conspiracy theories? What is the potential for transposing or trans-interpreting U.S. theories, or theories about U.S. conspiracy language, to a Middle Eastern context? The answer is at least in part a variable one, depending on the particular theory and, more importantly, the need to test an explanation against the unique elements of the Middle East: its specific historical experience, patterns of social organization, and styles of government and political economy. There are universalities in political behaviour, of course, but caution is no-

[39] Babak Dehghanpisheh, "Conspiracy Theories with a Bite", in: *Newsweek*, Dec. 8, 2010, http://www.thedailybeast.com/newsweek/2010/12/08/conspiracy-theories-with-a-bite.html (accessed Mar. 18, 2011).

netheless required to avoid an (over-)simplification or reductionism in cases where a theory is transferred from a western to a Middle Eastern context.

The first reaction of many critics of conspiracy theories, as mentioned, is to rush for a simple explanation for them: hence the earlier argument that 'cultural deterministic' explanations have limited utility. It is worth noting, however, that 'cultural deterministic' explanations are prominent, nonetheless, in explaining conspiracy theories in both the U.S. and the Middle East. One Arab writer, in lamenting the commonness of conspiracy theories in the region, claimed that they should be seen as:

> a clinical case that requires medical intervention more than just a quiet and relaxed discussion [...] If it were not for the existence of other races and nations with their own conspiracy theories, I would have thought that the concept was a patented Arab invention.[40]

Such remarks are not inherently different from Hofstadter's claim that the "paranoid style" is "a distorted style" and "a possible signal that may alert us to a distorted judgement",[41] or from Pipes' argument that a conspiracy theorist "discerns malignant forces at work wherever something displeases him; plots serve as his first method for explaining the world around him. He suspects a plot or cover-up even when other, less malign explanations better fit the facts".[42] In other words, the conspiracy theorist is foolish, illogical, even mentally challenged. Simplistic as such explanations are, the point remains that they find currency in various cultural settings.

Where conspiracy theories symbolize or express political concerns, shared identities, or anxieties, there is not a great difference in the political dynamics informing the actors engaged in articulating and transmitting the theories. Thus there is scope to assume a degree of theoretical transposability purely on the basis of shared characteristics applicable to the explanation: put simply, a minority in the U.S. that sees a distant, majority-dominated state or an opaque transnational force such as globalization or technological change at work and potentially at odds with the interests of a group at the political and social periphery, is not especially different from a minority in a Middle Eastern state that develops the same interpretations about the same actors or phenomena. Likewise, despite the different positions of the U.S. and the Middle East within trends such as globalization, the forces that

---

40 Mishari al-Thaidi, "More on Conspiracy Theories", in: *Arab News/ash-Sharq al-Awsat*, http://www.arabnews.com/9-11/?article=40&part=2 (accessed Jan. 9, 2006).

41 Hofstadter, *The Paranoid Style*, p. 6.

42 Pipes, *The Hidden Hand*, p. 10.

people fear can be remarkably similar: the facelessness and undemocratic characteristics of transnational companies and the power they are perceived to have gained from globalization figure prominently in conspiracy theories in both the U.S. and the Middle East. Likewise, theories about minorities often are similar, with anti-Semitic conspiracy theories being an especially prominent aspect of conspiracy theorizing in both places; albeit with the specific language varying – perhaps for obvious reasons of what is of gravest political concern – from a focus on Jewish banking, finance, and informal power more common in the U.S. and on Israeli actions and intent, and international Jewish (and non-Jewish) support for the Israeli state more common in the Middle East.[43] It is worth recalling the widespread belief in and popularity of the *Protocols of the Elders of Zion* for a long time in the U.S., the UK, and elsewhere in the West,[44] and that the *Protocols* are still cited in the Middle East today.[45]

Where the U.S. and the Middle East begin to diverge is in the applicability of more cultural-specific explanations, especially where historical experience or perspective is central to the conspiracy argument, and where the state-society relationship or the nature of the state and its stage of development is important explanatorily. Critical theory, postmodernism in particular, has, as noted earlier, been widely deployed in explaining U.S. conspiracy theories. There is some scope to include the anti-positivist ideas of critical theory when approaching conspiracy theories, especially as derived from sociological works, given their emphasis on the interpretation not only of texts and at face value, but of symbols and other communicated forms of meaning. However, this approach has far less utility in the Middle Eastern case in terms of explaining societal structures and conditions: it still has some validity in assessing intercultural dynamics and for understanding concepts such as multiculturalization, and, of course, in formulating explanations and contextualizations of U.S. conspiracism. Kravitz in this way has some basis in arguing, concerning the U.S. case, that:

---

43 On anti-Semitic conspiracy theories in the U.S. and the West cf. the extensive discussion in Pipes, *Conspiracy*.

44 Cf. the articles in: *The Times* (London), August 16–18, 1921 presented in Philip Graves, "The Source of 'The Protocols of Zion': An Exposure" (Jared Israel/ Samantha Criscione, "In 1921 Philip Graves Exposed the 'Protocols of Zion' as Phony", Sept. 26, 2002, http://emperors-clothes.com/antisem/times-pdf.htm [accessed Jan. 14, 2006]).

45 Cf. Steve Boggan, "The Anti-Jewish Lie that Refuses to Die", in: *The Times*, Mar. 2, 2005, http://www.timesonline.co.uk/printFriendly/0,,1-7-1506190,00.html (accessed Jan. 14, 2006).

> Conspiracy is the result of trying to imagine the totality of the late capitalist system, but it is also a cultural construct – stemming from that very same Western capitalist system – created both to cause and relieve the headache [of "imaging the totality of the world system" as he explains separately] [...] Thus conspiracy, despite its threatening nature, provides a rationale for the way the world is.[46]

However little of this is applicable in the Middle Eastern case: even if some arguments might be made about some components of it or related dynamics. These include: the impacts of neoliberalism and its encroachment into the Middle East; the confusion that Middle Easterners may share with Westerners about elements of the world around them and the constructed imaginings of other cultural settings; the Othering that sometimes occurs in the Middle East towards an external unilateral power seen as opaque and often nefarious. The variations between the two regions in terms of societal structures, urban orders, social isolation of the individual, and the individual's links to traditional family and kinship structures are nevertheless all very different, and all make a direct explanatory transposition of postmodernism onto the Middle East – at least in terms of how it is understood in the West – extremely complicated and ill-advised.

As an aside, it is worth noting that some other or associated critical approaches are more applicable to the Middle East and more transferable from a western context. Some ideas from Marxists and other thinkers have been adopted in the Middle East when debating the sources and impacts of conspiracism: while many in the West assume that such debate is relatively under-formulated in the Middle East, and although the scholarly literature in the region is far less voluminous than in the West, ideas can be located in the region and from both its intellectuals and among more popular commentators that are in fact very similar to critical theory ideas in the West, such as microcosmic and trans-cultural critiques of globalization and neoliberalism. Other non-Marxian approaches have been adopted to explain conspiracy theories in both the West and the Middle East, for example critical theory informed by psychological influences such as Freudian ideas. Finally, some of the tools deployed by critical theorists – perhaps the most obvious of which is deconstruction – are equally suitable in a Middle Eastern context: even with the language and linguistic variations between, say, Arabic and English, and the contextual differences in their cultural and historical settings, a deconstruction of the language of conspiracy theories retains some validity.

---

[46] Bennett Kravitz, "The Truth Is Out There: Conspiracy as a Mindset in American High and Popular Culture", in: *Journal of American Culture*, 22/1999, 4, p. 24.

An example assessable here of how critical theory may assist in explaining a conspiracy theory is that of the 2010 Sinai shark attacks already noted. The popular propensity to finger Mossad did, to some extent and at its simplest, reflect a wide public loathing and mistrust of Israel. To a western audience, of course, an Israeli role in training or remote-controlling a shark to attack tourists off Egyptian beaches seems extremely unlikely and a conspiracy theory along such lines self-defeating by its implausibility. However, paradoxically, it could be argued through a critical theory lens that the adoption of a conspiracy theory as explanation actually represents the implausibility of the events: recall that four people were injured in a single day on December 1, 2010, and on December 5 another was killed. For Egyptians facing economic ruin or hardship if tourism declined as a result, there may have been both explanatory value and self-empowerment in articulating an explanation that, on past experience of Mossad operations in Egypt, was no less plausible than the idea the chain of shark attacks was *not* planned. In developing or sharing these conspiracy theories, people were engaging in a form of everyday knowledge transmission, while denying their own powerlessness over events – in fact, claiming for themselves a power over the events in claiming to have uncovered and understood a nefarious plot against them. Such an explanation is little different in social origin and cultural structuralization to those that argue that conspiracy theories in the West arise in response to the confusion surrounding the postmodern world and its perceived threats: irrationality, by serving as self-empowerment or to clarify or even challenge that which is mysterious or fear-provoking, contains a form of rationality within or behind it.

The social and cultural variations between the U.S. and the Middle East stem in some part, of course, from different historical experiences and deviations between them in how, and to what extent, current circumstances are attributed to history. Minorities in the two places may possess similar histories of discrimination or marginalization, but at a wider societal level, among elites and majorities especially, the U.S. – in part because of historical dynamics – occupies a different place in the global power structure and enjoys an advantageous economic position. Its *actual* history is different, too: Middle Eastern majorities generally draw longer historical narratives as a distinct ethnos and, of course, because of Islamic identity. The experience of the Middle East with colonial and mandatory governments, whether Ottoman or western, is distinctly different from the U.S. as well, even if the U.S. can relate to fighting a conflict for national independence as some Middle Eastern states can. There are some limited ways in which history is (somewhat) similar, but more in how history is applied to conspiracy explanations or how grievances are framed with attempts at conspiratorial validation, rather than in shared historical dynamics or experiences.

The contemporary specifics of political systems in the two are important as well. There are problems of government legitimacy in the U.S., to be sure, deriving from the events of the 1960s and 1970s, such as the Kennedy assassination, the Vietnam War, the publication of the "Pentagon Papers", and Watergate, all of which undermined trust in government. Watergate in particular "contributed to a decline of Americans' trust in the federal government, already underway in the Vietnam years" that arguably continues to affect society's views of Washington to this day.[47] But that only really explains the state as a target of conspiracy theories – which it is in both the U.S. and the Middle East. In the latter, many states are actually a sponsor, narrator, and supporter of conspiracy theories, which sets them apart from the U.S. government, which might tolerate or accept conspiracy theories, but rarely enunciates them at individual leadership level and in effect never does so systemically.

The state in the Middle East does actually voice them, however, whether through leaders' speeches, state media, or other means. The Syrian president, Bashar al-Asad, articulated one during a visit by Pope John Paul II in May 2001: "We see [Israel] attacking sacred Christian and Muslim places in Palestine. [...] They try to kill the principle of religions in the same mentality in which they betrayed Jesus Christ and tried to kill the prophet Mohammed".[48] The Syrian media routinely makes claims about conspiracies, especially by Israel. One such example:

> It is very clear that after Iraq, Israel is now playing all its cards to foment tension in the region, by causing insecurity, political tension and resorting to military provocation. [...] Israel is not only exploiting the war on Iraq, but is also trying to carry out its plans of aggression against more than just one Arab and Islamic country.[49]

Former Iraqi President Saddam Hussein made many remarks similar to this, especially during periods when his rule was threatened, during the wars with

---

[47] Cf. Michael Schudson, "Notes on Scandal and the Watergate Legacy", in: *The American Behavioral Scientist*, 47/2004, 9, pp. 1231–1238, p. 1234.

[48] Ewan MacAskill, "Pope makes history in Syria, and angers Israel", in: *The Guardian*, May 7, 2001, http://www.guardian.co.uk/world/2001/may/07/israel.catholicism (accessed Sept. 12, 2007).

[49] From *Tishrin*, no details, qtd. in "Arab press worried about Syria", in: *BBC Monitoring*, Apr. 15, 2003, http://news.bbc.co.uk/2/hi/middle_east/2948989.stm (accessed Sept. 12, 2007).

Iran (1980–88) and the U.S. and its allies (1990–91 and 2003).[50] The state and its political elite do this for several reasons: to divert attention and distract critics, most obviously, and in more authoritarian contexts to crowd out alternative explanations of events or to confuse and disorientate the population.[51] In contrast with the U.S., the points here are two: that leaderships in the Middle East are struggling with problems of state formation that are completely different from the U.S., and that the organization of power and the separation of powers in the U.S. and the role of civil society make state conspiracism far more difficult to successfully accomplish. In short, state conspiracy theorizing is a Middle Eastern feature (and is found in a number of other places, including Russia, China, and elsewhere), but except for isolated examples by individuals in the political elite, conspiracy theories are not state-sponsored in the U.S.

4. Conclusion

For all the risks of neo-Orientalism or reductionism, the fact is that there are similarities in the sources of conspiracy theories in the U.S. and the Middle East, and indeed there are some broad explanations that hold across most states and cultures. There is scope to use U.S. theories about conspiracy theories, therefore, to inform an analysis of Middle Eastern ones, and potentially even some lessons from the Middle East for the study of the U.S. – especially some insights about universality where the actors in or characteristics of a conspiracy theory are the same or nearly so. There is a temptation towards this most often when the rhetoric is similar, as indeed it often is when minorities are expressing concerns about majorities or about the state, or where a majority is professing fears about external threats to the state, society, or an element of culture or shared values.

Yet it is important that the case for some transposability of conspiracy theory explanations not be overstated. The temptation of comparison ought to be resisted where similarities in explanation indicate a shared bias or dismissiveness on the part of the narrators, or where an oversimplification of theory might be to blame. Such cases provide little explanatory scope and little in the way of insight into the deeper meanings, signifiers, or potential

---

[50] On the case of Saddam Hussein, including several examples and more detail on the theories of state-narrated conspiracy theories than can be covered here, cf. Matthew Gray, "Revisiting Saddam Hussein's Political Language: The Sources and Roles of Conspiracy Theories", in: *Arab Studies Quarterly*, 32/2010, 1, pp. 28–46.

[51] On this cf. Gray, *Conspiracy Theories in the Arab World*, especially pp. 126–136.

impacts of conspiracy theories – which are, ultimately, as noted, a form of political language that ought to be understood and studied from its own points of departure, if not on its own terms. The transferral of explanations, therefore, requires testing and assessment both for applicability and bias.

Finally, but importantly, no matter what features are shared between the Middle East and the U.S. – from the human condition to minority dynamics to fears about powerlessness in the face of globalization or technological change – the two groups do have their own historical, political, and cultural points of departure and their own unique characteristics that they each not only fail to share, but often fail to appreciate about the other. There is the potential for – but also strict limitations upon – the transferability and transposability of explanations for conspiracy theories across any cultures, not least of all the U.S. and the Middle East.

V. Theorizing Conspiracy Theory

Alexander Dunst (Potsdam)

The Politics of Conspiracy Theories: American Histories and Global Narratives

1. Introduction

In 2002 the administration of George Walker Bush launched a diplomatic and media campaign to manufacture consent for the invasion of Iraq.[1] Saddam Hussein's regime and the terror network of al-Qa'ida were conspiring, Bush and his minions declared, to threaten the United States and its allies with weapons of mass destruction that could reach London, as an intelligence report famously claimed, "in 45 minutes".[2] A suspicious national and international citizenry, long schooled in the public relations of imperialist aggression, met the sabre-rattling with a mixture of disbelief, angry protest, and resignation.

Once American troops and their international support had occupied Iraq, it did not take long for critics to expose such war rhetoric as cynical ploys. Among the widespread condemnation of the media build-up to the invasion, one avenue of critique was conspicuously absent despite its ubiquity in U.S. and, arguably, global culture. Its classic formula, otherwise a frequent reference point for commentators, is to be found in the writing of historian Richard Hofstadter on "The Paranoid Style in American Politics". As he notes, "the central preconception of the paranoid style [is] […] the existence of a vast, insidious, preternaturally effective international conspiratorial network

---

1 Parts of an earlier version of this essay appeared in Slovene and English as: "Navadna paranoja: ponoven premislek o studiju (ameriske) zarote" / "Ordinary Paranoia: Rethinking (American) Conspiracy Studies", in: *Paranoia: Spellbound Spaces of Culture and Politics*, spec. issue of *Dialogi: Revija za Kulturo in Družbo*, 11/2011, 3/4, pp. 120–135.

2 Cf. "Address Before a Joint Session of the Congress on the State of the Union", Jan. 28, 2003, http://frwebgate.access.gpo.gov/cgi-bin/getdoc.cgi?dbname=2003_presidential_documents&docid=-pd03fe03_txt-6 (accessed Oct. 7, 2011); "A Policy of Evasion and Deception", in: *The Washington Post*, Feb. 3, 2003, http://www.washingtonpost.com/wp-srv/nation/transcripts/powelltext_020503.html (Oct. 7, 2011); and Glenn Frankel and Rajiv Chandrasekaran, "45 Minutes: Behind the Blair Claim", in: *The Washington Post with Foreign Policy World*, Feb. 29, 2004, http://www.washingtonpost.com/ac2/wp-dyn/A15697-2004Feb28 (accessed Oct. 7, 2011).

designed to perpetrate acts of the most fiendish character".[3] Elements of Hofstadter's diagnosis formed the basis of the story told by the Bush administration: from the construction of an absolute enemy to its deployment at political turning points.[4]

My point here is not to launch another attack on the Bush administration, this time by way of a pathologising diagnosis of its political paranoia. Nor do I intend to construct a genealogy of American conservatism that would see him and his associates as the true heirs to Joseph McCarthy and Barry Goldwater, the right-wing paragons Hofstadter reserved his ire for. An understanding of McCarthy, Goldwater, and now Bush, Jr., as the exceptions to an otherwise sound political system is best left to its liberal apologists. Besides, nothing would be easier than to show that conspiratorial rhetoric was never exceptional in America, never a fringe phenomenon, but has been part of mainstream politics from its beginnings. As Bernhard Bailyn argued in *The Ideological Origins of the American Revolution*, both proponents and opponents of independence from the British crown presented themselves as victims of a conspiracy, a belief Bailyn identified as a dominant intellectual pattern of the revolution.[5] To point to more recent examples: what should we make of Ronald Reagan's claims that the tiny Caribbean island of Grenada and its co-operation with Cuba posed an imminent threat to U.S. security – a contention deployed for its military invasion? Or Hillary Clinton's famous claim, made on live television, that her husband and then president Bill was the target of a "vast right-wing conspiracy"?[6]

What interests me here is not necessarily the truth content of Reagan's or Clinton's claims but the question why paranoid narratives such as these are so rarely understood as conspiratorial when they issue from the centres of power. In his recent and excellent study of *Conspiracy Theories in the Arab World*, which spends considerable time reviewing Americanist research on the topic, Matthew Gray repeatedly states that the U.S. government does not engage in conspiracy narratives even whilst discussing the Bush adminis-

---

3 Richard Hofstadter, "The Paranoid Style in American Politics", in: *The Paranoid Style in American Politics and Other Essays*, New York 1965, pp. 3–41, p. 14.

4 Hofstadter, "Paranoid Style", p. 3.

5 Bernard Bailyn, *The Ideological Origins of the American Revolution*, Cambridge 1992.

6 Cf. Stephen Zunes, "The US Invasion of Grenada", in: *Global Policy Forum*, Oct. 2003, http://www.globalpolicy.org/component/content/article/155/25966.html (accessed Oct. 7, 2011); David Maraniss, "First Lady Launches Counterattack", in: *The Washington Post*, Jan. 28, 1998, http://www.washingtonpost.com/wp-srv/politics/special/clinton/stories/hillary012898.htm (accessed Oct. 7, 2011).

tration's claims about links between Saddam Hussein and al-Qa'ida.[7] This is all the more remarkable given that Gray's study systematically broadens our view of who engages in conspiratorial rhetoric. He includes an uncommonly broad set of actors: "the state, political elites, political leaderships, social forces, and marginalized or disenfranchized individuals and groups, among others".[8] Gray is writing about the Middle East but his list and my earlier examples of conspiracy theories narrated by the political leadership in America force us, I believe, to ask how state and mainstream social actors have been systematically exempted from such diagnoses in a U.S. context.

I will attempt to give a very brief and necessarily incomplete answer to this question in the first section of this essay. There it forms part of a wider critique of what I will call, absent a more satisfying name, 'conspiracy studies', the interdisciplinary field of research that takes America's culture of conspiracy as its subject. We have already noted the seminal contribution to this field of Richard Hofstadter and will hear more about the intellectual and political context of his writings on the paranoid style later. Since the late 1990s, research on conspiracy theories has not only blossomed – a trend that owes as much to millenarian fears as to the attacks on New York's World Trade Center on September 11, 2001 – but undergone considerable revision. Distancing itself from the calculatedly ambiguous yet vehement pathologisation of dissent as paranoid initiated by Hofstadter, this revisionist conspiracy studies eschews overt pathologisation and insists, by varying degrees, on thinking conspiracy theories at a remove from psychopathology. Seen as distinct from paranoia, in principle, conspiracy theories are now understood as worthy of serious academic investigation, but are still viewed with a heavy dose of ambivalence as to their political and epistemological value.[9]

Like any dialectical negation, this reaction shares much with its preceding term. In what follows, I will argue that this revisionist conspiracy studies is defined by the logic of the ideological binary. Here, the positive re-evaluation of conspiracy theories depends on the continued abnegation of paranoia and gives rise to a ceaseless production and policing of the borders between sanity and madness that conceals an ultimate identity. As a consequence, a revi-

---

7 Matthew Gray, *Conspiracy Theories in the Arab World: Sources and Politics*, London 2010, pp. 78, 118, 168–169.

8 Gray, *Conspiracy Theories in the Arab World*, p. 6.

9 Among the most influential full-length studies within such a revisionist approach are Mark Fenster, *Conspiracy Theories: Secrecy and Power in American Culture*, Minneapolis 2008; Peter Knight, *Conspiracy Culture: From Kennedy to* The X-Files, London 2000; and Timothy Melley, *Empire of Conspiracy: The Culture of Paranoia in Postwar America*, Ithaca 2000.

sionist conspiracy studies perseveres with a research programme that locates paranoid narratives at the margins, privileges texts which seemingly distance themselves from paranoia, and remains blind to a systematic pathologisation employed to stifle political opposition. Revisionist conspiracy studies thus adheres to an intellectual tradition it routinely rejects, and reject what does not adhere to it.

Such complex ideological operations are not overcome by grand gestures. While quite understandable as a reaction to its long-standing demonisation, the countercultural investment of paranoia with progressive potential remains caught in the binary it strives to rebuff. Rather than repeat efforts to dissociate the two terms, or drop discussion of paranoia altogether, I will think about their distinctiveness as part of their inseparability. That is to say, what is commonly referred to as conspiracy theories will be understood as paranoid narratives, a form of story-telling partly determined by what I regard with Jacques Lacan as the epistemological mechanism of paranoia. Such a conception allows us to go beyond the static antitheses of conspiracy theorizing seen as either flawed and meaningless or illuminating and subversive and move towards an understanding of its structure and logic, its strengths and failures. Ultimately, I claim, rethinking conspiracy studies necessitates re-writing paranoia not as a madness outside reason but the madness *of* reason: to conceive it not solely as a paranoia about the state, but also as part of state reason.[10]

Throughout, my comments will be guided by Lacanian psychoanalysis and especially the radical revision of Lacan's thought in the mid-1970s. His writings on paranoia are arguably a privileged discourse for an attempt at rethinking America's culture of conspiracy. They equally resist the pathologisation and naïve idealization inherent in so many approaches to the topic and combine clinical insight with theoretical acumen. Arguing against the routine dismissal of their claims, Lacan asserted that the sometimes abstruse conclusions of conspiracy theories in no way negate a central element of truth. As he writes, "to misrecognize presupposes recognition".[11]

Let me insert a final comment, on method and its implications, before I turn to the main part of this essay. As I realized while writing this article, my

---

[10] For a recent article that emphasizes paranoia's function as a dispositif of state power but persists in attempting to separate its reasonable and unreasonable, necessary and pathological, manifestations, cf. Jonathan Bach, "Power, Secrecy, Paranoia: Technologies of Governance and the Structure of Rule", in: *Cultural Politics*, 6/2010, 3, pp. 287–302.

[11] Jacques Lacan, "Presentation on Psychical Causality", in: *Écrits: The First Complete Edition in English*, Bruce Fink (trans.), New York 2006, pp. 123–158, p. 135.

approach to conspiracy theories might be understood, somewhat reductively, as a return to Hofstadter, minus pathologisation. Freud is replaced with Lacan, but in both cases the relevance of psychoanalysis for the study of political and literary communication is asserted. The differences, however, are perhaps as revealing and, I hope, also productive for the further study of conspiracy theories. At first sight, the integration of paranoia into reason (in other words, its de-pathologisation) would seem to deprive us of the possibility of political or ethical evaluation. The reverse is true, I think. Moral judgments have never been a good guide to scholarly analysis, and the classification as irrational only ever removes from sight what it pretends to scrutinize. Thus, any critique of conspiracy theories should not be based on the moral condemnation of their supposed irrationality. Only a fair-minded account of their analysis of societal power relations can establish a truly political or ethical evaluation of conspiracy theories. Despite an occasional return to pathologising terminology, this is arguably what underpins most recent studies on the topic – but only at the cost of rejecting any connection to paranoia. Scholars like Gray, Mark Fenster, or Peter Knight do this because they find paranoia's ideological baggage of pathology unpalatable, and rightly so.[12] Yet if we remove this weight, we might be able to draw, once again, from the insights a psychoanalytic perspective has to offer.

2. A Critique of Conspiracy Studies

In a little-noticed aside in his introduction to the *Paranoid Style*, Hofstadter refers to the political scientist Harold Lasswell as "one of the first in the country to be dissatisfied with the rationalistic assumptions" of his profession and to have turned "to the study of the emotional and symbolic side of political life".[13] Although he has faded into obscurity today, to the student of modern American conspiracy theories Lasswell plays a role only rivalled by Hofstadter himself. After all, it was Lasswell's application of psychoanalytic terminology to political science in the 1930s that conceptualised political beliefs and actions as stemming from unconscious, and thus in the eyes of Lasswell and his followers, irrational sources.[14]

---

12 I offer a critique of their writings below.

13 Richard Hofstadter, "Introduction", in: *The Paranoid Style in American Politics*, pp. vii–xiv, p. ix.

14 Cf., for instance, Harold Lasswell, *Psychopathology and Politics*, Fred I. Greenstein (introd.), Chicago 1986; Harold D. Lasswell/Dorothy Blumenstock, *World Revolutionary Propaganda: A Chicago Study*, Freeport 1970.

At one stroke, Lasswell thus opened up a whole new field of study that would blossom from the 1940s to the early 1960s and examined politics as the projection, in his words, of "private motives upon public objects in the name of collective values".[15] Reversing this movement, scholars could now psychoanalyse political rhetoric they found dangerous or simply displeasing as the emanation of pathological minds. Such a negative view of politics was already inherently biased in favour of a status quo no longer in need of protest and reform. Yet Lasswell also detected the source of political engagement in an irrational hatred of existing authority and portrayed community organisers as paranoid agitators. During and after World War II Lasswell's former students at the University of Chicago adopted this methodological framework to studies of the national character of America's ideological and military opponents, from Nazi Germany to the Soviet Union.

Perhaps the most influential of these, Nathan Leites' *The Operational Code of the Politburo*, formed the central reference point for U.S. negotiators during the armistice talks at Panmunjon at the end of the Korean War. A product of the containment doctrine of the early Cold War, it portrayed the enemy as divorced from reality and incapable of rational decision-making.[16] "What accounts for the great strength of the Bolshevik belief that there are enemies with annihilatory designs?", asked Leites, an influential member of the Air Force think tank RAND, in 1955, only to give an unequivocal answer: "[A] major factor behind this central Bolshevik attitude [is] [...] the classical paranoid defense against latent homosexuality".[17]

Such psychoanalytic dissections of national character constituted the larger intellectual background for Hofstadter's later reliance on the famous study of American anti-semitism, *The Authoritarian Personality*. It was this volume, co-written by Theodor Adorno at Columbia University shortly before Hofstadter joined its faculty, and its authors' detection of the "paranoid style" that would form the basis of his work on the topic. Limiting themselves to interviews rather than in-depth analysis, Adorno and his collaborators blurred the boundaries between neurosis and psychosis, between psy-

---

15 Lasswell/Blumenstock, *World Revolutionary Propaganda*, p. 296.

16 On Leites in particular and the establishment of a military-academic complex after World War II in general, cf. Ron Robin, *The Making of the Cold War Enemy: Culture and Politics in the Military-Industrial Complex*, Princeton 2001. Much of the fascinating nexus of psychoanalysis and the development of early Cold War doctrines, in which Lasswell and then Leites played important roles, remains understudied.

17 Nathan Leites, "Panic and Defenses against Panic in the Bolshevik View of Politics", in: Werner Muensterberger (ed.), *Psychoanalysis and the Social Sciences*, vol. IV, New York 1955, p. 138.

chological mechanisms and symptoms. They detected surface traces of underlying psychological structures – ideas, traits, and 'touches' of paranoia. As a social type, the authoritarian character exhibited symptoms of psychosis that manifested themselves in what the authors called – in the case of one 26-year-old interviewee – "authentic paranoid style".[18] It was here, then, that the "paranoid style" was born.

In contrast to studies on National Socialism or the Soviet Union which had detected mental disease in elite as much as in mass psychology, *The Authoritarian Personality* now concentrated on prejudice as a popular phenomenon only. The reasons for this focus lay in the interest of its authors and the American Jewish Committee, which financed the project, in the mass psychology of fascism. It coincided with a conviction, increasingly shared by American and European scholars if not by the Frankfurt School, that communism and fascism shared a "totalitarian" character radically different from liberal democracies – a distinction that extended to the psychological makeup of its elites.[19] Unlike the professional agitators and organisers characteristic of totalitarian regimes, whose hunger for power, according to Lasswell and other social scientists, revealed their mental pathology, America's democratic checks and balances were believed to favour politicians with more diverse interests and balanced minds.[20] *The Authoritarian Personality*'s exclusion of political and social elites from analysis may have made it easier for Hofstadter to follow similar lines of inquiry in his essays on the paranoid style, but he shared his peers' suspicion of the common man. Part of a late modernist intelligentsia that increasingly isolated itself from ordinary citizens, Hofstadter decried the "irrationality of the public" at the same time that he lauded the "well-rationalized systems of political beliefs" of educated elites.[21]

In their inherent bias against popular movements and the common man's intellect, Hofstadter's writings on political paranoia were part of his much

---

18 T. W. Adorno et al., *The Authoritarian Personality*, New York 1969, p. 615. Of course, given the very different intellectual and political background of Adorno and the Frankfurt School, *The Authoritarian Personality* also differed in important regards from U.S. studies of national character, and Hofstadter's reading was extremely selective. I have written at greater length about the impact of *The Authoritarian Personality* on Hofstadter in my PhD thesis: Alexander Dunst, *Politics of Madness: Crisis as Psychosis in the United States, 1950–2010*, Nottingham 2010.

19 For the seminal contribution to this post-war consensus cf. Hannah Arendt, *The Origins of Totalitarianism*, 2nd ed., Cleveland 1958.

20 Cf. Harold D. Lasswell, "The Selective Effect of Personality on Political Participation", in: Richard Christie/Marie Jahoda (eds.), *Studies in the Scope and Method of 'The Authoritarian Personality'*, Glencoe 1954, pp. 197–225, p. 221.

21 Richard Hofstadter, *The Age of Reform: From Bryan to F.D.R.*, London 1962, p. 18.

more ambitious re-writing of American history. In his Pulitzer-Prize winning *The Age of Reform* he denounced the Populist and Progressive reform movements of the late nineteenth and early twentieth centuries as a provincial, quasi-delusional, and often anti-semitic mass revolt against modern government. In the mantle of a historical argument, Hofstadter struck out against both left and right: against a preceding generation of historians who saw America's past as determined by class struggle and argued for wider participation in the country's politics, as much as against the right's "cranky pseudo-conservatism of our time", in which he recognized a successor to the earlier reform movements.[22]

The "paranoid style" Hofstadter attributed to the pseudo-conservatives was characterised by an excessive coherence that ignored contradictory evidence and the construction of a totalising narrative which imagined history as conspiracy. Its adherents struck him as "absolutist", marked by "feeling[s] of persecution", and "paranoid leap[s] into fantasy".[23] By definition, for Hofstadter, such conspiratorial fantasies were limited to those standing outside the increasingly narrow frame of mainstream politics. Despite the fact that his main examples of the paranoid style were United States senators, thus leading representatives of the country's two mainstream parties, Hofstadter construed conspiracy theories as a popular sentiment only ever accommodated by the establishment or carried into the mainstream by populist demagogues who themselves lacked the rationality and sophistication distinctive of the true politician. The paranoid style, he wrote in a letter to a friend, only afflicted those out-of-power, and thus by definition exempted the moderate liberals of the 1950s and early 1960s.[24] Of course, this act of exclusion was aided by the clinical associations of the terminology Hofstadter used to describe conspiracy theories. Its political motivation was as clear: having cut themselves off from their popular and radical roots, liberals were increasingly coming under attack from conservatives, on the one hand, and a new participatory politics headed by the Civil Rights and students movements, on the other. Declaring them both irrational, even paranoid, and discrediting their historical record as much as their mass base, left the political arena to those who already inhabited centre stage.

---

[22] Hofstadter, *Age of Reform*, p. 19. Pseudo-conservatism was another term Hofstadter had borrowed from *The Authoritarian Personality*.

[23] Hofstadter, "Paranoid Style", pp. 17, 4, 11.

[24] Cf. David S. Brown, *Richard Hofstadter: An Intellectual Biography*, Chicago 2006, pp. 159–160.

Hofstadter's identification of conspiracy theories with a dangerous insanity was rarely challenged until the late 1990s, when literary scholars began to analyse a wave of popular conspiracy narratives that had attracted large audiences and garnered positive reviews from critics. In many of these more recent monographs, the authors reject Hofstadter's more overt pathologisations. As Fenster argues, Hofstadter's "understanding of it [conspiracy theory] as paranoid was confused and confusing in his own work, and has only become more simplistic and useless as it has been taken up by others".[25] Peter Knight in turn holds that "[i]n recent decades [...] the images and rhetoric of conspiracy are no longer the exclusive house-style of the terminally paranoid".[26] Such differentiation between conspiracy theory and paranoia opens up two paths for the former. Both, however, take the form of an ideological binary in which the recognition accorded to the former mirrors a continued pathologisation of the latter.

In the more traditional approach, closer to Cold War liberalism, conspiracy theories essentially still correspond in form to Hofstadter's understanding. Fenster thus writes that they "frequently lack substantive proof, rely on dizzying leaps of logic, and oversimplify the political, economic, and social structures of power". At the same time, conspiracy theories are now acknowledged as an important if ultimately unsound element of U.S. culture and seen as a "longstanding populist strain in American political culture [...] that is neither independent from nor necessarily threatening to the country's political institutions or political culture". All along, however, a distance is maintained between conspiracy theories and the "madness of paranoia".[27]

Here, Hofstadter's politically charged diagnoses of cultural and political texts – cultural pathology wielded as an intellectual weapon in a struggle for political influence – have sedimented into supposedly factual characteristics. A paranoid political tradition comprising both state and oppositional actors continues to be written as "a populist strain". Meanwhile Hofstadter's twin diagnoses of rigidity and totalisation have become the smallest common denominator of conspiracy theories. They are "wonderfully unified accounts of all the data at hand", characterized by "symmetrical totalities", and "rigid convictions".[28]

---

25 Fenster, *Conspiracy Theories*, p. 36.
26 Knight, *Conspiracy Culture*, p. 3.
27 Fenster, *Conspiracy Theories*, pp. 9, 11, 194.
28 Brian Keeley, "Of Conspiracy Theories", in: *Journal of Philosophy*, 96/1999, 3, pp. 109–126, p. 119; Ray Pratt, *Projecting Paranoia: Conspiratorial Visions in American Film*, Lawrence 2001, p. 17; Knight, *Conspiracy Culture*, p. 3.

The habitual rejection of Hofstadter's more unpalatable denigrations of paranoia thus retains the pathologising logic inherent in his understanding of conspiracy theory. Overt criticism goes hand in hand with an implicit continuation of what Michael Paul Rogin has called the "countersubversive tradition".[29] Aided as much by an isolated reading of Hofstadter's essay on the "paranoid style", which disregards an intellectual tradition in the social sciences that sought to discredit political opponents by associating them with insanity, as well as an absence of interest in contemporary re-considerations of paranoia, such scholarship reinforces rationality's long-standing power over madness.

The second, more strongly revisionist, approach may equally lack any consideration of this tradition, but its close textual analysis has considerably altered the way we look at conspiracy theories. Knight, for instance, has argued that they are frequently complex and self-reflexive, eschewing the rigidity and totalising intent of which they are so often accused. However, such arguments are undermined once again by the logic of the ideological binary. Like more traditional approaches, these studies balance their partial re-evaluation of contemporary conspiracy theories by the continued pathologisation of paranoia. In Knight's case this takes the form of a historical argument that pits today's "more insecure version of conspiracy-infused anxiety" against an older "paradoxically secure form of paranoia" described flippantly as "the exclusive house-style of the terminally paranoid".[30] Jodi Dean, for her part, endorses alien abduction narratives as a legitimate part of U.S. politics, only to accuse their critics of "irresponsible paranoia".[31] The binary opposition of the two terms enables the privileging of certain narratives as essentially sane and insists on the insanity of those it continues to label paranoid. As the philosopher Brian Keeley admits with admirable frankness, it allows "us clearly to distinguish between our 'good' and their 'bad' ones".[32]

What unites both versions is the continuous reassertion of the boundaries between reason and unreason. This presents a recurrent problem for any study of conspiracy theories, for, as I will argue from a Lacanian perspective, the lesson of any ideological binary, namely the ultimate inseparability of privileged and repressed terms, also holds true for this particular case. As

---

29 Michael Paul Rogin, *Ronald Reagan, the Movie, and Other Episodes in Political Demonology*, Berkeley 1987, p. xiii.

30 Knight, *Conspiracy Culture*, pp. 4, 3.

31 Jodi Dean, *Aliens in America: Conspiracy Cultures from Outerspace to Cyberspace*, Ithaca 1998, p. 136.

32 Keeley, "Of Conspiracy Theories", p. 126.

Keeley establishes in his article, "[t]here is no criterion or set of criteria that provide a priori grounds for distinguishing warranted conspiracy theories from UCTs [unwarranted conspiracy theories]". In the end, the only argument to distinguish reason from unreason, or warranted from unwarranted conspiracy theories, is the subversion of the distinction itself: the threat conspiracy theories pose to a narrowly-defined rationality, and thus sanity's power over madness. "It is this pervasive scepticism of people and public institutions entailed by some conspiracy theories", writes Keeley, "which ultimately provides us with the grounds with which to identify them as unwarranted".[33]

The implication of these recent studies of conspiracy theories in an earlier pathologisation of dissent extends to their research programme. Continuing Hofstadter's identification of conspiracy theories as a product of society's margins, conspiracy studies often takes as its subject narratives issuing from such sub-cultures as Alien abductees, right-wing extremism, and other forms of millenarianism. Even when the analysed texts are clearly a part of mainstream culture, such as the TV-series *The X-Files*, the dominant impulse is nonetheless to read them as a popular opposition to establishment politics. Such an interpretive thrust may be justified in some cases. But what is overlooked is the prominent use of paranoia as the circumscription rather than the expression of dissent. It is the participation of paranoid narratives in state reason, such as the Bush administration's claims about links between Iraq and al-Qa'ida, that usually goes unexamined, whether in the form of official government policy, political rhetoric, or popular culture. As a consequence, Hofstadter and his brand of elitist Cold War liberalism are handed a lasting ideological victory.

Attempts to overcome the binary logic of such accounts and redirect its central assumptions are rare. In general, they have remained at a stage of tentative suggestion, such as Martin Parker and Claire Birchall's proposition that the humanities and conspiracy theories share a common discursive structure.[34] Lacanian approaches to the nexus of conspiracy and paranoia remain surprisingly scarce. Most of these engagements have come from critics who apply them to the concrete analysis of narratives rather than a rethinking of conspiracy theories.

---

33 Keeley, "Of Conspiracy Theories", p. 123.

34 Martin Parker, "Human Science as Conspiracy Theory", in: Jane Parish/Martin Parker (eds.), *The Age of Anxiety: Conspiracy Theory and the Human Sciences*, Oxford 2001, pp. 191–207; Clare Birchall, "The Commodification of Conspiracy Theory", in: Parish/Parker, *The Age of Anxiety*, pp. 233–253, p. 249.

3. Re-thinking Paranoia with Lacan

From early on in his work, Lacan fundamentally questions traditional assumptions about knowledge and the distinction between reason and unreason. At the centre of his thought at this time lies the famous conception of the imaginary relation, man's identification of himself with an other, initiated by the "mirror stage".[35] This misrecognition of ourselves as our own image simultaneously creates the self or ego and the understanding of an opposite object. As an estranging construction of self as image or object "the imaginary dimension, with which man is always involved, [...] is constitutive of human reality".[36] The imaginary takes us beyond the immediacy of being characteristic of most animal life, and alienates us from its self-presence in a logic in which understanding of one element derives solely from its opposite term.

The knowledge of self and object as autonomous or self-same is based, for Lacan, on a fundamental error: imaginary knowledge, or *connaissance* in the original French, is necessarily a *méconnaissance*, a *mis*understanding. The decisive twist for our present purposes is Lacan's definition of this imaginary relation as constitutively paranoid, as it involves a process in which any object is defined solely by virtue of its reflection in the ego and vice versa. As a consequence, Lacan can not only speak of the "paranoiac structure of the ego", but identify paranoia as "the most general structure of human knowledge".[37] Paranoia thus becomes neither a logic radically distinct from sanity nor its excess; not a lack of insight but the very mechanism of the initial production of knowledge. Rather than constituting an entity that can be neatly distinguished from scientific understandings of the object world, paranoia is "constitutive of human reality".[38] That is to say, human reality presupposes an initial withdrawal from the self-sameness of animal being and the "dizzying leaps of logic", to quote Fenster once more, that constitute not a paranoia separate from knowledge, but knowledge *as* paranoia.[39]

The many revisions and reversals of his work notwithstanding, Lacan's conception of a necessarily delusional construction of imaginary reality al-

---

[35] Jacques Lacan, "The Mirror Stage as Formative of the I Function as Revealed in Psychoanalytic Experience", in: *Écrits*, pp. 75–81.

[36] Jacques Lacan, *The Seminar of Jacques Lacan: Book III: The Psychoses 1955–1956*, Jacques-Alain Miller (ed.), Russell Grigg (trans.), New York 1997, p. 120.

[37] Jacques Lacan, "Aggressiveness in Psychoanalysis", in: *Écrits*, pp. 82–101.

[38] Lacan, *The Psychoses*, p. 120.

[39] Fenster, *Conspiracy Theories*, p. 9.

ready contains the central thesis of his late work on madness. For much of the 1950s and 1960s, however, an imaginary paranoia could, if not bypassed, at least be controlled by man's integration into the symbolic, the world of inter-subjective speech and internalised authority. Correcting the strictly dyadic logic of the imaginary, the differential play of the signifier establishes a symbolic knowledge, or *savoir*, that could dispel the objectifications of imaginary *connaissance*. Such dialectisation is complicated by the definition of *savoir* as unconscious, and the resistance of modern reason to an understanding of knowledge that denies absolute mastery over it.

In line with this emphasis on the symbolic, Lacan's classic writings on psychosis define "paranoia" not exclusively as a logic common to all humanity. "Paranoia" here applies to the general structure of knowledge *and* its special case paranoid psychosis – seen from the privileged perspective of a hegemonic neurosis as an inability to advance beyond it. Due to a failure to internalise social authority, a submission to its norms and conventions that, in turn, allows for a certain amount of freedom within these rules, the paranoid psychotic is shackled all the more tightly to authority's unmediated power – to which delusion provides a personalized imaginary response. As Lacan writes, "what is refused in the symbolic order [...] reappears in the real".[40]

Having established Lacan's mature understanding of the term, we are in a position to clarify the central preconceptions about paranoia in conspiracy studies. As we have seen, conspiracy theories are routinely accused of overcoherence, "rigid convictions", and totalisation: arguments that can be traced to post-war liberalism's praise of irony and doubt and its pathologisation of the political commitment of left and right.[41] With Lacan we can argue that such a description of paranoia conflates two elements. On the one hand, paranoia's dyadic logic leads to absolute certainty. But this certainty only concerns the existence of the object in question. Its meaning remains highly volatile as the imaginary *connaissance* of paranoia is not stabilized by the differential knowledge of the symbolic. As Lacan writes, "any purely imaginary equilibrium with the other always bears the mark of a fundamental instability".[42] As a consequence, the paranoid narrative "varies, whether it has been disturbed or not", and the paranoiac "seeks, over the course of his delusion's evolution, to incorporate these elements [external stimuli or changes] into the composition of the delusion".[43] Common descriptions of

40 Lacan, *The Psychoses*, p. 13.
41 Knight, *Conspiracy Culture*, p. 3.
42 Lacan, *The Psychoses*, p. 93.
43 Lacan, *The Psychoses*, p. 18.

paranoid narratives as 'rigid' thus conflate the certainty of the existence of an object, frequently represented by the conspirator or persecutor in narrative, with a certainty of meaning.

A similar argument can be made in the case of so-called 'totalisation', part of the ideological arsenal traditionally levelled against the left. Two elements come together in this accusation: first, what we have discussed in terms of rigidity or over-coherence, the rejection of contradictory data in favour of establishing a unified narrative; secondly, and as a consequence of the first, the imposition of this narrative on others, and the political or economic imperatives said to follow from it. Two remarks seem pertinent here. As Freud already noted in his study of Daniel Paul Schreber, paranoia is a partial rather than a total delusion. Visitors were often surprised to find that the German judge talked affably about politics and literature but did not mention his paranoid cosmology in conversation with them.[44] While the exclusive presence of two terms, the opposition of self and other, means that the paranoid narrative is highly personalised, in the sense that its object relates directly to the self, such a truth is therefore also radically subjective, not the assumption of an objective reality to be imposed on others. This is not to argue that some conspiracy theories do not espouse comprehensive worldviews but that their total quality is not to be taken as a characteristic of paranoia, nor their paranoia as 'totalising'. As Lacan writes, the paranoid psychotic

> doesn't believe in the reality of his hallucination […] nothing is easier to obtain from the subject than the admission that what he can hear nobody else has heard. He says – *Yes, all right, so I was the only one who heard it, then.* […] Reality isn't at issue, certainty is.[45]

These arguments should not be regarded as theoretical hair-splitting. Rather, I believe that they describe conspiracy theories more accurately than much conspiracy studies has done to date. A more internally consistent understanding of paranoia as an epistemological structure, at once broader and more precise than previous conceptions, not only encourages us to question what we all too often take to be the undisputed qualities of conspiracy theories, but also to re-examine a cultural and political history that has been written according to these supposedly objective criteria. Two brief examples must suffice here. Does not the imaginary instability of meaning in paranoia

---

[44] Sigmund Freud, "Psycho-Analytical Notes on an Autobiographical Account of a Case of Paranoia (Dementia Paranoides)", in: *The Standard Edition of the Complete Psychological Works of Sigmund Freud*, vol. 12, J. Strachey (trans.), London, pp. 9–82, pp. 15–16.

[45] Lacan, *The Psychoses*, p. 75.

provide us with a precise explanation for why, as Fenster observes, "the classical conspiracy narrative [...] [is] vulnerable to continual unravelling"? And should not the same instability warn us of arguments that consign conspiracy theories of the past to an outdated "paradoxically secure form of paranoia" that rejects ambiguity and complexity?[46]

Turning now to Lacan's late writings on psychosis, it needs to be said that they move beyond a conception of madness as imaginary without invalidating the earlier understanding. The reversals of the later work on psychosis are summarized in Lacan's proposition that 'the Other does not exist'.[47] The Other as the subject's particular relation to the symbolic world is in itself lacking, that is to say, is without the fullness that the subject seeks in it. The subject's acquiescence to existing reality is thus dependent on an element of choice, and the fantasy of a full Other can be traversed for the subject's alternative construction of reality that seeks enjoyment not in the Other but in him- or herself.

In Lacan's writings of the 1950s, the symbolic order in its consistency, assured by the imposition of authority, the so-called 'Name-of-the-Father', provided an anchor for symbolic knowledge and joined it to the imaginary and the real. Once Lacan's increasing distance from structuralism leads to the insight into the *in*consistency of the Other, the 'Name-of-the-Father' becomes a fourth term that knots three radically distinct orders – a no longer privileged symbolic, the imaginary, and the real – into reality. As the product of such a fourth term, the social conventions of neurotic normality are similar in structure to the delusions of the psychotic and become only one of many impositions of contingent meaning on a baffling world. What distinguishes neurosis and psychosis is not their inherently rational or irrational nature. Psychosis is "not an irredeemable deficiency but rather another form of subjective organization".[48] Both are delusions in the strict sense of the word, but neurosis is a shared delusion in that it institutes a socially-accepted limit to meaning and behaviour and structurally displaces the object of desire from the subject. In contrast, psychotics must construct this limit one by one.[49] Accordingly, both neurosis and psychosis have to be understood as contingent attempts at interpretation, bridging a gap between a meaningless real and a meaningful structure whose passage is guaranteed by nothing but

46 Knight, *Conspiracy Culture*, p. 4.

47 Lacan, "The Mirror Stage", p. 688.

48 Véronique Voruz/ Bogdan Wolf, "Preface", in: Voruz/Wolf (eds.), *The Later Lacan: An Introduction*, Albany 2007, pp. viii–xviii.

49 I am grateful to Véronique Voruz for clarifying these structural distinctions between neurosis and psychosis.

its practice. Lacan here exposes the supposed epistemological privilege of sanity as a form of shared belief: precisely the subject's conviction in the inherent superiority of a supposedly sane organisation of reality. It is thus that Miller can write that "[e]veryone is crazy. It is only then that it becomes interesting to make distinctions".[50]

Such a conception of psychosis leads not, as one might assume from the identification of all reality as delusional, to a conceptual conflation. Sanity is not denied existence as a category but defined precisely as a sub-category of madness distinguished by its hegemonic status – madness which is supported by the acceptance of its norms and laws as rational. What has changed from early and mid-Lacan to the final phase of his teaching is that he no longer identifies psychosis solely with the imaginary, or a failure to control it. As the symbolic loses the status of a cure, a privilege extended to it under the presupposition of its fullness, the delusional act of reality-production now includes symbolic knowledge or *savoir*. The emphasis on sanity as hegemonic madness also introduces, more strongly than before, the potential for historical change and the possibility of making new distinctions.

Lacan's late writings also entail a re-definition of paranoia. With reference to Schreber, the paranoiac is now said to imagine that "the Other enjoys [him] in his passivized being", that is to say, an imagination of a personalized Other, frequently someone standing in for the abstract sphere of social laws, who enjoys in place of a subject that thereby feels robbed of its pleasure.[51] This refinement of Lacan's analysis adds an important aspect to our understanding. While earlier we noted the characteristic imaginary personalization inherent in paranoia, this final definition emphasises the centrality of *jouissance*. This enjoyment is attributed to authority figures in situations in which the subject is unable to become an active, enjoying participant in society.

Herein also lies the essential truth of paranoia, without which it is difficult to imagine why conspiracy theories should exert such fascination on the general population and academics alike. Its detection of a structure of authority or oppression speaks the truth of society – its structural responsibility, or the unbroken interrelation and movement between all constituents of the symbolic universe – and transforms it into the existence of conspiracy. In the meaning instituted by their portrayal of power, however, conspiracy theories

---

50 Jacques-Alain Miller, "A Contribution of the Schizophrenic to the Psychoanalytic Clinic", Ellie Ragland/Anne Pulis (trans. and ed.), in: *The Symptom*, 2/2002, http://www.lacan.com/contributionf.htm (accessed Nov. 29, 2010).

51 Jacques Lacan, "Présentation des Mémoires d'un névropathe", in: *Autres Écrits*, Paris 2001, p. 214.

also strengthen the belief in an authority whose potential disintegration is exposed by the need for such paranoid certainty in the first place. The paradox of conspiracy narratives thus lies in their exposure of the antagonisms they may want to repress and the reinforcement of a status quo they may wish to subvert.

4. Conclusion: Global Narratives

As mentioned above, Lacan understands paranoia not as a psychiatric pathology but as a human epistemology. Thus, his psychoanalysis can be seen as complementing existing macroscopic methodologies in the study of political conspiracy theories, or as laying the theoretical groundwork for the study of paranoid narratives in the humanities. Where the former emphasise the precise role and characteristics of existing conspiracy theories in a given context, a Lacanian framework can offer insights into their general function and logic. Such a theoretical basis would seem to be of particular interest for comparative approaches to conspiracy theories. Even at this early stage it seems clear that approaches focussing on the political culture of a given nation or region are constitutively unable to account for the truly global appeal of conspiracy theories exposed by transnational perspectives. As a consequence, they rely on universalising psychological assumptions. In the absence of convincing alternatives, they have tended to fall back on Hofstadter's Cold War adaptation of post-Freudian thought, the extent of whose ideological bias and intellectual shortcomings I have tried to make evident.

Yet it is only when we reject Hofstadter's definitions of conspiracy theories as a populist and irrational opposition to power that we can begin to ask questions long hidden by habitual pathologisation. Why and how have government and state actors deployed conspiracy theories in the U.S. and beyond, and to what effect? What role did conspiratorial rhetoric play in the popular justification and narration of the Cold War, or in the war against so-called global terrorism, still with us today? Very little work that goes beyond impressionistic and partisan denunciation has been done on conspiratorial theorizing as a tool of political persuasion and hegemony in the U.S. Perhaps, such work would help us to better understand the complex relationship between popular and establishment in its circulation.

As I hope these brief reflections indicate, the understanding of paranoia as an epistemological structure does not result in a totalising disregard for historically and culturally evolved differences. Difference remains meaningless without identity. To return to my initial example: to point to the conspiratorial narratives of government actors in the U.S. is not to equate them with their use in the Middle East, or elsewhere. Rather, the acknowledgment of such partial identity in mechanisms of political persuasion and control would seem to constitute the necessary foundation for a comparative analysis that goes beyond flawed Cold War distinctions between "authoritarian" and "liberal democratic" systems. Thus, we might begin to acknowledge that both western and non-western states make conspiracy theories a rational and potentially effective part of their political culture. We might then investigate where their use follows similar patterns and where it diverges. To phrase this in a somewhat different terminology, owed to Michel Foucault, we might ask: can the roles played by conspiracy theories in different national or regional contexts be traced to the constantly evolving and geographically uneven practices of bio-political governmentality?

Here as elsewhere, a Lacanian approach is no hindrance to specific case studies and political analysis, perhaps even the opposite. Lacanian psychoanalysis has long offered an account of the historical evolution of subjective structures that seems particularly well-placed for the analysis of a global culture of conspiracy. Observing the fragmentation of public discourse and the increasing pluralisation of norms and communities, Lacanians have posited a general weakening of existing structures of authority. Could the sometimes global currency of conspiracy theories today be understood as a reaction to such a crisis of authority – not of single governments and regimes – but of internalised forms of consent to existing power arrangements? Of course, such hypotheses must be tested and, if need be, adapted or rejected. Constructing a broad theoretical framework for such questions, however, allows us to compare and evaluate observations drawn from different actors, national cultures, and transnational networks that might otherwise remain isolated.

Perhaps it is worth returning to Richard Hofstadter one more time in closing. Surveying his essays on the historical evolution of the paranoid style, Hofstadter commented that they all dealt "with public responses to a critical situation or an enduring dilemma".[52] He also noted the international appeal of conspiracy theories and somewhat apologetically explained his exclusive focus on American culture by his chosen profession as a historian of the United States. The crisis of democracy confronted by Hofstadter and his peers in the late 1950s and 1960s ultimately took him in a very different direction. If we insist on his initial observations on the global currency of conspiracy theories and their mediation of political crisis we might today come up with very different answers to these very same questions.

---

52 Richard Hofstadter, "Introduction", p. viii.

Birte Christ (Gießen)

"What kind of man are you?": The Gendered Foundations of U.S. Conspiracism and of Recent Conspiracy Theory Scholarship

The conspiracy theorist most prominent in the U.S. American public imagination and most frequently discussed in recent scholarship on conspiracy theories is certainly District Attorney Jim Garrison in Oliver Stone's *JFK* (1991). Toward the film's resolution and just before Garrison's personal if not legal victory in the trial against Clay Shaw, Garrison's wife Liz confronts her husband – accusingly, desperately, even hysterically – with the question that serves as title for this paper: "What kind of man are you?"

My contention is that this is one of the central questions that every white male U.S. conspiracy theorist since the 1960s is struggling to answer for himself through the act of decoding the conspiracy, and that this is one of the central questions he indeed answers for himself when he eventually triumphs over the conspiracy cognitively and discovers the "true" narrative that knits disparate events and pieces of information together. The question "What kind of man are you?" may be rephrased in more academic terms as the question of how a man negotiates his masculinity: What makes him a man in his own view? What are the sources of his male self-esteem? What is it that enables his agency as a man? And what are the institutions and structures that support him in his masculine role? To assume that these questions drive the conspiracy theorist forward in his urge to emplot what he observes as skewed, fragmented reality means, in consequence, that conspiracy theorizing or "conspiracism"[1] functions not only to explain and overcome the theorist's perceived "own powerlessness"[2] – to use Mark Fenster's phrase – as a

---

1 I use the terms "conspiracy theorizing" and "conspiracism" almost interchangeably. "Conspiracism" is used to stress that what is usually referred to as "conspiracy theorizing" involves a number of activities and practices that the conspiracy theorist engages in which may be motivated in different ways and serve different functions, for example his suspicion that there must be a conspiracy going on, his attempts to get behind the conspiracy and identify the conspirators and their motives, or his struggle to publicly unmask the conspirators.

2 Mark Fenster, *Conspiracy Theories: Secrecy and Power in American Culture*, Minneapolis 2008, p. viii.

gender-neutral agent within the nation and within a globalized world: conspiracy theorizing also centrally functions to explain and overcome the theorist's perceived "own powerlessness" *as a man*. Conspiracy theorizing, I want to argue, is not only fuelled by a longing "for a perfectly transparent, accessible democracy",[3] but also by a longing for "perfectly transparent," that is, unambiguous gender roles and relations: as much as conspiracy theorizing is a populist intervention into national politics, it is also a populist intervention into *sexual* politics. Scholarship about conspiracy theories and their functions, then, needs to consider this nexus of conspiracism and negotiations of masculinity more thoroughly than it has done so far, although Hofstadter, whose work is still the point of departure for most studies, already recognized anxiety about unstable boundaries of gender as a "structuring principle" of conspiracy theorizing.[4]

I will develop my argument for recognizing gender as an important category for conspiracy theory scholarship in three steps. In section one of this essay, my goal is to demonstrate exemplarily that there is indeed this nexus between conspiracy theorizing and negotiations of masculinity which I have posited above. I will focus on Oliver Stone's *JFK* (1991), as one of the most widely discussed conspiracy narratives, and read it as a narrative that de- and re-constructs the conspiracy theorist's identity as a man, in other words, as a narrative that de- and re-constructs white "hegemonic masculinity".[5] I have chosen *JFK* specifically because almost all of the observations I am going to make have, in fact, been made by a host of scholars already. However, most of these observations have either been made in passing or they have not been analyzed with regard to their potential implications for the cultural functions of conspiracy theories. In my second section, an analysis of Sidney Pollack's *3 Days of the Condor* (1975) serves to show that neither is *JFK*'s concern with the conspiracy theorist's masculine identity an isolated case, nor are such concerns limited to the 1990s (and, perhaps, the post-Kennedy 1960s), but must be seen as a cultural tendency during the second half of the twentieth century. In section 3, I engage in an examination of the field of conspiracy theory scholarship. I will discuss in which ways recent studies on U.S. conspiracy culture which have paid attention to questions of gender and sexuality, particularly to paranoia as an expression of same-sex male desire and to women's conspiracy theorizing, may inform readings of conspiracy theories as narratives about the de- and re-construction of hegemonic masculinity. In

---

3 Fenster, *Conspiracy Theories*, p. ix.
4 Fenster, *Conspiracy Theories*, p. 39.
5 R. W. Connell, *Masculinities*, 1995, Berkeley 2005.

conclusion, I will take an even more meta-reflective stand on the dynamics of recent scholarship on conspiracy theory. I want to suggest that the turn towards de-pathologizing conspiracy theorizing and treating conspiracy theories as expressions of a populist engagement with the political and the welfare of the nation, after the "commodification of conspiracy theory"[6] in the 1990s and in the wake of Mark Fenster's, Peter Knight's, and Timothy Melley's seminal studies,[7] may be as much of a gendered intervention into the field of scholarship as conspiracy theorizing constitutes a gendered intervention into the public sphere.

1. *JFK* and the Restoration of Male Agency

Mark Fenster uses *JFK* as one of his examples of a classical conspiracy narrative which displays the genre's conventions in a paradigmatic way, in particular its narrative "pivots" which control the narrative speed or "velocity" in the plot's unfolding.[8] In this account of classical conspiracy narratives, Fenster suggests that a conspiracy theorist's "personal crises" contribute to establishing the "original motivations that led to or were caused by his or her finding the conspiracy".[9] Jim Garrison's personal crisis that forms the basis of his obsession to find the truth is, I argue, a crisis of masculinity – and Fenster himself has noted that Garrison's eventual restoration of a properly liberal democratic order is simultaneously a restoration of a *patriarchal* order in the public sphere of the courtroom *and* the private sphere of his own home and marriage.[10]

---

6 Clare Birchall, "The Commodification of Conspiracy Theory", in: Peter Knight (ed.), *Conspiracy Nation: the Politics of Paranoia in Postwar America*, New York 2002, pp. 233–253.

7 Cf. Fenster, *Conspiracy Theories;* Peter Knight, *Conspiracy Culture: From Kennedy to* The X-Files, London 2000; Timothy Melley, *Empire of Conspiracy: The Culture of Paranoia in Postwar America*, Ithaca 2000.

8 Fenster, *Conspiracy Theories*, p. 135.

9 Fenster, *Conspiracy Theories*, p. 122.

10 Cf. Fenster, *Conspiracy Theories*, p. 127. Laville and Thalmann have made the argument in more detail. In this section, I broadly follow their arguments. Thalmann, however, does not deal with the significance of the narrative pivots in this regard; Laville argues in much detail that *JFK* is about Garrison's negotiation of concepts of masculinity, but views this dynamic as entirely disconnected from readings of *JFK* as a conspiracy narrative. Helen Laville, "What kind of Man [sic] are you? – Masculinity in Oliver Stone's JFK [sic]", in: *49th Parallel: An Interdisciplinary Journal of North American Studies*, 5/2000, http://www.49thparallel.bham.ac.uk/back.issue5/laville.htm, no pag (accessed Sept. 23, 2010]; Katharina Thalmann, "'Men with Secrets': The Crisis of Masculinity and the Attractions of Conspiracy (Theory)", Unpublished Paper, University of Freiburg 2010.

I would like to take Fenster's analysis of *JFK* a step further by focusing on the two narrative pivots in the film which "initiate cognitive shifts of momentum"[11] and propel the protagonist forward in his search for and mastery of the conspiratorial plot. The first pivot, Garrison's chance conversation with Senator Long about the Warren Commission's version of the JFK assassination in early 1967, triggers Garrison's fixation on the case. The second pivot, Garrison's meeting with X just before the assassination of Martin Luther King, results in his taking action and bringing Clay Shaw to trial because X establishes the missing connections between pieces of information that Garrison has collected and reassures Garrison that "the truth is on [his] side". In terms of narrative structure, these pivots are instrumental in fuelling the protagonist's desire to uncover the conspiracy, but, at the same time, they are intimately tied to concerns about masculinity. The first pivot revolves around fears of the "unmanning" of the American nation; the second pivot symbolically reinvigorates American masculinity and the patriarchal social and political order. Whereas O'Donnell considers *JFK*'s "conver[sion] of the cold war into the singular narrative quest for 'manhood' and nationhood" the "most overbearing example [...] of transformation [sic] of the political into the personal",[12] I would argue that Garrison's (and Stone's) concerns are, vice versa, deeply rooted in personal concerns over masculinity that resonate with psycho-social concerns on a broader scale and are acted out in the realm of conspiracy theory and the political.

Leaving Washington D.C. on a plane, in an atmosphere of after-work banter between male professionals, Senator Long remarks to Garrison:

> Fucking out of control. All of these hippies running around on drugs. The way young people look, you can't tell a boy from a girl anymore. I saw a girl the other day. She was pregnant. You could see her whole belly. And you know what she had painted on it? "Love Child."

While both laugh smugly and shake their heads, indicating their dis-identification with the social dynamic Long has just described, both are concerned here about what Long obviously considers a disintegration of gender and sexual boundaries. More specifically, both men are concerned about the increasing feminization and hence, the unmanning of American "boys": you cannot tell them from girls anymore because they look exactly alike. Long leaves no doubt about who is responsible for the American man's emascu-

---

11 Fenster, *Conspiracy Theories*, p. 137.

12 Patrick O'Donnell, *Latent Destinies: Cultural Paranoia and Contemporary U.S. Narrative*, Durham 2000, p. 62.

lation. The pregnant "girl", proudly displaying her belly, and doing so in public, clearly claims ownership of her child which is declared a "child of love" rather than the child of a discrete father. The patriarchal lineage is in danger because women have taken over the control of reproduction. Not to put too fine a point on it, the two men fear the displacement of the rule of the phallus by the rule of the womb. This fear of women's growing power in society and, correspondingly, of the weakening of the American man – in brief: this national crisis of masculinity – is clearly an issue in U.S. Cold War culture already in the 1950s,[13] becomes projected into the 1960s, and is intensified by the rise of countercultural movements, here symbolized by the "hippie" "girl".

Looking down at the White House, Long comments next: "Uuuh, it's a mess down there, Jim", thus linking the "mess" of American men's loss of control over women to American men's loss of control in the realm of politics, specifically with regard to Vietnam, as Long continues: "We've bitten off more Vietnam than we could possibly chew. It figures with that polecat Lyndon in the White House." Garrison replies: "You know, I sometimes think things have gone downhill since Kennedy died", thus constructing Kennedy's death as the cause for both American men's increasing impotency on the battlefields abroad and in the bed at home. Long agrees and, in turn, points out inconsistencies in the Warren report and focuses on Lee Harvey Oswald's inability to fire the lethal shots from the window of the book depository three years earlier. This longer part of the conversation can be read as another expression of an increased confusion about phallic control, about who controls and who *can* still control the rifle and fire shots. The sexual subtext becomes even more obvious when Long claims that Oswald "got Maggie's drawers" during his time with the Marines, an expression for missing the target during shooting practice. Literally, it refers to failing to perform the sexual act and to being left with only "Maggie's" underwear in-

---

[13] Cf., for instance, Schlesinger's argument in *The Vital Center* (Arthur M. Schlesinger Jr., *The Vital Center: The Politics of Freedom*, Boston 1949) that an emasculated America will not be able to stand up against communism, which is taken up in even more alarmist tones in his *Esquire* essay in 1958 (Arthur M. Schlesinger Jr., *The Politics of Hope*, Cambridge 1962, pp. 237–246. For an analysis of Schlesinger's role in shaping articulations of the 1950s "crisis of masculinity" cf. K. A. Cuordileone, "Politics in an Age of Anxiety: Cold War Political Culture and the Crisis in American Masculinity, 1949–1960," in: *The Journal of American History*, 87/2000, 2, http://www.historycooperative.org/journals/jah//87.2/cuordileone.html [accessed Nov. 29, 2011]).

stead of her body.[14] Oswald, Long believes, was really just a "patsy", as Oswald had claimed himself, in a plot carried out by more potent riflemen. In Long's account, Oswald was duped by the conspirators in the same way the American public was; Oswald's victimization and his supposed ballistic and, in its figural meaning, his heterosexual non-performance becomes Long's and, by extension, Garrison's own.

Oswald "getting Maggie's drawers" may also be read as Oswald assuming a female role. Long, then, might be said to insinuate here that Oswald is a homosexual and hence might not only be commenting on the threat that heterosexual non-performance constitutes for the American nation, but on the even larger threat that "deviant" sexual performances pose. This argument is, again, very much in line with anti-communist discourses of the 1950s which cast communists as homosexuals. The film suggests at various other instances, too, that Oswald may have been homosexual. It compounds Garrison's struggle against his own loss of masculinity and patriarchal authority with the "demonization of a homosexual band", the underside of which is Garrison's homo-erotic "idealization of the beautiful 'dying king'" John F. Kennedy.[15] In the circular logic of this first decisive moment in *JFK*'s narrative, Oswald becomes the external signifier of that which Garrison grapples with personally and internally – heterosexual impotency and homosexual desire.

While I agree with analyses such as O'Donnell's that homophobia is a central motive for Garrison,[16] I would argue that a fear of women's power and, consequently, misogyny is even more decisive: the scene between Long and Garrison establishes American women's growing power over men as the ultimate source of Garrison's personal and American men's shared sense of crisis. Garrison's conflicts with his wife Liz as well as his flagging heterosexual (rather than his burgeoning homosexual) drive support such a reading that recognizes a "war of the sexes" rather than a "war of sexualities" as the ultimate motor of Garrison's quest for the "truth". On the Saturday night

---

[14] The expression developed in reference to the soldiers' drinking song "Those Old Red Flannel Drawers that Maggie Wore", popular during WW II. Maggie is a prostitute; the song claims about her drawers that "for a nickel they would drop" (cf. John Patrick, "Drinking Songs: The Old Red Flannel Drawer that Maggie Wore", 2006, http://www.csufresno.edu/folklore/drinkingsongs/html/categorized-by-song/red-flannel-drawers-that-maggie-wore-notes.htm [accessed Sept. 23, 2010]).

[15] Michael Rogin, "JFK: The Movie", in: *The American Historical Review*, 97/1992, 2, pp. 500–505, p. 503.

[16] Cf. Rogin, "JFK"; O'Donnell, *Latent Destinies.*

after his return from Washington and his meeting with Long, Garrison responds affirmatively to Liz's sexual invitation ("When I come up I wanna show you how Saturday night was invented!"), yet immediately afterwards runs along the corridor back to his study; the next shot shows a clock on the mantelpiece striking 3 a.m. and Garrison still in his study reading the Warren Report. Similar to Rogin's observations about the film's representation of homosexuality as both source and result of the national malaise, one can say that Garrison's heterosexual inadequacy becomes both source and result of his obsession with uncovering the conspiracy. On the one hand, the scene illustrates that Garrison is, in fact, unable to perform sexually and live up to the expectations towards masculine potency on "Saturday night". On the other hand, Garrison's unwillingness to be (sexually) available to Liz can be read as an act of resistance against the new, cold-war model of masculinity which his wife is imposing on him. This new model demands the husband's domestic presence and his cooperation in the upbringing of children. It also acknowledges women's sexual drive and hence considers a husband's sexual performance part of his central duties within such a companionship model of marriage.[17] From the moment Garrison buries himself in the 26 volumes of the Warren Report after his meeting with Long up until Liz Garrison's realization that her husband's suspicions of conspiracy are well-founded when Robert Kennedy is assassinated, Jim and Liz constantly fight over the time he spends on his public pursuit of Clay Shaw – a pursuit that monopolizes his private time and even his home where some of the meetings with his staff are held – and the time and interest he actually devotes to Liz and their children. Liz, frustrated with her husband, begins to believe the news reports that cast him as a liar and criminal, and consequently leaves the marital bed. This conflict reaches a climax on April 4, 1968 when Garrison has eyes and ears only for news about the assassination of Martin Luther King and dismisses a kidnapper's phone call to his home as unimportant. At this moment, Liz hurls her question at him: "What kind of man are you?" and prepares to leave her husband and take the children with her.

The second narrative pivot is instrumental in making Garrison the kind of man that he, at this later point of crisis, has already decided he can and wants to be. Thus, instead of giving in to Liz's accusations, he is now waiting for her to finally accept a traditional separation of male and female roles and spheres and, moreover, to legitimize his masculinity through public admiration – which she provides by attending the trial with Jasper, their oldest son, against

---

[17] Cf. Laville, "What kind of Man are you?"

her prior refusal[18] – and private, sexual availability – which she provides as soon as she realizes her husband is right about the conspiratorial plot at the heart of the JFK, MLK, and RFK assassinations.[19] Factually, Garrison's meeting with X shortly before the MLK assassination prepares his cognitive triumph in the Clay Shaw trial, the restoration of his agency in the public of the courtroom, and the restoration of control over his sexual and family life. Symbolically, the meeting restores the power of the phallus over the power of the womb and thus averts the scenario of personal and national threat that the first narrative pivot revolves around. Meeting at the steps of Lincoln Memorial, Garrison and X are shown traversing the National Mall until they sit down on a bench in Constitution Gardens, facing west. X's almost breathless monologue, visually accompanied by the films typical frenzied assemblage of archival material and re-enactments, provides Garrison with the master narrative of the conspiracy. The monologue is, however, also interspersed with shots of X and Garrison. Following the establishing shot, an aerial view of the Mall from the west and a quick shot of the Capitol at the far end, the camera follows the men as they are walking down the steps of Lincoln Memorial towards the Reflecting Pool, continues along the axis of the Mall, and slowly moves up until Washington Memorial is in full view. The camera thus indicates not only the geographic direction the two men are walking into, but shows in whose name and for which purpose they have come together: they are dedicated to the revitalization of the American democracy of George Washington, the nation's first and foremost patriarch. Washington Monument, symbolizing the origins and roots of American liberty, is not by coincidence America's most monumental materialization of the order of the phallus.

The staggered climaxes of revelation which X's narrative provides are accompanied by an increasing visual integration of the men sitting on the bench into the symbolically charged landscape of Constitution Gardens, with Washington Monument serving as the scopic anchor of a tableau of the two men who, at this moment, share the key to "crack" the corrupt administration and re-establish the order of Camelot. Half of the Monument is first seen in a medium close-up of the two men above X's left shoulder when they sit down. One of the next shots is a parallel to the close-up of Senator Long and Garrison on the plane, suggesting that this second narrative pivot must be read as an answer to the first one. Here, X and Garrison are framed by the camera in exactly the same position. When X expresses the same sentiment

18 Cf. Laville, "What kind of Man are you?".
19 Cf. Thalmann, "Men with Secrets", p. 11.

about the Kennedy assassination Garrison did on the plane, "I never thought things were the same after that", and both pause, the monument's base comes into view again. When X finally asks and answers the central question of "Who?", the camera shows both men for the first time from a low-angle distant shot, the whole monument visible behind them. As the "why" behind the conspiracy is revealed, three more low-angle shots elevate the men on the bench visually and at the same time frame them within the symbol of the phallic order – the monument appears first left and then right of the bench. X concludes his monologue not only by assuring Garrison that "the truth is on [his] side", but adds "bubba" as a form of address. Incongruent with X's otherwise detached manner and followed by almost ten seconds in which no word is spoken, this term of endearment stands out: calling Garrison "bubba", a Southern address used for the oldest brother of the family, X invites Garrison into the community, specifically into the brotherhood of those in the know and designates him as the ringleader who must take action. At the end of the second narrative pivot, "mastery" of the conspiracy and "fraternity" of the conspiracy theorists are completed. According to Strombeck, these are the two central goals of a conspiracism that is structured around concerns about male power and masculinity.[20]

A lot could be said about masculinity as a central concern in *JFK* beyond these two narrative pivots, yet its centrality at these important junctions of the film can vouch for its importance throughout. However, it may be argued that in this aspect *JFK*, generally considered one of the foundational conspiracy narratives of the conspiracy hype of the 1990s, exemplifies the structuring principles of a historically specific post-Cold War conspiracism, and that issues of masculinity are negligible in conspiracism of the 1960s to 1980s. As Peter Knight and others have claimed, end-of-the century conspiracism turns away from "the bipolar logic of the Cold War and its accompanying Manichean anxieties" and, consequently, is more concerned "with ongoing anxieties about race, class, gender and sexuality".[21] Garrison's conspiracy theorizing structured by concerns about masculinity in *JFK* must then be read as an ahistorical representation of conspiracism surrounding the Kennedy assassination that exclusively expresses concerns of the 1990s. As I have pointed out, however, *JFK* articulates the threat of a "crisis of masculinity" as part and parcel of the threat of communist infiltration or a defeat in Vietnam – and not as a concern that has been hitched onto the 1950s and

---

20 Cf. Andrew Strombeck, *None Dare Call It Masculinity: The Subject of Post-Kennedy Conspiracy Theory*, Diss. University of California, Davis, 1997, p. 2.

21 Knight, *Conspiracy Culture*, p. 230.

1960s from the perspective of the 1990s; the "bipolar logic of the Cold War" is always already played out in the similarly bipolar arena of gender relations. Yet the de- and reconstruction of male agency structures conspiracism not only in the 1950s and early 1960s but, I want to argue, throughout the Cold War. Sidney Pollack's *3 Days of the Condor* (1975) demonstrates this with regard to a male conspiracy theorist who could hardly be more different from D.A. and family man Jim Garrison: Joe Turner alias "Condor".

2. "Condor" and Counterculture: Restoring Male Agency in the 1970s

Jim Garrison, as I have shown, embodies a traditional model of masculinity which is inextricably bound to authority and the nation: the patriarchal rule of the phallus. That he perceives himself as, and restores his rule as, a patriarch by confronting the conspiracy becomes clear not only by the way in which the film integrates him visually into the brotherhood of American heroes – Founding Father George Washington and Civil War president Abraham Lincoln – in the pivotal scene with X. Other aspects of his character – and these become important in comparison with Joe Turner – are central to his embodiment of the patriarch: Garrison is one of the first defenders of the political order as he works as a prosecutor for the state; he believes in the institutions of the state and, when undermined, works towards their restoration; he exudes professionalism, seriousness, and seniority – none the least through his impeccable clothing and his statesmanlike bearing; he has a large family and rejects notions of sexual freedom, as we have seen in the scene with Senator Long; he rejects an encroachment of domestic and familial duties on his role as a public man.

3 Days of the Condor, by contrast, represents its protagonist Turner as someone who is sympathetic to the countercultural movements of the 1960s and 1970s and hence seems to embody an alternative version of masculinity as well. While Turner's masculinity as such has not been discussed, critics concur in describing him as an "antistereotypical character"[22] and as "a person with boyish ingeniousness who refuses to succumb to the conventions and routine procedures of his job".[23] Turner thus functions as a representative of the world

---

[22] Janet L. Meyer, *Sydney Pollack: A Critical Filmography*, Jefferson 1998, p. 81.

[23] Johannes Patzig, "Crisis of Americanism in Hollywood's Paranoia Films of the 1970s: The Conversation, Chinatown and Three Days of the Condor", in: *Philologie im Netz*, 40/2007, pp. 32–66, p. 60, http://www.fu-berlin.de/phin (accessed Sept. 27, 2010).

view held by the New Hollywood Cinema's young directors of the 1970s, part of which is a re-negotiation of the norms of masculinity.[24] Yet, as my analysis will show, this re-negotiation of masculinity is not as far-reaching as may be assumed; rather, Turner's mastery of the conspiracy is linked to his re-assertion of traditional norms of masculinity in ways similar to Garrison's.

First of all, Turner is characterized as a rebel against authorities, rules, and the state's institutions who is nevertheless likeable due to his personal charm and his humor. He does not share – and does not want to share – in the vestiges of patriarchal power as Garrison does. On the morning of the attack on the American Literary Historical Society, Turner is 17 minutes late for work, as Mrs. Russell points out sourly, and the conversations between his colleagues make clear that this is the rule rather than the exception. When Dr. Lappe opens Turner's office door to give him a job for the day, he and the viewer do not see Turner, but the face of Albert Einstein on a poster above Turner's empty desk. Echoing the Arthur Sasse photograph of Einstein with his tongue stuck out, the poster appears as an image of mad ingenuity and irreverence that serves as Turner's *alter ego*. In student-like manner, Turner rides a small moped to work, and he wears jeans and a wool hat which he uses to conceal his face facetiously in front of the security camera. Instead of apologizing about his late arrival, he jokes about his colleagues' pedantry of counting the minutes ("Make it twelve, there was fucking headwind!") and tells the security guard "At ease, Sarge!", thus ironically drawing attention to the incongruity of the peaceful, domestic setting of the A.L.H.S. – accentuated by a grandfather clock in the entrée and Dr. Lappe's tending to his house plants – and the high level of security they are surrounded with, suggesting that it is unnecessary, exaggerated, and perhaps not even efficient, as events some moments later will confirm. His constant if light-hearted rebellion against rules and authorities, then, is what ultimately saves his life when he leaves the building through the back door to get lunch for the team – against the protest of the security guard.

---

24 For studies that discuss *3 Days of the Condor*, cf. Meyer, Naziri, Patzig, Pratt, and Robnik. Naziri, Patzig, and Pratt discuss the film under the rubric of the "paranoia film", Meyer and Robnik are more interested in its role in the development of the New Hollywood Cinema. Cf. Meyer, *Sydney Pollack*; Patzik, "Crisis in Americanism"; Gérard Naziri, *Paranoia im amerikanischen Kino: Die 70er Jahre und ihre Folgen*, Sankt Augustin 2003; Ray Pratt, *Projecting Paranoia: Conspiratorial Visions in American Film*, Lawrence 2001; Drehli Robnik, "Allegories of Post-Fordism in 1970s New Hollywood", in: Thomas Elsaesser/Alexander Howarth/Noel King (eds.), *The Last Great American Picture Show: New Hollywood Cinema in the 1970s*, Amsterdam 2004, pp. 323–335.

Second, Turner subscribes to an alternative model of masculinity that abhors violence and admits to vulnerability. While Turner has served in Vietnam and is perfectly able to kill in self-defense later, he is anything but "hard-boiled" and refuses his agency's expectations of disallowing human feelings at all times. When Turner reports the attack on the A.L.H.S. to "the Major" from a phone booth, he is – apart from fearing for his life – exasperated at the Major's bureaucratic language, his refusal to admit that anything out of the ordinary has happened and that panic and anxiety are appropriate responses. During his second phone call with the CIA, Higgins asks him "Are you alright?" and Turner replies: "Are you insane? Everybody's dead!" Here, Turner not only rejects to follow CIA rules, but also to perform according to traditional notions of masculinity. He does not only experience, but embraces "feminine" hysteria and vulnerability as appropriate. This point is stressed when he associates himself with Mrs. Russell alias "Nightingale" who kept a gun in her drawer – the very gun that "Condor" now carries and later uses to kill the "mailman" – because she was afraid of being raped.

Third, Turner takes an altogether different stand on gender relations and sexual morality than Garrison does. He does not have a family and seems to favor what may be called serial monogamy. He has a relationship with his colleague Janice and used to be together with his colleague's wife Mae. The fact that his version of masculinity is opposed to and suspicious of those who represent patriarchal power is made explicit when Wabash asks "Is he homosexual?" in order to understand Turner's behavior. Moreover, the opposition of masculinities – traditional, hegemonic masculinities on the side of the conspirators, and an alternative version of masculinity on Turner's side – is highlighted in a move inverse to that in *JFK*: when the film first cuts to show the inside of the CIA office in New York, this is preceded by a shot of the phallic symbol of New York City – the towers of the World Trade Center; when the film first cuts to show the CIA headquarters in Langley, this is preceded by a shot of Washington Monument, which is particularly unmotivated on the plot level.

As Turner is characterized as a rebel against the patriarchal order and its institutions, as a representative of a 1970s "countercultural" masculinity, and as comfortable within this more flexible masculine role, one should assume that the reasons for his desire to find out the truth about the conspiracy do not lie in a personal crisis of masculinity. However, two narrative turning points in the film suggest otherwise: Turner realizes *that* a conspiracy must be going on and in order to regain his agency and find out *what* the conspiracy is about he needs to assert his masculinity by exerting power over a woman. In turn, this need to control a woman in those moments of crisis indicates that Turner, too, experiences a crisis of masculinity.

The first turning point occurs when Turner is shot at in a back alley instead of being taken "home" to headquarters by CIA agent Wicks. Turner then understands that he cannot trust anyone any longer. He runs and hides in a clothes store where he observes Kathy, follows her, and kidnaps her as she enters her car. Between the first and second narrative pivots, Turner is panicking, feeling that he cannot "think straight"; he is not in control of the events. At the same time, however, he moves closer and closer to possessing Kathy sexually as well, an act through which he will regain agency in face of the conspirators. He rummages through her closet, thus invading a private space which also belongs to her lover Ben who has left some of his shirts, and he forces her to lie down with him on her bed. By finally taking Ben's jacket and tying her up until his return, he symbolically already takes her lover's place. Throughout Kathy and Turner's conversation, his gun is linked to his sexual potency. When Kathy exclaims: "What are *you* scared for? *You*'ve got the gun!," Turner answers "Yes. And it is not enough", implying that physical power alone cannot solve the conspiracy and help him restore his agency – what he needs to assert is his sexual potency.

Turner regains his agency and can actively set out to solve the conspiracy only after he has slept with Kathy: only after he has fired his symbolic gun, he can also fire the actual one. The morning after they have spent the night together, he is suddenly able to cognitively draw the details of the conspiracy together. In consequence, he then shoots the "mailman" and begins to actively hunt for more data about the conspiracy by abducting Higgins with Kathy's voluntary support. Kathy makes clear to Higgins why she helps Turner and why he should cooperate, too: "Personally, I do it because he has this huge gun, and he's looking at us right now." This statement – delivered by Kathy with obvious joy in the *double entendre* – works on both the symbolic and factual level. For Kathy, it is Turner's sexual potency that has won her over to his side – and which, through the adjective "huge", magnifies the small handgun Turner is actually using; for Higgins, the reason to follow orders should be the gun which in turn signifies male physical power. As long as Kathy is available to Turner, he is in control of the conspiracy; the moment she leaves him to return to Ben, it is the contract killer Joubert who takes over and choreographs the showdown at Atwood's mansion in D.C. Turner, rejecting Joubert's suggestion that he should believe in no other truth than his own professionalism, continues to fight for agency in a world conspiring against him, but this agency has become uncertain.

Johannes Patzig, for instance, reads the ending of the film as showing a victorious Turner and the "(re)-birth" of "the traditional, mythical American hero: A solitary fighter, who takes on a brave struggle".[25] While I obviously disagree with Patzig's easy interpretation of Turner's masculinity as a "traditional" one, I would also insist that the ending cannot be interpreted as a promise of the reinvigoration of even an alternative masculinity, as he does by implication. Particularly in light of Kathy's central role with regard to Turner's agency and his ability to fight, the ending has to be read more ambiguously. When Turner no longer has sexual access to Kathy, Higgins's last words in the film are "How do you know they'll print it?", referring to the story Turner has told the *New York Times.* His abbreviated repetition "How do you know?" constitutes the final line of the film. Higgins's words leave Turner (and the viewer) in an epistemological crisis – he simply cannot "know" – and thus in a crisis of agency.

Garrison and Turner stand for different models of masculinity which are historically and generationally specific. Whereas in Garrison's case, the pre-condition for his mastery of the conspiracy is the establishment of traditional gender relations in his private life and his membership in the fraternity of great American men, in Turner's case, the pre-condition for his mastery of the conspiracy – at least for a short time – is the assertion of his sexual attractiveness and potency. Yet, what is important for my argument here is that in both narratives, a loss of control and the inability to interpret scattered pieces of evidence in the face of a conspiratorial plot are inextricably connected with a sense of crisis as a man. The examples of *JFK*, drawing an historically accurate picture of 1950s and 1960s "crisis of masculinity", and of *3 Days of the Condor*, one of the most widely discussed "paranoia" films of the 1970s, suggest that we need to pay more thorough attention to anxieties about male identity as a structuring principle of conspiracism throughout the Cold War era and after.

3. Some Observations about Gender and Sexuality in Recent Conspiracy Theory Scholarship

While the negotiation and construction of masculinity have not been thoroughly considered in recent scholarship on conspiracy theories,[26] gender and

[25] Patzig, "Crisis of Americanism", p. 62.

[26] Notable exceptions are two unpublished studies, Strombeck, "None Dare Call It Masculinity", and Thalmann, "Men with Secrets", as well as a published essay by Strombeck, "The Conspiracy of Masculinity".

sexuality are categories that *have*, in fact, been dealt with.[27] Recent studies that deal with gender, sexuality, and conspiracy in the U.S. American context generally do one of two things: one, they are interested in sexuality and, in line with Freud's notion of paranoia, focus on conspiracy theorists' homophobia as an externalized anxiety about their own male same-sex desire intertwined with the "oedipal logic"[28] that some conspiracy theories operate upon.[29] This first category of studies implicitly thinks through issues of masculinity, yet only through those that are linked to male sexuality and often neglects the way in which heterosocial and homosocial relations structure male identity. Moreover, they are often concerned with the "negative" of male identity construction, namely with what men strive to *dis*-identify from rather than what they strive to identify *with*. Two, they are interested in "gender and conspiracy" conceived of as *women's* conspiracy theorizing, especially in fictional(ized) conspiracy narratives.[30] This second category of studies neither

---

27 Studies with complete blind spots or explicit disregard towards gender and sexuality are rare. A recent case is Olmstedt, who flippantly remarks that "men love conspiracy theories, but women aren't immune to their charms" and states that "before the 1960s, most leading conspiracy theorists were men, but women began to play significant roles as conspiracism became democratized with the John Kennedy assassination", without substantiating this claim or returning to the issues of gender (cf. Kathryn S. Olmsted, *Real Enemies: Conspiracy Theories and American Democracy, World War I to 9/11*, Oxford 2009, p. 11).

28 Knight, *Conspiracy Culture*, p. 104.

29 Examples are Rogin, "JFK", O'Donnell, *Latent Destinies*, and Fenster, *Conspiracy Theories*, which have already been mentioned. They analyze homophobia as a motor for uncovering political conspiracies which, at first sight, do not have anything to do with homosexuality. By contrast, Sherry traces conspiracism which is explicitly directed against the homosexual community and homosexual individuals after WWII when, according to his analysis, general anti-gay sentiment is transformed into the scapegoating of specific gay agents or conspirators, cf. Michael S. Sherry, *Gay Artists in Modern American Culture: An Imagined Conspiracy*, Chapel Hill 2007; Wisnicki reads the fourth part of Proust's *À la recherche du temps perdu, Sodome et Gomorrhe*, as a narrative uncovering a global homosexual conspiracy of "inverts", cf. Adrian S. Wisnicki, *Conspiracy, Revolution, and Terrorism from Victorian Fiction to the Modern Novel*, New York 2008.

30 Examples are O'Donnell, *Latent Destinies*, in his chapter on "Engendering Paranoia" (pp. 77–110) and Melley, *Empire of Conspiracy*, in his chapter "Stalked by Love" (pp. 107–132) both of which are discussed in more detail below. – An example for an analysis of *non-fictionalized* women's conspiracy theorizing, which follows an entirely different argumentative path, is Peter Knight's brilliant chapter in *Conspiracy Culture* (2000) on "The Problem with No Name: Feminism and the Figuration of Conspiracy". He reads the "popular" or non-academic feminist discourses of Betty Friedan, Naomi Wolf, and Mary Daly as simultaneously embracing what he calls the "figuration of conspiracy" for rhetorical reasons and dis-

focuses on masculinity because it does not consider masculinity as a construct and thus as open to, and in as much need of, constant negotiation as femininity is. In other words, studies in this category universalize man as conspiracy theorist and consequently do not need to deal with his gendered identity. Conversely, such studies mark women conspiracy theorists as gendered and tend to reduce analyses of their conspiracism to gender-specific aspects.

I am interested here in Timothy Melley's study of fictionalized women's conspiracism in *Empire of Conspiracy* (2000) as an example of the second category. *Empire of Conspiracy* implicitly – yet more explicitly than other studies – offers a thesis on the decisive difference, in psycho-social terms, between men's and women's conspiracy theorizing. However, I will first look at O'Donnell's treatment of the same topic in *Latent Destinies* (2000) because O'Donnell's expansion of Freudian paranoia from a male to a male *and* female psychopathology constitutes the inverse argument to Melley's quite different use of Freud's own later description of a case of *female* paranoia. In their discussion of female conspiracism, both O'Donnell and Melley return to a psychopathological and thus to an almost Hofstadterian framework – an aspect which will become important for my conclusions.

In his chapter on "Engendering Paranoia" O'Donnell does not, as is typical and as Melley does, reduce women's conspiracism to gender-specific

avowing any proximity to conspiracy theorizing to demonstrate the seriousness of their writing. This goes hand in hand with their embrace of the "conspiracy figuration" for its naming of agents of the "conspiracy" against women and thus for its ability to rally concrete, activist support for the feminist agenda and their simultaneous rejection of conspiratorial thought by pointing toward institutions and general social conditions as responsible for female oppression. Feminists' conspiracy theorizing may thus be one more instance of the strategic use of conspiracy theories, some of which Rogin, for example, outlines in *The Intellectuals and McCarthy.* If, in feminists' hands whose primary agenda is to renegotiate women's gender identity, conspiratorial thought is directed against men, we might, by simple analogy, wonder whether the conspiratorial threat that is at the bottom of men's conspiracy theorizing may not be the threat of the gendered "other", women, displaced onto other political issues as has been argued for the 1950s. Moreover, Knight's analysis suggests that here, the "figuration of conspiracy" is used as an instrument of the "culture wars" (to use the terminology of the 1990s), as an instrument that is used to discredit the opponent in a struggle between ideological factions within the American public, rather than as a populist instrument into which dissatisfaction with the political elite and the political system is channeled. As such, we might take Knight's analysis as a starting point to reconsider, for example, parallels between conspiracy theories in the age of the culture wars and anti-Catholic and anti-Masonic conspiracy theories in the nineteenth century or even anti-Satanic conspiracy theories in the late seventeenth century.

aspects. Rather, he uses his discussion of female conspiracy theorists as a means to "neuter" female *and* male conspiracy theorists altogether. O'Donnell analyzes Thomas Pynchon's *The Crying of Lot 49,* Diane Johnson's *The Shadow Knows*, and Kathy Acker's *Empire of the Senseless.* To "engender" paranoia here means to speak about paranoia as an ailment of women – which is opposed to, or a re-interpretation of, Freud's original conception of paranoia as a *male* psychopathology. O'Donnell "engenders" paranoia through the theoretical move to include *female* psychopathology under the rubric of paranoia via Lacan and via Teresa Brennan's model of paranoia as a late capitalist aggression, resulting from the inability to control (commodified) objects of desire. He states that "what lies at the bottom of paranoia in these works is not a repressed homoerotic relation between men but a displaced relation to the maternal" – the original object of desire – "that manifest itself as a desire for semiotic wholeness ('the Truth')".[31] Yet, what O'Donnell is ultimately doing by theorizing women conspiracy theorists as "similarly" paranoid as men and by integrating them, due to their similarly "displaced relation to the maternal", into the fraternity of conspiracy theorists is to introduce gender as a category attached to the object of desire, but at the same time as a category erased in the desiring individual. Hence, conspiracy theorists of both genders become "unmarked", and negotiations of femininity or of masculinity as formations of identity do not figure in O'Donnell's analyses of supposedly "engendered" paranoia.

On the one hand, O'Donnell's argument works to avoid speaking of individual crises of masculine identity as one source of conspiracism. From a feminist standpoint it seems problematic that a struggle with gender identity first needs to be attributed to women conspiracists in order to do away with gender issues as a motivating force behind conspiracism altogether. Yet, at the same time and on a more abstract level, it is interesting that O'Donnell returns to seeing conspiracy theorists as individuals who feel threatened by issues of identity rather than by structural and political issues. He sees conspiracism as a phenomenon of the "ego's era" which is characterized by an anxiety of the ego to lose its ability to "dominate and control".[32]

Melley, in direct contrast to O'Donnell's point of departure, starts out by looking at Freud's description of a case of *female* paranoia in his chapter on "stalker novels" by Margaret Atwood and, again, Diane Johnson. Female paranoia is here characterized by a sense of surveillance and the threats of objectification (which Freud interprets as a struggle against lesbian desire in

31 O'Donnell, *Latent Destinies*, p. 81.
32 Brennan qtd. in O'Donnell, *Latent Destinies*, p. 77.

order to align his observations with his initial theory of paranoia) as well as domestic violence and rape. The fact that, in this chapter, paranoia "functions as a technology of gender"[33] and that Melley, if ironically, frames these conspiracy narratives within the gendered generic context of "romance" (the chapter's title is "Stalked by Love") drives home the point that the male conspiracy theorizing which he deals with in his other chapters is unmarked by gender.

What is interesting in Melley's analysis is that he shows Atwood's and Johnson's female conspiracy theorists to be less concerned about uncovering the conspiracy's plot, but rather, on a level of self-observation and meta-reflection, to be concerned about the question of whether they, personally, are the target of a plot (and this plot, they realize, might even be their own externalization of internal issues) or whether women in general are the target of that plot.[34] Put more simply, they are wondering: is the secret "plot" that they perceive revolving around them and their own psycho-social issues, or is it directed at a larger group of people (like women) or an institution (like liberal democracy) and hence revolving around political and social issues? Following Hofstadter's differentiation between paranoia and conspiracy, one could argue that these women protagonists are concerned with the question whether they experience paranoia, or whether they become victims of a conspiracy that they are in the process of uncovering. The protagonists of the narratives which Melley analyzes identify themselves first and foremost as female (endangered by eating disorders, domestic violence, and rape), and the interrelationship between anxiety about gender identity and the suspicion of a conspiracy stands out as the dominant concern.

Melley then, in contrast to O'Donnell, truly "genders" or "engenders" conspiracy theorizing: the fictional female conspiracy theorist needs to find out *whether* there is a conspiracy at all, while the fictional male conspiracy theorist's general mode of thinking is that there *is* a conspiracy which he needs to uncover and master. This male tendency to *posit* conspiracy, I would like to suggest, may be interpreted as a strategy to displace the *personal* struggle of identity with a *public* plot. The function of this displacement is to divert external attention from the male conspiracy theorist's struggle with gendered role expectations and to convert his inability to conform effortlessly to the ideals of hegemonic masculinity into public power. Internally, this may also allow him to avoid a painful confrontation with threats to, and possibly necessary reconsiderations of, his identity as a man.

---

33 Melley, *Empire of Conspiracy*, p. 117.
34 Melley, *Empire of Conspiracy*, p. 117.

Assuming that these fictionalized representations of conspiracy theorists contain a grain of truth, the gender division in how men and women tend to psychologically deal with crises of identity and interpretation – men externalize and emplot their psychological problems as a public conspiracy, whereas women at least suspect the perceived conspiratorial plot to be the result of their own psychological problems – explains why, in fiction as in reality, only few women engage in conspiracism: because it involves the outright, and for the most part never questioned, assumption of a public plot. One might also argue that, in consequence, when conspiracy scholarship comes across something that looks like women's conspiracy theorizing, however intermingled with much introspection and doubt as in Atwood's or Johnson's novels, it is quick to disqualify it by relegating it entirely to the private sphere. Women's conspiracy narratives in O'Donnell's and Melley's studies are not treated under the rubric of "conspiracy" but under the rubric of "paranoia".[35] Women characters' paranoia, one could argue, is never really granted the status of "theory", while men's paranoia is almost automatically elevated to this status.

What we can take away from these observations about gender in recent conspiracy scholarship is that in the wake of Fenster's call for de-pathologizing conspiracism in 1998 a split has occurred in scholarship. (Fictionalized) male conspiracy theorists become de-pathologized and treated as making interventions into the public sphere which need to be taken seriously; the psychologizing and pathologizing of conspiracism under the label of "paranoia" is largely shifted to (fictionalized) women conspiracy theorists who emerge as an object of analysis at this time. While, due to social conditioning, male conspiracy theorists may indeed tend to focus on public emplotment in their theorizing, and women may tend to become more interested in analyzing the private reasons for engaging in conspiracy theorizing, only paying attention to both the causes of conspiracy theorizing and its functions – no matter who is doing the theorizing – will yield a rounded and differentiated analysis.

What I would argue, then, from a perspective of gender criticism, is that perhaps conspiracy scholarship has reached a junction at which it would be worthwhile to develop an integrated approach which pays equal attention to private, psychological, identity-related causes of conspiracism and to the public, political interventions they are making – and thus combine the best of both worlds of conspiracy theory scholarship: Hofstadterian psychologizing and a focus on private causes and functions on the one hand, and Fen-

---

35 O'Donnell avoids the term "conspiracy" altogether, Melley partially conflates paranoia and conspiracy in his study.

sterian de-pathologizing and a focus on public causes and functions on the other.

Finally, I argue that this integration of approaches may only be achieved when scholars of conspiracism consider and question their own gendered motivations behind their theoretical moves when studying conspiracy theory. In other words, the dynamic, observed in fiction, that female conspiracy theorists tend to turn towards interrogating their own psychological implications in conspiracism, while their male counterparts posit a conspiracy and set out to uncover it and contribute to the public good, may be a dynamic that is replicated on the level of scholars engaging with conspiracy theory and their approaches – which may offer one explanation why female scholars of conspiracism, as this volume demonstrates, are the exception. In illustration of this point, it is illuminating to read Mark Fenster's *Conspiracy Theories* of 1998 and Elaine Showalter's *Hystories: Hysterical Epidemics and Modern Culture* of 1997 against each other.

Showalter's *Hystories* is often cited as a study that essentially deals with phenomena related to 1990s conspiracy theories that are supposedly more diffuse in their identification of "the conspirators".[36] Showalter equates "hysterical epidemics" with conspiracy theories in the sense that "hystories" are narratives that pinpoint secret agents behind widespread, national maladies.[37] As her title and terminology make clear, her point of departure is what may be considered the female counterpart to paranoia in Freud's gendered system of psychopathologies: hysteria. Conspiracy theory scholarship of the Hoftstadterian school and Showalter's study both link the mass phenomena of conspiracism/hystories to psychoneurotic disorders that are transformed into narratives that displace these disorders and their causes to external plots and agents. In an analytic movement inverse to Melley's reading of Freud's difficulties to make sense of a case of "paranoia" in a female patient,[38] Showalter examines Jean-Martin Charcot's analogous issues with categorizing male patients that displayed symptoms of hysteria.[39] She goes on to show how, between the World Wars and again increasingly from the 1960s onward, men are not diagnosed with hysteria any longer. Instead, men's psychoneurotic disorders are translated discursively into large-scale epidemics like the "Gulf War Syndrome" (which also affected men who did

---

36 Cf., for example, Jack Bratich, *Conspiracy Panics: Political Rationality and Popular Culture*, Albany 2008, p. 17.

37 Elaine Showalter, *Hystories: Hysterical Epidemics in Modern Culture*, 1997, London 1998, pp. 26–29.

38 Melley, *Empire of Conspiracy*, pp. 110–117.

39 Cf. Showalter, *Hystories*, pp. 62–72.

not serve in Iraq). In other words, they are removed from the realm of psychology and pathology and integrated into the realm of sociology and politics. Showalter then argues that a denial of psychoneurotic pathologies at the root of political dynamics such as "hysterical epidemics" is detrimental to American democracy. Fenster's study, as I have mentioned, inaugurated a shift in conspiracy studies toward viewing conspiracy theories primarily as interventions into the public sphere that were discussed with varying degrees of benevolence with regard to their function in American democracy by scholars that followed Fenster's footsteps.[40] The 2008 second edition with its turn away from "identify[ing] and describe[ing] causes"[41] of conspiracy theorizing once more emphasizes this shift away from psychology, and thus also from negotiations of individual identity and agency of those involved in it.

Showalter and Fenster make inverse theoretical moves that replicate the gender-specific obsessions of female and male conspiracy theorists respectively. By moving conspiracy theories into the realm of the public and political debate, Fenster may be said to mirror, on a theoretical level, the male conspiracy theorist's move *not* to confront his personal anxieties about his gender identity, but to externalize it. As the male conspiracy theorist re-casts personal struggles within a public plot, the male conspiracy scholar here moves his object of study into the political arena and thus lends it prestige and relevance as a point of public concern. By showing how symptoms of a psychological struggle with norms of sexual and gender identity are discursively transformed into public epidemics behind which responsible agents can be identified, Showalter mirrors the female conspiracy theorist who primarily finds psychological reasons for conspiracism, hence implicitly denounces conspiracism itself as an object of study and demands of scholarship to pinpoint and work against its origins. Whether or not these theoretical moves can indeed be attributed to the gender of the scholars can, of course, never be ascertained. However, the gendered split with regard to the basic question of what is even considered a conspiracy theory that occurs on the levels of conspiracy theorists and conspiracy scholarship, and that seems to be replicated on the level of conspiracy scholars, may let us pause to consider our own gendered motivations in our scholarly theorizing. The object

40 The most straightforward example of a study embracing this perspective is Olmstedt's *Real Enemies*: "I do not try to psychoanalyze these theorists and determine which elements in American culture and history led them to become 'paranoid.' I see these antigovernment conspiracy theories as an impulse, as an understandable response to conspiratorial government rhetoric and actions" (cf. Olmsted, *Real Enemies*, p. 11).

41 Fenster, *Conspiracy Theories*, p. 18.

of study and the scholarly field of conspiracism are gendered in multiple ways. In consequence, we need to pay more attention to conspiracy theorists' grappling with the question "What kind of a wo/man am I?" and to negotiations of gender identity as "structuring principles" of conspiracism. Moreover, we should ponder, in addition, the question of "What kind of a wo/man scholar am I?"

Mark Fenster (Gainesville)

Against the Cure

The contributions in this book collection ask a series of important questions about conspiracy theory's role within nations and across the Middle East, questions which focus on description and critique. In their detailed case studies of particular nations and conspiracy theories, or in their efforts to assess, translate, and apply the theoretical literature on conspiracy theories, the essays focus especially on issues of context and history. In this brief article, I want to view conspiracy theories from the opposite angle and with a more speculative approach. Rather than describing and/or critiquing conspiracy theories, I ask how and whether the non-conspiratorial state can respond to them.

Assume, if you will (and can!), that state actors are not involved in the conspiracy that others allege they lead. How does the non-conspiratorial state actor who does not herself want to engage in conspiracy theories respond to conspiracy theories that place her in a leading role? Put more directly, is there some political or administrative method that the state, as an institution, can deploy to placate those who allege that the state is merely a tool for some nefarious purpose? Can the state answer conspiracy theories and make them go away? Can conspiracy theorists be "cured"? And how do this collection's cultural, historical, and theoretical studies of conspiracy theory help, hinder, or comment on this search for a cure?

I discuss two methods that states can deploy below.[1] The first is disclosure, a largely defensive strategy which assumes that if the state is authentically transparent – that is, thoroughly visible to the public – then conspiracy theories' falsity will surely be revealed and widely accepted. The second is to proactively challenge and deny conspiracy theories by working within the intellectual and social communities which believe in them in order to disrupt

---

1 A third method arises with some frequency in autocratic regimes: allege the existence of other conspiracies perpetrated either by a foreign power or an enemy (racial or ethnic group, religion, political rival, etc.) within. I want to bracket this method for two reasons – because such states' own engagement in a conspiracy to subjugate their citizens and retain power precludes them from the universe of non-conspiratorial states I want to discuss, and because I am not interested in considering competing conspiracy theories but in whether there is a means for the state to step outside the epistemological cycle that conspiracy theory creates.

their formation and distribution. This approach assumes that conspiracy theories and theorists are impervious to the role that the first method ascribes to transparency and disclosure, and instead posits that only a more offensive strategy can disturb the information-sharing and opinion-formation processes which cause people to become and remain conspiracy theorists. The fact that neither approach is likely to work perfectly, if at all – indeed, each one identifies the other's fatal flaw – illustrates conspiracy theory's pervasive and continual challenge to the legitimacy of a particular government as well as to political order generally. It suggests that conspiracy theory cuts against the grain of the state by questioning its legitimacy, while it also runs parallel to political discourses and ideologies (specifically, populism of the democratic or authoritarian sort) which are themselves widely-held, and which popularly elected officials utilize. I consider the implications of this insight in a brief conclusion.

1. Method 1: The Transparent State Cannot Conspire

In 2006, WikiLeaks founder and head-honcho Julian Assange wrote several short posts and posted longer essays on his publicly available blog that offered a theoretical underpinning to his then-developing project to force disclosure upon recalcitrant and secretive states and powerful private actors.[2] He provocatively titled his most fully developed essay "Conspiracy as Governance", and described it as an effort to "understand the key generative structure of bad governance" – and, ultimately, to reach a pure "position of clarity" in order to "radically shift regime behavior".[3] The generative structure of illegitimate, dangerous, and corrupt governance, Assange argued, is "conspiratorial interactions among the political elite" that allow them to

---

2 The best account of these writings is Aaron Bady, *Julian Assange and the Computer Conspiracy; "To Destroy This Invisible Government"*, 2010, http://zunguzungu.wordpress.com/2010/11/29/julian-assange-and-the-computer-conspiracy-"to-destroy-this-invisible-government"/ (accessed Sept. 25, 2011). Cf. Peter Ludlow, *Rethinking Conspiracy: The Political Philosophy of Julian Assange*, 2010, http://leiterreports.typepad.com/blog/2010/12/peter-ludlow-on-the-political-philosophy-of-julian-assange.html (accessed Sept. 25, 2011). I offer my own take on Assange in Mark Fenster, "Disclosure's Effects: WikiLeaks and Transparency", in: *Iowa Law Review*, 97/2012, 3, pp. 753–807.

3 Julian Assange, *Conspiracy as Governance*, 2006, http://cryptome.org/0002/ja-conspiracies.pdf (accessed Sept. 25, 2011). That essay and another, Julian Assange, *State and Terrorist Conspiracies* (2006), are available as part of the same file on the Cryptome website. The former essay is a revision of the latter, written less than a month later, and a more authoritative version of Assange's argument.

communicate means to maintain and strengthen their "authoritarian power".[4] Conspiracies are "cognitive devices", he explained, that operate by accumulating, processing, and acting upon information.[5] They keep their strategies and plans secret from the public to avoid creating popular resistance and only allow them to be revealed when resistance is futile or incapable of overcoming "the efficiencies of naked power".[6] Secrecy thus plays a necessary and central role in what he terms "bad governance".

I want to set aside the uninteresting question of whether this constitutes a "conspiracy theory" in order to view Assange's argument on its own terms. The conspiracy that concerns him is the secretive nature of governance, and the opportunity for corrupt and exploitative behavior such governance enables; the remedy, he asserted in 2006 and then proceeded to set in motion, is to disclose the state's secrets and thereby not merely reveal the state's inner workings but also stop its ability to maintain secrecy and govern in a duplicitous and anti-democratic manner.[7] Assange has offered different accounts of his tactics over the past five years – in his 2006 article, his purpose appeared to be a radical campaign to bring down hierarchical structures of power, while at other times, especially in the wake of the 2010–2011 disclosures of documents obtained from the U.S. Departments of State and Defense, he described WikiLeaks as a more conventional journalistic project to make the state's inner workings more transparent to the public.[8] Whether understood, in Assange's anarchist mode, as an adversarial, radical challenge to the state that will lead to a direct democracy and popular sovereignty, or, when Assange presents himself as an investigative journalist and transparency advocate, as a reformist means to inform the public and make the existing state operate more efficiently and accountably, WikiLeaks claims that information disclosure is an essential element of a legitimate state.

This claim is not at all unique to WikiLeaks; indeed, it builds on longstanding assumptions made by modern political theorists about publicity's importance to a functional, accountable, and legitimate state. An open state is a better one, most liberal political theory holds, and it produces a more engaged and better-informed public than a closed, secretive state.[9] This ideal

---

4 Assange, *Conspiracy*, p. 2.
5 Assange, *Conspiracy*, p. 3.
6 Assange, *Conspiracy*, p. 2.
7 Cf. Assange, *Conspiracy*, pp. 2–3.
8 For a summary of these two explanations and citations of Assange's written works and interviews illustrating them, cf. Fenster, "Disclosure's Effects".
9 Cf. Mark Fenster, "The Opacity of Transparency", in: *Iowa Law Review*, 91/2006, 3, pp. 885–949.

also provides the foundational premise for the international transparency movement. Appearing under numerous guises – most prominently in efforts to force states to enact and enforce "a right to information", as well as anti-corruption reform movements led by the NGO Transparency International and more recently joined by international financial institutions like the World Bank – this movement has successfully pressured states from the Americas and Europe to parts of Africa and Asia into making themselves more visible.[10] While state bureaucracies, especially those involved in defense, intelligence, and law enforcement, continue to try to protect information, politicians from left to right publicly decry secrecy – especially that engaged in by their competition. Rare indeed is the electoral campaign that does not warn of the secret machinations of the other candidates, and of the dangerous threats that those candidates' secret alliances with nefarious special interests represent.

Conspiracy theorists also decry secrecy. Based on reinterpretations of publicly available information and especially on "secret" documents, their theories posit that additional information remains buried within well-guarded government repositories – an obsessive concern best captured in the fabulous tracking shot near the end of the final episode of *The X-Files*' first season in which the Cigarette Smoking Man buries key evidence of a conspiracy in a well-secured and immense vault of files. The state often, though not always, attempts to address such concerns with disclosure. Where the Warren Commission spectacularly failed in investigating and explaining a mysterious and traumatic event in a manner that answered all questions and challenges, the 9/11 Commission tried to succeed by holding open meetings and making the documents they obtained publicly available; where President Clinton used a strategy of ignoring conservative conspiracy theorists' allegations against him and his wife (such as Vince Foster's suicide) in the false hope that they would fade away, President Obama released his "long–form" birth certificate after years of speculation by an increasingly vocal "birther" movement. Surely such disclosures work, the state and liberal political theory suggests; surely, when state actors release as many authentic documents as they can, a rational, engaged public will no longer believe the most outlandish theories about secret power.

---

10 For a description of the transparency movement and its history since the aftermath of World War II, cf. Mark Fenster, "The Transparency Fix: Advocating Legal Rights and Their Alternatives in the Pursuit of a Visible State", in: *University of Pittsburgh Law Review*, 73/2012, 3, pp. 443–503.

But disclosure does not satisfy conspiracy theorists, nor does it always resolve the mysteries that theorists probe. Protests by the "9/11 Truth Movement" in 2006 and 2007 featured floats and human-sized copies of a "9/11 Truth Omission Report" [sic] with large, prominent holes cut out of them to represent the (presumably damning) information they failed to include. Obama's release of his "long form" birth certificate took much but not all of the momentum from the Birther movement, although in part its success in damping down conspiracies came from the (suspicious?) timing of the President's announcement, four days after releasing the birth certificate, of Osama bin Laden's assassination – photos of which were not released, a decision that itself prompted conspiracy theorists to allege that the entire event was faked. For those bitterly opposed to him, Obama is no more acceptable or legitimate than his Republican predecessor, despite his efforts, imperfect though they may be, to be more open, and he remains the suspect of far right conspiracy theories as well as from those who believe in a deep conspiracy that encompasses both political parties and the entire political system. Even setting aside some of the partisan or unreasonable aspects of such claims, the disclosure of more documents as a result of the John F. Kennedy Assassination Records Collection Act of 1992 has not curbed the theories, from the outlandish to the reasonable, surrounding Kennedy's murder.[11] Transparency – albeit the imperfect transparency that even the most ethical and open leaders of large modern states might attempt – will not quell conspiracy theories.

There are at least two reasons for this. One is that except in revolutionary breaks following the collapse of the state,[12] only the state can make the state transparent. Freedom of Information laws require, in the first instance, that the same bureaucracies that produce secrets disclose them. Even where government or non-government entities might review disclosure practices, like the judiciary or an independent ombudsman, the administrative obligation to disclose must be administered by bureaucrats administering laws that provide a certain degree of discretion and limited but potentially capacious classes of documents that need not be or cannot be disclosed. The state's disclosures, in sum, will not be perfect. Second, conspiracy theorists' radical

11 The Act appears at 44 U.S.C. § 2107.

12 Exemplary post-collapse disclosures occur when secret government archives are broken into following a revolution – as occurred when the Mubarak government fell in Egypt – and when a new government has little or no stake in preserving the informational privileges of the former government and so allows broad administrative access to secret files – as in, for example, the treatment of Stasi files from the former East Germany by the unified German state.

doubts of the state's legitimacy and honesty leave the state unable to satisfy conspiracy theorists and shut down their will to interpret official acts and information simply by producing documents and declaring itself transparent. In this regard, hardcore transparency advocates like Julian Assange and conspiracy theorists resemble each other. Their analogous populist distrust of the state focuses on official information practices, and in their shared desire for an unending flow of information, transparency advocates and conspiracy theorists demand perfect visibility of an imperfect, massive bureaucracy, and proclaim they will not rest until the truth is available and the state can finally be seen.[13]

An inference one can draw from the claim that transparency will abolish conspiracy theory is that the more open the state, the less likely people will believe in such irrational things as conspiracy theories; alternatively, if such theories are found non-crazy by being proved true, then the public will be able to hold accountable the conspirators. Put in the form of related hypotheses, one could posit:

- A society that becomes more open, and a state that discloses more information, will spawn fewer conspiracy theories and fewer of its citizens will believe in them.
- At any one time, an indexed map showing the relative openness of states will be consistent with an indexed map showing a state's role in conspiracy theories and the relative number of its citizens who engage in and believe in conspiracy theories.

These would be very difficult hypotheses to test, but based on polling data and empirical work on conspiracy theory belief (some of which is discussed in the paper I describe in the next section), my own sense is that if there were a relationship between transparency and conspiracy theory, it would show a weak correlation between the degree and strength of open government regimes and conspiracy theory belief. Different rates and styles of conspiracy belief are at least as closely tied to other historical, cultural, social, and political contexts as they are to the extent of government disclosure. This suggests that a reformed, transparent state – even if possible to achieve – cannot

---

[13] On the relationship between transparency and conspiracy theory, cf. the essays in Harry G. West/Todd Sanders, *Transparency and Conspiracy*, Durham 2003; in addition, Jodi Dean discusses the relationship between conspiracy theory and the information environment of what she calls the "technoculture" in *Publicity's Secret*, Ithaca 2002, pp. 69–78.

directly address and alleviate conspiracy theory belief through openness and information disclosure. As a secondary implication, this suggests that the assumption that transparency will necessarily lead to a more perfect state and a more active, engaged, and rational polis – an assumption that undergirds transparency advocacy and the WikiLeaks project – might not hold.

2. Method 2: It Takes a Conspiracy to Beat a Conspiracy Theory

In "Conspiracy Theories: Causes and Cures", Cass Sunstein and Adrian Vermeule, two prominent American law professors, exemplify the sunny prescriptive perspective of American policy intellectuals.[14] Drawing on academic literature that the authors in this volume (myself included) largely ignore, most prominently analytic philosophy and quantitative social science, they set out in search of the underlying cognitive and social causes for the development and circulation of conspiracy theories. After isolating the object of their concern – conspiracy theories that are false, harmful, unjustified, and resistant to correction – they explain why conspiracy theories arise and spread, and they prescribe steps that the state can take to counter or to "cure" them.[15] Their proposed cure is much more controversial than mere disclosure, which they dismiss as unlikely to be effective; indeed, their prescription is rarely spoken of in open company by those in or close to power. But before describing their cure, we need to take a closer look at their understanding of conspiracy theory's symptoms and causes.

Sunstein and Vermeule proudly disclaim psychological explanations and the search for a singular symptom – an approach most closely associated with at least the implication of Richard Hofstadter's "paranoid style" approach, if not precisely his intended meaning – and instead tie the rise and spread of conspiracy theories to a smorgasbord of related cognitive errors that social science and theories of epistemology help to uncover. In no particular order, Sunstein and Vermeule list the variety of ailments from which conspiracy theorists suffer when they retrieve and process information: their "crippled epistemologies" limit their knowledge of the world and leave them especially vulnerable to rumors and speculation; they are subject to "information cascades" through which their opinions are shaped and then solidified by a social and intellectual community of conspiracy theory believers; they come to believe in the most extreme version of their theories by picking

14 Cf. Cass Sunstein/Adrian Vermeule, "Conspiracy Theories: Causes and Cures", in: *Journal of Political Philosophy*, 17/2009, 2, pp. 202–227.

15 Sunstein/Vermeule, "Conspiracy Theories", p. 210.

up the signals and information of those surrounding them, who disproportionately share their own views; they are subject to and choose to indulge in emotional beliefs and moral panics; and they only accept as true and ultimately only have access to information that confirms the conspiracy theory they believe.[16] In Sunstein and Vermeule's view, then, conspiracy theorists may not necessarily be stupid, but they hang out with the wrong crowd and sup at the wrong data streams.

This model of conspiracy theory's causes portrays an abstract, bloodlessly deficient information environment. History, culture, and context have no place except in footnotes. Conspiracy theorists' cognitive and social dysfunctions result not from class or race or ethnicity or other social markers, which might explain the propensity – sometimes warranted and more based in fact – of certain populations or of certain broad social and political movements to form around or to include beliefs in a conspiracy. Rather, according to Sunstein and Vermeule, people come to believe in conspiracy theory because of the way they access and process information.

Not only is there no context in their account, it also contemplates no shades of grey or detail. To keep their explanatory model clean, they exclude allegations that prove true. They also remove both the playful and pervasive aspects of conspiracy theory – the fact that even those who don't "believe" in them can enjoy speculation about them, and that even those who may not fully or always believe may accept or be willing to contemplate the existence of one or a few such theories without self-identifying as conspiracy theorists or obsessing over them. They are uninterested in considering the extent to which conspiracy theories permeate or at least seep into political debate and mainstream populisms of the left and right. They focus only on the "hardcore" believers, as if that were a discernible, stable population at any one time or across time. Their model posits a binary: on one side are conspiracy theories, conspiracy theorists, their crippled epistemologies, and their uninformed and emotional social networks; on the other are rationality, rational actors, and reasonable political beliefs and debates. While they may not posit a psychological duality between the pathological and healthy, Sunstein and Vermeule propose in its stead an essential distinction between the cognitively functional and dysfunctional.

How, then, can the state respond? How can it "cure" the cognitively dysfunctional? Sunstein and Vermeule's model provides us with another reason to be skeptical of the claim that transparency and disclosure will cure conspiracy theory: conspiracy theorists and their theories resist contrary evi-

---

16 Cf. Sunstein/Vermeule, "Conspiracy Theories", pp. 211–218.

dence. They also persuasively identify the dilemma that the state faces: rebutting conspiracy theorists can lend legitimacy to their theories, but ignoring them – whether by refusing to rebut them or by attempting instead to address the presumptively more rational masses – may allow theorists greater traction with the general public as well as with potentially violent individuals (e.g., Timothy McVeigh).[17]

Unwilling to allow this dilemma to go unsolved, Sunstein and Vermeule offer their prescription: the state should deploy "(legal) tactics for breaking up the tight cognitive clusters of extremist theories, argument and rhetoric [through] *cognitive infiltration of extremist groups*".[18] They elaborate: "Government agents (and their allies) might enter chat rooms, online social networks, or even real-space groups and attempt to undermine percolating conspiracy theories by raising doubts about their factual premises, causal logic, or implications for action, political or otherwise".[19] Sometimes, government officials might "proclaim" their institutional affiliation; at other times, they could participate anonymously or "even with false identities".[20] The former method might not work, they caution, because "hard-core members" of the conspiracy community would discount the officials' statements, while the method of using undercover agents risks disclosure or discovery, "with possible perverse results" – that "the conspiracy theory may become further entrenched, and any genuine member of the relevant group who raises doubts may be suspected of government connections".[21]

I hope and assume the reader of this volume will see that this approach threatens much more than the "risks" and "costs" of exposure that Sunstein and Vermeule concede. The authors wish away the most pressing concern of this "tactic" with the parenthetical adjective "(legal)", while they only refer obliquely to "1960s-style infiltration with a view to surveillance and collecting information, possibly for use in future prosecution" – a veiled reference to the FBI's infamous counterintelligence and surveillance program code-

---

17 Cf. Sunstein/Vermeule, "Conspiracy Theories", pp. 221–224.

18 Sunstein/Vermeule, "Conspiracy Theories", p. 224; emphasis in original. For purposes of full disclosure, I am listed as one of several people who provided comments on an earlier draft; the focus of my comments were on the dangerousness of their proposed "cure" and the fact that it would be understood, especially by those in the conspiracy community, as akin to the illegal government programs that I describe below.

19 Sunstein/Vermeule, "Conspiracy Theories", pp. 224–225.

20 Sunstein/Vermeule, "Conspiracy Theories", p. 225.

21 Sunstein/Vermeule, "Conspiracy Theories", p. 225.

named COINTELPRO.[22] But COINTELPRO demands more than oblique mention, especially given the substance of Sunstein and Vermeule's proposal. An effort to fight lawful as well as unlawful dissent during the 1960s and 1970s, COINTELPRO was "designed to 'disrupt' and 'neutralize' individuals deemed to be threats to domestic security".[23] Its illegal activity was directly tied to FBI Director J. Edgar Hoover's contempt and detest for dissent of all sorts, and it confirmed every conspiracy theorist's (not to mention every civil libertarian's) paranoid fears of an Orwellian state.[24] Viewed in this context, Sunstein and Vermeule's suggestion that federal officials engage in undercover infiltration manifests a willful blindness to the past and to the enduring harm that COINTELPRO inflicted on the legitimacy of American law enforcement and domestic intelligence gathering – a blindness to the actual and existing state practices that they ignore when they define conspiracy theory as a set of isolated, cognitive errors. As any transparency advocate would proclaim, the state's secret infiltration and disruption of constitutionally protected political dissent would, like COINTELPRO, do lasting harm to the state's legitimacy and induce among the general population warranted suspicion of not only the participants but also those officials who played no part in the scheme.

Sunstein and Vermeule are not obscure academics. They are prominent faculty at one of the top law schools in the U.S., the school that President Obama attended. Their careers intersected with President Obama when all three of them taught at the University of Chicago Law School. Soon after the article's publication, Sunstein was appointed to serve in the Obama administration as the Administrator of the Office of Information and Regulatory Affairs, an office charged with overseeing the federal government's collection of information and information policies. This does not constitute a conspiracy; it merely illustrates that despite their distinct views – Obama was a community organizer and politician before and during his part-time teaching

---

22 Sunstein/Vermeule, "Conspiracy Theories", p. 224.

23 U.S. Senate Select Committee to Study Governmental Operations with Respect to Intelligence Activities, "Intelligence Activities and the Rights of Americans: Final Report", Book II, 1976, http://www.intelligence.senate.gov/pdfs94th/94755_II.pdf (accessed Sept. 25, 2011), p. 10.

24 Cf. Kathryn S. Olmsted, *Real Enemies: Conspiracy Theories and American Democracy, World War I to 9/11*, New York 2009, p. 10. Olmsted is the author of the best history of the Church and Pike Commissions, which investigated illegal and unauthorized intelligence activities and civil rights abuses by the intelligence and federal law enforcement agencies during the Cold War period (cf. *Challenging the Secret Government: The Post-Watergate Investigations of the CIA and FBI*, Chapel Hill 1996).

assignment at Chicago, while Sunstein and Vermeule are career academics; Obama and Sunstein are centrist-liberals on America's conservative political spectrum while Vermeule is relatively conservative – their ideas and understanding of the politically rational and dangerous dissent emanate from positions of discursive, institutional, and political power. Unsurprisingly, the libertarian left and conspiratorial right condemned the Sunstein and Vermeule proposal as part of a broader Obama administration plot to stifle dissent.[25] The argument that it takes a conspiracy to defeat a conspiracy theory thus illustrates that institutional elites can prove tone-deaf when they propose abstract policy solutions for a problem they understand in abstract ways.

3. Conclusion: No "Theory," No "Cure"

I want to draw two insights from this discussion. First, the prescriptions offered to "cure" conspiracy theory flow directly from the prescribers' theoretical apparatus. If you think that transparency can cure the state and its public and that conspiracy theory is caused by a lack of complete and authoritative information, then you assert that more transparency – which will produce more and more authoritative information – can cure conspiracy theory. Alternatively, if you think that conspiracy theory is symptomatic of cognitive failings, then you assert that the only cure is to address those failings. This is a neat trick for transparency advocates and policy entrepreneurs who can package their theories and description as the answers to the world's pressing concerns for policymakers, grant funding organizations, newspapers, and academic journals.

But where does that leave the papers from this book and the proceedings of the conference on which the book is based? There was no general theoretical apparatus on display; in fact, the papers come from across the interpretive and humanistic disciplines, armed with a motley assortment of methodologies, bibliographies, and terminologies. To the extent they offer or draw from one or more "theories", these theories are of the descriptive, contextual variety rather than of the "rigorous", testable kind. An underlying claim that seems to emerge from these papers is that conspiracy theories

---

25 Cf. Glenn Beck, *Sunstein's Cure for Conspiracy Theories*, 2010, http://www.foxnews.com/story/0,2933,591422,00.html (accessed Sept. 25, 2011); Glenn Greenwald, *Obama Confidant's Spine-chilling Proposal*, 2010, http://www.salon.com/news/opinion/glenn_greenwald/2010/01/15/sunstein (accessed Sept. 25, 2011); Paul Joseph Watson, *Obama Czar Wants Mandatory Government Propaganda On Political Websites*, 2010, http://www.prisonplanet.com/obama-czar-wants-mandatory-government-propaganda-on-political-websites.html (accessed Sept. 25, 2011).

arise in a particular context that results from a complex mix of social, political, religious, ethnic, racial, and cultural conditions. While surely this is true, it isn't particularly rigorous; indeed, it becomes interesting only in its application to individual cases. At best, a "cure" that arises from this claim would be related solely and directly to the conditions in which a specific set of conspiracy theories operate or in which conspiracy theories compete in a national or regional context.

To be clear, this is not a complaint. The second insight I think this essay offers is that the lack of a clear, insightful theory and an overriding cure is not a fault of or even a flaw in the work represented here. In its sensitivity to context, our interpretive work disdains – sometimes perhaps excessively – the supposed rigors of "hard" social science and the longing for prescriptive answers. It searches instead for situational insights; in so doing, it can offer insightful description and critique. Viewed in light of the alternatives presented above, which attempt to apply broad, theoretical claims in individual cases in order to posit doubtful cures, our caution about prescription seems well-founded. Our approach, if it could be described as a single thing, does at least as good if not a better job at explaining conspiracy theory as the presumptively rigorous and universalist ones. Our hesitancy to pronounce conspiracy theories as symptomatic of an underlying disease from which the public suffers, with an attendant cure that an academic discipline can readily provide, demonstrates a useful and worthy modesty. We offer no single theory, because we are skeptical of efforts to provide universal descriptions and models; we disdain talk of "cures" because we are skeptical of efforts to diagnose conspiracy theory as a singular disease.

Peter Knight (Manchester)

Plotting Future Directions in Conspiracy Theory Research

The present volume is a testament to the growing international scholarly interest in conspiracy theory as a complex cultural, psychological, and political phenomenon. It provides a snapshot of the variety of research being done in different disciplines on a variety of regions, historical traditions, and source materials. Its central premise of exploring conspiracy theories in comparative national and historical perspective opens up many new avenues of enquiry. In this chapter, I want to place this work in the context of other recent research on conspiracy theory, and to outline five areas for future inquiry: problems of definition, comparative approaches, modes of transmission, patterns of belief, and policy implications.

1. Definitions

Does conspiracy theory only become an identifiable epistemological category when it comes to be thought of as a social problem? Recent research has begun to map out the political context in which "conspiracy theory" as a term was developed as part of a wider set of concerns about mass hysteria and incipient totalitarianism. The story begins with Karl Popper's attack in *The Open Society and Its Enemies* on the intellectual error of the "conspiracy theory of society".[1] It was written in the depths of World War II, with Popper arguing that fascism and communism were twin forms of totalitarianism, each relying on conspiratorial interpretations of history to justify their political programmes. "Totalitarianism" became one of the buzz words of the Cold War in the U.S., with commentators ranging from Dwight Macdonald to Norman Mailer warning that mass culture threatened to create an American form of totalitarianism, by turning the masses into deindividualised and unthinking conformists, easily prey to populist demagoguery. Concern about an antidemocratic, conspiracist mindset continued in Harold Lasswell's work on political personalities and Franz Neumann's research on alienation and its connection to fear in the 1950s, before gaining academic and

---

1 Karl Popper, *The Open Society and Its Enemies*, London 1945.

popular currency with Richard Hofstadter's seminal study of the political pathologies of the "paranoid style" in the 1960s.[2]

Although we now have a clearer picture of the political and intellectual genealogy of the influential approach to conspiracy theory pioneered by the "consensus school" of American historians, there is still more research to be done on the origins of the term. First, there has to date been little detailed work on Popper's development of the term, and how it relates to Popper's overall project in *The Open Society* and the broader anti-totalitarianism debates of the period. Second, we still lack a complete etymology of the term in English, as well as other languages. Although Popper may have been the first to identify conspiracy theory as not merely a particular kind of explanatory framework but a political problem, the term has a longer genealogy. As Andrew McKenzie-McHarg has shown, the phrase dates back to at least the 1880s, when it was used by newspapers in the U.S. to account for different approaches that were being put forward to explain notorious murders from the period, with the "conspiracy theory" approach pitted against other possible lines of forensic inquiry, such as the "suicide theory".[3] Also in need of further research is how such competing explanations came to be seen as "theories", not in the older sense of broad, verifiable generalisations but as specific causal hypotheses. Finally, there is still much work to be done on the history of the concept of "conspiracy" and its relation to cognate terms such as conjuration, plot, cabal, and intrigue, not only in English but in other languages. We need to know more about the specific valences of each term in different historical and cultural contexts, as well as how they relate to changing legal definitions of conspiracy.[4]

---

[2] This intellectual history is told in Mark Fenster, *Conspiracy Theories: Secrecy and Power in American Culture*, Minneapolis 2008; and Jack Bratich, *Conspiracy Panics: Political Rationality and Popular Culture*, Albany 2008.

[3] Andrew McKenzie-McHarg, "How Did Conspiracy Theories Come to Be Seen as Theories?", Conference on Conspiracies Real and Imagined, University of York, Sept. 8, 2011.

[4] Some interesting work has started to appear in this vein, e.g. Timothy Tackett, "Conspiracy Obsession in a Time of Revolution: French Elites and the Origins of the Terror", in: *American Historical Review*, 105/2000, pp. 691–713. Tackett's research was based on a search for the term "conspiration" in the ARTFL database; however, as Peter Campbell notes, the focus on this one term is in danger of downplaying the importance of cognate terms (cf. Peter R. Campbell, "Perceptions of Conspiracy on the Eve of the French Revolution", in: Peter R. Campbell/ Thomas E. Kaiser/Marisa Linton (eds.), *Conspiracy in the French Revolution*, Manchester 2007, p. 38, n. 5).

The larger question thrown up by the recent historicisation of the term "conspiracy theories" is whether it still makes sense to think of them as a recognisable phenomenon with distinctive characteristics (rhetorical style, narrative structure, cultural function, psychological outlook, and political utility). Jack Bratich has argued forcefully that there is no such thing as a conspiracy theory, only panicked reactions to unpopular and dissenting views that are conveniently dismissed as beyond the pale of rationality by a system of governmentality whose main aim is to consolidate the political centre-ground as a non-partisan consensus.[5] Bratich's challenge to reorient the field of inquiry from the conspiracy theories themselves to the conspiracy panics that designate some views as conspiracy theories opens up new possibilities for research. As his book concentrates solely on recent case studies (such as AIDS and 9/11) that have emerged since the term "conspiracy theory" has entered public consciousness, it would be worth investigating to what extent the creation of conspiracy panics has been enabled by the availability of a simple, catch-all term, one that is now often elevated to the status of an identifiable political ideology: conspiracism. Presumably what were deemed to be exaggeratedly suspicious views on the part of a gullible public swayed by the seductions of demagoguery were also subjected to concerted attacks in earlier historical moments, but little research has been done on those kinds of episodes. It would also be helpful to compare Bratich's account of the operation of conspiracy panics in the U.S. with other nations, particularly more authoritarian ones, because Bratich's Foucauldian approach assumes that the technocratic, pathologising forms of governmentality in modern western societies are just as insidious as more direct forms of repression. Likewise, it would be useful to know more about what happens when some people willingly appropriate the label of conspiracy theorist, thus to some degree undermining the force of the delegitimisation of dissent that Bratich anatomises.

Bratich's work on conspiracy panics has not surprisingly itself come under attack for seeming to refuse to make distinctions between different kinds of conspiracy theory. Although much in sympathy with Bratich's cultural studies approach, Mark Fenster, for example, has noted that some conspiracy theories indeed deserve more vilification than others because their claims are far less plausible and are derived from or have typically been articulated

---

5 Bratich, *Conspiracy Panics.* Bratich's work can be seen as following in the footsteps of Michael Rogin, "*Ronald Reagan*", *The Movie, and Other Episodes in Political Demonology*, Berkeley 1987.

to undesirable political views.[6] If Fenster is right, we need to continue to research the political, rhetorical, and psychological mechanisms by which conspiracy thinking operates in order to make distinctions between particular conspiracy theories and communities, even if it is accepted that some of the labelling of particular views as "conspiracy theories" is a technique of governmentality.

From Hofstadter onwards most theories of conspiracy theory have been willing to grant that there have indeed been successful conspiracies, albeit in isolation rather than a single over-arching grand plan. Often a distinction is made between (implausible) conspiracy theories and what might be termed (plausible) theories of conspiracy, a division that is in keeping with Hofstadter's differentiation between small-scale and all-encompassing theories that see conspiracy as the "motive force of history" rather than an occasional disruption.[7] Many definitions of conspiracy theory have thus tended to move toward the prescriptive and normative: as Hofstadter notes, his characterisation of the "paranoid style" is meant to be "pejorative", confirming Bratich's sense that the term "conspiracy theory" is more an insult than a description.[8] In the last decade, a lively debate has emerged in analytical philosophy over the question of whether the truth claims of conspiracy theories are necessarily unwarranted or not.[9] While this debate has made some useful contributions in setting out what is at stake in the epistemology of conspiracy theory, it has also highlighted the difficulty of creating a watertight definition that covers the many different examples that seem naturally to come under an umbrella definition. Many commentators have ruefully acknowledged that the hermeneutic of suspicion that animates conspiracy thinking is shared by the larger project of legitimate scientific enquiry and critical thinking that would analyse it; as Freud himself noted ironically in his study of paranoia, "it remains for the future to decide whether there is more delusion

---

6 Mark Fenster/Jack Bratich, "Dialogues in Communications Research", in: *Journal of Communication Inquiry*, 33/2009, pp. 278–286; and "When Theorists Conspire: An Inter(re)view Between Mark Fenster and Jack Bratich", in: *International Journal of Communication*, 3/2009, pp. 961–972.

7 Cf. e.g. Daniel Pipes, *Conspiracy: How the Paranoid Style Flourishes and Where It Comes From*, New York 1997; and Michael Barkun, *A Culture of Conspiracy*, Berkeley 2003. A call to distinguish between conspiracy theories and legitimate inquiries into conspiratorial collusion and secrecy in politics is made in Jovan Byford, *Conspiracy Theories: A Critical Introduction*, Basingstoke 2011.

8 Richard Hofstadter, *The Paranoid Style in American Politics and Other Essays*, New York 1967, pp. 29, 5.

9 David Coady (ed.), *Conspiracy Theories: The Philosophical Debate*, Aldershot 2006.

in my theory than I should like to admit, or whether there is more truth in Schreber's delusion than other people are as yet prepared to believe".[10] Whenever a counterexample is brought forward that seems to undermine a particular understanding of how conspiracy theories work, the response is often that it does not actually count as a conspiracy theory at all.[11]

Usually the distinction between conspiracy theories and theories of conspiracy is made in order to shine a forensic light on the epistemological and political failings of the "paranoid style". However, some commentators have recently urged making a clearer distinction between legitimate and illegitimate conspiracy theories because they feel that serious research into political conspiracies has been tarnished by its association with the excesses of conspiracist fantasies. For example, the political scientist Jeffrey Bale recommends that academic researchers should overcome their prejudice of anything to do with conspiracy talk, and pay greater attention to the historical significance of actual covert and clandestine activities.[12] Instead of futile efforts to uncover signs of a vast, timeless conspiracy that is preternaturally efficient and ruthless, Bale recommends instead that researchers should pay attention to actual covert activities, that are more restricted in their scope, reach, and effectiveness, but which are nonetheless key components of modern states. Researchers should focus, for instance, on the activities of the Tsarist secret police that produced the forged *Protocols of the Elders of Zion* rather than the imagined plot for Jewish global domination supposedly documented in the *Protocols*. Bale's recommendation will of course not satisfy those die-hard believers in a vast, all-encompassing conspiracy; nor does it

---

10 Sigmund Freud, "Psycho-Analytic Notes on an Autobiographical Account of a Case of Paranoia (Dementia Paranoides)", in: James Strachey (ed.), *The Standard Edition of the Complete Psychological Works of Sigmund Freud*, 24 vols., London 1953–1974, pp. 12–79. There is an extended discussion of the connections between social science, the hermeneutic of suspicion, and theories of conspiracy theory in Martin Parker, "Human Science as Conspiracy Theory", in: Jane Parish/ Martin Parker (eds.), *The Age of Anxiety: Conspiracy Theory and the Human Sciences*, Oxford 2001, pp. 191–207.

11 Cf. e.g. Steve Clarke, "Conspiracy Theories and the Internet: Controlled Demolition and Arrested Development", in: *Episteme*, 4/2007, pp. 167–180. By using a very restricted definition of what is to count as a proper conspiracy theory, Clarke is able to reach the surprising conclusion that the Internet has brought about a reduction in conspiracy theories. The real problem with much of this work in philosophy, however, is the lack of engagement with the detailed case studies.

12 Jeffery M. Bale, "Political Paranoia v. Political Realism: On Distinguishing Between Bogus Conspiracy Theories and Genuine Conspiratorial Politics", in: *Patterns of Prejudice*, 41/2007, pp. 45–60.

obviate the need for historical, sociological, and psychological analysis of why people are seemingly so attracted to bogus conspiracy theories.

A similar concern to rethink the definition of conspiracy theory has recently been proposed by Lance deHaven-Smith, who puts forward the term "State Crimes Against Democracy" (SCADs) as an alternative. He defines SCADs as "concerted actions or inactions by government insiders intended to manipulate democratic processes and undermine popular sovereignty".[13] For deHaven-Smith, conspiracy theories "about assassinations, 9/11, and other suspicious events" have made the mistake of examining each event "in isolation". In contrast, the notion of a State Crime Against Democracy moves inquiry "beyond incident-specific theorizing. It delineates a crime category comparable to white collar crime, organized crime, and hate crime. SCAD research looks for patterns across events".[14] Ironically, the belief that there are not merely isolated conspiracies here or there in the historical record but that a single coherent thread unites them all into one master narrative is precisely what Hofstadter, Pipes, and others would regard as the telltale sign of a conspiracy theorist.[15] Although lumping together Watergate and the Gulf of Tonkin with the Kennedy assassination and 9/11 is unlikely to win deHaven-Smith many converts from those who would place the dividing line between bogus and realistic conspiracy research differently (with the former two cases deemed proven or probable, and the latter two as unproven or improbable), his intervention refocuses attention on what is at stake in the very terminology of conspiracism, and also on the need for research, both in the present and in other historical periods, into actual conspiracies and the way they have been imagined – and even the way that the latter has shaped the former.[16]

---

13 Lance deHaven-Smith, *Frequently Asked Questions about State Crimes Against Democracy (SCADs)*, http://www.dehaven-smith.com/faq/default.html (accessed Oct. 1, 2011). Cf. also deHaven-Smith, "Beyond Conspiracy Theory: Patterns of High Crime in American Government", in: *American Behavioral Scientist*, 53/2010, pp. 795–825.

14 DeHaven-Smith, *Frequently Asked Questions.*

15 DeHaven-Smith would presumably argue that the difference is that his social scientific perspective is more concerned with the social and political structures that make covert and clandestine actives part of the routine operation of state power in the postwar period, rather than a theory that posits a single, tightly-knit cabal that has been insidiously manipulating events behind the scenes for decades.

16 For a fascinating discussion about the nature of conspiracy in the Early American Republic, cf. Ed White, "The Value of Conspiracy Theory", in: *American Literary History*, 14/2002, pp. 1–31.

DeHaven-Smith's theory about the existence of an underlying pattern of high-level corruption within official structures of power is focused squarely on the U.S., but recent research into terrorism in general and al-Qaeda in particular has had to rethink the very idea of what constitutes a conspiracy. Although the Bush administration was very keen to portray the attacks of September 11, 2001 as the result of a clearly identifiable enemy with a traditional, hierarchical command-and-control structure and easily articulated ideology of hatred to western freedom, other commentators stressed that al-Qaeda was a loose, decentred network of related groups with varying political and theological outlooks in different locations around the world.[17] Moreover, although the belated official investigation into 9/11 concluded that the attacks were the result of a concerted conspiracy directed by Osama bin Laden and that conspiracy theories of insider foreknowledge or complicity on part of the Bush administration were unfounded, it nevertheless uncovered disconcerting evidence that suggested a far more troubling picture not just of incompetence and confusion on the part of the CIA and FBI but also a blurring together at the intersections between the bloated American intelligence apparatus, the network of al-Qaeda, private and state interests in Saudi Arabia, and organisations such as ISI in Pakistan – even if those connections did not amount to a conspiracy as such. Far from operating as a superhuman conspiracy with a single-minded focus on an overall goal, it is possible that different parts of the labyrinthine U.S. intelligence agencies were involved with some of the 9/11 attackers in contradictory and ambiguous ways that fall short of an actual conspiracy, but which nonetheless undermine the notion of complete American innocence.[18]

In addition to examining the definitions of conspiracy with regard to terrorism and intelligence agencies, it would be worth while exploring the mechanics and changing legal terminology of conspiracy in corporate bureaucracies, along with the history of corporate fraud and white collar crime. In

---

17 Cf. Jason Burke, *Al-Qeada: The True Story of Radical Islam*, London 2004; Richard Jackson, *Writing the War on Terrorism*, Manchester 2005.

18 Cf. Richard A. Clarke, *Against All Enemies: Inside America's War on Terrorism*, New York 2004. Clarke's suggestion that the CIA refused to share their knowledge of some of the 9/11 hijackers because they were trying to recruit them as agents (and would thus be exposed as operating illegally on U.S. soil) is used in the online film *Who Is Rich Blee?* (www.secrecykills.com [accessed Oct. 1, 2011]). Cf. also Rory O'Connor/Ray Nowosielski,
"Insiders voice doubts about CIA's 9/11 story", in: *Salon*, Oct. 14, 2011, http://www.salon.com/2011/10/14/insiders_voice_doubts_cia_911/ (accessed Nov. 4, 2011).

the American case, for example, the antimonopoly statutes implemented as a result of populist agitation in the late nineteenth and early twentieth century were designed to restrict the powers of the vast new corporations by outlawing "conspiracy in restraint of trade" in order to level the playing field of competition between small producers and the corporate behemoths.[19] Despite paying lip-service to the rhetoric of free market competition, many of the corporations created in the Great Merger Movement of 1898–1904 strived for monopoly rather than competition, to be achieved through horizontal and vertical integration. As rival firms were reorganised into a single entity through vertical and horizontal integration rather than a loose cartel, proving the existence of an actual price-fixing conspiracy was not an easy task. This is made harder still if collusion happens not through clearly documented acts of illegal, covert conspiracy but through tacit gentlemen's agreements, or through the institution of compartmentalisation and plausible deniability within corporate and government bureaucracies designed to insulate the leaders from the activities of those on the ground. What if low-level agents carry out illegal acts that they assume, through reading ambiguous signals, that their masters would wish – perhaps not consciously, but which represent their deepest, unconscious desires?[20] Is it still a conspiracy if one party merely assumes that the other is thinking in the same way and acts accordingly? What if collusion emerges not from an unspoken meeting of minds but from an unconscious convergence of interests? What if we take literally the legal doctrine of corporate personhood (the idea that corporations hold the same rights as individuals in the eyes of the law), and instead of endowing corporations with the kind of single-minded, ruthless agency that animates many conspiracy-minded personifications, we see the coherence of corporate subjectivity and intention as a convenient fiction?[21]

According to the Chandlerian account in business history, the managerial revolution of the nineteenth century introduced strict hierarchies of control, epitomised by the pyramid organisation charts pioneered by railroad corpor-

---

[19] The historical irony is that the statutes were most often used to suppress labour unions rather than corporations (cf. Michael Cohen, *"The Conspiracy of Capital": American Popular Radicalism and the Politics of Conspiracy from Haymarket to the Red Scare*, Diss. Yale University, 2004).

[20] This was the explanation given in the Iran-Contra hearings. Compartmentalisation and second-guessing the intentions of superiors is central to the representation of the CIA's possible involvement in the Kennedy assassination conspiracy in Don DeLillo's novel *Libra* (1988).

[21] Campbell Jones, "What Kind of Subject Is the Market?", in: *New Formations*, 72/2011, pp. 131–45.

ations in the 1850s.[22] These charts operate in a similar fashion to conspiracy theory diagrams of the structure of secret societies, in which power is concentrated in the hands of a small cabal at the top of pyramid. However, in the second half of the twentieth century, management theory turned to dynamic flow charts and flat structures of corporate organisation, that offer a very different model of decision-making processes than the traditional hierarchical ones. The way that the act of illegal conspiring (on the part of business and government bureaucracies) has been imagined has, unsurprisingly, also changed. For example, in a think-piece on state and terrorist conspiracies, Julian Assange, the founder of WikiLeaks, draws on mathematical metaphors of connected graphs. He characterises a conspiracy as a computational device, a closed network with inputs and outputs, rather than the product of individual, intentional agency. In effect, he imagines state conspiracies operating as a decentred system out of which arises co-ordinated behaviour, much like the Internet, the unregulated architecture of which ironically allows WikiLeaks to mount its counter-conspiracy campaigns of data liberation.[23] Or we could consider the fascinating drawings of Mark Lombardi, a conceptual artist who produced in the 1980s and 1990s vast detailed diagrams showing the connections between governments, corporations, and intelligence agencies in the financial scandals of the period. The drawings take their visual language from the diagrams produced by Social Network Analysis, but they also resemble representations of stellar constellations.[24]

More generally, conspiracy theories have been criticised for clinging to supposedly outmoded models of intentionality and causality that modern social science has rendered redundant. In his revisionist article on the rationality of conspiracy thinking in eighteenth-century America that challenges

---

22 Alfred Chandler, *The Visible Hand: The Managerial Revolution in American Business*, Cambridge, MA 1978. Among many other challengers to the Chandlerian story, cf. for example Richard White, *Railroaded: The Transcontinentals and the Making of Modern America*, New York 2011, which argues that America's transcontinental railroads in the nineteenth century were controlled by a nepotistic network of interlocking families and insiders, with the directors as petulant and backstabbing, lacking both the visible hand of managerial efficiency, and also the cold and sure touch of the hidden hand of the arch conspirator.

23 Julian Assange, *Conspiracy as Governance*, 2006, http://estaticos.elmundo.es/documentos/2010/12/01/conspiracies.pdf (accessed Oct. 1, 2011).

24 Cf. Robert Hobbs (ed.), *Mark Lombardi: Global Networks*, New York 2003. For a popular discussion of SNA and corporate conspiracy, cf. Andy Coghlan/Debora MacKenzie, "Revealed: The Capitalist Network That Runs the World", in: *New Scientist*, Oct. 24, 2011, http://www.newscientist.com/article/mg21228354.500-revealed--the-capitalist-network-that-runs-the-world.html (accessed Dec. 1, 2011).

Hofstadter's pathologising approach to the Founding Fathers, Gordon Wood nevertheless ends up agreeing with Hofstadter. Wood argues that, since the emergence of the social sciences in the nineteenth century, belief in hidden individual agency instead of structural causation is a sign of intellectual backwardness.[25] More recently, however, scholars such as Timothy Melley have noted how contemporary conspiracy theories at times imagine impersonal systems of power themselves as a conspiracy.[26] The personification of depersonalised structures of power in effect collapses Wood's distinction between the sophisticated social scientist and the naïve conspiracy theorist. In "We the Paranoid", an innovative online enquiry into contemporary conspiracy culture in the U.S., Peter Starr sees conspiracy theories grappling with the same problem that posthumanist thinkers such as Foucault returned to repeatedly, namely how in modern bureaucracies despotism can arise without an obvious despot.[27] Foucault's account of how all-pervasive power emerges from within a regime of bureaucratic surveillance rather than from the obvious brutality of state oppression goes a long way to explaining how it is possible for social control to emerge without any identifiable controllers intentionally pulling the strings, creating in effect a "conspiracy without conspirators".[28] However, Starr notes that, like the conspiracy theories it would seek to replace, Foucault's own account of despotism without a despot itself

---

25 Gordon Wood, "Conspiracy and the Paranoid Style: Causality and Deceit in the Eighteenth Century", in: *William and Mary Quarterly*, 39/1982, pp. 401–41. In "Conspiracy Myths and Conspiracy Theories", in: *Journal of the Anthropological Society of Oxford*, 20/1989, pp. 12–26, Geoffrey Cubitt takes issue with Wood's contention that conspiracy theories became merely an indicator of pathological thinking in the nineteenth century, arguing instead that they fulfilled important political functions in the religious divisiveness of France in the period, and that there was more continuity with pre-Englightenment conspiracy beliefs than Wood's notion of a sharp post-Enlightenment divide would suggest. Although Ralf Klausnitzer never mentions Wood directly, he nevertheless shows how the epistemological paradigm described by Wood continued to produce legitimate knowledge in Germany far into the ninetenth century, cf.: Klausnitzer, *Poesie und Konspiration: Beziehungssinn und Zeichenökonomie von Verschwörungsszenarien in Publizistik, Literatur und Wissenschaft 1750–1850*, Berlin 2007.

26 Timothy Melley, *Empire of Conspiracy: The Culture of Paranoia in Postwar America*, Ithaca, NY 2000.

27 Peter Starr et al., *We the Paranoid*, http://www.american.edu/cas/wtp/ (accessed Oct. 1, 2011).

28 The phrase "conspiracy without conspirators" has a much longer history. Cf. John Barrell, *Imagining the King's Death: Figurative Treason, Fantasies of Regicide*, Oxford 2003, which describes the attempts to create a legal distinction in the 1790s between fantasising and intending the king's death.

relies on repeated personification: the depersonalised and decentralised operation of power is presented rhetorically as a cunning arch conspirator, all-knowing and all-pervasive. In a similar vein, Slavoj Žižek suggests that the myth of an all-encompassing Jewish conspiracy is one of many versions of the "big Other", the "mysterious spectral agency" that is called into being to provide symbolic grounding for popular understandings of why history unfolds as it does; other contenders are divine Providence, the Marxist objective logic of History, and the Invisible Hand of the market.[29] Žižek's comments suggest new avenues for conspiracy theory research that would explore the broader history of why certain explanatory frameworks of collective causality have appealed at different historical moments.[30]

Along with the Invisible Hand metaphor used in neoclassical economics, disciplines such as cybernetics and ecology likewise claim to provide an alternative to conspiracy theory explanations, with their accounts of how complex, coordinated behaviour can emerge in the absence of a conscious coordinator, whether beneficent or malign. However, all three disciplines are reliant on the fiction that complex systems naturally desire to return to an equilibrium state, a utopian fantasy of self-organising and self-regulating behaviour that ignores the possibility that economic, ecological, and social systems might well have no such tendency to coordination. They also turn a blind eye to the possibility that human systems do not operate in the same way as natural ecosystems precisely because some groups do indeed conspire to control outcomes (and can more easily do so if the system is left to regulate itself).[31]

In addition to exploring the surprising rhetorical convergence between posthumanist accounts of power and humanist conspiracy theories, we also need to consider the relationship between conspiracy and related concepts such as complicity and collusion. Although conspiracy theories traditionally rely on a reassuringly clear notion of intentional agency (with the world neatly divided into evil conspirators and innocent victims), they often throw up anxieties about moral complicity. For example, in his analysis of *The Moneychangers*, Upton Sinclair's fictionalisation of the 1907 financial panic,

---

29 Slavoj Žižek, *The Ticklish Subject: The Absent Centre of Political Ontology*, London 1999, p. 339.

30 For a fascinating contribution to such a research agenda, cf. Stephen Kern, *A Cultural History of Causality: Science, Murder Novels, and Systems of Thought*, Princeton, NJ 2004.

31 Cf. Peder Anker, *Imperial Ecology: Environmental Order in the British Empire, 1895–1945*, Cambridge, MA 2001; Adam Curtis, "The Use and Abuse of Vegetational Concepts", on: *BBC2*, May 30, 2011.

David Zimmerman reads the novel not as a straightforward attack on the plutocratic insiders at the centre of the purported conspiracy but as an exploration of the problem of the degree of guilt of the outsiders who are caught up in the panic.[32] The evil intentions of conspirators might provide part of the explanation for "why bad things happen to good people", but conspiracy theories also often rely on notions of persuasion, influence, seduction, manipulation, corruption, contagion, or brainwashing to account for the involvement of those not part of the inner circle in the grand plan.[33] All of these terms can be seen as vernacular versions of what social scientists would now term hegemony or ideology, i.e. an explanation of why people seem to act in ways that serve not their own interests but those of the ruling class.[34]

It therefore makes sense for students of conspiracy theory to return to works of sociology such as C. Wright Mills' *The Power Elite*, which presents an account of how a ruling class can emerge from the fragmented and conflicted collusion of vested interests, without there ever being an explicit, conscious, and intentional conspiracy.[35] In a similar fashion, William Domhoff, the author of the influential study *Who Rules America?*, has insisted that his analysis of the way America is ruled by a small elite does not need a conspiracy theory: the moneyed elite openly and rationally pursue their transparent goals of self-advancement, and it does not take a secret conspiracy of obscure plotters for them to be able to achieve this.[36] The work of both Mills and Domhoff draws attention to the need for precise distinctions between conspiracy and collusion, or more accurately, a historical account of how the dividing line has been constructed in the popular imagination and encoded legally. Research on the shifting ways that conspiracy has been imagined – with conspiracy theory being but one of those ways – has much to learn from historians and theorists of organisational behaviour, corporate crime, and the sociology of elites.

---

32 Cf. David Zimmerman, *Panic!: Markets, Crises, and Crowds in American Fiction*, Chapel Hill, NC 2006, pp. 151–190.

33 Dieter Groh, "The Temptation of Conspiracy Theory, or: Why Do Bad Things Happen to Good People", in: Carl F. Graumann/Serge Moscovici (eds.), *Changing Conceptions of Conspiracy*, New York 1987, pp. 1–37.

34 Timothy Melley, "Brainwashed! Conspiracy Theory and Ideology in the Postwar United States", in: *New German Critique*, 103/2008, pp. 145–164.

35 C. Wright Mills, *The Power Elite*, New York 1956.

36 G. William Domhoff, *Who Rules America?*, Englewood Cliffs, NJ 1978; cf. also Domhoff, "There Are No Conspiracies", Mar. 2005, http://www2.ucsc.edu/whorulesamerica/theory/conspiracy.html (accessed Oct. 1, 2011).

2. Comparative Approaches

Much of the early scholarly work on conspiracy theories was focused on the United States. This might just be a coincidence: in his "Paranoid Style" essay, Hofstadter commented that he had chosen American examples merely because he happened to be a historian of the U.S., while in the same period historians on both sides of the Atlantic such as Norman Cohn and J. M. Roberts were turning their attention to the mythology of secret societies and the history of antisemitism in Europe.[37] Yet there is good reason to think that the focus in the 1960s and 1970s on the "paranoid style" was animated by a desire to understand why the U.S. seemed to have a peculiar affinity for the countersubversive imagination, driven in part, as we have seen, by anxieties about McCarthyism. Ironically, the consensus historians argued not that Americans were far more prone to populist paranoia than other nations, but that conspiracy theory functioned as a rhetorical safety valve that prevented the kind of violent, ideological class conflict seen in European history, and that therefore made American history exceptional. As recent critiques of the founding project of American Studies have argued, the consensus historians relied implicitly on a faith in American exceptionalism, the conviction that the history of the U.S. does not follow the same laws of historical development as other nations, and even that there is a God-given manifest destiny to the story of America.

The accusations of American exceptionalism highlight an important blind spot in the scholarly development of theories of conspiracy theory, my own work included. Although it is forgivable to begin like Hofstadter with the semi-arbitrary choice of American case studies as the material is so prominent in contemporary popular culture, often the inquiry subtly shifts from an analysis of conspiracism generally to the investigation of why America seems to have a peculiar affinity for conspiracy thinking. The work of the present volume and other recent contributions to an international history of conspiracy theory serves as a reminder that the U.S. has no monopoly on the conspiracist tradition. There is scope for many more local micro histories of the varying style and function of conspiracism in countries outside America and western Europe. In this regard, Matthew Gray's 2009 book on conspiracy theories in the Middle East is a landmark work, challenging Daniel Pipes' earlier, less convincing study of conspiracism in the region. Gray resists the temptation to see the prevalence of the discourse of conspiracy in the Middle

---

37 Norman Cohn, *Warrant for Genocide: The Myth of the Jewish World-Conspiracy and the Protocols of the Elders of Zion*, London 1969; and J. M. Roberts, *The Mythology of the Secret Societies*, London 1972.

East as the result of essential cultural differences (such as the so-called Arab mindset), instead looking to the diverging role and structure of the state in the U.S. and the Middle East as the reason for those differences.[38] It is therefore significant that the present volume takes as its guiding theme the question of how far American Studies approaches can be applied to conspiracism in the Middle East, and vice versa.

Likewise, there are several scholars who are beginning to work on conspiracy theories in Eastern Europe and Russia, providing an interesting update to the now considerable body of work on the *Protocols of the Elders of Zion*, beginning with Norman Cohn's classic study, *Warrant for Genocide*.[39] Further afield, anthropologists have begun to study how local versions of conspiracy rumours provide an expression of a sense of perplexed victimhood at the hands of vast, transnational forces, coupled with a desire to see these forces as not merely structural and inevitable but the product of specific, malign agency, whether human or supernatural. Anthropologists conducting field work in South Korea, for example, have discussed the turn to conspiracy-infused shamanic practices as a way of making sense of the devastating changes brought about by the economic strictures imposed upon the country by the IMF; or the use of "occult cosmologies" by the Christian minority in Indonesia to account for what the latter regard as the unseen powers of globalist Islam and state bureaucracy.[40] Although most work on conspiracy theories has focused on written texts or related media such as film, the work of anthropologists, folklorists, and journalists has introduced a welcome ethnographic methodology to the study of conspiracism.

In addition to exploring regional differences, I think that we also need to see if the conclusions reached by the large body of work on contemporary conspiracy culture apply to earlier historical periods, and, conversely, what

---

38 Matthew Gray, *Conspiracy Theories in the Arab World*, New York 2010; Daniel Pipes, *The Hidden Hand: Middle East Fears of Conspiracy*, New York 1996. The concern about "black paranoia" in the U.S. in the 1990s displayed the same essentialising logic (cf. Peter Knight, *Conspiracy Culture: From Kennedy to* The X-Files, London 2000).

39 Cf. e.g. John Heathershaw/Stephanie Ortmann (eds.), "Conspiracy Theories in the Post-Soviet Space", in: *The Russian Review*, 71/2012, 4, pp. 551–564; and Jovan Byford, "'Serbs Never Hated the Jews': The Denial of Antisemitism in Contemporary Serbian Orthodox Christian Culture", in: *Patterns of Prejudice*, 40/2006, pp. 159–180.

40 Cf. Harry G. West/Todd Sanders (eds.), *Transparency and Conspiracy: Ethnographies of Suspicion in the New World Order*, Durham, NC 2003; George E. Marcus (ed.), *Paranoia Within Reason: A Casebook on Conspiracy as Explanation*, Chicago 1998; and Knight, "Conspiracy Theories", in: Akira Iriye/Pierre-Yves Saunier (eds.), *The Palgrave Dictionary of Transnational History*, London 2009, pp. 194–197.

insights might be gleaned from studies of those earlier moments. Building on earlier important studies by scholars such as Geoffrey Cubitt and Rogalla von Bieberstein, there have been some useful recent developments in this area. For example, the existing scholarly interest in rumour and conspiracy theory surrounding the French Revolution has recently been expanded with Campbell, Kaiser, and Linton's edited collection.[41] Likewise, monographs by Albert Pionke and Adrian Wisnicki provide thoughtful studies of the fearful imagination of secret societies and foreign infiltrators in British Edwardian and Victorian literature, an intriguing counterpart to Robert Levine's 1989 book on the imagination of conspiracy in antebellum American literature.[42] Two monographs by Victoria Pagán and Joseph Roisman from the last decade have also explored the rhetoric of conspiracy in, respectively, Ancient Rome and Greece.[43]

However, this work raises the question of whether the approaches developed in the study of contemporary American conspiracy culture can indeed be applied wholesale to other regions, cultures, and historical periods. It also forces us to consider whether larger conclusions about the nature of conspiracy theory – its evolution, style, content, function – can be drawn by making cross-cultural and cross-temporal comparisons. Do conspiracy theories work in the same way everywhere? Do they draw on the same limited repertoire of images and narratives? Have they always worked in the same way, or are there significant evolutions as well as continuities? Although some of this recent work makes clear the local peculiarities of conspiracy thinking, it also highlights the surprising persistence and ubiquity of particular ideas across seemingly diverse and incompatible cultures. What are we to make of the fact, for example, that editions of the *Protocols of the Elders of Zion* are available not only on white supremacist and neo-fascist websites in the West, but also in the Middle East and even in Black Power bookshops in the U.S.? Although taking a comparative approach to the discourse of conspiracy promises to

---

41 Campbell/Kaiser/Linton (eds.), *Conspiracy in the French Revolution*. Cf. also, for example, Stefan Andriopoulos, "Occult Conspiracies: Spirits and Secret Societies in Schiller's *Ghost Seer*", in: *New German Critique*, 103/2008, pp. 65–81.

42 Albert Pionke, *Plots of Opportunity: Representing Conspiracy in Victorian England*, Columbus, OH 2004; Adrian S. Wisnicki, *Conspiracy, Revolution, and Terrorism from Victorian Fiction to the Modern Novel*, New York 2008; Robert S. Levine, *Conspiracy and Romance: Studies in Brockden Brown, Cooper, Hawthorne, and Melville*, Cambridge 1989.

43 Victoria Emma Pagán, *Conspiracy Narratives in Roman History*, Austin 2004; Joseph Roisman, *The Rhetoric of Conspiracy in Ancient Athens*, Berkeley 2006. With its focus on individual, legal denunciations, Roisman's book raises more questions than it provides answers about the social and political functions of conspiracy accusations in Ancient Greece.

open up interesting new areas of inquiry, it is currently impeded because only a minority of recent scholarly research has been translated into other languages. There is surely scope for a European-wide scholarly network on conspiracy theories that would enable the sharing of research.

Comparative approaches to conspiracy theories have much to offer, not least in providing sharper answers to the question of what is distinctive about the "paranoid style" in U.S. politics and culture. Yet I would also argue that there is a need for future research on conspiracy theories to take not just a comparative but a transnational approach. For example, in addition to examining how conspiracy theories work differently *within* the U.S. and the Middle East, we also need to explore how each region imagines the other *through* the lens of conspiracy. Furthermore, many contemporary conspiracy theories explicitly target vehicles of global, transnational governance such as the United Nations and the Trilateral Commission, organisations that are often lumped together in the conspiracy rhetoric under the umbrella terms "The Illuminati", "The Zionist Occupied Government" (ZOG), or "The New World Order". In the countersubversive demonology that erupted repeatedly in Europe and the United States in the nineteenth and twentieth centuries, the accusation often made against the imagined conspirators was that they secretly swore allegiance to alien and typically transnational powers (the Pope, the Grand Master of the Masonic lodges, the international Communist Party, and so on).

However, even if conspiracy fears have often latched onto transnational institutions, it must be remembered that they frequently have served to bolster a sense of group and often national identity precisely by imagining it under threat. Indeed, the history of conspiracy thinking is intertwined with the history of the legitimation and evolution of the state. Although recent cultural studies research in the U.S. has tended to concentrate on contemporary conspiracy theories emerging from the grassroots and directed toward the state, we also need to consider the longer history of conspiracy theories emanating from the grassroots but appropriated by the state, as well as conspiracy theories generated by the state and directed against minorities or ordinary people – and how each interacts with the others.[44] If we resist the

---

[44] For an interesting historical account of the shift from fears of infiltration of the American state to fears that the government itself is the source of conspiracies, cf. Kathryn E. Olmsted, *Real Enemies: Conspiracy Theories and American Democracy, World War I to 9/11*, Oxford 2009. However, unlike Barkun who identifies a change in the social origin and political function of conspiracy theories after World War II, Olmsted dates this transition from red scares to Fed scares to much earlier in the twentieth century with the increase in the power and reach of the Federal government.

temptation to ascribe the turn to conspiracy explanations to essential cultural differences, then we are obliged to examine the relationship between different police systems, media traditions, and regimes of transparency in order to account for both the similarities and differences thrown up by comparative research. Do conspiracy theories tend to thrive more in authoritarian political systems (such as post-Soviet Russia and parts of the Middle East) in which the flow of public news and information is restricted and controlled, producing a corresponding mistrust of official channels, sources, and narratives; or, ironically, do they flourish in considerably more democratic and transparent countries such as the U.S. in which the political reality fails to live up to an unrealistic utopian faith in egalitarianism and the rights of sovereign individualism? Likewise, how have the ways in which conspiracy is imagined and the contexts in which it is denounced been shaped by shifting conceptions of the state in western Europe since the Early Modern period, from one that views secrecy as an essential and natural attribute of state power to one which prioritises ideals of transparency in the political arena? There is thus still much research to be done on the role of conspiracy-mongering as a technique of state power, and also the state's inability to imagine unrest as anything other than a top-down conspiracy.[45]

3. Patterns of Belief

A good deal of research has been conducted on the different tropes, images, narratives, and epistemological structures of the discourse of conspiracy in different regions and media, as well as the varying political and cultural uses that conspiracy theories have served. We still know comparatively little, however, about the individual psychology of conspiracy beliefs, especially in terms of detailed empirical work. Although cultural studies scholars have followed the path Hofstadter opened up by examining the symbolic dimension of conspiracy beliefs, they have nonetheless criticised him and those subsequently working in the same vein for relying too heavily on undeveloped quasi-psychoanalytical explanations, such as Freud's understanding of paranoid projection as a result of repressed male homosexuality.[46] If some

---

[45] On the tendency of the state to resort to conspiracy explanations, cf. e.g. John Plotz, *The Crowd: British Literature and Public Politics*, Berkeley 2000; and Kim Wagner, *The Great Fear of 1857: Rumours, Conspiracies and the Making of the Indian Uprising*, Oxford 2010.

[46] For a brilliant cultural materialist reinterpretation of Schreber, cf. Eric Santner, *My Own Private Germany: Daniel Paul Schreber's Secret History of Modernity*, Princeton 1996.

scholars have warned that too much attention is paid to psychological issues in the study of conspiracy culture, others have argued in contrast that there is too little. Some empirical psychologists have begun to conduct experiments to identify the factors of individual psychological make-up that affect the propensity to believe in conspiracy theories, including cultural difference. Karen Douglas, for example, has devised experiments to test whether the endorsement of conspiracy theories is influenced by a person's willingness to conspire; while Viren Swami has examined personality and individual differences as predictors of 9/11 conspiracist belief in Britain.[47]

The value of this empirical psychological work is that it engages in some detail with conspiracy theorists, unlike many of the cultural and political studies that tend to reach conclusions about the nature of conspiracy belief from the analysis of textual evidence at arm's length. Although an ethnographic approach is of course not possible for historical case studies, there is a noticeable lack of participant observer and oral history research on the sociology of contemporary conspiracy theories.[48] This is no doubt in part because the proselytising tendencies of conspiracy theorists are often matched by an all-pervasive suspiciousness. However, some journalists have begun to use interviews as a more direct way to understand the appeal of conspiracy theories for their believers. The journalist Jonathan Kay's recent book *Among the Truthers*, for example, is a thoughtful attempt to generate larger conclusions about conspiracy theories based on interviews with 9/11 truth movement activists. Although some of its generalisations are not warranted by the limited evidence base and it is overly alarmist, *Among the Truthers* has made the effort to understand conspiracy theory beliefs not in isolation but as part of an individual's broader outlook; Kay is also concerned to explore how conspiracy theories circulate within and are defined by particular communities.[49]

---

[47] A useful round-up of work in psychology is provided by Viren Swami and Rebecca Coles, "The Truth Is Out There: Belief in Conspiracy Theories", in: *The Psychologist*, 23/2010, pp. 560–563.

[48] Notable exceptions include Patricia Turner, *I Heard It Through the Grapevine: Rumor in African-American Experience*, Berkeley 1993; and Bridget Brown, *They Know Us Better Than We Know Ourselves: The History and Politics of Alien Abduction*, New York 2007.

[49] Jonathan Kay, *Among the Truthers: A Journey Through America's Growing Conspiracist Underground*, New York 2011. Other explorations by journalists include Jon Ronson, *Them: Adventures with Extremists*, London 2001; Francis Wheen, *How Mumbo-Jumbo Conquered the World: A Short History of Modern Delusions*, London 2004; and the more textual study, David Aaronovitch, *Voodoo Histories: The Role of Conspiracy Theory in Shaping Modern History*, London 2009.

The lack of an understanding of the social dynamic of conspiracy belief is one of the weaknesses of recent empirical psychological studies. There is a tendency in some of this work to view conspiracy theories as the result of a particular personality type, rather than a habit of mind that is not merely confined to a minority. A related problem with that work is the tendency to produce universal conclusions about the psychological mechanisms of individual conspiracy belief from a sample that is very particular and local (usually undergraduate students at the researcher's own institution). Although the psychological studies use careful statistical analysis to scale their findings to be representative of the population as a whole, they are always necessarily limited to western European or the U.S., and therefore raise the question of whether their conclusions apply to other regions and cultures.[50] Likewise, they beg the question of whether conspiracy beliefs have always functioned in the same way, or whether they are relative to specific historical moments. The hypotheses generated by empirical psychologists can be very valuable, but they have generally failed to engage fully with the historical, cultural, and political approaches to conspiracy theories – and vice versa. We therefore need to develop research programmes that combine the systematic approach of empirical psychology with analytical insights into the social dynamics of conspiracy communities in different historical periods and cultural contexts.[51] It would be intriguing, for example, to apply some of the generalisations reached by social psychologists to earlier historical case studies, and, conversely, to design new empirical experiments to test some of the conclusions reached by historical studies. At the very least, scholars working in each area need to be more familiar with the literature produced in other disciplines.

One broad topic in conspiracy theory research that would benefit from a greater convergence of psychological, psychoanalytical, and cultural approaches is the dynamic of gender and sexuality. Little work has been done on the often unspoken fact that most conspiracy theorists are men and that most conspiracies are imagined to be the result of men plotting with other men.[52]

---

50 Conversely, the anecdotal evidence employed by journalists gets to the heart of the social element of conspiracy beliefs, but it lacks the statistical rigour that would enable us to judge whether its interviewees are indeed representative of wider trends.

51 In *"Ronald Reagan", The Movie*, Rogin attempts to synthesise the symbolist and realist approaches to conspiracy theory through the use of Melanie Klein's theories of paranoia.

52 In addition to Birte Christ's contribution to the present volume, exceptions would include Rogin, "Kiss Me Deadly: Communism, Motherhood, and Cold War Movies", in: *Representations*, 6/1984, pp. 1–36; Andrew Strombeck, "The Conspi-

Why do conspiracy theories seem to appeal predominantly to men? What difference does it make when women are imagined as conspirators, or when plotting men are feminised? What is the psychic investment of conspiracy theorists in repeatedly imagining the homosocial bonding rituals of secret societies? What, as Birte Christ asks in this volume, is the psychic investment of male theorists of conspiracy theory in seeking to master their specialist subject? To what extent do popular explanations of the attractions of conspiracy thinking (seduction, persuasion, influence, brainwashing) rely on sexualised metaphors? What is the relationship between what Timothy Melley has called "agency panic" and contemporary anxieties of masculinity?[53] Is that dynamic only a recent phenomenon?

Although we should rightly be wary of the universalising conclusions of pop Freudianism, the investigation of gender and sexuality in conspiracy thinking – and indeed the study of conspiracy theories in general – would benefit from an engagement with some of the questions raised by psychoanalytic theory. For example, one of the really puzzling features of conspiracy thinking is that it is structured both by a compulsion to reach an ultimate revelation, and a seemingly contradictory drive to keep the investigation going. There might well be straightforward, rational explanations for this apparent paradox (not least the possibility that for some of the most prominent contemporary conspiracy theorists such as Alex Jones and David Icke conspiracism is their livelihood), yet the notion of conflicting psychic impulses is one where, say, Lacanian theory might usefully be employed.[54]

4. Modes of Transmission

In addition to understanding more about what makes particular conspiracy narratives attractive to believers, we need further investigation of the way that conspiracist ideas are *transmitted* in varying historical and regional contexts. Many commentators have noted how particular conspiracy tropes, images, and story elements are endlessly recycled and recombined, but comparatively little work has been done on documenting how particular theories are circulated and adapted. Leaving aside the many existing studies of the origins and afterlives of the *Protocols*, some new research into the modes of

---

racy of Masculinity in Ishmael Reed", in: *African American Review*, 40/2006, pp. 299–311; and Michael S. Sherry, *Gay Artists in Modern American Culture: An Imagined Conspiracy*, Chapel Hill, NC 2007.

53 Melley, *Empire of Conspiracy*.

54 Cf. Starr, "We the Paranoid", ch. 3.

transmission of conspiracy theories is beginning to emerge. At the macro level, we could point to Lindsay Porter's *Who Are the Illuminati?*, an exemplary genealogy of myths about the Illuminati, from David Icke in the twenty-first century, via evangelical Christians, the John Birch Society, Nesta Webster and the *Protocols*, all the way back to Abbé Barruel in the eighteenth century.[55] At the micro level, Andrew McKenzie-McHarg's contribution to the present volume is a good advertisement for the rewards of careful historical research into the precise routes by which particular conspiracy ideas are conveyed from individual to individual across borders.[56] However, in investigating the intellectual and cultural circuits by which conspiracist ideas have been relayed, we must not forget the material, political factors that have promoted particular beliefs, from the forging of the *Protocols* by the Tsarist secret police to the role of the Soviet intelligence agencies in promoting false conspiracist rumours about the origins of AIDS, or the role of right-wing think tanks in bank-rolling the Birther movement.

Further research in this area needs to focus on two aspects in particular: to what extent do new media technologies bring revolutionary possibilities for the formulation of conspiracist ideas, and what role do these new technologies of transmission play in creating new social networks of belief? We need to consider how conspiracy ideas have been enabled by the development of print media, the successive emergence of pamphlets, newspapers, radio, film and television, all the way through to contemporary digital forms of communication such as web sites, blogs, and social media. (We also need to think of different genres in which conspiracies have been feverishly imagined – plays, novels, political tracts, satirical cartoons, and so on – as technologies of transmission in their own right.)[57] Although much recent popular and scholarly attention has understandably been focused on what the Internet means for conspiracy theory, there is much to be gained from an examination of how conspiracy ideas circulated in and were shaped by the new print cultures of the eighteenth century. According to Jürgen Habermas's

---

55 Lindsay Porter, *Who Are the Illuminati?*, London 2005.

56 New technologies such as automated data-scraping of websites offer ways of tracking conspiracy memes and urban legends through the online landscape.

57 There has been surprising little scholarly attention paid to visual representations of conspiracy. Two exceptions are Ian Haywood, "The Dark Sketches of a Revolution: Gillray, the Anti-Jacobin Review, and the Aesthetics of Conspiracy in the 1790s", in: *European Romantic Review*, 22/2011, pp. 431–451; and Amy Wiese Forbes, "The Lithographic Conspiracy: How Satire Framed Liberal Political Debate in Nineteenth-Century France", in: *French Politics, Culture, & Society*, 26/2008, pp. 16–50.

influential account, the private modes of selfhood promoted by the consumption of literary texts in the "republic of letters" nevertheless engendered a public sphere of ideas, an idealised notion of a dispersed yet orderly polity.[58] But to what extent did the Enlightenment ideal of a rational public sphere generated through the anonymous circulation of texts conjure up the nightmarish flipside of a decentred and deterritorialised network of like-minded conspirators, whose power to influence and manipulate from afar seemed to defy local structures of control?[59]

Similar questions about the relationship between conspiracy theory and the project of the Enlightenment have been raised in relation to the Internet. On the one hand, an influential strand of libertarian cyber-utopianism has argued that the structure of the Web encourages a more democratic and participatory approach to media information. For some, the chaotic, unregulated online marketplace of ideas is enough to ensure a healthy scepticism among the public; others have suggested that in the absence of authoritative media sources the "wisdom of crowds" will produce a convergence toward the truth; and those animated by a "hacktivist" ethic urge that all official data should be freed to create a regime of transparency in which government conspiracies would have nowhere left to hide. On the other hand, less sanguine commentators have wondered whether the trend toward social networking in Web 2.0 creates not so much a utopian digital public sphere but balkanised echo chambers that reinforce and radicalise existing beliefs. We need therefore detailed, empirical studies of online conspiracy communities, and how they intersect with "offline" political groups. But we also need to consider to what extent the very architecture of the Internet shapes contemporary conspiracy culture. How, for example, do search engines like Google exacerbate the spread of conspiracist ideas, not merely by enabling the rapid connecting of disparate documents from around the globe, but by using algorithms that in effect put popularity above accuracy, and, increasingly, serve up answers that are no longer universal but are tied into the user's previous history of surfing, more a projection of our existing prejudices and paranoias than an objective gateway to information that might challenge our views? What is the significance of the fact that by far the most popular recent conspiracy theories have been promulgated through slick yet home-made online videos

---

58 Jürgen Habermas, *The Structural Transformation of the Public Sphere: An Inquiry Into a Category of Bourgeois Society*, Thomas Burger (trans.), Cambridge, MA 1989.

59 For an interesting investigation of the connections between secrecy and publicity, cf. Bryan Waterman, "The Bavarian Illuminati, the Early American Novel, and Histories of the Public Sphere", in: *The William and Mary Quarterly*, Third Series, 62/2005, pp. 9–30.

such as *Loose Change* and *Zeitgeist: The Movie*?[60] In what ways does the ease of creating associative links and weaving together existing documents push conspiracy theories to ever more complex and integrative forms?

5. Policy Implications

From Karl Popper onwards, conspiracy theory has been seen not merely as an epistemological curiosity but as a matter for serious political concern. The debate whether conspiracy thinking is troubling, politically useful, or merely entertaining, and whether it is on the wax or the wane, has continued over the last half century. In the last decade, however, it has come to seem a more pressing political issue, in the West at least.[61] The main reasons put forward are the rise of the Internet, the erosion of trust in both government and media, and the dangers of terrorism. In the U.S., public concern with conspiracy theories has been prompted principally because of conspiracist reactions to the attacks of September 11, 2001. Just a month after the attacks, President Bush warned against the "outrageous conspiracy theories" that were beginning to circulate in other countries, and the U.S. State Department felt the need to create web pages designed to identify for users – presumably thought to be from abroad – the common traits of conspiracy theories, as well as to debunk particular conspiracy theories (e.g. AIDS was manufactured by the U.S. as a biowarfare weapon) that seemed to misinterpret America's benevolent intentions in global politics.[62] The 9/11 Commission likewise felt compelled to tackle popular conspiracy theories head-on even if it meant engaging in a fruitless "whack-a-mole" project, as the Commission's chairman Philip Zelikow put it.[63] This desire to address and challenge con-

---

60 Cf. Michael Butter/Lisa Retterath, "From Alerting the World to Stabilizing Its Own Community: The Shifting Cultural Work of the *Loose Change* Films", in: *Canadian Review of American Studies*, 40/2010, pp. 25–44.

61 Similar issues have been raised about the difficulties of countering conspiracy theories about HIV/AIDS in sub-Saharan Africa (cf. Nicoli Nattrass, *Denying AIDS: Conspiracy Theories, Pseudoscience, and Human Tragedy*, New York 2009).

62 *Conspiracy Theories and Misinformation*, http://www.america.gov/conspiracy_theories.html (accessed Oct. 1, 2011). On Bush's comment, cf. Knight, "Outrageous Conspiracy Theories: Popular and Official Responses to 9/11 in Germany and the United States", in: *New German Critique*, 103/2008, pp. 165–193.

63 Zelikow qtd. in Carol Morello, "Edgy Online Sites Feed Conspiracy Theories to a Distrustful Public", in: *Washington Post*, Oct. 9, 2004. On official government commissions and conspiracy theories in the U.S., cf. Chara Van Horn, *The Paranoid Style in an Age of Suspicion: Conspiracy Thinking and Official Rhetoric in Contemporary America*, Diss. Georgia State University, 2010.

spiracy theories is in contrast to earlier blue riband government commissions such as the Warren Commission that on the whole refused to engage with popular suspicions directly.

Most recently an article co-written by the Harvard Law professor Cass Sunstein advocated the "cognitive infiltration" of online conspiracy sites by those working either directly for or on behalf of the intelligence agencies.[64] This article would not be so significant were it not for the fact that Sunstein in 2009 was appointed as the Administrator of the Office of Information Affairs in the Obama administration. We are left wondering whether this policy idea has gained any traction within the administration; at the very least, it would be interesting to know whether Sunstein played any part in Obama's decision to finally release his long-form birth certificate in April 2011 in an effort to defuse the Birther movement. The birth certificate case demonstrated the impossible bind that most attempts to counter conspiracy theories face. Ignoring the Birther movement as beneath contempt only seemed to stir up accusations of a cover-up; yet directly refuting the birthers with evidence merely generated even more convoluted conspiracy scenarios. Likewise, the labelling of birthers as closet racists by some in the liberal media only served to muddy the waters.

Policy makers are thus beginning to ask the question of how conspiracy theories spread, and which methods of tackling them are most likely to be effective. In the UK, for example, the independent think tank Demos produced a report in 2010 dealing with conspiracy theories. *The Power of Unreason* looks at the role of conspiracy theories within extremist groups with violent tendencies.[65] It concludes that conspiracy theories within these groups act to radicalise members, by buttressing extremist ideologies and sustaining the group's sense of cohesive identity. According to the authors, conspiracy theories on the web in the specific context of violent, extremist groups act in effect as an echo chamber, isolating believers from potential challenging views. One of the authors' policy recommendations is to infiltrate these digital information silos, albeit not with the use of clandestine agents in the way that Sunstein countenanced. This research was followed up in 2011 with *Digital Fluency: Truth, Lies and the Internet*, a report examining the skills deficit of young British people in assessing the validity of the information they en-

---

64 Cass Sunstein/Adrian Vermeule, "Conspiracy Theories: Causes and Cures", in: *Journal of Political Philosophy*, 17/2009, pp. 202–227.

65 Jamie Bartlett/Carl Miller, *The Power of Unreason: Conspiracy Theories, Counter-Terrorism and Extremism*, 2010, http://www.demos.co.uk/publications/thepowerofunreason (accessed Oct. 1, 2011).

gage with online, making it difficult to distinguish between plausible and far-fetched ideas.[66] The report made various policy recommendations, perhaps the most important of which is a call for schools to teach digital fluency. Jonathan Kay's *Among the Truthers* makes a similar recommendation for combating the power of conspiracy theories. Kay suggests developing university courses on the history of conspiracy thinking, in the hope that the more people are able to recognise the patterns of thought and rhetorical tropes that encourage conspiracy theories the less likely they are to succumb to them.

The key recommendation from other commentators, however, is greater official transparency, as Mark Fenster's contribution to the present volume discusses.[67] If governments and powerful institutions are more willing to override the default assumption of keeping all their decision-making and operations secret, the argument goes, then conspiracy theorists would have less reason to concoct fantasies. What "open democracy" (in the current buzzword on both sides of the Atlantic) would reveal is not the machinations of a master conspiracy, it is thought, but the mundane, messy, and at times incompetent stumbling toward consensus in large bureaucracies. Although it is undoubtedly true that unnecessary secrecy breeds conspiratorial fears, it is also likely that enforcing greater transparency in government agencies would merely result in key decisions being taken "off the record" and immune to proper accountability – in effect creating the very processes of back-room deals that conspiracy theorists are so concerned about. If policy makers are to turn to scholars of conspiracy theories for advice on how to counteract their influence, then it is all the more the important that we develop research into the definitions, comparative dimensions, modes of transmission, and patterns of belief.

---

66 Bartlett/Miller, *Digital Fluency: Truth, Lies and the Internet*, 2011, http://www.demos.co.uk/publications/truth-lies-and-the-internet (accessed October 1, 2011).

67 Cf. also Clare Birchall, "'There's Been Too Much Secrecy in This City': The False Choice Between Secrecy and Transparency in U.S. Politics", in: *Cultural Politics*, 7/2011, pp. 133–156; and Birchall, "Transparency, Interrupted: Secrets of the Left", in: *Theory, Culture and Society*, 28/2011, pp. 60–84.

Bibliography

The bibliography lists the studies cited and mentioned in the volume that deal with conspiracy and conspiracy theorizing.

Aaronovitch, David, *Voodoo Histories: How Conspiracy Theory Has Shaped Modern History*, London 2009.

Abalakina-Paap, Marina et al., "Beliefs in Conspiracies", in: *Political Psychology*, 20/1999, 3, pp. 637–647.

Bailyn, Bernard, *The Ideological Origins of the American Revolution*, Cambridge 1992.

Bale, Jeffrey M., "Political Paranoia v. Political Realism: On Distinguishing Between Bogus Conspiracy Theories and Genuine Conspiratorial Politics", in: *Patterns of Prejudice*, 41/2007, pp. 45–60.

Barkun, Michael, *A Culture of Conspiracy: Apocalyptic Visions in Contemporary America*, Berkeley, CA 2003.

Bayat, Asef, "Conspiracies & Theories", in: *ISIM Review*, 18/2006.

Birchall, Clare, *Knowledge Goes Pop: From Conspiracy Theory to Gossip*, Oxford 2006.

Bratich, Jack, *Conspiracy Panics: Political Rationality and Popular Culture*, Albany, NY 2008.

Bronner, Stephen, *A Rumor about the Jews: Anti-Semitism, Conspiracy, and the Protocols of Zion*, New York 2003.

Butter, Michael, *Plots, Designs, and Schemes: American Conspiracy Theories from the Puritans to the Present*, Berlin/Boston 2013.

Byford, Jovan, *Conspiracy Theories: A Critical Introduction*, Basingstoke 2011.

Campbell, Peter R./Kaiser, Thomas E./Linton, Marisa (eds.), *Conspiracy in the French Revolution*, Manchester 2007.

Caumanns, Ute/Niendorf, Mathias (eds.), *Verschwörungstheorien: Anthropologische Konstanten – historische Varianten*, Osnabrück 2001.

Clarke, Steve, "Conspiracy Theories and the Internet: Controlled Demolition and Arrested Development", in: *Episteme*, 4/2007, pp. 167–180.

Coady, David, "Conspiracy Theories and Official Stories", in: *International Journal of Applied Philosophy*, 17/2003, 2, pp. 199–211.

– (ed.), *Conspiracy Theories: The Philosophical Debate*, Aldershot 2006.

Coale, Samuel Chase, *Paradigms of Paranoia: The Culture of Conspiracy in Contemporary American Fiction*, Tuscaloosa, AL 2005.

Cohen, Michael, *"The Conspiracy of Capital": American Popular Radicalism and the Politics of Conspiracy from Haymarket to the Red Scare*, Diss. Yale University, 2004.

Cohn, Norman, *Warrant for Genocide: The Myth of the Jewish World-Conspiracy and the* Protocols of the Elders of Zion, London 1969.

Coward, Barry/Swann, Julian (eds.), *Conspiracies and Conspiracy Theory in Early Modern Europe*, Aldershot 2004.

Critchlow, Donald T. et al. (eds.), *Political Conspiracies in America: A Reader*, Bloomington, IN 2008.

Cubitt, Geoffrey, "Conspiracy Myths and Conspiracy Theories", in: *Journal of the Anthropological Society of Oxford*, 20/1989, pp. 12–26.

–, *The Jesuit Myth: Conspiracy Theory and Politics in Nineteenth-Century France*, Oxford 1993.
Davis, David Brion (ed.), *The Fear of Conspiracy: Images of Un-American Subversion from the Revolution to the Present*, Ithaca, NY 1971.
–, *The Slave Power Conspiracy and the Paranoid Style*, Baton Rouge 1970.
–, "Some Themes of Counter-Subversion: An Analysis of Anti-Masonic, Anti-Catholic, and Anti-Mormon Literature", in: *The Mississippi Valley Historical Review*, 47/1960, 2, pp. 205–224.
Dean, Jodi, *Aliens in America: Conspiracy Cultures from Outerspace to Cyberspace*, Ithaca, NY 1998.
Fathi, Schirin (ed.), *Komplotte, Ketzer und Konspirationen: Zur Logik des Verschwörungsdenkens – Beispiele aus dem Nahen Osten*, Bielefeld 2010.
Fenster, Mark, *Conspiracy Theories: Secrecy and Power in American Culture*, Minneapolis 2008.
Fenster, Mark/ Bratich, Jack, "Dialogues in Communications Research", in: *Journal of Communication Inquiry*, 33/2009, pp. 278–286.
Goertzel, Ted, "Belief in Conspiracy Theories", in: *Political Psychology*, 15/1994, pp. 731–742.
Goldberg, Robert A., *Enemies Within: The Culture of Conspiracy in Modern America*, New Haven, CT 2001.
Graf, Arndt/Fathi, Schirin/Paul, Ludwig (eds.), *Orientalism and Conspiracy*, London 2011.
Gray, Matthew, *Conspiracy Theories in the Arab World: Sources and Politics*, London 2010.
–, "Explaining Conspiracy Theories in Modern Arab Middle Eastern Political Discourse: Some Problems and Limitations of the Literature", in: *Critique: Critical Middle Eastern Studies*, 17/2008, 2, pp. 55–174.
Groh, Dieter, "The Temptation of Conspiracy Theory, or: Why Do Bad Things Happen to Good People", in: Graumann, Carl F./Moscovici, Serge (eds.), *Changing Conceptions of Conspiracy*, New York 1987, pp. 1–37.
Gugenberger, Eduard/Petri, Franko/Schweidlenka, Roman, *Weltverschwörungstheorien: Die neue Gefahr von rechts*, Wien 1998.
Hofstadter, Richard, "The Paranoid Style in American Politics", in: *The Paranoid Style in American Politics and Other Essays*, London 1966, pp. 3–40.
Hünemörder, Markus, *The Society of the Cincinnati: Conspiracy and Distrust in Early America*, New York 2006.
Jameson, Fredric, "Cognitive Mapping", in: Nelson, Cary/Grossberg, Lawrence (eds.), *Marxism and the Interpretation of Culture*, Urbana, IL 1988, pp. 347–357.
Johnson, George, *Architects of Fear: Conspiracy Theories and Paranoia in American Politics*, Los Angeles 1983.
Keeley, Brian L., "Of Conspiracy Theories", in: *Journal of Philosophy*, 96/1999, 3, pp. 109–126.
Klausnitzer, Ralf, *Poesie und Konspiration: Beziehungssinn und Zeichenökonomie von Verschwörungsszenarien in Publizistik, Literatur und Wissenschaft 1750–1850*, Berlin 2007.
Knight, Peter, *Conspiracy Culture: From Kennedy to* The X-Files, London 2000.
–, "Conspiracy Theories", in: Iriye, Akira/Saunier, Pierre-Yves (eds.), *The Palgrave Dictionary of Transnational History*, London 2009, pp. 194–197.
– (ed.), *Conspiracy Theories in American History: An Encyclopedia*, Santa Barbara 2003.

–, "Outrageous Conspiracy Theories: Popular and Official Responses to 9/11 in Germany and the United States", in: *New German Critique*, 35/2008, pp. 165–193.

Knox, J. Wendell, *Conspiracy in American Politics, 1787–1815*, New York 1972.

Kravitz, Bennett, "The Truth Is Out There: Conspiracy as a Mindset in American High and Popular Culture", in: *Journal of American Culture*, 22/1999, 4, p. 23–29.

Levine, Robert S., *Conspiracy and Romance: Studies in Brockden Brown, Cooper, Hawthorne, and Melville*, Cambridge 1989.

Locke, Simon, "Conspiracy Culture, Blame Culture, and Rationalisation", in: *The Sociological Review*, 57/2009, 4, pp. 567–585.

Marcus, George E. (ed.), *Paranoia within Reason: A Casebook on Conspiracy as Explanation*, Chicago 1998.

Melley, Timothy, "Brainwashed! Conspiracy Theory and Ideology in the Postwar United States", in: *New German Critique*, 35/2008, 1, pp. 145–164.

–, *Empire of Conspiracy: The Culture of Paranoia in Postwar America*, Ithaca, NY 2000.

Miller, Shane, "Conspiracy Theories: Public Arguments as Coded Social Critiques: A Rhetorical Analysis of the TWA Flight 800 Conspiracy Theories", in: *Argumentation and Advocacy*, 39/2002, 1, p. 46.

Mintz, Frank P., *The Liberty Lobby and the American Right: Race, Conspiracy and Culture*, Westport 1985.

Nefes, Türkay Salim, *Towards a Sociology of Conspiracy Theories: An Investigation into Conspiratorial Thinking on Dönmes*, Diss. University of Kent, 2010.

O'Donnell, Patrick, *Latent Destinies: Cultural Paranoia and Contemporary U.S. Narrative*, Durham 2000.

Olmsted, Kathryn S., *Real Enemies: Conspiracy Theories and American Democracy, World War I to 9/11*, Oxford 2009.

Pagán, Victoria Emma, *Conspiracy Narratives in Roman History*, Austin 2004.

Parish, Jane/Parker, Martin (eds.), *The Age of Anxiety: Conspiracy Theory and the Human Sciences*, Oxford 2001.

Pfau, Michael William, *The Political Style of Conspiracy: Chase, Sumner, and Lincoln*, East Lansing 2005.

Pigden, Charles, "Popper Revisited, or, What Is Wrong with Conspiracy Theories?", in: *Philosophy of the Social Sciences*, 25/1993, 1, pp. 3–34.

Pionke, Albert, *Plots of Opportunity: Representing Conspiracy in Victorian England*, Columbus, OH 2004.

Pipes, Daniel, *Conspiracy: How the Paranoid Style Flourishes and Where It Comes from*, New York 1997.

–, *The Hidden Hand: Middle East Fears of Conspiracy*, Basingstoke 1996.

Popper, Karl, *The Open Society and Its Enemies*, Princeton, NJ 1966.

–, *The Open Society and Its Enemies: 2*, The High Tide of Prophecy: Hegel, Marx, and the Aftermath, New York 2005.

Pratt, Ray, *Projecting Paranoia: Conspiratorial Visions in American Film*, Lawrence 2001.

Reinalter, Helmut (ed.), *Verschwörungstheorien: Theorie, Geschichte, Wirkung*, Innsbruck 2002.

Roberts, J. M., *The Mythology of the Secret Societies*, London 1972.

Robins, Robert/Post, Jerrold, *Political Paranoia: The Psycho-Politics of Hatred*, New Haven, CT 1997.

Rogin, Michael Paul, *Ronald Reagan, the Movie, and Other Episodes in Political Demonology*, Berkeley, CA 1987.

Roisman, Joseph, *The Rhetoric of Conspiracy in Ancient Athens*, Berkeley, CA 2006.
Sherry, Michael S., *Gay Artists in Modern American Culture: An Imagined Conspiracy*, Chapel Hill, NC 2007.
Showalter, Elaine, *Hystories: Hysterical Epidemics and Modern Culture*, London 1997.
Simmel, Georg, "The Sociology of Secrecy and Secret Societies", in: *American Journal of Sociology*, 11/1906, 4, pp. 441–498.
Strombeck, Andrew, "The Conspiracy of Masculinity in Ishmael Reed", in: *African American Review*, 40/2006, pp. 299–311.
–, *None Dare Call It Masculinity: The Subject of Post-Kennedy Conspiracy Theory*, Diss. University of California, Davis 1997.
Sunstein, Cass/Vermeule, Adrian, "Conspiracy Theories: Causes and Cures", in: *Journal of Political Philosophy*, 17/2009, 2, pp. 202–227.
Swami, Viren/Coles, Rebecca, "The Truth Is Out There: Belief in Conspiracy Theories", in: *The Psychologist*, 23/2010, pp. 560–563.
Tackett, Timothy, "Conspiracy Obsession in a Time of Revolution: French Elites and the Origins of the Terror", in: *American Historical Review*, 105/2000, pp. 691–713.
Tibi, Bassam, *Die Verschwörung: Das Trauma arabischer Politik*, Hamburg 1994.
Turner, Patricia, *I Heard It through the Grapevine: Rumor in African-American Experience*, Berkeley, CA 1993.
Von Bieberstein, Rogalla, *Der Mythos von der Verschwörung: Philosophen, Freimaurer, Juden, Liberale und Sozialisten als Verschwörer gegen die Sozialordnung*, Wiesbaden 2008.
Wagner, Kim, *The Great Fear of 1857: Rumours, Conspiracies and the Making of the Indian Uprising*, Oxford 2010.
Ward, E. (ed.), *Conspiracies: Real Grievances, Paranoia, and Mass Movements*, Seattle 1996.
West, Harry G./Sanders, Todd (eds.), *Transparency and Conspiracy: Ethnographies of Suspicion in the New World Order*, Durham, NC 2003.
White, Ed, "The Value of Conspiracy Theory", in: *American Literary History*, 14/2002, pp. 1–31.
Wisnicki, Adrian S., *Conspiracy, Revolution, and Terrorism from Victorian Fiction to the Modern Novel*, New York 2008.
Wood, Gordon, "Conspiracy and the Paranoid Style: Causality and Deceit in the Eighteenth Century", in: *The William and Mary Quarterly*, 39/1982, 3, pp. 402–441.

List of Contributors

MICHAEL BUTTER is Professor of American Studies at the University of Wuppertal. He is the author of *The Epitome of Evil: Hitler in American Fiction, 1939–2002* (Palgrave, 2009) and *Plots, Designs, and Schemes: American Conspiracy Theories from the Puritans to the Present* (de Gruyter, 2014) and coeditor of *Arnold Schwarzenegger: Interdisciplinary Perspectives on Body and Image* (Winter, 2011) and *American Studies/Shifting Gears* (Winter, 2009).

BIRTE CHRIST is Assistant Professor of American Literature and Culture at Justus Liebig University Giessen. Her research interests include gender studies, popular cultural forms, and law and literature. She is the author of *Modern Domestic Fiction: Popular Feminism, Mass-Market Magazines, and Middle-Class Culture, 1905–1925* (Winter, 2012) and has published on issues ranging from counterfactual narration to contemporary political figures from a gender studies perspective.

BARBARA DE POLI teaches History of Islamic Countries at Ca' Foscari University in Venice. She has conducted extensive fieldwork in Arab Countries, especially Morocco, for several years. Her main research interests concern the relationship between institutions, Islam and society. She is also specialized on Egyptian Freemasonry. Among her publications: *I musulmani nel terzo millenio. Laicità e secolarizzazione nel mondo islamico* (Carocci, Roma 2007) and *Il sorriso della mezzaluna. Umorismo, ironia e satira nella cultura araba* (with Paolo Branca and Patrizia Zanelli, Carocci, Roma 2011).

ALEXANDER DUNST teaches American Studies at the University of Potsdam, Germany, and holds a PhD in Critical Theory from the University of Nottingham. His research and teaching focuses on twentieth-century cultural history and the relations between state and cultural forms. He has published in journals such as *Parallax*, *New Formations* and *Textual Practice* and is currently finishing a book manuscript titled "Mad America: Psychosis and Cultural Politics from the Cold War to War on Terror".

SCHIRIN FATHI is an independent scholar of Islamic and Middle Eastern Studies. She has taught and done research at institutes in Germany, the U.S., South Africa, Jordan, Lebanon, and Israel. She is the author of *Jordan – An Invented Nation?* (Deutsches Orient-Institut, 1994), *Lexikon des Nahostkonflikts*

(Palmyra, 2001) and *Komplotte, Ketzer und Konspirationen* (transcript, 2010). Schirin Fathi has taught and published further on issues relating to the Arab-Israeli conflict, nationalism and identity building, and the compatibility of Islam and democracy.

MARK FENSTER is Cone, Wagner, Nugent, Hazouri & Roth Tort Professor at the Levin College of Law, University of Florida. He is the author of *Conspiracy Theories: Secrecy and Power in American Culture* (University of Minnesota Press, 2008), which is in its second edition. He has also published extensively on transparency as an ideal of governance, which is the subject of his current book in progress.

MATTHEW GRAY is The Sheikh Hamdan bin Rashid al-Maktoum Associate Professor at the Centre for Arab and Islamic Studies of the Australian National University, Canberra, where he specializes in the politics and political economy of the Middle East. He is the author of *Conspiracy Theories in the Arab World: Sources and Politics* (Routledge, 2010), and of various journal articles and book chapters on conspiracy theories, political language, and other topics in the politics and political economy of the Arab world.

CHRISTOPHER HERBERT is an Assistant Professor of History of Columbia Basin College in Pasco, WA. He completed his PhD at the University of Washington in 2012. His current project examines the intersection of race, gender, and colonialism in the gold rushes of California and British Columbia. He has also published in the *Pacific Historical Review*.

SEBASTIAN M. HERRMANN is assistant lecturer in American Studies at the University of Leipzig. He has recently finished his dissertation on *Presidential Unrealities: Epistemic Panic, Cultural Work, and the US Presidency*. He is also the founding editor of *aspeers*, the first and currently only graduate journal for European American studies, a teaching and publication project on the MA level he has chaired for four consecutive years serving as head editor and instructor for the first four issues of the journal. He has also co-edited a volume on *Ambivalent Americanizations: Popular and Consumer Culture in Central and Eastern Europe* (Winter, 2008) and one on *Participating Audiences, Imagined Public Spheres: The Cultural Work of Contemporary American(ized) Narratives* (Leipziger Universitätsverlag, 2012). He has studied at Leipzig and Cornell University, has received stipends from the Evangelisches Studienwerk Villigst and the Fulbright Commission, and holds degrees in American studies and computer science.

Christoph Herzog is Professor of Turcology at the University of Bamberg, Germany. He studied Middle Eastern and modern European history in Freiburg, Germany and in Istanbul. In 1995 he completed his Ph.D. thesis on *Geschichte und Ideologie. Mehmed Murad und Celal Nuri über die historischen Ursachen des osmanischen Niedergangs* (Schwarz, 1996). His second monograph *Osmanische Herrschaft und Modernisierung im Irak. Die Provinz Bagdad, 1817–1917* (Bamberg University Press) on the late history of Ottoman Iraq appeared in 2012.

Brian C. Johnsrud is completing his PhD in Stanford's interdisciplinary Program in Modern Thought and Literature. He studied English literature and media studies at Montana State University and received Masters degrees in medieval literature and cultural anthropology from the University of Oxford. His research considers how the Crusades and other violent histories have served as popular metaphors for US/Middle East relations since the First Gulf War. He has published on the U.S. revision of Iraqi school history textbooks in 2003 and the role of social media and cultural memory in the reception and interpretation of the Abu Ghraib torture photographs.

Peter Knight teaches American Studies at the University of Manchester, UK. He studied at St Andrews, York and Nottingham, and has been a visiting fellow at New York University and Harvard. He is the author of *Conspiracy Culture* (London/New York, 2000) and *The Kennedy Assassination* (Edinburgh University Press, 2007), and is the editor of *Conspiracy Nation* (New York University Press, 2002) and *Conspiracy Theories in American History: An Encyclopedia* (ABC-Clio Inc, 2003). He is currently completing a book on popular readings of the market in Gilded Age America.

Andrew McKenzie-McHarg is is a research associate at the Forschungszentrum of the University of Erfurt in Gotha. He has recently completed a study on the emergence of the term "conspiracy theory" and has otherwise worked on secret societies, Radical Enlightenment and notions of the "underground" in eighteenth- and nineteenth-century Germany.

Türkay Nefes is a research fellow at the St. Antony's College and the Sociology Department of the University of Oxford. He completed a PhD at the Sociology Department of the University of Kent in 2010. His doctoral research, titled "Towards a Sociology of Conspiracy Theories: An Investigation into Conspiratorial Thinking on Dönmes", examines the content, propagation and political effects of anti-Semitic conspiratorial accounts about Dönmes (Converts) in Turkey. He has published on this topic and others in journals such as *Journal of Sociology*, *International Sociology*, and *Journal of Historical Sociology*.

ANNIKA RABO is professor in the Department of Social Anthropology, Stockholm University. She has conducted fieldwork in the Middle East, mainly in Syria, since the late 1970s focusing on a variety of topics related to state-citizens relationships. She is currently involved in projects focusing transnational connections in education and welfare and has recently finished a project on transnational Syrian families and family law.

MAURUS REINKOWSKI is Professor of Islamic and Middle Eastern Studies at the University of Basel. In the years 2008–2010 he was Senior Fellow at the Freiburg Institute of Advanced Studies. Extended research stays in the Middle East (amongst other in Israel 1991–92, 95–96 and in Turkey 1996–98). His field of specialization is the history of the late Ottoman Empire and the modern Middle East. Among his major publications in English are the volumes *Legitimizing the Order: The Ottoman Rhetoric of State Power* (Brill, 2005; edited jointly with H. Karateke, University of Chicago) and *Helpless Imperialists: Imperial Failure, Fear and Radicalization* (Vandenhoeck & Ruprecht, 2012; edited jointly with Gregor Thum, University of Pittsburg).

STEPHAN SCHMID is senior risk analyst for the MENA region at EXOP Ltd., a risk management firm with headquarters in Konstanz, Germany. Simultaneously, he is PhD Candidate in the Program Arab and Middle Eastern History at the Department of History and Archaeology at the American University of Beirut. He studied Political Science, Islamic Studies and Semitic Philology at the University of Erlangen-Nuremberg from where he earned his M.A. His fields of specialization are the history of secret societies, the phenomenon of political Islam as well as international politics in the Middle East.

ANDRÉ SLEIMAN received his Ph.D. in Sociology at the École des hautes études en sciences sociales (EHESS), Paris. His dissertation addresses the emergence and evolution of the federal projects in Lebanon since 1975. His research mainly focuses on ethnicity and nationalism in the Middle East. His previous research focused on power sharing, ethno-federalism and secularism in Lebanon and the Near East.

Aaron Winter is Lecturer in Sociology at the University of Abertay. He holds a BA in Political Science from York University, an MA in Philosophy and Social Theory from the University of Warwick and a DPhil in Social and Political Thought from the University of Sussex. His research examines the extreme-right and organised racism in the United States and Canada, terrorism and conspiracy theory. He is co-editor of and a contributor to *Discourses and Practices of Terrorism: Interrogating Terror* (Routledge, 2010) and the author of *White Separatism and the Politics of the American Extreme-Right: Civil Rights, 9/11 and a Black Man in the White House* (Ashgate, forthcoming).

Kolibri 360 GmbH
Ferdinand-Jühlke-Straße 7
99095 Erfurt, Deutschland
produktsicherheit@kolibri360.de